THE ARDEN SH

THIRD SE
General Editors: Richard Prou
and David Scott

THE TWO
GENTLEMEN
OF VERONA

THE ARDEN SHAKESPEARE

ALL'S WELL THAT ENDS WELL	edited by G. K. Hunter*
ANTONY AND CLEOPATRA	edited by John Wilders
AS YOU LIKE IT	edited by Juliet Dusinberre
THE COMEDY OF ERRORS	edited by R. A. Foakes*
CORIOLANUS	edited by Philip Brockbank*
CYMBELINE	edited by J. M. Nosworthy*
HAMLET	edited by Ann Thompson and Neil Taylor
JULIUS CAESAR	edited by David Daniell
KING HENRY IV Part 1	edited by David Scott Kastan
KING HENRY IV Part 2	edited by A. R. Humphreys*
KING HENRY V	edited by T. W. Craik
KING HENRY VI Part 1	edited by Edward Burns
KING HENRY VI Part 2	edited by Ronald Knowles
KING HENRY VI Part 3	edited by John D. Cox and Eric Rasmussen
KING HENRY VIII	edited by Gordon McMullan
KING JOHN	edited by E. A. J. Honigmann*
KING LEAR	edited by R. A. Foakes
KING RICHARD II	edited by Charles Forker
KING RICHARD III	edited by Antony Hammond*
LOVE'S LABOUR'S LOST	edited by H. R. Woudhuysen
MACBETH	edited by Kenneth Muir*
MEASURE FOR MEASURE	edited by J. W. Lever*
THE MERCHANT OF VENICE	edited by John Russell Brown*
THE MERRY WIVES OF WINDSOR	edited by Giorgio Melchiori
A MIDSUMMER NIGHT'S DREAM	edited by Harold F. Brooks*
MUCH ADO ABOUT NOTHING	edited by Claire McEachern
OTHELLO	edited by E. A. J. Honigmann
PERICLES	edited by Suzanne Gossett
THE POEMS	edited by F. T. Prince*
ROMEO AND JULIET	edited by Brian Gibbons*
SHAKESPEARE'S SONNETS	edited by Katherine Duncan-Jones
THE TAMING OF THE SHREW	edited by Brian Morris*
THE TEMPEST	edited by Virginia Mason Vaughan and Alden T. Vaughan
TIMON OF ATHENS	edited by H. J. Oliver*
TITUS ANDRONICUS	edited by Jonathan Bate
TROILUS AND CRESSIDA	edited by David Bevington
TWELFTH NIGHT	edited by J. M. Lothian and T. W. Craik*
THE TWO GENTLEMEN OF VERONA	edited by William C. Carroll
THE TWO NOBLE KINSMEN	edited by Lois Potter
THE WINTER'S TALE	edited by J. H. P. Pafford*

* Second series

THE TWO GENTLEMEN OF VERONA

Edited by
WILLIAM C. CARROLL

The Arden website is at
http://www.ardenshakepseare.com

The general editors of the Arden Shakespeare have been
W. J. Craig and R. H. Case (first series 1899-1944)
Una Ellis-Fermor, Harold F. Brooks, Harold Jenkins and
Brian Morris (second series 1946-82)

Present general editors (third series)
Richard Proudfoot, Ann Thompson and David Scott Kastan

This edition of *The Two Gentlemen of Verona,* by William C. Carroll
Published 2004 by the Arden Shakespeare
Reprinted 2007

Editorial matter © 2004 William C. Carroll

Typeset by DC Graphic Design

Arden Shakespeare is an imprint of Thomson Learning

Thomson Learning
High Holborn House
50-51 Bedford Row
London WC1R 4LR

Printed in China

British Library Cataloguing in Publication Data
A catalogue record for this book is available from the British Library
Library of Congress Cataloguing in Publication Data
A catalogue record has been requested

ISBN: 978-1-903436-94-3 (hbk)
NPN 9 8 7 6 5 4 3 2 1

ISBN: 978-1-903436-95-0 (pbk)
NPN 9 8 7 6 5 4 3

The Editor

William C. Carroll is Professor of English at Boston University, Boston, Massachusetts. His publications include *The Great Feast of Language in 'Love's Labour's Lost'*, *The Metamorphoses of Shakespearean Comedy* and *Fat King, Lean Beggar: Representations of Poverty in the Age of Shakespeare*; in addition, he has edited Thomas Middleton's *Women Beware Women* for the New Mermaid series and *Macbeth: Texts and Contexts* for the Bedford Shakespeare.

CONTENTS

Contents

LIST OF
ILLUSTRATIONS

GENERAL EDITORS' PREFACE

The Arden Shakespeare is now over one hundred years old. The earliest volume in the first series, Edward Dowden's *Hamlet*, was published in 1899. Since then the Arden Shakespeare has become internationally recognized and respected. It is now widely acknowledged as the pre-eminent Shakespeare series, valued by scholars, students, actors and 'the great variety of readers' alike for its readable and reliable texts, its full annotation and its richly informative introductions.

We have aimed in the third Arden edition to maintain the quality and general character of its predecessors, preserving the commitment to presenting the play as it has been shaped in history. While each individual volume will necessarily have its own emphasis in the light of the unique possibilities and problems posed by the play, the series as a whole, like the earlier Ardens, insists upon the highest standards of scholarship and upon attractive and accessible presentation.

Newly edited from the original quarto and folio editions, the texts are presented in fully modernized form, with a textual apparatus that records all substantial divergences from those early printings. The notes and introductions focus on the conditions and possibilities of meaning that editors, critics and performers (on stage and screen) have discovered in the play. While building upon the rich history of scholarly and theatrical activity that has long shaped our understanding of the texts of Shakespeare's plays, this third series of the Arden Shakespeare is made necessary and possible by a new generation's encounter with Shakespeare, engaging with the plays and their complex relation to the culture in which they were – and continue to be – produced.

THE TEXT

On each page of the play itself, readers will find a passage of text followed by commentary and, finally, textual notes. Act and scene divisions (seldom present in the early editions and often the product of eighteenth-century or later scholarship) have been retained for ease of reference, but have been given less prominence than in the previous series. Editorial indications of location of the action have been removed to the textual notes or commentary.

In the text itself, unfamiliar typographic conventions have been avoided in order to minimize obstacles to the reader. Elided forms in the early texts are spelt out in full in verse lines wherever they indicate a usual late twentieth-century pronunciation that requires no special indication and wherever they occur in prose (except when they indicate non-standard pronunciation). In verse speeches, marks of elision are retained where they are necessary guides to the scansion and pronunciation of the line. Final -ed in past tense and participial forms of verbs is always printed as -ed without accent, never as -'d, but wherever the required pronunciation diverges from modern usage a note in the commentary draws attention to the fact. Where the final -ed should be given syllabic value contrary to modern usage, e.g.

> Doth Silvia know that I am banished?
> (*TGV* 3.1.219)

the note will take the form

219 **banished** banishèd

Conventional lineation of divided verse lines shared by two or more speakers has been reconsidered and sometimes rearranged. Except for the familiar *Exit* and *Exeunt*, Latin forms in stage directions and speech prefixes have been translated into English and the original Latin forms recorded in the textual notes.

COMMENTARY AND TEXTUAL NOTES

Notes in the commentary, for which a major source will be the *Oxford English Dictionary*, offer glossarial and other explication of verbal difficulties; they may also include discussion of points of theatrical interpretation and, in relevant cases, substantial extracts from Shakespeare's source material. Editors will not usually offer glossarial notes for words adequately defined in the latest edition of *The Concise Oxford Dictionary* or *Merriam-Webster's Collegiate Dictionary*, but in cases of doubt they will include notes. Attention, however, will be drawn to places where more than one likely interpretation can be proposed and to significant verbal and syntactic complexity. Notes preceded by * discuss editorial emendations or variant readings from the early edition(s) on which the text is based.

Headnotes to acts or scenes discuss, where appropriate, questions of scene location, Shakespeare's handling of his source materials, and major difficulties of staging. The list of roles (so headed to emphasize the play's status as a text for performance) is also considered in commentary notes. These may include comment on plausible patterns of casting with the resources of an Elizabethan or Jacobean acting company, and also on any variation in the description of roles in their speech prefixes in the early editions.

The textual notes are designed to let readers know when the edited text diverges from the early edition(s) on which it is based. Wherever this happens the note will record the rejected reading of the early edition(s), in original spelling, and the source of the reading adopted in this edition. Other forms from the early edition(s) recorded in these notes will include some spellings of particular interest or significance and original forms of translated stage directions. Where two early editions are involved, for instance with *Othello*, the notes will also record all important differences between them. The textual notes take a form that has been in use since the nineteenth century. This comprises, first: line reference, reading adopted in the text and closing square bracket; then: abbreviated reference, in italic, to the earliest edition to adopt the accepted reading, italic semicolon and noteworthy alternative reading(s), each with abbreviated italic reference to its source.

Conventions used in these textual notes include the following. The solidus / is used, in notes quoting verse or discussing verse lining, to indicate line endings. Distinctive spellings of the basic text (Q or F) follow the square bracket without indication of source and are enclosed in italic brackets. Names enclosed in italic brackets indicate originators of conjectural emendations when these did not originate in an edition of the text, or when the named edition records a conjecture not accepted into its text. Stage directions (SDs) are referred to by the number of the line within or immediately after which they are placed. Line numbers with a decimal point relate to entry SDs and to SDs more than one line long, with the number after the point indicating the line within the SD: e.g. 78.4 refers to the fourth line of the SD following line 78. Lines of SDs at the start of a scene are numbered 0.1, 0.2, etc. Where only a line number and SD precede the square bracket, e.g. 128 SD], the note relates to the whole of a SD within or immediately following the line. Speech prefixes (SPs) follow similar conventions, 203 SP] referring to the speaker's name for line 203. Where a SP reference takes the form e.g. 38+ SP, it relates to all subsequent speeches assigned to that speaker in the scene in question.

Where, as with *King Henry V*, one of the early editions is a so-called 'bad quarto' (that is, a text either heavily adapted, or reconstructed from memory, or both), the divergences from the present edition are too great to be recorded in full in the notes. In these cases the editions will include a reduced photographic facsimile of the 'bad quarto' in an appendix.

INTRODUCTION

Both the introduction and the commentary are designed to present the plays as texts for performance, and make appropriate reference to stage, film and television versions, as well as introducing the reader to the range of critical approaches to the plays. They discuss the history of the reception of the texts within the

PREFACE

Editing comedy is no laughing matter, as I have discovered. Still, editing *The Two Gentlemen of Verona* has been a distinct pleasure as well as a challenge. Like all editors, I stand on the shoulders of those who came before me, and I want to express my particular admiration for the Arden First Series edition of *Two Gentlemen* by R. Warwick Bond and the Arden Second Series edition by Clifford Leech: I learned much from both of them, and I am still amazed at the depth of their scholarship. Among other modern editions, I also found much to admire and ponder in the New Cambridge edition by Kurt Schlueter, the Bantam and *Complete Works* by David Bevington, the Penguin by Norman Sanders and the New Folger Library edition by Barbara A. Mowat and Paul Werstine.

All current Arden editors enjoy an enormous, invaluable resource: the wisdom, imagination and industry of the general editors. David Scott Kastan and Ann Thompson have been wonderfully supportive throughout and helpful in their suggestions and comments. This edition of *Two Gentlemen*, though, owes its single greatest debt to the third of the general editors, Richard Proudfoot, who has served virtually as my co-editor (as I suspect he does for all the editions), making helpful suggestions, probing my suppositions and reading everything in this edition rigorously, imaginatively and sympathetically. He has brought a director's eye to the project as well (after much prompting, I learned of his production of the play at Worcester College, Oxford, in 1960), raising questions about stagecraft as frequently as those about F lineation. I wish to express my particular gratitude to him.

Other members of the Arden team have proven equally important. Three of my fellow editors, Virginia and Alden Vaughan (*The Tempest*, 1999) and James R. Siemon (*Richard III*, forthcoming), read drafts of my Introduction, talked through various issues with me over the years and provided strong support, especially through the occasional meetings, usually over dinner or drinks, of our informal group, or conspiracy, the Boston Arden Editors. I am additionally grateful to Virginia Vaughan for inviting me to present a portion of my Introduction to her advanced seminar at Clark University, Worcester, Massachusetts, and to Jim Siemon – for everything, as a colleague and friend of nearly thirty years.

In the period when this edition was first proposed and while most of the work was done on it, the entire Arden project was headed by the incomparable Jessica Hodge, whose work as publisher was exemplary in every way. She has an uncanny ability to judge her editors' capacities and to support and nudge them in just the right combinations. It has been astonishing to see how quickly and how effectively Margaret Bartley has taken over the reins, in my case providing the same kind of support and leadership over the last stages of this edition. Giulia Vincenzi has proven to be enormously helpful in a variety of ways, from connecting me to the various elements of production to helping secure photos and permissions from many different sources. It is also a pleasure to acknowledge the superlative work done by my copy editor, Nicola Bennett, who has served as virtually another co-editor (indeed, she is herself co-editing *Edward III*); her scrupulous eye, her suggestions, her sense of both the textual and the dramaturgical elements of the project have been of the greatest importance, and this edition is vastly the better for her involvement.

Much of the work on this edition was done at the Folger Shakespeare Library in Washington, D.C. I have profited from conversations with many wonderful people there, including Barbara A. Mowat, Gail Kern Paster, Richard Kuhta and Georgianna Ziegler. The Reading Room staff – under the expert direction of Elizabeth Walsh – makes the Folger not only the most efficient place on earth in which to do research in the early modern period but also, in my opinion, the friendliest and most inviting. The good humour of the staff, in the face of my often bumbling questions and requests, made the daily experience of work pleasurable as well as rewarding. I am also grateful to the Cambridge University Press for permission to reprint a revised version of '"And love you 'gainst the nature of love": Ovid, Rape, and *The Two Gentlemen of Verona*', originally published in *Shakespeare's Ovid: The 'Metamorphoses' in the Plays and Poems*, ed. A.B. Taylor (Cambridge, 2000).

Closer to home, I wish to thank Provost (and earlier, Dean) Dennis B. Berkey for important financial support on a number of occasions, which most recently allowed me to employ Melissa Ware Pino for a summer's meticulous assistance in gathering resources for the stage history of *Two Gentlemen*. My colleagues in early modern studies, Laurence Breiner, Christopher Martin and William Riggs, along with Jim Siemon, have been a source of intellectual stimulation and great collegiality for many years, and daily life is much the richer because of them – as it also is because of Coppélia Kahn, my co-chair of the Shakespeare Seminar at Harvard's Humanities Center for several years. A number of my former doctoral students – now embarked on their own careers – have enriched my teaching and scholarly life over the years, and although I did not inflict any part of this edition upon them, their influence is still palpable: Michael Friedman (who has himself written interestingly on *Two Gentlemen*), Andrew Hartley, Claudia Limbert, John McKernan, Kirk Melnikoff, Kaara Peterson, Marie Plasse, Dana Sonnenschein, Penelope Staples, Edward Washington and Bin Zhu among others.

And closest to home, I owe the greatest debt, as always, to my wife Carol and son David, who have watched and supported my work on this project with unfailing love and confidence.

William C. Carroll
Boston, Massachusetts

INTRODUCTION

THE PLAY

'Cease to Persuade'

The Two Gentlemen of Verona occupies a prominent position in the First Folio of 1623 – the second play, after *The Tempest*. Its position may only reflect the fact that it was one of the plays prepared by the scrivener Ralph Crane, four of which are grouped together at the beginning of the Folio (see p. 117), but *Two Gentlemen* does amply demonstrate Shakespeare's richly exuberant comic powers at work. When Francis Meres in 1598 listed six of Shakespeare's comedies as examples, proving that he 'is the most excellent' author of both comedy and history, *Two Gentlemen* was the first play mentioned (Chambers, *WS*, 2.194). Exactly four centuries later, the screenwriters Tom Stoppard and Marc Norman, in their 1998 Academy Award-winning film, *Shakespeare in Love*, show the beautiful Viola De Lesseps (played by Gwyneth Paltrow) joining a dashing young Shakespeare (Joseph Fiennes) as a male-disguised actor in a play that starts out as *Romeo and Ethel, the Pirate's Daughter* and winds up as *Romeo and Juliet*; Viola becomes Shakespeare's muse, and his professional career takes off. Viola's original incentive to meet Shakespeare (often overlooked in accounts of the film) is a production of a Shakespeare play, full of high comic scenes with a dog and rich, romantic language. Unnamed in the film, the play is of course *The Two Gentlemen of Verona*. We see Viola listening to the opening lines of the play, clearly thrilled by its poetic language, and Queen Elizabeth (Judi Dench) openly laughing at a scene with 'Will Kemp's' Lance and

1

throwing his dog Crab a piece of food. Shakespeare, however, watching offstage, shakes his head at the audience's low taste as they enjoy the performance of 2.3 with Lance and Crab.[1] The popularity of *Two Gentlemen* continues as a running joke throughout the film as the 'Henslowe' character hopes that Shakespeare will have a dog in the next play, *Romeo*, as well ('You mean, no dog of any kind?', Norman & Stoppard, 86).

Like all of Shakespeare's plays, *Two Gentlemen* has attracted the attention, if not the unfailing admiration, of the greatest editors and actors of the past four centuries and its stage history proves surprisingly rich. However, many readers and audiences have judged *Two Gentlemen*, as one of Shakespeare's earliest plays, to be aesthetically inferior to most of his others: 'early' comes to connote 'immature', hence relatively incompetent, in contrast to a play written later, which is more 'mature' (how could it not be?) and (almost by definition) therefore more successful. The final scene of the play, with Proteus's attempted rape of Silvia and Valentine's forgiveness of his friend, ranks as one of the most controversial in the Shakespearean canon. Its dramaturgical difficulties have been seen as the inept product of a callow and inexperienced playwright, consequently leading to questionable conclusions about the play's composition (see p. 129).

I aim to break this critical cycle, not by mounting a new (and doomed) argument about the play's aesthetic perfections, but by enlisting and, if possible, augmenting some stimulating recent critical and theoretical work on the early modern period and also related texts to cast light on Shakespeare's dramatic strategies in *Two Gentlemen*. Thus, the Introduction that follows begins by placing the play in relation to sixteenth-century discourses of

---

1   Later, Viola is shown in a near-swoon as she listens to the mediocre actor playing Valentine speak the lines at 3.1.174–84 (Queen Elizabeth dozes off at this point); Viola will herself recite these lines – and is vastly superior to the professional actor – later in the film, in her audition for a part in Shakespeare's new play. Speaking as one who is about to be banished from his beloved, as Valentine does in these lines, is a perfect foreshadowing of Viola's fate.

friendship, which have been seen to contextualize (although not satisfactorily for modern tastes) Valentine's behaviour at the end of the play. I hope that this edition, in exploring the early modern discourse of male friendship, will show how Shakespeare's use of the tradition is more complicated and indeed more searching than what has sometimes been seen as a rather immature, incompetent appropriation of it. Indeed, the fact that Shakespeare re-engages with the friendship tradition in his last play, *The Two Noble Kinsmen* (written around 1613 in collaboration with John Fletcher), counters any argument that the interest was merely one of an immature playwright. The controversial ending of *Two Gentlemen* presses the social demands of male friendship to their absurd limits, deliberately unsettling the audience by providing the form of closure but also leaving unresolved disturbing questions about desire, friendship and identity.

The Introduction then moves on to a consideration of other topics of significance: the bearing on the play of the story of the Prodigal Son, the problematics of the cross-dressed boy actor (the first in a Shakespearean comedy), metamorphosis as a central motif revealing the play's indebtedness to Ovid and Lyly, the use of letters, the identity of Crab's breed, the play's confused geography and its dramaturgy. The Introduction concludes with an examination of the play's stage and critical histories and issues relating to its text and date.

The Early Modern Discourse of Male Friendship

The dominant cultural context of *The Two Gentlemen of Verona* appears to be registered in the discourse of male friendship, derived from an amalgam of advice pamphlets, courtesy books (see Fig. 1), personal essays, letters, epigrams, paternal advice to sons, ballads, prose and verse romances (e.g. Book 4 of Spenser's *Faerie Queene*, the legend of friendship), plays (e.g. John Lyly's) and debates, among other written texts, as well as from an unwritten code of behaviour reflected in the fading glories of an honour culture (as James, 308–465, has described it) and a common set of foundational texts in the Tudor educational

1 Title-page of Richard Brathwait's *The English Gentleman*, 1630

system.[1] The dissemination of the precepts of friendship was extraordinarily widespread, yet two figures stand out as essential in every account: Aristotle and Cicero. Aristotle's comments on friendship were widely known and quoted, though they were not concentrated into a single essay. Cicero's essay *De Amicitia*, on the other hand, was at the heart of the entire textual field. Generations of schoolboys read and translated this essay and took up its moral lessons, even more than its style, in a widening arc of transmission.[2] Cicero's essay was translated into English three times before 1600,[3] yet almost anyone could have learned the essay's basic insights elsewhere, from both elite and popular culture. Among the most important of friendship texts was one evidently known to Shakespeare, Sir Thomas Elyot's *The Boke Named the Governour*, published in 1531, reprinted seven times by 1580, and widely cited and imitated.[4] Elyot devoted two chapters in Book 2 to themes and legends of friendship.

Cicero's essay establishes, if it does not historically originate, the basic tenets of friendship theory.[5] The first of these, as in John Harington's translation (reprinted by Ruth Hughey), is the moral necessity that 'frendshippe can bee but in good men' (Hughey, 147, l. 361). Cicero notes that 'there shoulde be among all men, a certain felowship' (Hughey, 148, ll. 387–8) and also that there are forms of natural friendship that are very strong (parent–child, for example), yet these are not so strong as the real thing. True friendship completes or perfects the individual. So close do true friends

---

1   For the play's other major contextualizing discourse, the tradition of romance derived most directly from George of Montemayor's *Diana*, see pp. 41–6.

2   See Baldwin for the authoritative study of Cicero's place in the early modern school curriculum.

3   By John Tiptoft (first Earl Worcester), from the Latin, printed 1481; by John Harington of Stepney, from a French version, printed 1550; and by Thomas Newton, who reworked Harington's translation but also made use of Latin texts, printed 1557 (Hughey, 295).

4   See the useful survey of Elyot's importance in the tradition by Mills; Hutson and Shannon further analyse the friendship literature from different perspectives.

5   In *A Type or Figure of Friendship*, A4^{r-v}, Walter Dorke's codification lists them in numerical order, from 1 to 20, with a final definition that includes all the others: 'Friendship is a perfect consent and agreement with benevolence and charity in all things, appertaining as well towards God as men.'

become that, in the most famous phrase of the entire tradition, 'of two he wold almost make one' (Hughey, 172, l. 1233).[1] Later writers erase Cicero's modifier 'almost' and assert the paradox of unity more forcefully: for Sir Thomas Elyot friendship is 'a blessed and stable connexion of sondrie willes, makinge of two parsones one in havinge and suffringe' (Elyot, 129–30); for Richard Edwards in 1564 'true friends should be two in body, but one in minde, / As it were one transformed into another' (*Damon and Pythias*, ll. 333–4); and for John Bodenham in 1600 'The summe of friendship is, that of two soules / One should be made, in will and firme affect' (Bodenham, 94). Similar examples could be multiplied almost indefinitely. With true friends, Montaigne, in his essay 'Of Friendship', argues,

> All things being by effect common betweene them; wils, thoughts, judgements, goods, wives, children, honour, and life; and their mutuall agreement, being no other than one soule in two bodies, according to the fit definition of *Aristotle*, they can neither lend or give ought to each other.
>
> (Montaigne, 1.203–4)

Such 'perfect amity', he continues, 'is indivisible' (Montaigne, 1.204).[2]

Along with 'One soull . . . in bodies twain' ('Of Friendship', Tottel, 1.106), the other most frequently quoted tenet of friendship is that, in Harington's translation of Cicero, 'he surely is a

---

1   The phrase seems already common by the time of Aristotle: 'all the proverbs agree in this; for example, "Friends have one soul between them" [and] "Amity is equality"' (Aristotle, Book 9, Chapter 8). The Latin is '*efficiat paene unum ex duobus*' (Cicero, *De Amicitia*, 188). Aristotle devotes the entirety of Books 8 and 9 of the *Nichomachean Ethics* to the subject of friendship.

2   As Potter, 55, notes, Montaigne's essay was 'clearly in Shakespeare's mind at the time when he wrote *Two Noble Kinsmen* . . . not in the relationship of Palamon and Arcite, but in Emilia's dialogue with Hippolyta in 1.3'. Shakespeare seems not yet to have read Montaigne as early as 1593. Florio's translation of the *Essays* was only printed in 1603, but there is evidence that Shakespeare might have seen a manuscript version around 1600 (see Yates, 213, 244).

freend, that is an other I' (Hughey, 172, ll. 1223–4). The Latin here is '*alter idem*' (Cicero, *De Amicitia*, 188), which might be better translated as 'another the same', but most writers took up the idea that the friend is indeed an '*alter ego*', another I or self.[1] Thus for Erasmus, in his *Adagia* (Book 1, section 1, adage 2), 'A friend is another self' ('*Amicus alter ipse*') and 'a second self'; for Elyot, 130, 'a frende is properly named of Philosophers the other I'; and for Walter Dorke, B2ʳ, the friend is 'as it were an *Alter ego*, that is another himselfe'. For Bacon, even this mystical paradox does not go far enough:

> it will appear, that it was a Sparing Speech of the Ancients, to say, *That a Frend is another Himselfe*: For that a *Frend* is farre more then *Himselfe*. Men have their Time, and die many times in desire of some Things, which they principally take to Heart; The Bestowing of a Child, The Finishing of a Worke, Or the like. If a Man have a true *Frend*, he may rest almost secure, that the Care of those Things, will continue after Him.
>
> (Bacon, 86)

Among the other key elements of the Ciceronian tradition are the frequently repeated insights that true friendship is generally not found 'in theim, whiche live in honour and rule' (Hughey, 166, l. 1031) and that true friendship must be carefully distinguished from flattery. These two precepts link friendship theory to political concerns. For some writers, no one needs a true friend to speak the blunt truth more than princes and kings, yet no one is less able to accept such friendship, in part because 'it is a chiefe poinct in freendeship, the higher to bee equall with the lower . . . the betters in degree, ought to equall theim selves with their inferiours' (Hughey, 168–9, ll. 1095–6, 1120–1).[2] This levelling effect, and

---

1 Henry H.S. Croft (Elyot, 130, n. 1) says that 'Zeno . . . originated the expression which afterwards passed into a proverb', and notes that Cicero also uses '*alter ego*' in the *Letters to Atticus*.

2 Cf. Dorke, A4ᵛ: 'Among Friends all things should be common.'

the privileging of personal autonomy over the power of the state, leads, as Laurie Shannon has shown, to an overlapping of friendship discourse with resistance theory. The Tyrant is, in the political field, the equivalent of the false friend; as Shannon notes, in many friendship narratives there is a triangle of desire among two friends and the ruler or tyrant who demands their loyalty (Shannon, 50–3, 125–55). But not all stories move in this direction, and in *The Two Gentlemen of Verona* Shakespeare follows another track.

For almost all (male) writers, friendship is a possibility among men only, not among women; 'the ordinary sufficiency of women', Montaigne asserts,

> cannot answer this conference and communication, the nurse of this sacred bond: nor seeme their mindes strong enough to endure the pulling of a knot so hard, so fast, and durable . . . this sex could never yet by any example attaine unto it, and is by ancient schooles rejected thence.
>
> (Montaigne, 1.199)

Women's friendships, of which there are numerous examples and accounts, are 'commonly portrayed in the Renaissance, but normally as coexistent with marriage', rather than in opposition to it (Shannon, 55, n. 2). Shakespeare, however, does depict some women as strong friends, as in Helena's reminiscence in *A Midsummer Night's Dream*, which employs the standard tropes of friendship:

> We, Hermia, like two artificial gods
> Have with our needles created both one flower,
> Both on one sampler, sitting on one cushion,
> Both warbling of one song, both in one key,
> As if our hands, our sides, voices, and minds
> Had been incorporate. So we grew together,

> Like to a double cherry, seeming parted,
> But yet an union in partition,
> Two lovely berries moulded on one stem;
> So, with two seeming bodies but one heart,
> Two of the first, like coats in heraldry,
> Due but to one and crownèd with one crest.
> And will you rend our ancient love asunder,
> To join with men in scorning your poor friend?
> (*MND* 3.2.203–16)

As with male friends, romantic love here injects discord into the now past-tense ideal friendship; 'two seeming bodies but one heart' have now split apart, and at the end of the play the two couples will leave behind same-sex friendship for marriage. In *As You Like It*, Celia defends Rosalind's loyalty in similar terms:

> If she be a traitor,
> Why, so am I. We still have slept together,
> Rose at an instant, learned, played, eat together,
> And wheresoe'er we went, like Juno's swans
> Still we went coupled and inseparable.
> (*AYL* 1.3.70–4)

They will be coupled in a different way at the end of the play, however, each going off to marriage. Interestingly, the language of these two female friendships is similar to the language Shakespeare uses for the male friendship in *The Winter's Tale*, that of Polixenes and Leontes, expressed by Polixenes as a matter of past union:

> We were as twinned lambs that did frisk i' the sun
> And bleat the one at th' other. What we changed
> Was innocence for innocence; we knew not
> The doctrine of ill-doing, nor dreamed
> That any did. Had we pursued that life,
> And our weak spirits ne'er been higher reared

With stronger blood, we should have answered heaven
Boldly 'Not guilty,' the imposition cleared
Hereditary ours.

(WT 1.2.67–75)

These accounts of ideal friendship are all about lost childhood innocence. Hermione's ironic response to Polixenes – 'By this we gather / You have tripped since' (*WT* 1.2.75–6) – confirms this in *The Winter's Tale* and could be directed at any of these Shakespearean friends, male or female. All these same-sex friendships are changed by romantic desire and ultimately marriage.[1] Yet despite the use of similar language to describe both male and female same-sex friendship (and *A Midsummer Night's Dream* even explores conflict between friends over love), none of these plays really derives from the Ciceronian friendship tradition of idealization, which took men as its exemplars: Damon and Pythias, Orestes and Pylades, Theseus and Pirithous, Achilles and Patroclus, and Titus and Gisippus, among other pairings; women's friendships were not the same.

If female–female relations could not really be true friendship, neither could male–female relations. The question, again, was one of stability, as Montaigne argues:

the affection toward women . . . is a rash and wavering fire, waving and divers: the fire of an ague subject to fits and stints, and that hath but slender hold-fast of us. In true friendship, it is a generall and universall heat, and equally tempered, a constant and setled heat, all pleasure and smoothnes, that hath no pricking or stinging in it, which the more it is in lustfull love, the more is it but a ranging and mad desire in following that which flies us.

(Montaigne, 1.198)

---

1 Cf. the friendship of Emilia and Flavina described in *TNK* 1.3.49–82, which seems to contradict this. Emilia's powerful description ends with the assertion 'That the true love 'tween maid and maid may be / More than in sex dividual' (81–2), yet Flavina died when each girl was eleven years old (54), hence before 'stronger blood' came into existence.

In John Lyly's *Endymion*, 3.4.114–16, Eumenides, torn between his desire for Semele and his friendship with Endymion, comes to realize that 'The love of men to women is a thing common and of course: the friendshippe of man to man infinite and immortall' and wise old Geron confirms, at 3.4.122–6, 'all thinges (friendship excepted) are subject to fortune: Love is but an eye-worme, which onely tickleth the heade with hopes and wishes, friendshippe the image of eternity, in which there is nothing moveable, nothing mischeevous' (Lyly, 3.50). Cicero asserts that 'it is love (*amor*), from which the word "friendship" (*amicitia*) is derived' (Cicero, *De Amicitia*, 139) or, as Harington more ambiguously translates, 'love, wherof freendly love and freendshippe commeth, is the chiefe cause, to fastne good willes together' (Hughey, 152, ll. 519–21), but all of Cicero's examples, as with later writers, are men, and in the early modern period a clear misogynist line emerges.[1] True friendship, in virtually all cases, could only exist between men. At first glance, Edmund Tilney's *The Flower of Friendship* (1573) might seem to be the exception. The flower of friendship is in fact marriage, but though Tilney does move a certain distance towards defining marriage as a companionate relationship or friendship, he never connects marriage to the traditions of Aristotle and Cicero.[2]

The idealization of the power and transcendent virtue of male–male friendship lies at the heart of the male friendship tradition as Shakespeare explores it in *The Two Gentlemen of Verona*. In most pre-Shakespearean works engaged with the

---

1   Elyot, 122, follows Cicero more closely: 'love, called in latine *Amor*, whereof *Amicitia* commeth, named in englisshe frendshippe or amitie'.
2   Metaphors of marriage were, however, often inserted into friendship theory, as in Thomas Churchyard's *A Spark of Friendship* (1588): friendship is 'the only true love knot, that knits in conjunction, thousands together: and yet the mysterie and maner of the working is so great, that the ripest wittes may waxe rotten, before they yeeld reason, and shewe how the mixture is made: that two severall bodies shall meete in one minde, and bee as it were maried and joined in one maner of disposition, with so small a shewe of vertue, and so little cause, that may constraine both parties to be bound and fast locked in a league of love' (Churchyard, C1ʳ). Cf. *Son* 116.1–2: 'Let me not to the marriage of true minds / Admit impediments.'

11

tradition, the bonds of friendship between two male friends – what Eve Kosofsky Sedgwick terms homosocial bonds – prove stronger than male–female desire. Usually, one of the young men falls in love with a woman, but the prior friendship with a male friend produces enormous anxiety and conflict; or one male friend falls in love with his friend's beloved, leading to conflict and anxiety on both sides. The nature of such male–male friendship is both platonic and to some extent erotic, and its power is sufficient to cause a man to renounce his own life to save his friend (as in the stories of Damon and Pythias and Titus and Gisippus), to renounce his wife or fiancée in preference to the bond with another man, or even, in perhaps its most extreme form, to offer his female beloved to his friend.

This idealization of male–male friendship reflected a Neoplatonic exaltation of both selfless devotion to and ideal union with another, as well as mastery over sexual desire. Once achieved, such friendship produced powerful, even therapeutic, effects, such as, in Bacon's phrasing, 'the Ease and Discharge of the Fulnesse and Swellings of the Heart, which Passions of all kinds doe cause and induce . . . no Receipt openeth the Heart, but a true *Frend*' (Bacon, 81), while some formulations of friendship's power moved toward the mystical, as in Cicero: 'Wherfore in frendship the absent be present, the nedie never lacke, the sicke thincke them selves whole, and that which is hardest to be spoken, the dead never die' (Hughey, 150, ll. 453–6).

Early modern texts stressing the powerful emotional bonds of male–male friendship frequently figured this closeness as a clearly physical intimacy. A typical example may be seen in Lyly's description of the friendship of Euphues and Philautus:

> after many embracings and protestations one to an other, they walked to dinner, where they wanted neither meate, neither Musicke, neither any other pastime, and having banqueted, to digest their sweet confections,

they daunced all that afternoon, they used not only one
boord but one bedde, one booke (if so be it they thought
not one to[o] many.) Their friendship augmented every
day, insomuch that the one could not refraine the company of the other one minute, all things went in
common betweene them, which all men accompted
commendable.

(*Euphues*, ll. 13–21; Lyly, 1.199)

As Alan Bray, among others, points out, 'the public signs of a
male friendship – open to all the world to see – could be read in
a different and sodomitical light to the one intended' (Bray, 53);
although the conventions of friendship 'were set a world away'
from the discourse of sodomy, still the 'signs of the one were
indeed sometimes also the signs of the other' (Bray, 47; see
Fig. 2).[1] Bruce Smith also traces the themes of male friendship
through a wide range of early modern literature (particularly in
relation to the ways in which it is distinguished from but also
allied to master–servant sexual relations), noting the 'improbable,
magical circumstances that allow friendship to be reconciled with
marriage' in the early plays of Shakespeare (Smith, *Desire*, 69).

Jeffrey Masten, in his study of 'the sanctioned homoeroticism
of male friendship' (Masten, 37), argues that the very first lines
of *Two Gentlemen*, in which 'male friendship and Petrarchan
love . . . speak a remarkably similar language', insert the play
'into a discourse of homoerotic male friendship' (Masten, 39).
Citing such passages as Proteus's soliloquy rationalizing his
betrayal of Valentine ('Valentine I'll hold an enemy, / Aiming at
Silvia as a sweeter friend', 2.6.29–30), Masten notes 'the extent
to which courtship is in this play constantly collapsing into

---

1 Jardine, 'Companionate', 239, argues that we should read texts that 'elide professional male friendship and sodomy in a "discourse of sodomy" as part of the period's
   mistrust of concealed, irregular networks of co-operation of all kinds, where these
   interfered with the recognized, public socially structuring forms' – i.e. of marriage
   and the reproduction of the lineal family.

2 Detail from title-page of Richard Brathwait's *The English Gentleman*, 1630

friendship', revealing 'not the opposition of male friendship and Petrarchan love but rather their interdependence' in a social order in which 'texts and women circulate among gentlemen' (Masten, 41, 37). The final scene, in his view, 'stages the play's ultimate collaboration of male friendship and its incorporation of the plot we would label "heterosexual"'' in the play's 'ongoing project, the (re)constitution of Valentine and Protheus as gentlemanly subjects' (Masten, 46, 47).

Some critics describe the idealization of male friendship as a kind of fantasy of denial, an embodiment, in psychoanalytic terms, of the paralysis of normative development from same-sex to other-sex erotic relations – representing an adolescent phase of withdrawal or self-protection prior to the establishment of a heterosexual relationship.[1] It may also be seen, as Bray suggests, as a discourse produced by a cultural lack: 'some of the conventions of friendship are missing . . . in society at large', one of which is 'the assumption that both masters and their close servingmen would be "gentle" men' (Bray, 50); missing elements of a mutating class structure are thus supplied through the discourse of idealized friendship. One might also note here changing conceptions of marriage in the early modern period, in which romantic companionate[2] relations are elevated as equal or superior to purely arranged marriages based on economic considerations. The idealization of male friendship as superior to male–female love (which was considered not romantic or companionate but merely lustful, hence inferior in some accounts (see p. 10)) therefore performs a project of cultural nostalgia, a stepping back from potentially more threatening social arrangements to a world of order, a world based on a 'gift' economy of

1 See Garber, 31–2, and Adelman, 75. Haslem, 129, notes that the 'female communicative bond' established between Julia and Lucetta in the first half of the play 'is in effect discarded, erased, en route to achieving the male–female love relationship'.
2 Among works on companionate marriage in the early modern period, see Fletcher, 'Marriage', Jardine, 'Companionate', and Macfarlane.

personal relations among male social equals rather than one based on a newer, less stable economy of emotional and economic risk.[1] The offer of the woman from one male friend to another would therefore be the highest expression of friendship, from one point of view, a low point of psycho-sexual regression from another, or, from still another viewpoint, a fantastic instance of a patriarchal culture's 'traffic in women' (Gayle Rubin's term). Elements of all these viewpoints inform the final scene of *Two Gentlemen*, if not the entire play.

Shakespeare's *Sonnets* also depict the painful disruption of an idealized male friendship by heterosexual desire for a third party. Dating the sonnets seems a permanently difficult task (see Duncan-Jones, 1–29), but some were certainly written by 1598, when Francis Meres lists them in *Palladis Tamia*, in which he also mentions *Two Gentlemen* (see p. 129). Although there are verbal links between various Shakespeare sonnets and *Two Gentlemen*,[2] the basic situation – the friendship and subsequent conflict between two male friends – is what most strongly links the play to many of them. For example, in *Sonnet* 36, the speaker, even as he agonizes over his friend's betrayal, invokes the standard propositions of friendship theory: 'Let me confess that we two must be twain, / Although our undivided loves are one . . . In our two loves there is but one respect, / Though in our lives a separable spite' (*Son* 36.1–2, 5–6). The speaker's plight is perhaps most evident in *Sonnet* 42, in which his young friend finally betrays him with his own mistress. The triangle of desire is paradoxically, but not convincingly, invoked as something positive. The speaker excuses the young man and his mistress because, since he and his friend 'are one' (13), his mistress, in loving his friend, still loves him and, moreover, he and his friend are further united in loving the same woman:

---

1 Thus Valentine's attempt to steal away with Silvia is denounced by her father in terms of class inferiority and social overreaching; see 3.1.153–60.
2 See notes on 1.2.133; 2.1.66; 2.6.1–43, 7; 3.1.340; 5.4.8–9, 75.

> That thou hast her it is not all my grief,
> And yet it may be said I loved her dearly;
> That she hath thee is of my wailing chief,
> A loss in love that touches me more nearly.
> Loving offenders, thus will I excuse ye:
> Thou dost love her, because thou knowst I love her,
> And for my sake even so doth she abuse me,
> Suff'ring my friend for my sake to approve her.
> (*Son* 42.1–8)

The next lines may remind us of Proteus's soliloquy in 2.6:

> If I lose thee, my loss is my love's gain,
> And losing her, my friend hath found that loss;
> Both find each other, and I lose both twain,
> And both for my sake lay on me this cross:
> But here's the joy, my friend and I are one;
> Sweet flattery! Then she loves but me alone.
> (*Son* 42.9–14)

The penultimate line, with its invocation of the two-in-one figure, is a desperate and unconvincing attempt to remove the 'cross' that weighs the speaker down. The sonnets do not resolve the conflict, as *Two Gentlemen* will (whether or not convincingly) by bringing all the parties together in the final scene.

Given its built-in anxieties and conflicts, the discourse of friendship found expression throughout the drama of the early modern theatre. Plays ranging from Marlowe's *Edward II* to the anonymous *A Knack to Know a Knave* make use of friendship material, as Mills shows, and at the end of his career Shakespeare reworked the story of Palamon and Arcite in *The Two Noble Kinsmen* (see p. 33–5). In 1566, Richard Edwards's *Palamon and Arcite* (of which only one song survives) was performed before an audience that included an appreciative Queen Elizabeth (Potter, 46), and a play entitled 'palaman & arset' was performed several times in the autumn of 1594 (Henslowe, 24); Henry Chettle was paid for working on a 'damon and Pytheas' in 1599/1600 (Henslowe, 63) – possibly a reworking of Richard Edwards's play by that name – and the Admiral's Men performed the aptly-titled (in light of *Two Gentlemen*) play, also by Chettle, 'love partes frenshippe' in 1602 (Henslowe, 202), which is not extant.[1]

Among the most relevant precursors to *Two Gentlemen*, Richard Edwards's *Damon and Pythias*, performed in 1564 by the Children of the Chapel Royal, is not a source of *Two Gentlemen* in the strictest sense of the term as directly-copied plot, but the 'two gentlemen of Greece' (as the list of 'the Speakers names' has it) anticipate the two gentlemen of Verona in several ways. A related male friendship text, the anonymous German translation of another English play, the *Tragaedia von Julio und Hyppolita*, was performed in about 1600 and printed in 1620 in the collection *Englische Comedien und Tragedien* (Cohn, 118). This play also contains a few slight resemblances to *Two Gentlemen*, but again not sufficient to establish it as a source, though Leech thinks it likely that some connection exists (Ard^2, xxxix–xl). The friendship of Damon and Pythias effortlessly transcends romantic love, but in *Julio und Hyppolita* the two gentlemen of Rome, Romulus and Julius, clash over the love of Hyppolita with tragic consequences: Julius's betrayal of his friend Romulus is never resolved, and the play ends with Romulus killing Julius, and then with Hyppolita and Romulus each separately committing suicide.

Unfortunately, what may be the *Ur-Two Gentlemen*, the anonymous play *The History of Titus and Gisippus*, acted in 1577 by the rivals to the Children of the Chapel Royal, Sebastian Westcott's Paul's Boys, is now lost (Chambers, *Stage*, 4.93, 152). The well-known story of Titus and Gisippus depicts one gentleman of Athens, Gisippus, who makes the ultimate sacrifice in the name of friendship, the offer of his beloved to his friend Titus, a gentleman

---

1 According to Henslowe, 200, it was co-written by Henry Chettle and 'mr smyth'; on Smith, see Chambers, *Stage*, 4.50. The plays of John Lyly provided a particularly rich vein of material for Shakespeare; see Hunter, *Lyly*, and pp. 58–9.

of Rome. Although the text of this play has not survived, several versions of the story were in print in the sixteenth century. The central version in Continental literature was that of Boccaccio, while the dominant version in England was that of Sir Thomas Elyot in *The Boke Named the Governour*. There were also at least two verse accounts of Titus and Gisippus in English: William Walter's translation (*c.* 1530) of Philippo Beroaldo's 1491 Latin version of Boccaccio and Edward Lewicke's 1562 version, adapted from Elyot (these two verse narratives of the story can be found in Wright), as well as an earlier Latin play performed around 1544–5, written by John Foxe (whose text has survived), and one performed around 1547–53 produced by Ralph Radcliff (Foxe, 9). There were numerous other versions in Italian, French and German.

The main outlines of the Titus and Gisippus story may serve as a lens through which we can see more clearly what Shakespeare was up to in *Two Gentlemen*, particularly in the infamous final scene. The following discussion will focus initially on the sexual dynamics of the Titus and Gisippus story, and then much more specifically on what is unique, in the early modern discourse of male friendship, to this story and to *Two Gentlemen* – the offer of the female by one male to another.

Titus and Gisippus and the Offer

Titus and Gisippus are linked with Damon and Pythias, among others, as equal paragons of male friendship in many texts of the period, such as Spenser's *Faerie Queene* and Lyly's *Euphues*.[1] Unlike the 'two gentlemen of Greece', however, or the two

---

1   See Lyly, *Euphues*, ll. 22–5: 'Assure your selfe that *Damon* to his *Pythias*, *Pylades* to his *Orestes*, *Titus* to his *Gysippus*, *Theseus* to his *Pyrothus*, *Scipio* to his *Laelius*, was never found more faithfull then *Euphues* will be to his *Philautus*' (Lyly, 1.198); and *FQ*, 4.10.27: 'great *Hercules*, and *Hylas* deare; / Trew *Jonathan*, and *David* trustie tryde; / Stout *Theseus*, and *Pirithous* his feare; / *Pylades* and *Orestes* by his syde; / Myld *Titus* and *Gesippus* without pryde; / *Damon* and *Pythias* whom death could not sever: / All these and all that ever had bene tyde / In bands of friendship, there did live for ever, / Whose lives although decay'd, yet loves decayed never'.

Germans of Rome, or the two gentlemen of Verona, Titus and Gisippus are from different cities, from Rome and Athens respectively. This geographical distinction, however, is largely masked by a repeated insistence on the identity of the two young men: these friends are not simply alter egos of one another but doppelgangers, for, as children, they were 'so like, that without moche difficultie it coulde nat be discerned of their propre parentes, whiche was Titus from Gisippus, or Gisippus from Titus . . . they semed to be one in fourme and personage' (Elyot, 134); no one could distinguish between them, Titus claims, 'but by our owne insignement or showinge, in so moche as there were put about our neckes lacis of sondry colours to declare our personages' (Elyot, 146–7).[1] When Gisippus, pressured by his friends and family, falls in love with Sophronia, Titus too is struck by Cupid's arrow, falling in love with Sophronia as well, and then is struck deadly ill from his guilt and despair, blaming Gisippus's praise of her for his own treasonous desire. René Girard would describe the resulting triangle as a consequence of mimetic desire – Titus desires Sophronia just because Gisippus does[2] – but Titus himself puts a slightly different interpretation on it:

> Why wolde ye have me see that, whiche you youre selfe coulde nat beholde without ravisshinge of minde and carnall appetite? Alas, why forgate ye that our mindes and appetites were ever one? And that also what so ye liked was ever to me in like degree pleasaunt?
>
> (Elyot, 139)

---

1   This account follows, as Shakespeare did, Elyot's version in Book 2, Chapter 12, of *The Boke Named the Governour*, rather than Boccaccio's. See Sargent on Shakespeare's use of Elyot. In Boccaccio, by contrast, the friends are not said to look identical. In Foxe's play, derived largely from Elyot, 'except for your clothing there's almost no difference between you' (Foxe, 97).

2   Girard makes a similar argument about *Two Gentlemen*: 'Valentine and Proteus can be friends only by desiring alike and, if they do, they are enemies' because 'The *mimesis* of desire is both the best of friendship and the worst of hatred' (Girard, 233 and 242). Østergaard offers a refutation of Girard's argument.

Given their essential unity, then, Titus must desire the same thing or person as his twin Gisippus, and Gisippus acknowledges that he had 'remembred nat the commune astate of our nature . . . the unitie of our two appetites' (Elyot, 140). The resemblances and the differences from the situation in *Two Gentlemen* are readily apparent. In Shakespeare, the two gentlemen are closely linked but they are physically and psychologically distinguished, the distinctions between Shakespeare's two gentlemen running partly along Ovidian lines (see pp. 25–7).

In the Titus and Gisippus story, the offer of Sophronia is made by Gisippus in order to save Titus's life; in *Two Gentlemen*, Valentine makes the offer to Proteus freely, at the sign of Proteus's penitence and supposed return to normality. Proteus's sickness is only psychological and is already past (assuming his repentance is sincere) when the offer is made, whereas Titus is said literally to be near death. In Shakespeare, moreover, the offer is not accepted – at least, there is no textual indication that it is; Julia faints (see 5.4.84 SDn.) before either Proteus or Silvia can speak.[1] Silvia, in fact, never speaks again. It is a critical moment in the play, to which I will return; I want to emphasize here that the offer of the beloved is not accepted in Shakespeare.

In Elyot's Titus and Gisippus story, however, Titus does accept Gisippus's offer of Sophronia, with virtually no psychological conflict in either party. The means by which the transaction is effected are worth a closer look. Gisippus's plan to switch places with Titus on his wedding day rests on the physical near-identity of the two men, and the peculiarity of the Greek wedding ritual

---

1 Seeing the play not as an exploration of romantic desire but as 'a comic exploration of the nature and function of a gentleman', Slights, 72, believes that Valentine's offer is no more than 'a courteous gesture that will give Proteus a chance to be his best self' – a chance that Proteus never takes up, it would seem, because Julia faints immediately. Rossky, 210, on the other hand, sees the play as 'a good-humored satirical lark, most of all in its controversial ending', and believes that 'almost everything Elyot does to prompt our acceptance of friendship over love, Shakespeare alters to create comic absurdity' (Rossky, 213). For theatrical and editorial efforts to evade the nature of the offer, see pp. 92–5.

that, 'natwithstandinge any ceremony done at the time of the spousayles, the mariage natwithstandinge is nat confirmed, untill at night that the husbande putteth a ringe on the finger of his wife, and unloseth her girdell' (Elyot, 142)[1]. What follows, then, is a male-oriented bed trick, in which Titus simply takes Gisippus's place in the marriage bed, deceiving not only the servants of the household but the bride herself. In the actual bed scene, there is no reference to darkness, so Titus's face is visible, and, unlike many bed tricks in Renaissance drama, here the lovers speak with one another, in exchanging vows and ring. 'What thinge els' they did, Elyot discreetly remarks, 'they two onely knewe it' (146).[2]

Shakespeare seems not to have been the dramatist who would pass up the chance to use a bed trick. In *All's Well That Ends Well*, he takes up a bed trick that is in his source material (William Painter's *The Palace of Pleasure*, 1566), while in *Measure for Measure*, he invents a bed trick that does not exist in any of the source materials (see Doran, 385–9). In the Renaissance versions of the Titus and Gisippus story following either Elyot or Boccaccio, the offer of the woman is not only accepted, but it is accomplished through a bed trick. The bed tricks in *Measure for Measure* and *All's Well* work against the male – in the dark, he cannot distinguish his wife from the woman whose place has been taken; in both cases, he rightly believes he is deflowering a virgin (the aptly named Diana in *All's Well*) or even a nun (Isabella in *Measure for Measure*), though wrong about that virgin's identity. The blindness of the

---

1 The requirements specified in the wedding ritual here, as RP notes, 'correspond with the conditions imposed by Bertram on Helena in *AW* 3.2.57–60'.
2 The bed trick in Elyot is therefore not really crucial to Gisippus's plan. In Lewicke, 'Then Titus he stept in full light, / Anon to bed he did prepare, / The maide assone eke as she might, / Lay downe by Titus naked bare, / Not knowing of the subtill s[n]are, / But thought it had bene Gisippus' (Wright, 195). In Boccaccio, 783, by contrast, the bedroom is darkened, as is usual in most bed-trick narratives. Walter's translation gives 'Gesippus chambre where as the bride lay / Titus chambre annexed was unto / Which had a litle dore & secret way / From the one to the other for to go / Gesippus the candell light quenched tho / And to Titus chambre fast he hastid' (Wright, 149). Foxe completely effaces the actual scene, simply having Titus enter afterward, singing '*O dies festus*' ('Oh happy day') (Foxe, 100–1).

man in these stories figures male desire as primally aggressive and narcissistic; the woman is reduced to a maidenhead, undistinguishable from any other maidenhead. Thus the usual bed trick enacts a male rape fantasy, one which is magically resolved: the virgin/nun taken in the dark turns out to be the man's wife after all, a woman both sexual and virginal. Eventually, the exposure and guilty knowledge of their actions leads the men to some kind of penitence or apparent reformation.[1]

But in Elyot's version of the Titus and Gisippus story, not only does Sophronia not know she is marrying and sleeping with Titus, but even when she does, they seem to live happily ever after; there is no record of her reaction to the truth, or any sense of how she is reconciled to the situation.[2] But how could there be, given that she is the merest token in the transactions of male friendship? Shakespeare does not follow the Titus and Gisippus story beyond the offer, even with the dramatically appealing intricacies of the story's bed trick. Here, as in the Sherlock Holmes story, we have the curious case of the dog – not Crab – which did not bark in the night. Moreover, what for Shakespeare is the climactic moment of his play, in the final scene, comes relatively early in the various versions of Titus and Gisippus (Titus has slept with Sempronia by 2.2 of Foxe's five-act play). Shakespeare has thus foregrounded what is only part of a much longer narrative in Elyot and Boccaccio and, in the greatest contrast to their accounts, the offer is not even accepted in *Two Gentlemen*. Yet the mere fact of the offer being made constitutes what has traditionally been seen as the most objectionable moment in the play, or the main cause of its 'failure' (see Slights and Small).

The Rape and the Offer

Proteus's attempted rape of Silvia in 5.4, like Valentine's offer, is frequently seen as another objectionable moment in the play. (For

---

1 See Desens for a useful survey of the bed trick in this period.
2 In Boccaccio, 784, by contrast, she becomes angry and tells her father.

the history of the staging of this scene, see p. 95–9.) Where does the attempted rape come from? No attempted or completed rape exists in any of the available analogues of *Two Gentlemen*: in Elyot's version of Titus and Gisippus, Sophronia goes willingly with Titus under a misapprehension, and in *Julio und Hyppolita*, the female is simply deceived into accepting a new lover. However objectionable these actions may be, neither involves the physical assault which Proteus undertakes. Unlike the offer, which has a clear source in the Titus and Gisippus story, the attempted rape seems to be Shakespeare's invention. The rape motif, however, does figure in other material that may have influenced the play.

In traditional source studies of the play, Ovid is referenced almost exclusively in relation to Proteus's name (see Giamatti, Scott and List of Roles, 3n.), to Julia's allusion to Ariadne (see 4.4.165–6n.), to Valentine's allusion to Hero and Leander (see 1.1.21–6) and to more general themes of transformation (see Carroll, *Metamorphoses*, Barkan and Bate). Ovidian influence, however, clearly informs the play at the end as well as in these other moments, for love in the *Metamorphoses* itself is all too frequently enacted as rape; indeed, Charles Segal has gone so far as to term Ovid's poem an 'epic of rape' (Segal, 93). The most Ovidian element in the play, in some respects, is thus not Proteus's name, but the attempted rape itself.

Perhaps one way in which to reconceive Ovid's influence on Shakespeare in *Two Gentlemen* is to consider Valentine as no less Ovidian than Proteus, and to see the two gentlemen as in essence one man split into two parallel but distinct figures.[1] One mark of this linkage is that the key Ovidian term is used of both of them: Proteus exclaims in the opening scene, 'Thou, Julia, thou hast metamorphosed me' (1.1.66), while Speed notes of Valentine,

---

1 Simmons, 862, calls them subject (Valentine) and anti-subject (Proteus).

'now you are metamorphosed with a mistress' (2.1.27–8).[1] At its worst in the play, metamorphosis is a kind of disease, comic in Valentine, but almost demonic in Proteus, whose helplessly metamorphic condition represents a terrifying triumph of unconstrained desire. The two gentlemen, then, enact alternative but equally Ovidian conceptions of male desire.

Certainly the name Proteus immediately evokes Ovid's figure of instability, shape-changing and aggressive desire, even rape – the '*Protea . . . ambiguum*' of *Metamorphoses*, 2.9. In the *Ars Amatoria*, Ovid muses on the 'hearts of women', which 'have as many fashions as the world has shapes'. The wise man, he goes on,

> will suit himself to countless fashions, and like Proteus
> will now resolve himself into light waves, and now will be
> a lion, now a tree, now a shaggy boar . . . And so comes it
> that she who has feared to commit herself to an hon-
> ourable lover degrades herself to the embraces of a mean
> one.
>
> (*Art*, 1.755–70)

So most Renaissance authors see Proteus in Ovid's tradition, in the words of Spenser, as 'that old leachour, which with bold assault / That beautie [Florimell] durst presume to violate' (*FQ*, 3.4.36; see Nohrnberg, 593–6).

The Ovidian link to Valentine is perhaps less obvious but equally significant. Valentine's love is considerably less violent and aggressive than that of Proteus. Valentine's very name was understood as synonymous with 'a lover' (*OED sb.* 2) and perhaps love-token ('There's not a hair on's head but 'tis a Valentine',

---

1   The Folio reads 'metamorphis'd' in both cases. Bate, 43, notes that the *OED* gives these passages as the earliest English uses of the term, though he notes as well that it appears in Marlowe's *The Jew of Malta*, 1.2.381 (Marlowe, 1.281), which may pre-date *Two Gentlemen*. The only other instance in Shakespeare of this word as a verb occurs in the twin play of *Two Gentlemen*, *Two Noble Kinsmen*, where Emilia hears of the battle between Palamon and Arcite: 'Were they metamorphosed / Both into one! – Oh, why? There were no woman / Worth so composed a man' (*TNK* 5.3.84–6).

3.1.191–2), and Saint Valentine is the patron saint of lovers. A.B. Taylor suggests that 'As well as being a saintly name, it is significant that "Valentine" was also used in the sixteenth century to refer to God himself' (ABT; see *OED sb*. 2b). Taylor also suggests that 'Valentine's "moderate" Ovidian love is also enriched by profound and mysterious Christian values', giving 'a deep resonance to the lines in which he forgives Proteus after the rape' (ABT).

Valentine's secular antecedents are perhaps signalled most effectively by his own dismissive allusion to Hero and Leander as 'some shallow story of deep love – / How young Leander crossed the Hellespont' (1.1.21–2). Yet Valentine will find himself in a similar position in the third act, when he is intercepted on his way to Silvia's chamber with the hidden ladder, which 'Would serve to scale another Hero's tower, / So bold Leander would adventure it' (3.1.119–20). With its echoes of Ovid's *Heroides* (18 and 19) and *Amores* (2.16.31), and of Marlowe's poem (see 1.1.21–6n.), this allusion links Valentine to the Ovidian tradition of the amatory poem, amply represented in Renaissance literature generally and regularly invoked by Shakespeare. Valentine thus takes his place among other rebellious young male lovers, such as Troilus and Pyramus, thwarted from their loves by hostile conditions or blocking fathers. The Duke clinches this train of associations when, after reading Valentine's letter to Silvia, he exclaims,

> Why, Phaëton, for thou art Merops' son,
> Wilt thou aspire to guide the heavenly car,
> And with thy daring folly burn the world?
> Wilt thou reach stars because they shine on thee?
> (3.1.153–6)

The Duke associates Valentine with one of the most dangerous of mythological rebellions against the father (tragically linked with Juliet at *RJ* 3.2.3), while also suggesting that Valentine is overreaching socially ('Go, base intruder, overweening slave, / Bestow thy fawning smiles on equal mates', 3.1.157–8). Valentine will crash and burn only figuratively, his fate as a lover following along with but stopping short of those of Pyramus, Leander and Phaëton. Valentine's love, moreover, by leading him into reckless, although partly comic, rebellion links him with Proteus. In *Two Gentlemen*, Shakespeare can therefore be seen to be bringing together two figurations of male desire from the narratives of the two gentlemen of England and Italy, Elyot and Ovid. By the end of the play, the desires of both Proteus and Valentine culminate in the attempted rape and the offer, and in the light of the rest of the play these two moments may therefore be understood together.

If *Two Gentlemen*, like other friendship texts, depicts the conflict between love and friendship, by the fifth act there is very little conflict for Proteus, as sexual desire has completely overcome him. Just before he attacks Silvia, Proteus justifies his desire for her by asking, 'In love / Who respects friend?', to which Silvia replies, 'All men but Proteus' (5.4.53–4). Proteus's name accurately reflects the transforming and deforming power of desire (which afflicts Valentine as well, as we see in 2.1). His assault on Silvia follows with an admission that language has failed to 'change' her likewise, thereby, in his logic, necessitating 'force' – the repeated keyword:

> Nay, if the gentle spirit of moving words
> Can no way change you to a milder form,
> I'll woo you like a soldier, at arms' end,
> And love you 'gainst the nature of love – force ye.
>   (5.4.55–8)

Proteus's assault reflects not only the failure of persuasive language, then, but the collapse of 'love' itself.[1] To love against the

---

1 Cf. *Diana*, 76 (a few pages before the main line of narrative that Shakespeare followed), in which an attempted rape is observed: 'I never thought that love could bring a lover to so foule an extreme, as with violent hands, and such unseemly force to sease upon his beloved.'

nature of love is not only to employ force, but to understand the female other merely as an object. Proteus then reiterates the necessity for force ('I'll force thee yield to my desire', 5.4.59), to which Valentine, when he interrupts, demands that Proteus 'let go that rude uncivil *touch*' (5.4.60; emphasis added). The rescue as well as the attempted rape objectifies the woman as body, as possession. Once he has his possession – the now completely subdued Silvia – back, Valentine directs his comments entirely to Proteus – to the issues of trust, of Proteus's repentance and of his own forgiveness as their bond is re-established, at which point Valentine then makes the infamous offer: 'All that was mine in Silvia I give thee' (see 5.4.82–3n.).

Valentine's offer of Silvia stands in direct relation, therefore, to Proteus's attempted rape of Silvia: the offer is the structural equivalent, in terms of male friendship, to the attempted rape, in terms of male desire. The woman is no less the object of possession ('All that was mine'). The conflict of possession continues when Turio enters to claim Silvia – 'Yonder is Silvia, and Silvia's mine' (5.4.123) – and Valentine answers him in the same terms with which he thwarted Proteus: 'Here she stands; / Take but possession of her with a touch – / I dare thee but to breathe upon my love' (127–9). The word 'touch' is thus the verbal signal of male authority over and possession of the female body. Earlier in the play, protesting against Lucetta's advice not to follow Proteus, Julia argues in more mystical terms that ironically anticipate Proteus's later rationalization at 5.4.55–8: 'Didst thou but know the inly touch of love / Thou wouldst as soon go kindle fire with snow / As seek to quench the fire of love with words' (2.7.18–20). And Proteus himself employs the same term in referring to the power of Orpheus's lute:

> For Orpheus' lute was strung with poets' sinews,
> Whose golden touch could soften steel and stones,
> Make tigers tame and huge leviathans
> Forsake unsounded deeps to dance on sands.
>
> (3.2.77–80)

But the 'golden touch' of music and the 'inly touch of love' give way at the end to Proteus's 'rude uncivil touch' of violence and possession.[1]

Turio, coward that he is, quickly backs down from Valentine's challenge – 'I claim her not, and therefore she is thine' (5.4.133). Then, however, another male, Silvia's father the Duke, assumes the authority to decide who shall possess Silvia, as he demonstrates when he bestows her on Valentine:

DUKE

          ... Sir Valentine,
Thou art a gentleman, and well derived;
Take thou thy Silvia, for thou hast deserved her.

VALENTINE

    I thank your grace; the gift hath made me happy.
                        (5.4.143–6)

The circle of transactions concerning Silvia is then interrupted by Julia and paralleled by the business with the rings that she is carrying. Although at this point in the play the reintroduction of the rings (recalling the initial exchange of rings between Proteus and Julia at 2.2.5–6) is a reminder of male and female reciprocity, the treatment of the rings generally in the play reflects the masculinist ideology of possession. Often in Shakespeare the 'ring' has a sexual connotation – it was a slang term for the female genitalia (Rubinstein, 220–1; cf. *AW* 4.2.59–62). In *Richard III*, when Lady Anne accepts a ring from Richard, in the famous wooing scene, she hopefully but erroneously says, 'To take is not to give' (1.2.205). Like Richard, Proteus attempts to give a ring (that given to him by Julia) in order to win Silvia's 'ring', i.e. her sexuality (Proteus, in fact, goes further than Richard, attempting to

---

1 Cf. *MM* 5.1.146–7 (Angelo is supposedly 'as free from touch or soil with [Isabella] / As she from one ungot'), *WT* 1.2.415–16 (Leontes supposes Polixenes to 'have touched his queen / Forbiddenly') and Helena's magical touch in *AW* 2.1.76–7 ('whose simple touch / Is powerful to araise King Pepin').

exchange one woman's 'ring' for another). Unlike Lady Anne, however, Silvia knows that taking and giving are linked, reciprocal actions for men, the object of which is possession of the female 'ring'[1] – she consequently refuses him. To 'force' the woman ''gainst the nature of love' is thus the logical conclusion in this male economy of sexual transactions.

In the Titus and Gisippus story, the bed trick is the exchange mechanism of sexual property between the two men. Just as the bed trick is the complement to the offer in Titus and Gisippus, so the attempted rape is the complement to the offer in *Two Gentlemen*. By substituting an attempted rape for the rape fantasy (the bed trick) as the action which mirrors the offer, Shakespeare drastically raises the emotional temperature of the play. But it should also be noted that both the rape and the offer are merely attempted; neither is completed. The more violent the staging of the attempted rape, therefore, the more extraordinary and generous, and consequently objectionable, Valentine's forgiveness seems.[2]

In *Two Gentlemen*, Shakespeare transforms the nature of the offer from an almost routine mechanism of exchange in Elyot to a dark and disturbing, essentially Ovidian, view of masculine desire, figured by the possession of the female body through rape, and also reflected in the father's power to bestow the daughter as a gift; the attempted rape and the attempted offer are thus equivalent, or at least parallel, enactments of an ideology of male possession. Yet in *Two Gentlemen*, where neither action is completed, both ultimately lead to the same thing: marriage. Shakespeare understood, better than most, how powerful, transforming and at times destructive a force male desire could be, and he learned this, in

---

1   The circulation of the rings at the end of *The Merchant of Venice* (especially Gratiano's play-ending lines, 5.1.306–7: 'while I live I'll fear no other thing / So sore as keeping safe Nerissa's ring') makes the sexual meaning even more explicit.

2   For a traditional reading of the theme of forgiveness, deriving it from the medieval 'play of forgiveness', see Hunter, *Comedy*, 1–41.

large part, from his reading of Ovid. *Two Gentlemen* is not quite Shakespeare's first problem play, but the problems it stages, by way of Elyot and Ovid, may seem to resist a totally satisfactory conclusion. Yet, as Masten, 37, observes, the presumably opposed ideologies of male friendship and romantic love[1] end in the same place: the reformation and restoration of the heterosexual couples.

In his comprehensive survey of friendship literature, Mills claims that Elyot's use of the Titus and Gisippus narrative produces something new: 'For the first time in the sixteenth century the medieval emphasis on love and the classical doctrines of friendship come into dramatic conflict in English literature – but not the last' (Mills, 103). It would be slightly more accurate to note that writers from Cicero onward had considered whether true friendship could exist between male and female, and whether romantic love could develop into the idealized form of friendship; the answers were invariably negative. The Titus and Gisippus narrative, we should recall, offered Shakespeare not only the thematics of friendship but the kind of romance plot to which he was repeatedly attracted. Moreover, simply introducing a character named (and with the characteristics of) Proteus into a friendship plot automatically destabilizes the genre, since true friendship depends absolutely on fidelity and constancy, the inverse of the protean. The equivalents to Titus and Gisippus in *Two Gentlemen*, finally, are similar only in that each is transformed through desire. The very first scene depicts the two in the process of separation, both philosophically – 'He after honour hunts, I after love' (1.1.63) – and geographically. Shakespeare's fondness

---

1 By 'romantic love' is meant the set of concepts derived from Petrarchan conventions and the tradition of romance. Shakespeare seems continually to appropriate these rhetorical and philosophical stereotypes for his own purposes – for example, in *Sonnet* 130 ('My mistress' eyes are nothing like the sun') and in such plays as *As You Like It* and *All's Well*, where aggressive and autonomous female characters pursue the men they love, even to the extent of themselves initiating marriage proposals. The character of Julia represents a major step in their direction.

for twins onstage – in *The Comedy of Errors* and *Twelfth Night* –
could have had no more obvious site of fulfilment than in the plot
of *Two Gentlemen*, yet he resisted similarity to insist on difference.
Some of the awkward or ideologically exposed moments in the
play result from this dramaturgical deconstruction of the generic
rules of the friendship tradition.

Friendship Discourse After Two Gentlemen

The conflicts between friends over matters of love continued to
engage writers in the early modern period, though treatments and
attitudes varied. Few provided a more telling parody of the
friendship genre than Ben Jonson in *Bartholomew Fair* (1614),
when Leatherhead stages Littlewit's 'motion' or puppet-play:
'The ancient modern history of Hero and Leander, otherwise
called *The Touchstone of true Love*, with as true a trial of friendship
between Damon and Pythias, two faithful friends o' the Bankside'
(5.3.5–8). We are told that Marlowe's story is 'too learned, and
poetical for our audience', so Littlewit has been asked 'to reduce it
to a more familiar strain for our people' (5.3.92–3, 96–7). Jonson
thus brings together the essentially incompatible traditions of the
amatory poem and friendship discourse, as Shakespeare had done
in *Two Gentlemen* (where the Hero and Leander story shadows
Valentine in particular). After Leander enters Hero's room at the
Swan Inn, Cokes asks to see 'the friendship', and Leatherhead
obliges:

> *Now gentles, to the friends, who in number, are two,*
> *and lodged in that ale-house, in which fair* Hero *does do.*
> Damon *(for some kindness done him the last week)*
> *is come fair* Hero, *in Fish Street, this morning to seek:*
> Pythias *does smell the knavery of the meeting,*
> *and now you shall see their true friendly greeting.*
> (5.4.207–12)

This mythic friendship is 'reduce[d]', however, to a comically
grotesque exchange of insults ('*You lie, like a rogue . . . A pimp and*

a scab', 5.4.220–2) and fighting ('*Pink his guts*, Pythias', 5.4.238).
Leatherhead assures his audience that their conflict is but 'show':

> *Thus gentles you perceive, without any denial,*
> *'twixt* Damon *and* Pythias *here, friendship's true trial.*
> *Though hourly they quarrel thus, and roar with each other,*
> *they fight you no more, than does brother with brother.*
> *But friendly together, at the next man they meet,*
> *they let fly their anger, as here you might see't.*
>
> (5.4.255–60)

And in the next few moments, they insult both Hero ('*a whore*')
and Leander ('*whore-master knave*'), and '*Here the* puppets *quarrel
and fall together by the ears*' (5.4.297 SD). Jonson's parody of
Marlowe's poem and Richard Edwards's play reaches far, mocking
both the language and the conventions of each tradition. Jonson
may have had an even closer target in mind, too, for when Winwife
and Quarlous, at the request of Grace Wellborn, select and write
down names for 'the next person that comes this way' (4.3.45) to
choose between, and so determine which of them she will
marry, Winwife declares 'And mine [is] out of the play, Palemon'
(4.3.64). The reference is undoubtedly to the friendship play by
Shakespeare and Fletcher, *The Two Noble Kinsmen*, performed in
1613 (Potter, 35).

Although *The Two Gentlemen of Verona* cannot be proven to be
Shakespeare's first play, and *The Two Noble Kinsmen* cannot quite
be proven to be his last (Potter, 12–16), nevertheless it is striking
that Shakespeare would return to the conflicts of the friendship
tradition, by way of Chaucer's *The Knight's Tale*, at the very end
of his career. Even the title of the later play reflects that of the
earlier one, the 'gentlemen' now 'noble', the close friends now
even closer 'kinsmen' (cousins, nephews to King Creon). The
authors of *Two Noble Kinsmen* do not, however, combine their tale
with a romance story supplying a plot-convenient second female,
as Shakespeare does in *Two Gentlemen*, but they still dramatize the
paradigmatic friendship story of male friends who both love the

same woman. Some of the extremes of the plot[1] lead Potter to wonder whether 'At such moments . . . to see the play as a parody of friendship literature', while other scenes, she notes, 'seem to draw on that very literature' (Potter, 57). The play expresses an ideal vision of friendship:

> We are an endless mine to one another;
> We are one another's wife, ever begetting
> New births of love; we are father, friends, acquaintance,
> We are, in one another, families;
> I am your heir and you are mine.
>
> (*TNK* 2.2.79–83)

This passage also insists on the homosocial displacement of the normative heterosexual relation ('We are one another's wife'). Yet, as Potter, 57, points out, this vision is 'only constructed' after Palamon and Arcite are faced with what they assume is life-long imprisonment and serves, therefore, as 'a replacement' for marriage, which seems impossible.[2]

Much had changed in Shakespeare's career and, presumably, in his attitudes since *Two Gentlemen*, yet *Two Noble Kinsmen* deploys, at some points, a comparable ambivalence about the friendship tradition, and suggests, as *Two Gentlemen* does, that romantic desire is a vastly stronger power than male–male friendship. In the play's final scene, when Arcite is brought in, dying, Palamon declares 'I am Palamon, / One that yet loves thee dying', to which Arcite responds, in the familiar terms of friendship theory, with a kind of Gisippus-like offer:

> Take Emilia
> And, with her, all the world's joy. Reach thy hand;

---

1 Palamon and Arcite try to kill each other, and, even when accepting they should both die, Palamon desires to see the death of his friend first, so that he can ensure Arcite cannot claim the woman (*TNK* 3.6.179).

2 Although 2.2 has generally been attributed to Fletcher, there and elsewhere, as Potter, 32, argues, Fletcher 'seems to have been working on, or in the light of, Shakespearean material'.

> Farewell. I have told my last hour. I was false
> Yet never treacherous. Forgive me, cousin.
> One kiss from fair Emilia. [*Emilia kisses Arcite.*]
>   'Tis done.
> Take her. I die.
>   (*TNK* 5.4.89–95)

Rather than saving one friend's life, as Gisippus's offer does, the equivalent moment in *Two Noble Kinsmen* ends with one friend's death.[1] Bruce Smith (*Desire*, 70) argues that *Two Noble Kinsmen* 'reenacts the plot of *The Two Gentlemen of Verona*, but with a much sharper sense of the sexual and emotional complexities that are entangled in the earlier comedy's simplicities'. One could just as easily – and less teleologically – argue that the later play's death of the rival friend/lover is a 'simplicity' of narrative that *Two Gentlemen* refuses in its final scene, where the 'sexual and emotional complexities' are pushed to a dramatic extreme – often shocking and sometimes seeming neither morally nor intellectually satisfying onstage, like life itself.

The Prodigious Son

As he is departing Verona with Crab in 2.3, Lance tells the audience, 'I have received my proportion, like the prodigious son' (2.3.2–3) – his malapropism, deliberate or not, meaning that he has received his 'portion' or inheritance as the Prodigal Son did; 'prodigious', meaning 'Of extraordinarily large size' (*OED a.* 4), may also allude to Will Kemp's physical size (see 2.3.3n.),[2] but the word more generally meant 'ominous, portentous' (*OED a.* 1; cf. *MND* 5.1.407: 'mark prodigious') or 'unnatural' (*OED a.* 2), either of which may well reflect on Lance, Proteus or Valentine. The reference to the Prodigal Son has a relevance to *Two Gentlemen* as a whole. Proteus and Valentine are not only two

---

1   The final scene of *Two Noble Kinsmen* has always been assigned to Shakespeare.
2   For a discussion of the possible casting of Kemp as Lance, see pp. 126–7.

gentlemen, two travellers, two separate and then two rival suitors, but also two sons seeking love and fortune apart from their families. The play's recurring family structure, in fact, is that of the child leaving home: some going willingly, others sent forth. While the underlying narrative of the child's journey to a new life outside the family can be seen throughout Shakespeare's plays, J.L. Simmons observes that

> The young man's departure from home in quest of knowledge, a lost twin, or (in the case of Petruchio) a wife structures three of the earliest comedies; and the fourth, *Love's Labor's Lost*, varies the paradigm only by transposing 'home' so far as is possible into a defamilialized male zone.
>
> (Simmons, 858)[1]

In *Two Gentlemen*, however, Shakespeare depicts not only sons but daughters as well following this trajectory away from the parent.

The parable of the Prodigal Son was widely known in early modern England[2] and is, according to Richmond Noble, 277, 'the most frequently mentioned Parable of the Gospels in [Shakespeare's] plays'. The parable serves as a deep narrative for many plot lines in several of Shakespeare's plays, perhaps the most obvious being the development of Prince Hal from *I Henry*

---

1 Simmons, 857, argues that *Two Gentlemen* is 'self-referentially the self-fulfilling purpose behind Shakespeare's departure from Stratford – his playwrighting debut', though he provides no evidence or argument that *Two Gentlemen* is Shakespeare's 'debut'. Such speculation is not new; Salingar, 243, in noting similarities between *Comedy of Errors*, *The Taming of the Shrew* and *Two Gentlemen*, suggests reading into these plays 'something of the author's inner struggle for adjustment, as a young provincial trying his fortunes in London'.

2 Young, 20, notes that 'following the issue of *The New Church Calendar* in 1561, it was established that the parable of the Prodigal Son should be read three times every year in church, on 4 March, 3 July, and 29 October, provided that those dates did not coincide with a Sunday or a Holy Day'.

IV to *Henry V*.[1] This parable provides the basic plot of many morality and classical plays acted in the latter part of the sixteenth century by children's acting troupes, and well into the seventeenth century even in the public theatres (e.g. *The London Prodigal, c.* 1603–5, by the King's Men); these plays moralistically warn against the wages of sin and the ways in which youth may go astray. In the prodigal son plays performed in the public theatres, sympathy for the protagonist is deflected

> by linking prodigality to other vices – lechery, gambling, despair – and by exploiting the pathos of his abandoned fiancée or wife, and sometimes his children. The forsaken woman always remains faithful to the prodigal, some-times disguises herself as a page in order to be near him, and brings him to contrition and repentance by some overpowering display of her virtue.
>
> (Shapiro, *Children*, 121)

At the same time, and increasingly in the early seventeenth century, though, a parallel counter-tradition had taken hold, in which, as Michael Shapiro argues, 'the London children's troupes . . . [developed] the parable satirically, by evoking sympathy for the prodigal, mocking the adult world through miniaturization and mimicry, and supplementing the Biblical narrative with episodes taken from conny-catching pamphlets and jest books' (Shapiro, *Children*, 212–13; see also Young, 230–47). Full-blown parodies of the public theatre's prodigal son plays by children's companies – e.g. *Eastward Ho!* (Queen's Revels, 1605) and *The Knight of the*

---

1   See Young, 174–225, for a useful account of 'princely prodigals'. Among the other references in Shakespeare are: *MW* 4.5.7: 'the story of the Prodigal'; *CE* 4.3.17–18: 'he that goes in the calf's skin that was killed for the Prodigal'; *MV* 2.6.15, 18: 'How like a younger or a prodigal . . . How like the prodigal doth she return'; *AYL* 1.1.37: 'What prodigal portion have I spent'; *1H4* 4.2.33–4: 'a hundred and fifty tattered prodigals lately come from swine-keeping'; *2H4* 2.1.142–3: 'the story of the Prodigal'; and *WT* 4.3.93–4: 'Then he compassed a motion of the Prodigal Son'. The plot of *All's Well* also follows the prodigal son pattern.

Burning Pestle (Queen's Revels, 1607) – soon followed (see Young, 247–78). The plot of the parable was also appropriated for vastly different satiric purposes by playwrights of so-called 'city comedy'.[1] In *Two Gentlemen*, the prodigal son plot structures much of the main plot even as it is burlesqued in Lance's opening soliloquy.

Lance's situation does not fit the plot of the parable very precisely, as there seems to be no brother nor is he notably wasteful, but the situation of the child leaving the family behind does apply to him and runs throughout *Two Gentlemen*. In many of Shakespeare's plays there are few references to mothers, and, likewise, in *Two Gentlemen* there is only one – Lance's single allusion to his, the 'wood' ('mad' (see 2.3.26n.) but also perhaps wooden, artificial) woman, represented by his left shoe, the smelly one 'with the hole in it' (2.3.17): 'Now come I to my mother: O, that she could speak now, like a wood woman! Well, I kiss her. Why there 'tis – here's my mother's breath up and down' (2.3.25–8). There are, however, plenty of references in the play to fathers, from whom the younger generation is separating. Valentine's father, never seen in the play, waits for him offstage in 1.1, 'My father at the road / Expects my coming, there to see me shipped' (53–4), and is said to be 'in good health' (2.4.48) by the Duke. Julia's unseen father 'stays' for her to come to dinner at 1.2.130, while Proteus seems to refer to him as a potential blocking agent to their love: 'O, that our fathers would applaud our loves / To seal our happiness with their consents' (1.3.48–9). Fathers in comedy, and in New Comedy particularly, of course, rarely applaud their children's loves, at least at the beginning of the plays (cf. Egeus in *A Midsummer Night's Dream*). Valentine and Julia willingly journey from home, leaving behind their unseen families – Valentine's quest 'To see the wonders of the world abroad' (1.1.6) will take him to a single destination, Milan, where love will

1   On the earlier history of the prodigal son play, see Norland, 149–60, and Young, 1–173.

overcome him, while Julia, who has already found love, will undertake 'A journey to my loving Proteus' (2.7.7) as a 'true-devoted pilgrim' (9). The quest motif is repeated later in the play.

In contrast to his Veronese friends, Proteus has a father much in evidence onstage, Antonio, who is 'resolved', 'peremptory' and determined to 'suddenly proceed' (1.3.66, 71, 64) – in short, the typical father-figure of comedy who, wittingly or not, thwarts the romantic desires of his child. But it is Silvia's father, the Duke, who most clearly serves as the Bad Parent in the play, planning to marry off his daughter to the idiotic Turio, accepting and abetting Proteus's treachery to his friend, denouncing his daughter's lover in class-inflected terms and banishing him. He is not simply a father, moreover, but the Duke. But as in *A Midsummer Night's Dream*, when Theseus sets aside the law that Egeus had invoked in the opening scene, at the end of *Two Gentlemen* the Duke is prevailed upon as a father to accept his daughter's choice ('I here forget all former griefs, / Cancel all grudge, repeal thee home again', 5.4.140–1), and as a Duke to forgive and pardon the Outlaws (5.4.156–7). Valentine promises, at the end of the play, that they will all celebrate together, 'One feast' in 'one house' (5.4.171), but it is no longer their parents' houses. Lance had left 'all our house in a great perplexity' (2.3.7–8) and, in a way, the prodigal children of the play did so as well. The quest, the journey out, ends (at least in comedy) with a return to a reconstituted 'house', one of 'mutual happiness' (5.4.171).

The comic hysteria of Lance's family in 2.3, sending the Prodigal Son forth into the world, is one of the play's great set-pieces. The enormous grief of the family over his departure – the father weeping so hard he cannot speak a word of blessing, the speechless mother, the moaning sister (28–9), the grandmother weeping 'herself blind' (12), but also the 'maid howling' and the 'cat wringing her hands' (7) – contrasts most strikingly with Crab's mute indifference (9–10; see pp. 69–73), but it also contrasts with the departures of the four lovers from their families. In those that know of their child's departure there is nothing like this grief; indeed, in the case of Proteus, and presumably in that of Valentine, there is a strong parental belief that the son must go forth into the world (1.3.66–7), and Silvia's father is not afraid to lose his daughter – the marriage to Turio is all arranged – but rather to lose the economic commodity she represents. The prodigal daughters of *Two Gentlemen*, Julia and Silvia, undertake journeys for love, to Verona and to the forest, while the journeys undertaken by the two prodigal sons, Proteus and Valentine, are, initially, explorations of their own identities – both are 'metamorphosed' (1.1.66; 2.1.27–9). The careful use of this verb, unusual in Shakespeare (see p. 25, n. 29), referring to the two friends, signals that their quests will be internal as well as external. Confusion of identity appears most openly in Proteus, in his rationalizing soliloquy in 2.6:

> I cannot leave to love, and yet I do;
> But there I leave to love where I should love.
> Julia I lose, and Valentine I lose;
> If I keep them, I needs must lose myself.
> If I lose them, thus find I by their loss,
> For Valentine, myself, for Julia, Silvia.
>   (2.6.17–22)

The intertwined identities of the various figures, resulting from the triangular desire of Valentine–Silvia–Proteus, will have to be clarified at the end of the play. And while the lovers will finally be correctly paired off, they will also go off together as 'one'.

The prodigal son motif substantially overlaps with the male friendship tradition: both concern the process of the individuation of male identity – or, more generally, of masculinity itself.[1] As Shakespeare plays out the parable in *Two Gentlemen*, the sons leave their families in search of a place in society, but the 'hunt' for 'honour' (1.1.63) is soon short-circuited by love. Loss of self is associated with being in thrall to sexual desire, as in Proteus's

1 See Adelman, Garber and Kahn.

soliloquy, but also with immaturity. Sexual and psychological maturity evolve as the child leaves behind the limitations of the 'fraternal or sororal bond . . . which must yield priority to a marital and sexual bond' (Garber, 38). So, in *Two Gentlemen*, Lance will find his maid or 'milkmaid' (3.1.265); the 'cate-log of her condition' (3.1.269) he and Speed read mocks the convention of the romantic blazon. So too Valentine and Proteus come to the crisis point of individuation and separation in 5.4 and, in the attempted rape and the offer, seem to regress (to assume a normative vocabulary) into immature narcissism, only to be shocked out of it by Julia's revelation of herself. The Duke will welcome home those other prodigal sons, the Outlaws – 'Forgive them what they have committed here, / And let them be recalled from their exile', Valentine asks, 'They are reformed, civil, full of good / And fit for great employment' (5.4.152–5) – and Proteus will be pardoned with the mildest 'penance' (5.4.168) imaginable. In *Two Gentlemen*, in the end, every son receives his 'proportion', which – in the word's sense of 'equity' – may not be a malapropism after all.

Who is Julia? Romance and the Boy Actor

The prior discussion has emphasized the male friendship tradition and suggested its primacy in Shakespeare's thinking about *Two Gentlemen*, yet the indebtedness to Elyot's tale of Titus and Gisippus is only part of the story – the other part of which is Shakespeare's use of a romance love-quest narrative from George of Montemayor's *Diana*.[1] The tale of Felix and Felismena, which appears in Book 2 with in the much longer narrative concerning Diana and Syrenus, bears many resemblances to Julia's pursuit of

---

1 Arthur Brooke's *The Tragical History of Romeus and Juliet* provided still other romance material; see notes on 1.1.5–8; 2.4.179–80, 189–92, 204–5; 2.6.9–10; 2.7.40–3; 4.1.27; 4.3.29–31. See also Allen.

and betrayal by Proteus.[1] In *Diana*, Felismena disguises herself as a page to follow her beloved Felix, who has been sent by his father to a foreign court; there, he falls in love with the lady Celia. Upon her arrival, Felismena becomes page to Felix, is sent on an errand to Celia and so on. In an anticipation of *Twelfth Night* rather than *Two Gentlemen*, Celia falls in love with the disguised Felismena. Ultimately, the solution to this dilemma is the death of Celia; much later, Felismena saves Felix from danger and they are reunited.

The 'friendship' narrative as found in Elyot, then, presents Shakespeare with a triangle of desire of two men and one woman, whom one male friend gives to the other in order to save his life. The 'romance' narrative as found in *Diana*, on the other hand, provides Shakespeare with a triangle of desire consisting of two women and one man, resolved by the death of one of the women.[2] Shakespeare in effect merges the two triangles of desire from both narratives, retaining many built-in conflicts in each but bringing their resolutions to a collision point, where the offer is not accepted nor the death of the other woman required. Shakespeare achieves, unsatisfactorily in some views, a resolution of his own narrative by using a second woman in order to break the triangle of desire and allow for the marriage of both men.[3]

---

1 See Ard[2], xlii–xliv, and Harrison for a detailed discussion of the resemblances and differences between *Two Gentlemen* and *Diana*. For major resemblances and direct borrowings, see also notes on List of Roles, 1; 1.1.5–8; 2.2.16–18; 2.7.25–32, 40–3; 4.2.29–31; 4.4.97–103, 97–8, 141–70, 187, 189; 5.3.8; 5.4.103. Among the more significant resemblances, in addition to Felismena's pursuit of Felix in disguise as the male page 'Valerius' (see 5.3.8n.), are her arrival at an inn and hearing him serenade Celia (= Silvia), and much of the conversation between the two women (= 4.4 in *TGV*); see *Diana*, 88–90. See p. 128 for the circulation and publication of *Diana* as it relates to the dating of *Two Gentlemen*.

2 In *Two Noble Kinsmen*, by contrast, the death of one of the men is required for resolution.

3 Wells, 'Failure', 171, sees the play as a failure because of 'its overall organisation . . . It shows Shakespeare accepting dramatic conventions with one hand and throwing them overboard with the other.'

3 A comically unromantic version of Sir Eglamour in Robin Phillips's RSC
production, 1970, at the Aldwych Theatre, London

In bringing together a romance narrative and a male friendship
plot, moreover, Shakespeare also brings together what might at
first glance seem discrepant, almost contradictory, conceptions of
female agency. Silvia, the centre of the male friendship plot, does
not confidently initiate action on her own behalf. She is the object
of desire for Valentine, Turio and Proteus, and, although she
pursues her desire for Valentine, she gets him to write a love letter
as a declaration of her own intentions rather than taking the initiative in writing it herself (2.1.152–5). She does undertake a
journey to follow her beloved, but not alone; she is accompanied
by a male companion, Eglamour (4.3.22–6; see Fig. 3). Despite
her general caution, however, Silvia is by no means a passive
Griselda-figure, for she insists on the fidelity of her own love,

denounces Proteus's betrayal, flees from an enforced marriage to Turio to join her banished Valentine and struggles against Proteus's attempted rape.[1] In Silvia, Shakespeare created a formidable woman character, more intelligent than any of the men who desire her. Silvia's strong characterization in most of the play explains in part the continuing efforts of directors and editors to invent positive stage actions for her during her long silence in 5.4 (see pp. 104–8). The romance heroine Julia, by contrast, does write a letter directly to Proteus (1.3.45–7) and, like her model Felismena in *Diana*, rather than finding a male escort for her journey to her beloved, she adopts a male identity and undertakes the journey alone. She actively, and far less cautiously, expresses and seeks to fulfil her desire. In this aspect Julia anticipates, as many critics have noted, such later Shakespearean heroines as Portia, Rosalind and Viola.[2]

When Julia agrees to take on the disguise of a man, she follows in the steps of innumerable heroines of romance narratives. In *Diana*, Felismena says

> I determined to adventure that, which I thinke never any woman imagined: which was, to apparell my selfe in the habit of a man, and to hye me to the Court to see him, in whose sight al my hope and content remained.
>
> (*Diana*, 87)

This claim to uniqueness is more than a little ironic, however, given the dozens of such disguised heroines in earlier saints' lives,

---

1 The Silvia of Robin Phillips's 1975 production seems to have been taken as far away from the direction of passivity as is really plausible: 'a capricious daughter of wealth and power' with the 'quick, intuitive mind of the accomplished flirt', this Silvia, according to one reviewer, in her final encounter with Proteus 'managed to be provocative and challenging, and then visibly excited by his advances, rather than resolute and admonitory and, finally, frightened. You felt she was enjoying herself, and that the touch of chagrin in her silence following Valentine's intervention was as much the result of being prevented from dealing with Proteus in her own way as of finding herself, for once, not the center of attention' (Jackson, 26).

2 In her pursuit of an unfaithful and unworthy lover, Julia also anticipates Helena in *All's Well*.

chivalric romances, romantic epics, ballads and novellas.[1] Among the best-known examples is that of Zelmane in Sidney's *Arcadia*: she disguises herself as a page named 'Diaphantus' and serves her beloved, Pyrocles, until her death (Pyrocles – conversely and confusingly – disguises himself as an Amazon, adopting Zelmane's name, in order to be near his beloved).[2] Such cross-dressings, so common in literary romance, were considerably rarer on the public stage until the 1590s. In *Clyomon and Clamydes* (written *c*. 1570–83) the lovelorn Neronis, having escaped from imprisonment, enters, '*in the Forrest, in mans apparell*', lamenting the 'painfull Pages show' she must assume, but reasoning that any 'good Lady' will 'say it is an honest shift, the which I have devised' (*Clyomon*, E4ᵛ); she later enters '*like a Sheepheards boy*' and then again '*like the Page*' (*Clyomon*, F4ʳ and G1ʳ). In George Whetstone's *Promos and Cassandra* (1578), one of Shakespeare's sources for *Measure for Measure*, Cassandra enters one scene 'apparelled like a Page', with the usual misgivings: 'Unhappy wretche, I blush my selfe to see, / Apparelled thus monstrous to my kinde' (Whetstone, Part 1, 3.7). In Robert Greene's *James IV* (written *c*. 1591?), Queen Dorothea is forced into '*man's apparell*' (4.4.1 SD), and is even desired, as a 'man', by Lady Anderson; Dorothea's servant Nano advises her to carry a sword as a 'show' of her masculinity (3.3.110). The two young women of Lyly's *Gallathea* (1585) also disguise themselves as boys: Gallathea is already in disguise when the play begins, and Phillida soon follows, complaining 'I shall be ashamed of my long hose and short coate, and so unwarily blabbe out something by blushing at every thing' (1.3.20–2; Lyly, 2.436).[3] Despite these earlier examples,

---

1 These are some of the genres considered by Shapiro in his useful survey of antecedents (Shapiro, *Gender*, 29–62 and 207–20).
2 See Bullough, 1.253–6.
3 The lost play 'The history of felix & philiomena', performed in 1585 (Chambers,

especially *Gallathea*, the fact remains that Shakespeare is among the first playwrights to introduce this romance motif into the theatre, and he is certainly the first to develop the idea to the sophisticated levels we see in *Two Gentlemen*.

Julia is the first Shakespearean heroine to disguise herself as a male but by no means the last: she is followed in later plays by Portia, Jessica, Rosalind, Viola and Imogen, and possibly also Violante in *The History of Cardenio* (Shakespeare's lost play, of which Lewis Theobald's adaptation, *Double Falsehood*, is presumed to be the only surviving version). Her dialogue with Lucetta in 2.7 works through what would become typical Shakespearean concerns. She will take on a disguise to 'prevent / The loose encounters of lascivious men' (40–1), an ironic anticipation of Proteus's attempt on Silvia in 5.4. Her disguise will be that of 'some well-reputed page' (43) – a page is the traditional male disguise – and as a result, her hair will have to be cut short (44), according to Lucetta, though Julia proposes instead that it be knit up 'in silken strings / With twenty odd-conceited true-love knots' (45–6), thus signalling her desire, rather than concealing it. But her breeches cause these two women the greatest difficulty. Lucetta insists that, to appear as a man, Julia 'must needs have them with a codpiece' (53), and when Julia protests that the codpiece 'will be ill-favoured' (54), Lucetta insists that 'A round hose, madam, now's not worth a pin / Unless you have a codpiece to stick pins on' (55–6; see 2.7.56n.). Julia, like almost all such heroines in similar situations, fears that 'undertaking so unstaid a journey . . . will make me scandalized' (60–1) but proceeds nevertheless (see Figs 4 and 5).

Julia's first appearance as 'Sebastian' in Milan in 4.2 is not a happy one, for it permits her to see Proteus betraying her in his

---

Stage, 4.160), evidently a dramatization of the story of Felix and Felismena in *Diana*, would also have shown the young woman in disguise.

4 Julia (Helen Mirren) as Sebastian and Proteus (Ian Richardson) in Robin
   Phillips's RSC production, 1970, at the Aldwych Theatre, London

wooing of Silvia. Listening to the song, 'Who is Silvia?', Julia –
whose identity is far more mysterious than Silvia's at this
point – condemns Proteus's fickleness in ironically self-reflecting
terms – 'I would always have one play but one thing' (4.2.69; see
n.). As Proteus attempts to woo Silvia, Julia comments, through a

5   Julia (Lesley Vickerage) as Sebastian in Edward Hall's RSC production, 1998, at the Swan Theatre, Stratford-upon-Avon

series of asides (4.2.103–4, 115, 123–4), on their dialogue, in effect giving Julia the privileged position of vision in the play. In 4.4, Proteus employs the disguised Julia as his page to 'with some discretion do [his] business' (63), but mainly, so he says, because Sebastian's demeanour suggests 'good bringing-up, fortune and truth' (65–7). As every audience anticipates, the 'business' Proteus has in mind is for Sebastian to woo Silvia on his behalf – again, a familiar situation in romance narratives (see 4.4.97–103n. for the same situation in *Diana*) – but here Shakespeare creates in the disguised character a self-consciousness representing something new on the stage, which we find in all his later plays with disguised heroines. For the rest of the play, Julia frequently speaks on two levels, as her identity, signalled by her pronouns, shifts back and forth between 'Julia' and 'Sebastian'.

When Julia, as Sebastian, challenges Proteus by expressing pity for the woman he once loved, he asks why. Julia's answer is evocative:

> Because methinks that she loved you as well
> As you do love your lady Silvia.
> She dreams on him that has forgot her love;
> You dote on her that cares not for your love.
> 'Tis pity love should be so contrary;
> And thinking on it makes me cry 'Alas'.
>
> (4.4.77–82)

In *Twelfth Night*, such a speech, with its sly final pun on 'a lass', would stir the unwitting male to some expression of sympathy, but not here; and the emotional power of Sebastian's speeches (e.g. 4.4.156–70) would move 'his' hearer to instant interest in the speaker as well as his speech. In *Twelfth Night*, Shakespeare would engineer a comic resolution of the confusion caused by disguise through the use of twins. In *Two Gentlemen*, though, there is no magical splitting of a 'Cesario' into component male and female parts; rather, Julia must simply suffer, until Proteus is once again transformed.[1]

When Silvia asks 'Sebastian' for a physical description of Julia – 'How tall was she?' (4.4.155) – she prompts Julia to make another allusion to playing:

> About my stature; for at Pentecost,
> When all our pageants of delight were played,
> Our youth got me to play the woman's part,
> And I was trimmed in Madam Julia's gown,
> Which served me as fit, by all men's judgements,
> As if the garment had been made for me;
> Therefore I know she is about my height.
> And at that time I made her weep a-good,
> For I did play a lamentable part.
> Madam, 'twas Ariadne, passioning
> For Theseus' perjury and unjust flight,
> Which I so lively acted with my tears
> That my poor mistress, moved therewithal,
> Wept bitterly; and would I might be dead
> If I in thought felt not her very sorrow.
>
> (4.4.156–70)

This remarkable speech, bringing together the Christian calendar, popular festivity and classical legend (see 4.4.156–7n. and 165–6n.), leads to subtle and touching ironies about emotion, playing and Julia's situation. Julia has become Ariadne and the

---

1 MacCary, 108, argues that 'through transvestism [Julia] has acquired those traits which Proteus himself feels the need of in his own nature, and so, in loving her he remakes himself in his own image. She becomes both Silvia and Valentine to him, the idealized image of himself and the woman who first projected that image to him.' This process (similar to what happens to Orlando in *As You Like It* or Orsino in *Twelfth Night*) is what one would perhaps like to see, but the play does not provide sufficient evidence, in my view. Proteus's abrupt repentance at 5.4.73–7 and equally abrupt return to love for Julia – 'What is in Silvia's face but I may spy / More fresh in Julia's, with a constant eye?' (5.4.113–14) – offer little ground for MacCary's argument, and, furthermore, could be construed as exterior and superficial.

tears 'so lively acted' in the speech are now her own real 'sorrow' (although of course still acted). The past is then replayed, for just as Sebastian's 'poor mistress', watching the performance of Ariadne, 'wept bitterly', so Silvia is emotionally drawn to identify with Julia – 'I weep myself to think upon thy words' (4.4.173). The multiple levels of comment on the power of acting here reflect the wit and self-consciousness of a young playwright making discoveries about the stage's possibilities. Theseus's unjust flight, in any event, will not be repeated in *Two Gentlemen*: he will escape into *A Midsummer Night's Dream* and *Two Noble Kinsmen*, but Proteus will be transformed and reconciled to Julia once again. Although similarly sophisticated moments of self-consciousness about dramatic art, in relation to the heroine's gender disguise, may be found in the vast array of romance poems and narratives that stand behind the play, what particularly distinguishes Shakespeare's treatment of the subject is his self-consciousness about the physical reality of the boy actor beneath the female role.

Much recent scholarly work has engaged with the material conditions, metadramatic thematics and erotic suggestiveness of the boy actor on the early modern stage (see, for example, Shapiro, *Gender*, Levine and Orgel). *Two Gentlemen* does not seem to go as far as *As You Like It* (Rosalind's Epilogue, 16–18: 'If I were a woman I would kiss as many of you as had beards that pleased me') or *Antony and Cleopatra* ('I shall see / Some squeaking Cleopatra boy my greatness / I'th' posture of a whore', 5.2.218–20) in acknowledging its own practice, nor does *Two Gentlemen* become as complex in cross-gender, transvestite homoerotic wooing as *As You Like It* or *Twelfth Night*. That said, the language of *Two Gentlemen* does at times reveal the boy actor: for example, when Julia, sent by Proteus to give her own ring to Silvia, asks, 'How many women would do such a message?' (4.4.88), and when 'Sebastian' relates how 'he' played the 'lamentable' (one full of lamentation; one to be lamented) female part of Ariadne. In the latter speech, we learn that the trick of female impersonation is to wear the right signifying costume – the woman's gown that fits Sebastian perfectly 'As if the garment had been made for' him (4.4.161) – and to give a 'passioning' performance, with 'tears' (4.4.165–7), a stereotypical 'female' signifier, like the codpiece for the male. Except that here these signifying marks do not, of course, correctly designate the gender beneath.

The verbal equivocations about Julia's gender are intensified in the final scene, once she reveals herself at 5.4.98–100 yet remains in the page's costume. Proteus, Valentine and Silvia now know her identity as a woman, but because she continues to the end of the play in the garments of the boy 'page' (5.4.162) she is seen by the Duke as a 'boy [who] hath grace in him', to which Valentine replies 'more grace than boy' (5.4.163–4). This exchange highlights the androgynous aspects of the boy actor and further destabilizes any supposedly clear demarcations of gender. In his discussion of the 'body beneath' the woman's clothing on the early modern stage, particularly in regard to scenes of women characters in bed or undressing to reveal themselves, Peter Stallybrass effectively demonstrates the impossibility of fixing gender, noting that

> all attempts to fix gender are necessarily *prosthetic*: that is, they suggest the attempt to supply an imagined deficiency by the exchange of male clothes for female clothes or of female clothes for male clothes; by displacement from male to female space or from female to male space; by the replacement of male with female tasks or of female with male tasks. But all elaborations of the prosthesis which will supply the 'deficiency' can secure no essence. On the contrary, they suggest that gender itself is a fetish, the production of an identity through the fixation upon specific 'parts'.
>
> (Stallybrass, 77)

Any consideration of the boy actor in *Two Gentlemen*, and the potential erotic charge of the phenomenon in general (see Orgel), must take account of the fact that Shakespeare's introduction of the female-disguised-as-male-page was relatively daring in the early 1590s (as indeed later). Antitheatrical writers like John Rainoldes were constantly inveighing against the moral dangers of the boy actor let alone the multiplied effects of the further transformation of the female character into the boy page:[1]

> The apparell of women . . . is a great provocation of men to lust and leacherie: because a womans garment being put on a man doth vehemently touch and move him with the remembrance and imagination of a woman; and the imagination of a thing desirable doth stir up the desire.
>
> (Rainoldes, 97)

In *Two Gentlemen*, the moral debate over cross-dressing is touched upon in Julia's speech in the final scene:

> O Proteus, let this habit make thee blush.
> Be thou ashamed that I have took upon me
> Such an immodest raiment, if shame live
> In a disguise of love.
>
> (5.4.103–6)

Here the female character expresses the shame of dressing as a male in her description of the disguise as 'immodest', but she also qualifies this by describing it as a 'disguise of love', consequently subverting the shame by projecting it onto the cause – Proteus. Finally, therefore, adopting the clothes of the opposite sex is presented as less of a moral issue than changing faith or infidelity: 'It is the lesser blot, modesty finds, / Women to change their shapes than men their minds' (5.4.107–8). Any moral dubiety arising from the boy actor playing a female is also partly subverted by having the female character disguised as a page, and at the end of the play the boy playing Julia remains in a more suitable male

---

1 Among the vast literature on antitheatrical discourse, see Barish.

costume: Julia's revelation of her identity does not involve remov-
ing, or threatening to remove, her clothing.

Yet one boy actor does remain in his female garments at the
end of the play, as Silvia, and is involved in the defining moment
that engages the whole nexus of clothing, gender and the 'body
beneath': the attempted rape. There one of Rainoldes's 'beautiful
boyes transformed into women' (Rainoldes, 34) is threatened with
rape – heterosexual, in terms of the play, homosexual, in terms of
the 'body beneath'. The threat is of course deflected, yet despite
this, and despite leaving Julia dressed as a boy, the play does not
shy away from gender complications. The audience is left visually
at the end with a semiotic asymmetry: three men and one woman,
identified as two couples, walk toward 'one mutual happiness'. In
Two Gentlemen Shakespeare has begun to explore, with some con-
siderable sophistication, the dramatic possibilities raised by the
material reality of the boy actor: the boundaries of gender identity, a metadramatic self-consciousness about his own craft and the
erotic frisson of transvestite wooing.

Metamorphosis: Ovid and Lyly

Ovid is not named in *Two Gentlemen*, as he is in other early comedies – 'Ovidius Naso was the man', *LLL* 4.2.123; 'As Ovid be an
outcast quite abjured', *TS* 1.1.33; 'the most capricious poet, honest Ovid', *AYL* 3.3.5–6 – but his presence is felt throughout the
play.[1] Ovid's texts (the *Heroides* and the *Metamorphoses* especially)
resonate not only in particular allusions (e.g. Proteus's name, his
account of 'Orpheus' lute . . . strung with poets' sinews' (3.2.77),
the double invocation of Hero and Leander (1.1.21–2, 3.1.119–20)
and Julia's claim to have played the 'lamentable part' of 'Ariadne,
passioning / For Theseus' perjury and unjust flight' (4.4.164–6)),
but more generally in the relentless instability experienced by

---

1   For substantial accounts of Ovid's influence on Shakespeare, see Baldwin; Barkan;
    Bate; Carroll, *Metamorphoses*; and Taylor, *Ovid*.

many of the figures in the play – the transformations of character, the shifting of allegiances, the erosion of resolve, the instability of language. Some of the characters' difficulty and unhappiness result from the fact that 'were man / But constant, he were perfect. That one error / Fills him with faults' (5.4.109–11). The potential for that 'error' qualifies any idealized notion of constancy (e.g. Julia's), man being, as Valentine observes of Turio, 'a kind of chameleon', who can 'change colour', sometimes uncontrollably (2.4.24–5, 23).

As in most of Shakespeare's comedies, love constitutes the great agent of transformation in *Two Gentlemen*. In the first scene, Proteus rhapsodizes, 'I leave myself, my friends and all, for love. / Thou, Julia, thou hast metamorphosed me' (1.1.65–6), and Speed notes of Valentine, 'now you are metamorphosed with a mistress, that when I look on you, I can hardly think you my master' (2.1.27–9). The iterated verb draws attention to the drastic perceptual changes in these characters. Even the comic dialogue affirms the power of love to alter vision:

> VALENTINE   How esteem'st thou me? I account of her
>   beauty.
> SPEED   You never saw her since she was deformed.
> VALENTINE   How long hath she been deformed?
> SPEED   Ever since you loved her.
> VALENTINE   I have loved her ever since I saw her, and
>   still I see her beautiful.
> SPEED   If you love her, you cannot see her.
> VALENTINE   Why?
> SPEED   Because Love is blind. O, that you had mine eyes
>   . . . you, being in love, cannot see to put on your
>   hose.
>
> (2.1.57–72)

Such exchanges are in effect an illustration of Theseus's observation that 'Lovers and madmen have such seething brains, / Such shaping fantasies, that apprehend / More than cool reason ever comprehends / . . . The lover . . . / Sees Helen's beauty in a brow of Egypt' (*MND* 5.1.4–11). Appropriate to this idea is the chameleon, invoked twice in the play, not only as a central emblem of change, as at 2.4.23–5, but also for its alleged ability to live on air as a lover lives on nothing (2.1.159–60). Love's power to subdue all other desires (e.g. for nourishment) and the irresistibility of its power are played out particularly in Proteus, who, confronted with Silvia's beauty, announces his own helplessness: 'now my love [for Julia] is thawed, / Which like a waxen image 'gainst a fire / Bears no impression of the thing it was' (2.4.197–9). Metamorphosis represents a potentially dangerous condition, then, an energy that transforms and deforms, alters vision, undermines resolve.

Yet there are centres of constancy in the two women, Julia and Silvia; their love for Proteus and Valentine remains immovable, giving the lie, for example, to the Duke's easy confidence in Silvia's malleability:

> This weak impress of love is as a figure
> Trenched in ice, which with an hour's heat
> Dissolves to water and doth lose his form.
> A little time will melt her frozen thoughts,
> And worthless Valentine shall be forgot.
>
> (3.2.6–10)

However, this 'figure' of transformation stays inertly rhetorical, for Silvia remains constant in her love for Valentine. Julia, even more remarkably given his betrayal of her, remains constant to Proteus. Both women change in other ways: Julia changes on the outside, but it is still a 'disguise of love' (5.4.106), and Silvia changes in her filial duty, but only to avoid an 'unholy match' with Turio (4.3.30; see 4.3.29–31n.). Metamorphosis would accordingly seem to be the inescapable underlying condition of the world of *Two Gentlemen*, and some changes are shown to be better than others. The very self-consciousness of Julia's transformative disguise seems a far healthier shift than the helpless compulsiveness of Proteus, who hypocritically tells Valentine of

Silvia's mourning, 'she hath offered to the doom [of banishment], / Which unreversed stands in effectual force, / A sea of melting pearl, which some call tears' (3.1.220–2). The play continually reveals, however, that few things stand 'unreversed': the Duke's proclamation of banishment has no more final authority than any of the vows and oaths sworn by Proteus.

Proteus's changeability is both his vice and the means of his regeneration, for he can recover as quickly as he fell. His sudden repentance – 'My shame and guilt confounds me. / Forgive me, Valentine' (5.4.73–4) – may seem psychologically absurd, but it works thematically, as does the forgiveness of the Outlaws in the forest, who are at the end said to be 'reformed' (5.4.154), their original 'worthy qualities' (5.4.151) and noble shapes recovered; they are now 'civil, full of good / And fit for great employment' (5.4.154–5).

Perhaps the most complex verbal exploration of metamorphosis in *Two Gentlemen* is during the constant Julia's first encounter with the inconstancy of Proteus. Just after the song in 4.2, 'Who is Silvia?', Julia (disguised as a boy), in the ensuing dialogue with the Host, uses language relating to musical modulation or change to attack Proteus's change of heart and inconstancy. The music 'jars so' (4.2.65) because the musician 'plays false' (4.2.57):

> HOST   Hark, what fine change is in the music!
> JULIA   Ay, that change is the spite.
> HOST   You would have them always play but one thing?
> JULIA
>   I would always have one play but one thing.
>   (4.2.66–9)

The final line in this passage embraces both music and theatre. The metaphor, itself ironic in relation to Julia's disguise (she is herself the living proof that to 'play' is always and inevitably to be more than 'one thing'), enacts multiplicity both in its variety of meaning and in disguising Julia's real concerns from the Host. The passage as a whole illuminates how positive change – the variety and flux of the music – is undermined by negative inconstancy, manifested by Proteus and later culminating in his attempt forcibly to change Silvia.

The recurring interest in metamorphosis and transformation in *Two Gentlemen* may rightly be traced to Shakespeare's extensive indebtedness to Ovid, but it may equally be indebted to the Ovidianism of John Lyly's drama: many of his plays – *Sapho and Phao*, *Gallathea*, *Endymion*, *Midas*, *The Woman in the Moon* and *Love's Metamorphosis* (with its heroine, Protea) – feature central acts of transformation: the spiritual and psychological changes of moonstruck lovers, the man-into-ass transformation in *Midas*, the promised sex-change at the end of *Gallathea*.[1] One passage in *Midas* (written *c*. 1589) sounds a particularly resonant note with the concerns about constancy in love in *Two Gentlemen*:

CAELIA. Indeed men varie in their love.

ERISTUS. They varie their love, yet change it not.

CAELIA. Love and change are at variance, therefore if they varie, they must change.

ERISTUS. Men change the manner of their love, not the humor: the meanes how to obteine, not the mistresse they honor. So did *Jupiter*, that could not intreat *Danae* by golden words, possesse his love by a golden shoure, not altering his affection, but using art.

CAELIA. The same *Jupiter* was an Aeagle, a Swan, a Bull; and for every Saint a new shape, as men have for every mistres a new shadow. If you take example of the gods, who more wanton, more wavering? if of your selves, being but men, who wil think you more constant then gods?

(2.1.8–20; Lyly, 3.123–4)

---

1   On Lyly's own indebtedness to earlier drama, see Jeffrey; on the relation between Lyly and Shakespeare, see Hunter, *Lyly*, 298–349. For Shakespeare's specific indebtedness to Lyly, see notes on 2.6.1–43; 3.1.93–5, 100–1, 102–5, 269–355, 293, 319; 5.4.53–4.

Lyly's Caelia thus already knows what Shakespeare's Julia must discover in *Two Gentlemen*. The idea that 'Love and change are at variance' receives a complex embodiment in the characters of Julia and Proteus.

'Pox of your love letters'

Many of Shakespeare's plays have letters in them, and in many plays these letters prove crucial to the plot – in *King Lear*, above all. The substantial traffic in letters in *Two Gentlemen* – six or possibly seven letters circulate – reflects issues of textuality and representation that spread throughout the entire play.[1] Unlike *King Lear*, however, all of the letters in *Two Gentlemen* are love letters: Proteus's letter to Julia, referred to at 1.1.92–3, then received, torn up and read in 1.2; Julia's letter to Proteus, on which he meditates at 1.3.45–50 (in response to Antonio's enquiry, he claims it to be 'a word or two / Of commendations sent from Valentine' (1.3.52–3)); Silvia's letter to Valentine (2.1.155), written by Valentine himself at the request of Silvia; Valentine's letter to Silvia (3.1.137), intercepted and read by her father; Lance's 'cate-log' (3.1.269) of his mistress's virtues, read aloud by both him and Speed, and referred to as one of the 'love letters' (367–8) and a 'letter' (369); Proteus's letter to Silvia in 4.4 given to Julia to deliver along with a ring at 83–4 (she gives it to Silvia, at 122, who tears up this letter at 129 SD); 'this letter . . . a paper' inadvertently given by Julia to Silvia at 4.4.119–21 (presumably one of Proteus's former letters to Julia and possibly, as in many productions, the letter from 1.2, now comically repaired).

These letters, variously delivered and read, or intercepted and torn up, become metonymies for sexual desire. Their errant and self-referential paths effectively reflect the confusions and failures

---

1   For a survey of Renaissance precursors of the letter device in Act 1 of *Two Gentlemen*, see Guinn. Bond (xxx) suggests that the numerous letters derive from Lyly's novel *Euphues*, but Bullough, 1.204, convincingly demonstrates that Shakespeare 'found more in Lyly's plays than in his moral romance'.

of the main love plots.[1] Speed's curse at 3.1.367–8, after he learns that his master has been waiting for him while he has been reading Lance's letter – 'Pox of your love letters' – may be a 'possible self-parody by the author on the unusually frequent use of letters' (Cam[2]) in the play, but it also speaks to what the sometimes ineffectual letters signify. Invoking the 'pox' was a standard imprecation in Shakespeare's time (*OED sb.* 3), but it more directly referred to the facial lesions caused by, hence shorthand for, syphilis or 'any venereal disease' (*OED sb.* 1a). A more sinister association, therefore, lies behind the love-letter device – if the letters achieved their aims, and sexual intercourse followed, then the pox might well result. Elsewhere in the play disease is associated with love, again by Speed, who, speaking of Valentine's transformation since his love of Silvia, refers to the 'pestilence' (2.1.19), another cause of pockmarks. The play's plot, like the letters, keeps moving the lovers toward union, but then veering away from it.

The vagrant letters figure the errancy of desire in a number of ways. For example, Silvia's trick in 2.1, of getting Valentine to write to himself, comically but problematically characterizes Valentine as obtuse, as Speed's choric comments confirm (2.1.125–30). But this self-letter-writing scene also enacts an adolescent/romantic approach to love, since writer and recipient are the same, collapsed together in an 'autoerotic strategy' that 'negotiates fearful desire' (Simmons, 870).[2] In the first scene, Valentine scorns a 'love-book' and mocks the story of Hero and Leander as 'some shallow story of deep love' (1.1.19, 21), but by 3.1 he presents himself to the pretending Duke as the expert on

---

1　As Kiernander, 36, observes, 'The characters cannot relate to one another directly but only through various highlighted mediating devices – messengers, letters, portraits and a gift. The signals these media are intended to transmit are subject to a great deal of interference.' For a more general consideration of 'the slippage between sign and referent' in the play, see Smith, 'Sign'.

2　Kiefer, 70, notes that there is no self-letter-writing in Elyot's narrative. Wall, 151, observes that Silvia 'cleverly escapes the sexuality of textuality by having Valentine write love letters to himself. Like Julia, she preserves her modesty by refusing the letter.'

such matters, advising how easily a maiden in a tower can be liberated by casting up a rope ladder 'with a pair of anchoring hooks', which 'Would serve to scale another Hero's tower, / So bold Leander would adventure it' (3.1.118–20). But Valentine, whose very name marks him as a 'lover', finds himself figuratively, as Leander does literally, out of his depth. Judging the letter he writes for her, Silvia concedes that 'the lines are very quaintly writ' (2.1.113), while he advises the Duke that the necessary ladder will be 'quaintly made of cords' (3.1.117). All this ingenious business revolves around the 'quaint', or female sexual organs (*OED sb.*[1]), but every approach is deflected in some way. Valentine's own letter not only is not delivered to Silvia, but is seized and read aloud by the Duke, thereby short-circuiting the male–female connection to a male–male discourse which results in Valentine's banishment. In the end, Valentine's claim to Silvia will be renewed not by him directly, but by her father's making her a 'gift' (5.4.146) to Valentine, an exchange between men.

Lance's 'love letter' in 3.1 serves as a reductive parody of Valentine's two letters, as it does not even have a designated recipient and is nothing more than a 'cate-log of [a maid's] condition' (269).[1] The 'cate-log' constitutes his nameless beloved (though she might be a Kate, see 269n.) as the sum of her virtues, vices, skills and bodily parts, a comically unromantic blazon that distills desire into legalistic language ('*Inprimis*', '*Item*') shot through with sexual double entendre. Lance's beloved can fetch and carry, sew/sow, milk, knit, wash and scour, is '*too liberal*' (337), and has '*more hair than wit*' (342), a formulation so daunting that Lance must construe it at length. Perhaps as a result of her liberality, she has no teeth (330) and may be undergoing one of the cures for venereal disease (see 3.1.304–5n.). It turns out that Lance's 'love letter' may also be linked to the pox.

Proteus's letter to Julia is actually delivered to her by Lucetta in a scene that comically figures the embodiment of desire in

---

1 There is a similar scene in Lyly's *Midas* (published 1592), 1.2.20–87 (Lyly, 3.120–1).

textuality. When Lucetta stoops to pick 'a paper up' that she 'let fall', Julia asks 'And is that paper nothing?' (1.2.73–4). Something might come of nothing, but before anything can happen Julia tears the letter into pieces, only to attempt to reassemble them, fragment by fragment, as if each is a part of Proteus's sundered body: 'Poor wounded name, my bosom as a bed / Shall lodge thee till thy wound be throughly healed; / And thus I search it with a sovereign kiss' (1.2.114–16; see Fig. 6). She will 'search' (like a surgeon's knife or, in another connection, a lance) the wound she has given with a healing kiss, but she will also 'fold' their two names 'one upon another' (128) and, as if the names were their physical bodies, urge them 'Now kiss, embrace, contend, do what you will' (129). All this erotic activity is directed toward paper and ink, however, and is doomed (like so many erotic offerings in the play) not to be reciprocated.[1] The paper is decidedly not 'nothing', but Julia will herself have to become 'nothing', i.e. lose her identity by becoming a boy, in order to pursue and secure Proteus for her own.[2]

Julia later delivers Proteus's letter to Silvia in 4.4. Just before she does, however, she mistakenly delivers 'a paper' she 'should not' (4.4.121). Presumably this is a letter from Proteus to herself (either the one from 1.2, repaired, or another). This confusion of the two letters neatly reflects the improper substitution of one sexual partner for another. At first rebuffing the second letter, Silvia then tears it into pieces, asserting that Proteus's lines 'are stuffed with protestations / And full of new-found oaths, which he will break / As easily as I do tear his paper' (127–9). The mirroring of Julia's letter-tearing scene in 1.2 of course links the two women together, as the objects of Proteus's desire, but also

---

1   In her wide-ranging essay on 'scenes of reading' in this period, Wall, 148, sees Julia's scene as an exception to such scenes in other texts 'in which female desire and writing are perceived as blotted' (i.e. sinful).
3   Bullough, 1.208–9, notes that there is a comparable letter scene in *Julio und Hyppolita*, but none in *Diana*.

Act 1. TWO GENTLEMEN OF VERONA. *Sc.1.*

Julia. *Go, get you gone; and let the papers lie:*

Publish'd by F & C.Rivington.London.Jan.8.1803.

6 Julia and Lucetta in 'Act 1, Scene 1' (1.2), Henry Fuseli, 1803

distinguishes them because Silvia really means it, and does not put the pieces back together.

The letters in 4.4 are accompanied, significantly, by the 'ring' (4.4.69) Julia gave Proteus at their parting at 2.2.5. The sexual association of the woman's ring is here linked with the transmission of the letter, as Silvia makes clear: 'Though his false finger have profaned the ring, / Mine shall not do his Julia so much wrong' (134–5). Sexuality and textuality are thus nearly synonymous. In the final scene, moreover, once she is aware of Proteus's brutal intentions, Silvia excoriates his infidelity in terms of language (my emphases in following quotations): 'I do detest false *perjured* Proteus . . . *Read* over Julia's heart, thy first, best love, / For whose dear sake thou didst then rend thy faith / Into a thousand *oaths*, and all those *oaths* / Descended into *perjury* to love me' (5.4.39–49). Proteus's response is to renounce what he takes to be 'the gentle spirit of moving *words*' (5.4.55) and resort to brute force. Valentine's rebuke of Proteus continues the theme: 'Who should be trusted, when one's right hand / Is *perjured* to the bosom?' (5.4.67–8). Julia, too, will employ the same term: 'How oft hast thou with *perjury* cleft the root!' (5.4.102).

The vagrancy and instability of language in *Two Gentlemen* indicate a far more complex and ambiguous world than the naive lovers imagine at the beginning of the play. Julia, for example, before she knows of Proteus's betrayal, equates constancy in language with constancy in love:

> But truer stars did govern Proteus' birth.
> His words are bonds, his oaths are oracles,
> His love sincere, his thoughts immaculate,
> His tears pure messengers sent from his heart,
> His heart as far from fraud as heaven from earth.
>
> (2.7.74–8)

The possibility and danger of inconstancy, however, are soon revealed. Sexual desire is the principal source of change in the play and it impacts on language as well as human nature; it erupts through the play's puns, malapropisms, oaths and letters, and its possible association with the 'pox' suggests its manifestation as a disease of corruption, where language is not only affected but infected. A linguistic prophylaxis protecting language from this disease is not easy to attain, however, when language is as vulnerable to change – hence, fallen – as human nature is:

> O heaven, were man
> But constant, he were perfect. That one error
> Fills him with faults, makes him run through all th' sins;
> Inconstancy falls off ere it begins.
>
> (5.4.109–112)

Sexuality and textuality, therefore, become recurrently and inextricably linked. Observing Valentine's obtuseness as Silvia invites him to receive the very letter he has written at her direction, Speed exclaims, 'she woos you by a figure'; when Valentine asks 'What figure?', Speed elaborates, 'By a letter, I should say' (2.1.137–9). The puns here are thick, as 'figure' means rhetorical trope (so that 'by a figure' means 'indirectly') and mathematical integer, and 'letter' means an epistle as well as a letter of the alphabet. The transmission of desire through the textual – literally embodied in all the letters – is also reflected in the play's frequent habit of seeing much of the world in textual terms: Proteus promises Valentine that he will pray for him 'Upon some book I love', rather than on a 'love-book' (1.1.19–20); Lucetta gives Julia Proteus's letter when her mistress laments 'I would I knew his mind' (1.2.33); Julia, in asking for counsel from Lucetta, tells her 'e'en in kind love I do conjure thee, / Who art the table wherein all my thoughts / Are visibly charactered and engraved, / To lesson me' (2.7.2–5); and Julia's 'lesson' will be how to disguise herself as a 'page'.[1] In the following scene, Silvia's father, the Duke, asks Valentine to 'lesson' him on how to court a pretended lover in order to draw out Valentine's thoughts and secret intention to elope with

---

1 Wall, 151, notes a similar linking of Mistress Page 'to printed pages and intermediary boy-servants' in *MW* 2.1.62–70 and 2.2.107–115.

Silvia. Valentine advises the Duke to 'Win [his love] with gifts if she respect not words' (3.1.89). Proteus resorts to 'gifts', trying to give Silvia a dog (appropriately referred to as a 'jewel' at 4.4.46). He will learn the falsity of the stock proposition that 'Dumb jewels often in their silent kind / More than quick words do move a woman's mind' (3.1.90–1). True love in the world of *Two Gentlemen* can only be expressed by and attained with true and constant words, as Julia pleads, 'Be calm, good wind, blow not a word away' (1.2.118). Proteus, who has no respect for words, claims 'truth hath better deeds than words to grace it' (2.2.18). His statement, as well as ironically prefiguring the attempted rape in 5.4, where 'the gentle spirit of moving words' (55) is sacrificed for 'force' (58), is also a response to Julia's parting 'without a word' (2.2.16), her grief-filled silence itself an expression of truth. It is fitting then that at the end of the play Proteus will learn the importance of silence as well as constant words, as both he and Julia are silent after their final reconciliation at 5.4.118–19. A grieving Lance also knows the value of silence when, in the scene that follows and parallels the parting scene of Julia and Proteus, he stops Pantino's mouth 'For fear thou shouldst lose thy tongue'. Where, Pantino asks, should he lose his tongue? Lance replies, 'In thy tale' (2.3.44–6; see 2.3.45–7n.).

Losing her tongue is ultimately Silvia's fate, as she will fall silent after the attempted rape in 5.4.[1] Her silence has sometimes been seen as evidence for an unfinished text or just poor dramaturgy, but Jonathan Goldberg has argued that her name is her destiny, since in the final scene she arrives 'in the place her name determines, the woods', where she ends up 'voiceless', 'placed within discourse that is not her own' (Goldberg, 68–9).[2] Goldberg also notes a similar phenomenon in Valentine's name, which

---

1 Lavinia of course suffers actual rape and loss of her tongue in *Titus Andronicus*.

2 Working through the song at 4.2.38–52, which tells that 'She excels each mortal thing', and the play's 'master text . . . Ovid's *Metamorphoses*', Goldberg goes on to connect Silvia to the Ovidian narrative of Philomela (see 5.4.5n.).

means 'lover' (see List of Roles, 2n.): 'Appearing *in* a letter, a valentine . . . *is* a letter, a folded slip of paper on which the name of a lover is inscribed' (Goldberg, 71). For Goldberg, 72, then, speaking of both Valentine and Silvia, 'it can come as no surprise that their first scene together is played around a letter'. Ultimately, Goldberg, 74, sees Silvia as 'doubly disabled since her power is a trope within a discourse that she cannot control' and Valentine's 'figurative submission to the discourse that gives him his name is what disables him from recognizing himself within the discourse to which he submits'. In Goldberg's argument, words become 'bonds' in an imprisoning sense. Yet essentially *Two Gentlemen* promotes the constancy of words while illustrating how, like all the other pieces of paper floating throughout the play, they can be contaminated by instability, even 'perjury', torn up and fractured.

Who is Crab?

What breed of dog is Crab? Or is Crab in fact a dog? Some stage 'dogs' were performed by actors in costume in the early modern period. In *The Witch of Edmonton*, 'Dog, *a Familiar*', listed among the dramatis personae, appears frequently in the play and speaks a number of lines, including 'Bow, wow!' (Rowley, *Witch*, 4.1.154), while Shakespeare, in *The Tempest*, employs '*diverse Spirits in shape of dogs and hounds*' (*Tem* 4.1.254.1–2). Henslowe's inventory list includes 'j black dogge' (Henslowe, 321, l. 92). Still, there seems little doubt that actual dogs did appear onstage, as is made clear by entry stage directions in *Every Man Out of His Humour*, 3.2.0.1: 'one *leading a dog*' (Jonson, 1.338), and in Middleton and Dekker's *Roaring Girl*, 2.1.364.1: '*Enter . . . with water-spaniels and a duck*'. Although there is no mention of dogs in the entry stage direction near the beginning of the Induction of *Taming of the Shrew* (*TS* Induction 1.14.1–2), still the conversation that follows about the Lord's 'hounds' – named Merriman, Clowder, Silver, Bellman and Echo (*TS* Induction 1.15–28) – suggests they may have entered with the '*Lord from hunting, with his train*', and in *A Midsummer Night's Dream*, Moonshine enters with some kind of canine, 'this dog my dog' (*MND* 5.1.255). So Crab was a dog, not an actor.[1]

The breed of dog one owned was a reflection of one's social standing. A gentleman, for example, would have been likely to own a greyhound, spaniel or hound (reflecting, as in *Taming of the Shrew*, the nobility's love of hunting). Some masters showed 'more care for their dogs than of their servants', according to one Stuart writer, who goes on to note, in a phrase reminiscent of Lance's self-sacrifice for Crab, 'often the servant is beaten for the dog' (Thomas, 103). The lower down the human social scale, the less refined the breed of dog, and the greater the number of complaints about their uncleanliness and impurity. During times of high plague mortality, special officers (after 1563) were appointed 'to "murder" and bury dogs found loose in the streets', and many parishes supported their own dog-killer (Wilson, *Plague*, 39). Crab was therefore probably a 'cur' (4.4.47), a mutt in modern terms, on the large side, as he is 'as big as ten' (4.4.55) of the type Proteus had bought for Silvia; Crab's excretal energies (see 4.4.36n.) also mark him as low and, as several critics have observed (Brooks, Beadle), associate him with humans in the play, particularly with Proteus.[2]

Reviewers of productions over the years have been at pains to identify Crab's breed if possible – 'a handsome cream colored setter named Otis' (Jorgens, 229), 'a fine quiet animal of the Newfoundland breed' (Salgado, 80), an 'Irish greyhound' (Eagles, 97), 'a salt-and-pepper schnauzer mix' (*Times*), a 'wolfhound' (Thomas, *Stratford*), 'an Australian sheepdog' (Pressley), 'a drooling, wrinkled, black-and-brown bloodhound with drooping ears

---

1 Real dogs were also apparently used in *Clyomon and Clamydes* ('*Enter father* Coryn *the Shepheard, and his dog*', *Clyomon*, F2ᵛ), Jonson's *The Staple of News* (when Peniboy Senior interrogates his dogs, Lollard and Block, one of whom 'pissed against my lady's gown', 5.4.55; Jonson, 4.356), *The Merry Devil of Edmonton* ('*Enter* Brian . . . *and his hound*', *Merry Devil*, 4.169) and Heywood and Brome's *The Late Lancashire Witches* ('*Enter Boy with the Greyhounds*', *Witches*, E1ʳ), among other plays.
2 The attribution of human characteristics to dogs seems to be a fundamental habit of human psychology (see Thomas, 92–142).

and melancholy eyes' (Shaltz, 35) and so on – but often the animal is just 'a mongrel' (Jackson, 27) or a 'scruffy mutt' (Peterson[3], 31). One Crab at Stratford, Ontario, Canada is memorably described as 'a beast of markedly indeterminate breed but vaguely resembling a beagle on stilts that had passed through the hands of a headshrinker' (Pettigrew, 55). See Figs 7–10.

Of more significance than the exact breed is that Crab is so often said to be without emotion: 'a deadpan equal to Buster Keaton's' (*Times*), a 'virtuoso of doggy deadpan' (Peterson[3], 31). He is invariably described as besting the human actors: 'if any actor needed a lesson in the art of picking up one's cue, or in the far subtler art of stealing the stage by doing absolutely nothing, he had only to watch the performance of Crab' (Speaight, 447).

7   Lance teaching his dog Crab, Henry Bunbury, 1794

Crab's complacent 'deadpan' lack of affect is in one sense a performance, for dogs can be trained to do many things onstage, but

8 Crab (Woolly) and Lance (Richard Moore) pointing to a shoe in David Thacker's RSC production, 1992, at the Barbican Theatre, London

the comic richness stems from Crab's lack of interaction of any kind, beyond the occasional gaze at the audience. One reviewer of Edward Hall's 1998 production found its Crab 'unsurpassed in the theatrical history of this play' as 'the embodiment of

9 Lance and Crab, Walter Crane, 1894

R. Cruikshank, Del.   C. W. Bonner, Sc.

The Two Gentlemen of Verona.

Launce. **Didst thou ever see me do such a trick?**

Act IV. Scene 2.

10 'Act 4, Scene 2' (4.4), showing Lance and Crab, R. Cruikshank, 1831

indifference . . . he is indeed a very "stone", incapable of fidelity, infidelity, or any other emotion' (Thomas, *Stratford*).[1] The dog's lack of emotion contrasts with Lance's tearful recounting of his farewell to his family, and Lance's fidelity to his dog – he is willing to be beaten in his place (4.4.25–8) – is not reciprocated; hence Crab is to Lance as Proteus is to Julia (see Fig. 11).

The association with Proteus continues with the substitution of Crab for Proteus's gift dog for Silvia (only referred to), the 'little jewel' (4.4.46; see n.), as small as a 'squirrel' (4.4.53). This would undoubtedly have been a lady's lap-dog, 'usually a toy spaniel in the early sixteenth century and a pug in the seventeenth' (Thomas, 107): 'The smaller they be', according to Dr Caius, in his treatise *Of English Dogs* (1576),

> the more pleasure they provoke, as more meete play fellowes for minsing mistrisses to beare in their bosoms, to keepe company withal in their chambers, to succour with sleepe in bed, and nourishe with meate at bourde, to lay in their lappes and licke their lippes as they ride in waggons.
>
> (Fleming, 21)

Cute they may be, but Caius also found them 'instrumentes of folly for them [i.e. the ladies] to play and dally withall, to trifle away the treasure of time, to withdraw their mindes from more commendable exercises, and to content their corrupted concupiscences with vaine disport' (Fleming, 20–1). Proteus aligns himself earlier with just such a lap-dog in his contemplation of Silvia's rejection of his advances: 'Yet, spaniel-like, the more she spurns my love, / The more it grows and fawneth on her still' (4.2.14–15). Significantly, Proteus's emblem of dog-like devotion is stolen, never reaching its intended recipient, and the real nature of Proteus's pursuit of

---

1 The deadpan, unresponsive nature of stage dogs was also commented on in other plays of the period. Thus, the Boy in *The Late Lancashire Witches* complains 'A Hare, a Hare, halloe, halloe, the Divell take / These curres, will they not stir, halloe, halloe, / There, there, there, what are they growne so / lither and so lazie?' (*Witches*, E1ʳ).

11 Frontispiece to Howard Staunton's 1858 edition, showing Lance, Crab, Proteus and Julia as Sebastian

Silvia is figured by the replacement gift, in the form of Crab, which is offensive, urinating on Silvia (4.4.35–7). The substitution anticipates the attempted rape, and Crab, an inversion of dogdom's proverbial human-like trait of fidelity, comes to symbolize 'the transgressor in Proteus' (Brooks, 99).

Whatever the dog does onstage, even if it is nothing, the audience will attribute human qualities to it, so that it will simultaneously seem to engage on the level of the play (showing interest or boredom) and on the level of natural animal behaviour. As States, 379, notes, 'we have an instance of Bergson's comic formula in reverse: the living encrusts itself on the mechanical – *mechanical* here meaning the prefabricated world of the play; in short, we have a real dog on an artificial street'. If Will Kemp had played Lance (see p. 127), the audience would also have been engaged on two levels with the actor as well as with the dog. The humour generated by the dog depends absolutely on Lance as the unexpected straight man. When Lance asks, 'When didst thou see me heave up my leg and make water against a gentlewoman's farthingale? Didst thou ever see me do such a trick?' (4.4.35–8), he is speaking to Crab, yet we might also see here a metadramatic turn to the audience, many of whom could indeed have seen Kemp play tricks onstage. Upstaged by a dog, Kemp would have found it necessary to improvise, as he so often did, while also sticking to a witty script – a complex stage moment reflecting Weimann's account of the gradual professionalization of the clown in this period. The human actor usually comes off second-best, however, and in the few productions when Crab's scenes are not particularly funny, the dog rarely gets the blame.

Verona–Milan–Mantua–Padua

Were it not for the final word of the play's title, we might be hard-pressed to identify just which Italian city was home to Proteus, Valentine and Julia. The name 'Verona' is mentioned only four times in the play: when the Duke pretends that 'There is a lady of Verona here' (3.1.81; F has 'in *Verona*'), when Valentine identifies his destination to the Outlaws (4.1.17), when the Third Outlaw claims to have been banished from Verona (4.1.46) and when, at the end of the play, Valentine threatens Turio not to claim Silvia, or 'Verona shall not hold thee' (5.4.127). No Elizabethan audience could otherwise have identified the location of the first act of the play except from its title, presumably used in announcing performances. Those in the audience who had read descriptions of Italy – by English travellers[1] or in translated accounts – might have expected some reference to the two most remarkable landmarks of Verona, the Piazza Bra and the Arena, one of the largest surviving Roman amphitheatres in the world, but *Two Gentlemen* offers no such reference.[2] The 'Verona' of the play seems, instead, to be a fairly generic small town, from which the ambitious youth leave to go to the sophisticated court world of Milan. The sole distinguishing geographic feature of Shakespeare's Verona in *Two Gentlemen* is that its river (the Adige, not named in the play) seems to have a tide, even though it is far inland.[3] The river Thames of course did have tidal effects; as Gurr, 'Localities', 62, notes, all Shakespeare's 'cities are versions of London'.

---

1 Typical descriptions of Italy in the period include, for example, that of Fynes Moryson (not published until 1617, but based on travels in the mid-1590s). He saw Verona as 'built in the forme of a Lute, the necke whereof lies towards the West, on which side the River . . . doth not only compasse the City, but runs almost through the center of the body of this Lute' and described 'many ruines of an old Theater, and old triumphall arches'; near the walls on the south side of the city, he reported, 'lies a stately Monument of an old Ampitheater, at this day little ruined, vulgarly called Harena, and built by Luc: Flaminius . . . It passeth in bignesse all the old Amphitheaters in Italy' (Moryson, 1.377–9). For William Thomas, writing in 1549, however, Verona was just one of many small towns under the dominion of the State of Venice (Thomas, *History*). Thomas Coryat (*Coryat's Crudities*, printed 1611) writes that 'the worthiest and most remarkable of all [the city's monuments] is the Amphitheater commonly called the Arena' (Coryat, 2.19); a meticulous five and a half page description of the city follows.

2 The map of Verona in the *Civitates Orbis Terrarum* (1593), for example, depicts the Arena in the middle of the city, and also provides a greatly magnified close-up in the bottom right corner (Braun, 3.49).

3 Shakespeare had a much more sharply focused conception of Venice, which is only natural given its much greater importance in contemporary history and its prominence in all visitors' accounts of Italy; many scholars have usefully studied the depth of this knowledge (see Levith, McPherson, Marrapodi, 143–209). For a useful overview of Italian settings in English Renaissance drama, see Hoenselaars.

Many scholars over the years have commented, at times derisively, on Shakespeare's faulty knowledge of Italian geography; journeying by water from Verona to Milan, to cite the prime example from *Two Gentlemen*, hardly seems plausible. In an effort to vindicate Shakespeare, however, some scholars have pointed out the existence of inland water routes through northern Italy, and indeed one can see even today remains of the Roman maritime fleet in the museum on Lake Garda.[1] Those not inclined to credit Shakespeare with such detailed knowledge of the waterways of northern Italy may point to his knowledge of Arthur Brooke's *Romeus and Juliet* (1562), a narrative that undoubtedly lies behind *Two Gentlemen* and that is set in Verona. Such knowledge as Brooke affords, however, is thin and generalized, as the opening lines of his poem demonstrate:

There is beyonde the Alps, a towne of auncient fame
Whose bright renoune yet shineth cleare, Verona men it
    name,
Bilt in an happy time, bilt on a fertile soile,
Maintened by the heavenly fates, and by the townish toile.
The fruitfull hilles above, the pleasant vales belowe,
The silver streame with chanell depe, that through the
    towne doth flow,
The store of springes that serve for use, and eke for ease
And other moe commodities which profite may and please,
Eke many certaine signes of thinges betide of olde,
To fill the houngry eyes of those that curiously beholde

---

1   See Draper. The Oxfordians, champions of the Earl of Oxford's authorship of Shakespeare, have a different stake in the question of Shakespeare's geographical knowledge, as the title of Magri's article indicates ('No Errors in Shakespere: Historical Truth and The Two Gentlemen of Verona'). Once the historical accuracy of the play's references is shown, according to her argument, it can be aligned with the personal knowledge of the Earl of Oxford, who visited northern Italy in 1575–6; the same process is applied to the confusions (only apparent, in this view) between Duke and Emperor in Milan (see List of Roles, 1n.).

Doe make this towne to be preferde above the rest
Of Lumbard townes, or at the least compared with the best.
                                                    (*Romeus*, ll. 1–12)

   Verona is named in *Two Gentlemen* solely, however, as the place
of origin and the point of departure for five of the main characters. Milan is where most of the action takes place, the location of
the Duke's (or Emperor's) court – clearly, in the play's terms, a
larger, more sophisticated world where the full flowering of the
Italian Renaissance might be found. (Reports of English travellers
like Thomas Coryat and Fynes Moryson concur.) Pantino tells
Antonio that the court of Milan is the best place to send his son,
Proteus, where he can be made 'a perfect man . . . tried and
tutored in the world' (1.3.20–1):

> There shall he practise tilts and tournaments,
> Hear sweet discourse, converse with noblemen
> And be in eye of every exercise
> Worthy his youth and nobleness of birth.
>   (1.3.30–3)

Milan is presented as a powerful but uncharacterized place in
the play. No Milanese landmarks are described, yet the play does
register one very precisely – 'Saint Gregory's well' (4.2.81), identified by Bond as 'an actual well near Milan'. There is also a forest
somewhere near Milan, on the way to the third Italian city cited in
the play, Mantua, as well as a 'mountain foot' (5.2.44). Mantua is
the home of the Second Outlaw (4.1.49) and Silvia's destination
in her flight to Valentine (4.3.23), as the Duke confirms (5.2.45).
Otherwise nothing is said about the city, nor does the action ever
move there.

   The fourth city mentioned in the play, Padua, is either a joke,
a confusion by Shakespeare or an error in the transcription and
printing process. In the Folio, Speed welcomes Lance 'to *Padua*'
(see 2.5.1n.), which, like many other editors, I have emended to
'Milan'; yet the F reading has been successfully played as Speed's
joke greeting to a confused Lance. Padua is frequently alluded to

in early modern England, primarily for its historic university. Clifford Leech interprets the anomalous '*Padua*' and other geographical confusions as evidence of revision of the text underlying F – even going so far as to argue for a chronology of progressive composition (see p. 126).

These four cities appear or are referred to in a set of Shakespeare's early Italianate plays. 'Verona' is referred to in *Two Gentlemen* and *Taming of the Shrew* (Petruchio is from Verona, 1.2.1), and of course *Romeo and Juliet* is set in Verona (again, without reference to its two most famous landmarks).[1] Michael Cassio's ship in *Othello* is said to be 'A Veronessa' (2.1.26). 'Milan' is referred to in *Two Gentlemen*, *King John* (twice), *Much Ado About Nothing* (once), and, in *The Tempest*, Shakespeare depicts a Milan of power politics and conspiracy leading to Prospero's exile (1.2.57–151) rather than the noble court of *Two Gentlemen*. 'Mantua' is referred to in *Two Gentlemen*, *Taming of the Shrew* ('Litio' is said to have been born in Mantua (2.1.60) and the Pedant of 4.2 is a native of Mantua) and *Romeo and Juliet* – Romeo flees to Mantua, where Juliet was originally supposed to have joined him. *Taming of the Shrew* is set primarily in Padua, and there are additional references in *The Merchant of Venice* (the home of Portia's cousin, 'Doctor Bellario', 3.4.50, whose identity she assumes in the trial scene) and *Much Ado About Nothing* (Benedick's home, 1.1.34). The plays that are set in or refer substantially to northern Italy – *Taming of the Shrew*, *Two Gentlemen*, *Romeo and Juliet* – are 'romantic' in nature, with many shared themes and images, suggesting, but not proving, that they may have been composed at approximately the same time. Certainly the references to Verona and Mantua in *Two Gentlemen* and *Romeo and Juliet* are linked to Arthur Brooke's *Romeus and Juliet*, which lies behind both plays (see Melchiori). Shakespeare's Italy in these plays, then, is the Elizabethans' romantic Italy, not that other Italy which was home to Machiavelli, Catholicism, poison and

---

1 See Locatelli on the fictional world of *Romeo and Juliet*; she demonstrates how 'Verona' is a 'renaming' of London.

treachery in general as seen in early modern tragedies. There may be outlaws on these roads, but they are all 'gentlemen' capable of reformation.

Dramaturgy

The dramaturgical requirements of *Two Gentlemen* are relatively straightforward: a stage with two doors and an upper acting area (Silvia's 'window', 4.2.16; see Figs 12 and 13). Relatively few props are necessary: the various letters in the play (see pp. 59–60), a coin (1.1.127), a glove (2.1.1), the two rings (2.2.5–6), Lance's shoes (2.3.13–17), staff (2.3.18–19) and hat (2.3.20), the 'corded ladder' (3.1.40) and 'cloak' (3.1.136) for Valentine, musical instruments (4.2.25) and the 'picture' of Silvia (4.4.115–16). The chief costume change would seem to be Julia's disguise as 'Sebastian' (described at 2.7.39–56). Various productions of the play (see pp. 84–92) have introduced much, much more in the way of scenery and properties, but the play can be performed with relative economy of means.

The play requires a minimum of eleven actors. Originally it could have been performed by a company of eight or nine adult actors, three boy actors and possibly one or two additional hired men, as indicated in the casting chart (see Appendix).[1] These figures of course are based on a number of assumptions – for example, that the actor playing Lance (presumably Kemp) did not double any parts (though he could have), that a different boy played each of the three different female parts (though one could have doubled Lucetta and Silvia) and that all three Outlaws were onstage in the final scene (two might have been sufficient). Some scholars, assuming that 1594 is the date around which the earliest performances of *Two Gentlemen* took place, have attempted to identify which actors in the play's original company (at that time

---

1   Bradley, 50, 232, believes that probably a minimum of eight adult actors (maximum ten) and three or four boy actors was required; King, 82, believes that the play required nine adult actors, three boys and three men playing minor speaking roles.

12 Balcony scene, 4.2, with Proteus (Barry Lynch) and Silvia (Josette Bushell–Mingo) above in David Thacker's RSC production, 1992, at the Barbican Theatre, London

13 Balcony scene, 4.2, with Proteus (Dominic Rowan) and Silvia (Poppy Miller) above in Edward Hall's RSC production, 1998, at the Swan Theatre, Stratford-upon-Avon

the Chamberlain's Men) would have played individual parts. Thus Grote, 23–4, argues that John Heminges and Augustine Phillips would have played Proteus and Valentine, George Bryan the 'more authoritative of the two fathers, the Duke of Milan, with [Thomas] Pope as the more conventional father Antonio, doubling the Host in Milan' – though Pope was known primarily as a comic actor.[1] Such speculations offer little hope of certainty, yet if anything is probable and plausible in the casting of the play it is Kemp's role as Lance (see p. 127).

While the dramatic strategies employed in the play are not as striking (e.g. Bottom's entrance with an ass head in *A Midsummer Night's Dream*) or as radical (e.g. Hermione's revivified statue in *The Winter's Tale*) as in some later plays, Shakespeare does utilize over-hearing scenes (4.2), layered disguises, mis-delivered letters and dogs, and dramatic irony in addition to the frequent 'duets' on which Beckerman and others have commented (see 1.1.70–141n.).[2] Shakespeare also brings together, as he was to do later in his work, the rustic clown and the witty servant – the latter developed from Plautus and Lyly.[3] Shakespeare seems to have learned from Lyly generally in terms of dramaturgy and characterization (for more specific indebtedness to Lyly, see p. 58, n. 56). Hunter speaks of the 'Lylian kind of structure' of *Two Gentlemen* and the organization of the play's themes in the form of debates – e.g. love versus honour. This structure is apparent in other plays of Shakespeare, but, Hunter argues, not in such a 'rudimentary form' as in *Two Gentlemen*. Yet even in such an early

---

1   Thomas Pope has often been assumed to have played Speed (Chambers, *WS*, 1.83), but Grote, 23–4, argues that Speed, called a 'boy', 3.1.255, and 'sweet youth', 2.5.2, must have been played by a boy actor.

2   Wells, 'Failure', 163, observes that 'Shakespeare's technique in this play is limited almost exclusively to three devices: soliloquy, duologue, and the aside as comment.'

3   Speed is the typical Lylian page – witty, critical of both his master and his master's friend, ultimately linked to the tricky servant of Plautine comedy. Yet Hunter, *Lyly*, 314–15, notes that 'Lyly's servants have a simple and definite set of characteristics – quick wit, love of mischief, empty bellies', but that Lance and Speed 'are much more difficult to define' (for example the Lylian Speed certainly has wit, but he is outwitted by the more clownish Lance in 2.5). See Campbell and Salingar.

play, Shakespeare introduces more complex elements, particularly in terms of characterization. Hunter maintains, however, that such complexity is inadequately supported by too heavy a reliance on the simplicity of a Lylian structure: 'the debate theme of *Two Gentlemen* is quite incapable of controlling the history of Proteus in whose complex nature will and reason are seen at psychological odds' (Hunter, *Lyly*, 324).

THE AFTERLIFE

The Theatrical Tradition

While *Two Gentlemen* was certainly known in Shakespeare's lifetime, as Francis Meres's comments in 1598 make clear (see p. 129), no record exists of any staging of *Two Gentlemen* from the time of its composition in the 1590s until Benjamin Victor's adaptation was performed at David Garrick's Theatre-Royal in Drury Lane, in London, in 1762–3. Given this late starting point, and the play's general lack of popularity, its subsequent performance history, if not extensive, is nevertheless surprisingly rich.[1] After Victor's version reintroduced the play, productions of it were

---

1 Carlisle and Derrick, in their useful survey of the play's stage history, put the case in very negative terms: 'just twenty-four productions of it on the London stage since Shakespeare's time . . . At Stratford-upon-Avon there have been only ten since . . . 1879', even fewer productions in New York ('only five full-length productions') and only four at Stratford, Ontario, Canada in forty years (Carlisle & Derrick, 126, 148, n. 2). Accepting this survey as the final word, however, would be like accepting as mountains in the world only those peaks over 27,000 feet high. *Two Gentlemen* is a popular play in regional theatre throughout the United States, and attendance figures can be impressive, so the impact of regional theatre and festivals should not be underestimated. Osborne, 172, moreover, points out that 'there were seven separate performance editions of the comedy published between 1774 and 1850' (i.e. Bell 1774, Butters 1800, Kemble 1808 and 1815, Oxberry 1823, Cumberland 1830 and French 1845). Finally, in the five-year period 1996–2000, according to the *SQ* bibliography (vols 48–52), the play was performed in twenty-one different states and the District of Columbia in the United States; at the Royal National Theatre, the Royal Shakespeare Theatre, Shakespeare's Globe Theatre and four other venues in England; at Stratford, Ontario, in Canada; and in Moravia, Warsaw, Paris, Aachen, Tokyo, Sofia and Munich.

mounted by most of the great actor-managers of the eighteenth and nineteenth centuries: the play was produced in London at Covent Garden in 1784, by John Philip Kemble at Drury Lane in 1790 and again in 1808 at Covent Garden (with Kemble, now fifty years old, performing the role of Valentine), by William Charles Macready at Drury Lane in 1841 (after his earlier production at Bristol in 1822), by Charles Kean in 1848 at the Haymarket Theatre, by Samuel Phelps at Sadler's Wells in 1857 and by William Poel in 1892, 1896 and 1910, among others. In New York, the play was directed by Charles Kean in 1846[1] and by Augustin Daly in 1895. This is not the production history of a *Hamlet* or *Romeo and Juliet*, to be sure, but the play attracted the attention of the period's major theatrical figures, several of whom made substantial alterations and 'improvements' to its text.[2]

The twentieth century saw productions of *Two Gentlemen* by Harley Granville-Barker at the Court Theatre, in London, in 1904 and at a variety of other venues in the first three decades of the century. Two notable productions in the 1950s continued to provoke interest in the play: Denis Carey's in 1952, at the Bristol Old Vic, and Michael Langham's in 1956, at the Old Vic in London. At Stratford-upon-Avon, major directors, starting with Ben Iden Payne in 1938, regularly revived the play: Peter Hall in 1960, Robin Phillips in 1970, John Barton in 1981, David Thacker in 1991 and Edward Hall in 1998. *Two Gentlemen* was the only play produced by the new resident company during the Shakespeare's Globe Theatre's 'Prologue Season' in London in 1996, directed by Jack Shepherd, and the Royal National Theatre Company put on another production in London three years later, in 1999, at the Cottesloe Theatre, directed by Julie Anne Robinson. The play also continued to flourish in the United

---

1   It is often assumed that Kean's was the first production of *Two Gentlemen* in America, but Roppolo, 118, notes a production at Caldwell's American Theatre in New Orleans, 28 December 1831.

2   In relation to Kemble, Macready and Kean – I only discuss here their productions of 1808, 1841 and 1846 respectively.

States, with Adrian Hall's New York production of 1994, and in Canada, at Stratford, Ontario, with productions in 1975, directed by Robin Phillips, and in 1984, directed by Leon Rubin. Musical versions of *Two Gentlemen* have ranged from the operatic, produced by Frederick Reynolds and Henry Bishop at Covent Garden in 1821, to the rock musical, directed by Mel Shapiro in New York in 1971. Don Taylor directed the play for television in the BBC Shakespeare series in 1983, bringing the play to a wider audience than ever before. *Two Gentlemen* is now produced many times each year – in summer festivals, in schools and universities, and in elite theatre venues around the world. This is not the place to offer a full performance history of the play, but rather to highlight some of the major production issues to which actors and directors have responded over the centuries.[1]

It is noteworthy that the first recorded production of the play was of an adaptation, Benjamin Victor's. As well as contending with the issues of the offer, the attempted rape and Silvia's silence, Victor introduced other substantial changes, which subsequent directors followed to a greater or lesser degree. The dialogue concerning the decorative codpiece for Julia, of course, vanished from the text – evidently one of the many 'weeds' with which 'this comedy abounds' ('Advertisement' in Victor).[2] Victor also established a structure, followed for many years, in which 2.2 and 2.7 are moved back into the first act, thus bringing all the 'Verona' locations into consecutive sequence; 2.3 (Lance's weeping scene) is moved to Milan, the lines about boarding ship deleted. Kemble would follow this logic in his 1808 adaptation.[3]

Victor was also the first to amplify the roles of Lance and Crab considerably by inventing two scenes in the fifth act. Lance enters,

---

1 Schlueter reviews the stage history up to 1981, and the essay by Carlisle and Derrick is very useful. Friedman offers a valuable if not complete stage history; his account of the Victor and Kemble adaptations is illuminating.

2 See Derrick, 'Depth', for a survey of cuts in the women's parts in nineteenth-century productions.

3 One reason for this reordering of scenes might have been the constraints of shifting pictorial scenery, which had not been a problem in Shakespeare's theatre (RP).

'*in a fright, follow'd by* Crab', terrified of the Outlaws, who indeed enter and '*present their guns at* Launce', taking him and Crab prisoner (Victor, 49–50). Later, Speed puts on a disguise, pretending to be one of the Outlaws, and pushes the trick on Lance – now steadily weeping – even further. Crab, he says, is behaving better than his master, to which Lance, in a reasonably 'Shakespearean' passage, objects:

> No – no – he has no bowels – he is hard-hearted – I knew that before – He won't shed one tear if you were to execute me (his best friend) before his face – when I should drown myself in tears, if you were to put him to the least torture – but we are not all made alike – and yet, we are sometimes doom'd to suffer alike –
>
> (Victor, 54)

The joke is revealed and Lance is almost Falstaffian (as in *Merry Wives of Windsor*) in surprise: 'I am disgrac'd! I am undone. Who the devil would have thought of such a masquerade trick as this?' (Victor, 55). The 'Advertisement' to the printed text leaves the reader to judge whether these added scenes 'contribute any thing to the representation, or afford any amusement'. Evidently Kemble believed they did, as he includes a similar episode – Victor's two scenes now compressed into one – with Lance and Crab once again lost in the forest: 'they say, it's inhabited by goblins, monsters with three throats, that swallow men up alive' (Kemble, 66). Captured by the Outlaws – so cruel that one is shown '*Striking at the Dog*' – Lance is rescued (in contrast to Victor's version) by Speed, who leads them happily offstage. Macready eventually deleted these added scenes, and Kean, following Macready, sarcastically comments in the preface to the printed text of his adaptation: 'some profane hand has made *Launce* to re-appear in the fourth and fifth acts, and talk nonsense, of which we are quite certain even *Crab* would have been ashamed' (Kean, v). Evidently shame has little place in the theatre, however, for subsequent productions, while not including these added scenes, gave full play to the Lance–Crab scenes, some of them lasting an extraordinarily long time as the actor milked every pause in the text, while the dog scratched, licked, micturated or simply stared at the audience. As the 'Henslowe' character says in the film *Shakespeare in Love*, 'Love and a bit with a dog, that's what they like' (Norman & Stoppard, 18).

Proteus has been variously depicted as sinister from the beginning of the play, as a haplessly naive innocent and as a confused young man sexually attracted to Valentine as well as Julia and then Silvia. Valentine has been portrayed as an obtuse pretty boy and as a naive young man who, learning the hard way, turns into a near-heroic mature figure. Turio, on the other hand, is nearly always – and rightly so – depicted as a dense dolt and the coward of Act 5. Victor (followed by Kemble) goes considerably further with Turio, making him '*Enter . . . singing*' (in Act 2) with additional lines revealing him to be even more full of himself than Shakespeare's text allows. Victor carries this through into 5.1:

> Well – I am certainly a person of considerable attractions! Lady Silvia cannot remain much longer unsubdu'd by a man of my accomplishments! My last serenade was powerful! [*Sings an affected voluntary.*] But I must practice my new song – This must bring her down. What! a man of my estate! my figure! my parts! to be baffled thus long! 'tis insufferable, and must not be endur'd.
>
> (Victor, 46–7)

These additions, too, were eventually dropped from productions, directors apparently having concluded that Shakespeare makes Turio quite foolish enough in the original.

The play has been set in locations ranging from a vaguely Renaissance Verona and Milan around 1500 (Macready placed the opening scene, in a further bid for historical accuracy, before the 'Tombs of the Scaligeri' (Carlisle & Derrick, 135)) to Verona Beach, New Jersey (Wager), from settings of the American Wild West or Little Italy mafiosi around 1900 (Jorgens, 228) to the chic

1990s Milan of Gucci and Armani (Edward Hall; see Fig. 14); in Phillips's 1970 production, 'Verona was a high-class resort, Milan an open-air university' (Thomson, 'Necessary', 121; see Fig. 15). One of the most successful twentieth-century productions was that of Thacker in 1991, set in the 1930s of Noel Coward (see Fig. 16). This production began with approximately fifteen minutes of songs (from a big-band orchestra and blonde chanteuse) by George and Ira Gershwin, Irving Berlin and Cole Porter, among others, to which couples in period evening wear danced. Once the play began, intervals between scenes were created in which the singer and orchestra would perform another song; the songs were cleverly chosen for their relevance to the themes of the play – 'Night and Day', 'Love is the Sweetest Thing', 'Love Walked In', 'I'm in the Mood for Love', 'Still of the Night' and, inevitably, 'The Glory of Love' (Thacker, Promptbook). As Peter Holland notes, the music and setting 'validated' the 'characters' obsession with love' (Holland, 87).

14 Opening scene in Edward Hall's RSC production, 1998, at the Swan Theatre, Stratford-upon-Avon

15 Opening scene in Robin Phillips's RSC production, 1970, at the Aldwych Theatre, London

16 Closing scene in David Thacker's RSC production, 1992, at the Barbican Theatre, London, with orchestra in the background

Two Gentlemen has often been linked to music, perhaps in part because of its song, 'Who is Silvia?', well known in its setting by Schubert. One of the earliest productions of the play was the operatic version by Reynolds and Bishop in 1821. The text has not survived, but the titles and placement of the songs were printed. The texts of the songs, in the form of solos, duets, choruses, and even a round by the Outlaws, have been selected from the whole range of Shakespeare's works: the sonnet-loving Julia, rather inappropriately, sings 'That time of year thou mayst in me behold' in Act 1 and 'When in disgrace with fortune and men's eyes' in Act 3, and a chorus of Outlaws sings 'Now the hungry lions roar' in Act 4 (see Reynolds). The production featured, according to a playbill, a 'Carnival in the Great Square of Milan' with an 'Emblematical Procession of the Seasons and the Elements', including, under the heading of 'Water', 'Cleopatra's Galley . . . seen sailing down the river Cydnus' (Odell, 2.160). One reviewer describes how

> The Queen lay classically sofa'd upon the deck, and the Nymphs and Cupids flew and fanned about her with picturesque fidelity. This was followed by a splendid scene of the Palace of Pleasure, all gaiety and glory, which was also succeeded by a view in the Duke's gardens, with a lake, a castle, a bridge, and an artificial mountain reaching to the clouds, the explosion of which discovered a gorgeous Temple of Apollo, rich in all that is bright and brilliant; and dazzling the spectators until the drop scene covered the catastrophe.
>
> (Salgado, 79)[1]

---

1 During one performance of this production the actor playing Proteus, 'while fencing in the banditti scene at the close of the fifth act', apparently gave an 'accidental wound' to 'Mr. A.', whose 'piercing shriek' did not signal any 'really dangerous' injury, 'although the cheek was laid open' (Salgado, 80).

Despite, or perhaps because of, these alterations, this production was a significant success with a very substantial run of 'twenty-nine performances during the first season' (Odell, 2.140). At the opposite musical extreme to Reynolds was the 1971 production of the New York Shakespeare Festival: a rock musical with a large number of black and Hispanic actors. Adapted by the playwright John Guare and Mel Shapiro and directed by Mel Shapiro, the production made Verona into San Juan and Milan into New York: 'We saw that the play was not only for the city, it was about the city, about going to the city' (Guare, 5). The production was successful enough to transfer to Broadway and to win a Tony Award as Best Musical of the season.

While actors and directors have exercised their ingenuity on many aspects of *Two Gentlemen*, especially in terms of the play's setting and the Lance–Crab scenes, by far the most important and controversial moments of every production have concerned the much-maligned final scene. Act 5, Scene 4, of *Two Gentlemen* stages the play's most crucial moment, the turning point in the friendship tradition of the Titus and Gisippus narrative – Valentine's offer of his beloved Silvia to his now suddenly penitent friend Proteus, who has just attempted to rape her:

> Then I am paid,
> And once again I do receive thee honest.
> Who by repentance is not satisfied
> Is nor of heaven nor earth, for these are pleased;
> By penitence th'Eternal's wrath's appeased.
> And that my love may appear plain and free,
> All that was mine in Silvia I give thee.
>
> (5.4.77–83)

Throughout the recorded stage history of *Two Gentlemen*, critics, audiences, adapters, directors and actors have been trying to understand, rationalize or simply evade this moment of the offer. Victor's adaptation, for example, simply omits the offensive line – 'All that was mine in Silvia I give thee' – in favour of a more general reconciliation ('Thy Valentine, and Julia, both are thine', Victor, 53). The lines of forgiveness are then moved to follow 5.4.115–17 (see 5.4.115–17n.). Julia's fainting is explained by an invented line, in which Proteus says, 'I merit death' (Victor, 52). The efforts of subsequent directors and actors to mitigate or erase this moment have been well documented.[1] Although some critics at the time denounced Victor's alterations, Kemble also dispensed with the offer. Macready, in his 1841 production, made wholesale changes to the text, including adding lines and transposing speeches, but he did restore the offer for the first time in decades (see Macready, Promptbook). Little has been written about Samuel Phelps's 1857 production, but it may be deduced that the offer was not evaded, from comments Phelps makes in the introduction to his 1858 edition of the play: 'this surrender . . . may have been intended by Valentine merely as a test of the sudden penitence of Proteus' (Cam[2], 37). In Iden Payne's production of 1938, the offer was again simply and silently omitted; one viewer claimed that 'no one who did not know the story would have guessed that anything had been left out' (Cam[2], 39). But the offer is a crucial moment in Shakespeare's source material and likewise integral to the discourse of male friendship as explored in *Two Gentlemen* (see pp. 3–32).

Later productions of *Two Gentlemen* also attempted to squirm out of the moment: Carey's production of 1952 again deleted the offer, while in Peter Hall's 1960 production the infamous line 'was spoken so that it was hardly noticed' (Brown, 132). Hearkening back to Victor's invented line, Langham's 1956 production prompted Valentine's offer by 'a threat of suicide with a pistol by the repentant Proteus' (Byrne, 471). In one American production of 1977, the director evidently found the ending 'incomprehensible and unplayable, so this Valentine offered Sylvia to Proteus sarcastically. It was a challenge to a fight' (Jorgens, 229), while in an Oregon production of 1974, the offer 'was all a ruse, a device

---

1 See the stage history in Cam[2], 17–49, and Carlisle & Derrick.

93

conceived by Valentine and Silvia and communicated to the audiences by pantomimed gestures' (Carey, 'Oregon', 420).[1] Describing Barton's 1981 production, Stanley Wells speaks of how the impact of the infamous line was lost by 'deliberately running it over with action' (Cam[2], 48), while Roger Warren describes this moment in the same production as Valentine trying to bring off the line 'as another piece of conventional behaviour, the kind of gesture Valentine would think was expected of him, while desperately hoping that Proteus wouldn't accept the offer' (Warren[1], 144). In the BBC production, a hesitant and deeply moved Valentine makes the offer to an engaging and profoundly penitent Proteus, as they embrace each other; Silvia's face is not shown while the offer is made or just after.[2] In Leon Rubin's production of 1984, the troublesome line of the offer was emended to 'All my love to Silvia I also give to thee', in order to make it clear 'that Valentine was not simply handing Silvia over to the man who had just attempted to rape her' (Warren[2], 190). But Valentine's offer entails precisely the handing over of Silvia.[3]

Productions have sometimes minimized the offer by staging Julia's faint nearly simultaneously, as in Edward Hall's 1998 production.[4] This stage business served to overshadow Silvia, whose

1 In a comparable denial of the authenticity of the offer, a 1966 production in Ashland, Oregon, had Julia, thinking she was alone, reveal herself as a woman, unaware that Valentine was watching, before the offer; this meant that Valentine could then 'pretend to yield Silvia to Proteus, confident that the shock of such a thing [would] lead Julia to reveal herself [to everyone else] and thus demonstrate her love so overwhelmingly that even Proteus [would] be shamed' (Smith, 'Festivals', 413).

2 Derrick, 'Crucial', 4, after analysing contradictory readings of this scene by reviewers, argues that 'Proteus clearly perceives the offer as a noble gesture of friendship, not an actual offer, because he does not even look toward Silvia but rather falls into an embrace with Valentine.'

3 Guare makes the literal meaning of the offer abundantly clear; Valentine makes the offer word for word as it is in F and Proteus clearly accepts – 'Oh, thank you' (Guare, 78). Small wonder that Julia faints – but the cause is equally likely her pregnancy (Proteus 'sees she is pregnant. He feigns innocence', Guare, 78).

4 One reviewer notes, Proteus's repentance in this production was 'so convincing that Valentine's subsequent offering of Silvia to Proteus, said with his back turned to the woman he loves, slips by virtually unnoticed as an extreme example of forgiveness' (McCauley, 11).

silence in relation to the offer has often been seen as another complicating factor. One of the simplest (and most evasive) ways of
dealing with Silvia's reaction was employed in a 1950 production:
'in a dead faint since her rescue from rape, she doesn't respond at
all' (Peterson[1], 4).[1] Robinson's production in 1999 depicted Silvia
with her head rested on her knees, her face only partly visible.
Emphasizing the importance of the women, however, Thacker's
1991 production, having staged the offer straightforwardly, used
Silvia as an instrument of reassurance for the audience:

> After Proteus' 'My shame and guilt confounds me'
> (5.4.73) Barry Lynch left a colossal pause, showing
> Proteus considering the possibility of conning Valentine
> again, before finally resolving on genuine repentance. If
> the audience hesitated slightly as to the genuineness of
> the repentance . . . it was Silvia's silent intercession, a
> calm gesture of moving towards Proteus, that reassured
> them.
>
> (Holland, 90)[2]

I rehearse this performance tradition to document briefly the
theatrical and editorial energy expended over two centuries on the
infamous offer. It is widely considered an embarrassment in *Two
Gentlemen* and, many feel, ought to be negotiated away in some
manner. How it is played can imply profoundly different conceptions of Valentine's character, of the homosocial relation between
Proteus and Valentine and of Silvia's silence. Yet while editors,
adapters and directors have considered the offer (which is not
even accepted) highly offensive, the attempted rape of Silvia has

---

1   Thaler, 746, attributes Silvia's silence to an equally convenient 'breathlessness after
her struggle' – evidently a very long one – with Proteus.

2   The promptbook (confirmed by the Archive Video) shows that Silvia came behind a
kneeling Proteus ('Sl x Behind P', Thacker, Promptbook), while Valentine made the
offer, in effect signalling her approval. Both couples then embraced just before the
Duke and Outlaws entered at 5.4.119 SD.

by contrast been found dramatically acceptable, even compelling, and does not have a similar revisionary theatrical history:

PROTEUS

    Nay, if the gentle spirit of moving words
    Can no way change you to a milder form,
    I'll woo you like a soldier, at arms' end,
    And love you 'gainst the nature of love – force ye.
      [*Seizes her.*]

SILVIA

    O heaven!

PROTEUS   I'll force thee yield to my desire.

VALENTINE [*Comes forward.*]

    Ruffian, let go that rude uncivil touch,
    Thou friend of an ill fashion!

                        (5.4.55–61)

Even Victor retains the attempted rape. Although he softens Proteus's words very slightly, he adds the generally-accepted stage direction ('*He seizes her*') to make the action unmistakable:

Pro. . . . I'll move you like a soldier, at arms end,
    And force you.   [*He seizes her.*]
Sil. O Heavens!
Val. [*comes forward*] Ruffian! let go that rude, uncivil touch!

                        (Victor, 51)

Rowe, Pope, Theobald, Johnson, Malone and others all leave the lines intact. Kemble, along with other efforts to reclaim Valentine's character, follows Victor in eliminating the offer, but he retains the attempted rape, though also softening Proteus's words by eliminating 'And love you 'gainst the nature of love – force ye' and 'I'll force thee yield to my desire':

    Pro. Nay, if the gentle spirit of moving words
        Can no way change you to a milder form,

I'll woo you, like a soldier, at arms' end.
Sil. O heaven! –
[*As* PROTEUS *goes to seize* SILVIA, VALENTINE *rushes between them.*]
Val. Ruffian, forbear that rude, unhallow'd touch! –
Thou friend of an ill fashion!

(Kemble, 68–9)

How then should the attempted rape, as important and contro-versial as the offer, be staged? In Macready's production, Proteus seized Silvia and threatened rape before Valentine intervened, 'Drawing [his] sword'; Proteus also 'draws his sword . . . is about to attack him, but recognizing Val, drops sword . . . staggers back' (Macready, Promptbook). In Kean's production, the text was soft-ened even more than in Victor's adaptation. The lines were to be 'All spoken as rapidly as possible!', but the stage action left no doubt about what was happening: 'He seizes Silv by the waist – they change places – when Val speaks, he quits her instantly' – this, too, was to be 'All done very rapidly!' (Kean, Promptbook). In Iden Payne's production, when Proteus 'threatened to rape Silvia, Valentine managed to get between them well ahead of real danger' (Cam[2], 39). In Peter Hall's production, however, 'The threatened rape of Silvia was a broad joke . . . Proteus' repentance was a sentiment to laugh at' (Brown, 132). This line was taken even further in a 1997 Oregon production, which consistently downplayed the danger through Proteus's ludicrous costume and Silvia's dominance in the scene.[1]

Phillips's 1970 production, however, reinforced a darker stage tradition, and Proteus's madness ended in a graphic attempted

---

1 At their entrance in 5.4, 'Silvia is clearly in command, not fleeing from but merely followed by a whining Proteus . . . Her "O heaven!" is not a cry for help but an exas-perated expression of impatience with Proteus' annoying behavior. In the brief scuffle that follows, Silvia easily pushes Proteus around . . . Silvia's own strength lands her supine on the floor, and Proteus ends up, quite accidentally and rather to his surprise, on top of her . . . This menacing, unintended stage picture . . . lasts scarcely the blink of an eye' (Armstrong, 37).

rape before he was interrupted. In the BBC production, Proteus grabs Silvia's arm, then rips off the mask she is wearing and begins to grab at her before Valentine almost instantly interrupts, sword in hand. This tendency toward more graphic and violent stage action was continued in Thacker's production when Valentine stopped Proteus's assault 'by physically wrestling him to the floor – echoing, now in desperate earnest, the playful rough-housing of act one' (Nelsen, 16). Edward Hall's production included an awkward, complicated hesitation in Valentine as Proteus attacked Silvia, perhaps resulting from astonishment at his supposed friend's action, perhaps from a darker, voyeuristic interest. And Robinson's production had Proteus throw Silvia down, rip off his own jacket and straddle her before Valentine intervened.

The most extreme possibilities of this moment were realized in several stagings toward the end of the twentieth century. In a 1990 production by The Acting Company at Bucknell University, Pennsylvania, the attempted rape of Silvia was 'horrifyingly real-istic', according to one account:

> She and Proteus overturn a couch in a struggle that lasts several minutes, and, when she resists, he slaps her viciously. This rapist means business. Valentine's inter-vention is equally brutal – he only just resists bringing a log down on his betrayer's skull with killing force. The image visually echoes their opening wrestling bout, while the overturned couch – belly exposed, guts gaping – rein-forces the sudden, visceral exposure of their friendship's violent potential. The play's ironic and sobering com-ment is that, in such a context, rape makes brutal sense.
>
> (Peterson[1], 34)

An all-female production in 1988 in Melbourne, Australia, made the attempted rape 'as uncomfortable as possible', for the young actresses (aged between ten and sixteen) as well as the audience (Schafer, 245). And in a feminist production at the University of

Kansas in 1989, director Dolores Ringer went even further, staging not an attempted but a completed rape, with the added outrage that Valentine observed the entire episode (Friedman, 63). Beyond the lack of textual authority for this interpretation, such staging undermines the offer itself, since Proteus has already taken what Valentine would offer. This line of staging reached its nadir in a 1991 production in New York, in which the play opened, 'simply and horribly, with [Silvia's] enacted rape . . . Two premises are established: no timely intrusion by Valentine . . . will prevent the rape, and the play is viewed backwards, leading inevitably to that accomplished evil' (Peterson[2], 24).[1] Whether these premises are worth establishing is of course another question.

The theatrical history of the offer, then, reveals a continuing effort to minimize or even erase it, from rewriting the scene to overrunning the lines with action, while the theatrical history of the attempted rape, by contrast, reveals a growing effort to maximize it, from its inclusion even in softened form in the earliest adaptations, to increasingly violent modern stagings and even the representation of an actual rape. Moreover, the attempted rape is, along with Lance and Crab in 4.4, the most frequently depicted scene in the play (see Figs 17–19). The different textual and performance histories of these paired actions, in which an offer made in friendship is frequently considered more heinous, more of an embarrassment onstage, than an attempted rape, may partly be explained by the collapse of the discourse of male friendship, even as early as the eighteenth century. Yet the attempted rape and the offer are mirroring actions (see pp. 28–30). Not to stage them for what they are is therefore to miss a profound, and profoundly disturbing, connection between them which the play insistently makes.

---

1 Or perhaps the nadir was reached in a 1978 production, in which 'Eglamour was shown to be enamoured of Silvia and so angry at her for not preferring him that he attempted to rape her even before Proteus got his turn at the poor girl' (L. Barber, 213).

17 Act 5, Scene 3' (5.4), Amy Zambi, 1803

If the offer and the attempted rape are the two most conspicuous problems of the final scene, the nature of Proteus's repentance is equally significant in any assessment of the play's meaning (see Fig. 20). The earliest adaptations, those of Victor and Kemble, invent a scene which Shakespeare does not show, Proteus's rescue of Silvia from the Outlaws, apparently as a way of rehabilitating Proteus morally, or at least making him appear in a much more positive light prior to Valentine's forgiveness of him. Kemble's is the more elaborate treatment, following Victor's precedent:

> *Pro.* Ha! Silvia's voice! – Love, guide my weapon sure!
>   Unhand the lady, slaves; – or meet your death.
> [PROTEUS *strikes the Sword out of* CARLOS's *hand,*
> *who flies: – he then engages* STEFANO, *who finds himself*
> *overpowered, and escapes.*]

18 Frontispiece to Nicholas Rowe's 1709 edition, showing 5.4

Painted by T. Stothard R.A.   Engraved by J. Heath, Historical Engraver to his Majesty and A.R.A.

TWO GENTLEMEN OF VERONA.

Val.   *Ruffian let go that rude uncivil touch.*

Act 5. Scene 4.

Published March 1 1801. by J. Heath, Russell Place Fitzroy Square & G. & J. Robinson, Paternoster Row.

19 Act 5, Scene 4, Thomas Stothard, 1818

20 Valentine rescuing Silvia from Proteus, Holman Hunt, 1851

> Prosperous adventure! – and most blest encounter! –
> Madam, this service I have done for you.
>
> (Kemble, 67)

Most productions, however, have tried to stage Proteus's actions in the final scene, particularly his speech of repentance, without recourse to such revision. His brief five lines –

> My shame and guilt confounds me.
> Forgive me, Valentine; if hearty sorrow
> Be a sufficient ransom for offence,
> I tender't here. I do as truly suffer
> As e'er I did commit.
>
> (5.4.73–7)

– have seemed inadequate to generations of directors and critics, yet a slow pace of delivery alone has been sufficient to evoke a profound, and therefore convincing, sense of Proteus's shame (as in Shepherd's Globe production with Mark Rylance). One interpretation of the speech, noteworthy for its extreme ambivalence, was that of Barry Lynch in Thacker's production. Friedman, 63–5, in his useful account of the contradictory audience responses to Lynch's performance, observes that Lynch seemed to convey either profound sincerity or sly duplicity in alternate performances, or somehow all at once. Friedman quotes Robert Smallwood's review:

> At some performances that little enigmatic flicker of a smile seemed to be discernible before he began to speak. When it was, the repentance was clearly a pure sham, and they were all being duped; when it was not, we had genuine penitence and thus the possibility of a comic ending: extraordinary that a half millimeter flicker of the lip muscles should change a dramatic genre.
>
> (Friedman, 65)

In addition to the attempted rape and the offer, the passivity of the women at the end of the play, so perplexing to many critics, has also afforded ample opportunity for directorial ingenuity. Janet Adelman perfectly articulates the issues:

> in order for the play to enact this fantasy [that allows both relationships' simultaneous fulfilment], the autonomy of both Silvia and Julia as fully realized figures has to be sacrificed: Silvia stands by silently as she is swapped from Valentine to Proteus, who has just tried to rape her (indeed, she never speaks after the rape attempt); and Julia is not permitted to notice, or to care, that her man is a would-be rapist. The sacrifice of the autonomy of these hitherto sensible characters suggests the extent to which the deepest concern of the play is with the male bond.
>
> (Adelman, 79)

Two stage responses to the unease Adelman describes have become nearly conventional. One stage tradition stems from Victor, who transfers Valentine's lines of reconciliation at 5.4.115–17 – 'Come, come, a hand from either. / Let me be blest to make this happy close. / 'Twere pity two such friends should be long foes' – to Silvia, with the added stage direction, '*She joins the hands of* Protheus *and* Julia; *and then takes the hand of* Valentine *to give to* Protheus' (Victor, 53); Kemble follows suit, with slight changes.[1] Moreover, as Victor also moves Valentine's earlier controversial lines of forgiveness at 5.4.77–83 to follow Silvia's rejoining of the hands here, Valentine's forgiveness follows Silvia's. Kemble accepts the same logic. While few productions since these adaptations have transferred the lines, the end of the twentieth century began to see many show Silvia silently joining the hands of the two estranged men or otherwise orchestrating the coming together of happy, unified couples at the very end of the play. Thacker's production, according to Thomas Clayton, showed that Silvia's

> stance and facial expression are so eloquent a mute plea
> for forgiveness that Valentine must be thought partly to
> be moved by and partly to reflect (on) it in his response,
> which in effect articulates the spirit seen in Silvia.
>
> (Clayton, 18)

In this production, the offer did not signify the alienation of Silvia but her inclusion: 'In order that his renewed love may be plainly seen to be freely given, "all" his love that was in Silvia he gives to, shares with, Proteus, even while it remains with Silvia (and even Valentine himself)' (Clayton, 18). From one perspective, having Silvia presiding over, or enforcing, the reconciliation of the two men makes her seem wiser than the men – she knows that their

---

1 'Give me your hand, sweet Julia; – yours, sir Proteus; – / Let me be bless'd to reconcile your vows: – [SILVIA *joins their Hands.*] [*To* VAL.] Nor must you hold out enmity for ever' (Kemble, 71).

friendship is something too valuable to be lost. Thus Silvia seems to be the dominant figure, yet from another perspective, she seems to preside acceptingly over her own marginalization.

A second tradition of staging concerns the final exit. It usually depicts the continuing bond of the men, while maintaining the autonomy of the women in their direct, if silent, response to it. In a 1978 production, at Great Lakes Shakespeare Festival, Lakewood, Ohio, for example,

> Valentine and Proteus started off stage, arm in arm, almost forgetting the ladies entirely. When they remembered and returned, Silvia and Julia turned the tables by suddenly linking arms and marching off together themselves, to the dumbfounded stares of their mates.
>
> (L. Barber, 213)[1]

In a 1994 production, at Illinois Shakespeare Festival, Normal, Illinois, all the men again left the stage to Julia and Silvia:

> The women appear stunned as they sit together on a tree-log at centerstage. Valentine and Proteus return moments later, smiling and holding their arms out to them as if nothing has happened. Julia and Silvia stand and walk away, then turn and glare fiercely at the men. The lights go out.
>
> (Shaltz, 35)

In these productions, a happy ending was denied – as if the female characters' autonomy could only be asserted by their refusal to participate in the play's heterosexual pairings. In a more positive

---

1   In a 1977 production, in Washington, D.C., 'When the two men caught themselves as they were about to walk off with each other instead of with their ladies at the end, it was funny partly because it seemed so in keeping with their earlier distracted states' (Roberts, 'D.C.', 236). At the end of the Australian all-female production of 1988, 'the two "boys" walked off hand in hand, leaving the girls behind in wistful silence. Then they joined up, not so happily, and walked off together. Basically the girls had been forgotten; the boys were so much into each other that they'd forgotten their lovers. It's very teenage' (Schafer, 244).

version, Edward Hall's production ended with the two women embracing at centre stage, in a moment of sisterly bonding that contrasted with the men's rivalry. In Shepherd's production, Julia's 'ambivalence about her reunion with Proteus' in marriage was highlighted in various ways, so that, as the stage cleared, 'Their final exit trail[ed] the beaming departure of the others as a diminished shadow' (Nelsen, 'Prologue', 7).[1] Wager's 2001 production, on the other hand, staged a far more conventional final tableau that cleverly demonstrated the normative progression from homosocial to heterosexual relations: Proteus and Valentine embraced on one side of the stage, and Silvia and Julia embraced on the other, the two gentlewomen mirroring the union of the two gentlemen. Then, in a moment of general recognition, the same-sex couples separated to re-form as the destined heterosexual couples, Proteus and Julia, Valentine and Silvia.

Some productions have thus found ways to suggest not only Silvia's approval of the offer but even her orchestration of the restoration of Proteus and Valentine's friendship and the reunion of Proteus and Julia by means of transferred or invented lines or, more often, symbolic stage actions. Other productions have found ways to represent the women's resistance to what the men of the play have arranged, often in the form of stage actions or groupings after the final line. In Phillips's 1970 production, the 'portentous delivery' of the final line itself 'cast doubt on the prospect it promises: "One feast, one house, one mutual (*pause*) happiness (*with an interrogatory vocal rise*)"' (Thomson, 'Necessary', 121). In all these stagings, whether the necessity and desirability of the heterosexual pairings have been reconfirmed or subverted, an agency and self-determination have been granted Silvia and Julia that otherwise seem absent in the final scene.

1 According to Brown, 'Free', 129, Phillips's 1970 production was far more melancholy than most, ending 'with a silent tableau as all the characters remain on stage where Shakespeare's text asks for an *exeunt*; at this point the director introduced a further character, a silent, black-visaged Launce who slowly threads his way through the silent figures' – rather like the Coming of Death, apparently.

One can hardly fault directors for creating stagings that seek to rationalize what they see as the play's difficulties. Most of these stagings are efforts to produce more seemingly logical or realistic psychological motivations in Valentine and Silvia, and virtually all fill in Silvia's long silence. Every effort to make Silvia speak, however, with transferred lines or silent action, ignores how the play has depicted Silvia as more or less constituted by masculine discourse. Silvia's famous silence begins after her 'O heaven!' at 5.4.59, but Julia (still dressed as a 'page' or 'boy') also falls silent after her reconciliation with Proteus at 5.4.118, when he tells her that he has his 'wish forever' and she replies, 'And I mine'. The male characters do all the talking at the end while the women's silence is ambiguous.

The Critical Tradition

The critical history of *Two Gentlemen* begins with Francis Meres's listing of '*Gentlemen of Verona*' in 1598 as one of six plays exemplifying the claim that Shakespeare is among 'the best for Comedy' (Chambers, *WS*, 2.194); for the next two centuries, however, its critical history continues primarily through the comments of the play's editors, some of whom were distinguished literary figures themselves, and few of whom rated the play as among the 'best'. The play's perceived aesthetic shortcomings effectively blocked significant critical commentary for a long period, as did the more general judgement that comedy was a less 'serious' genre than tragedy or history, hence less deserving of comment.

Although there is no record of a performance until 1762, *Two Gentlemen* was certainly known and occasionally alluded to by earlier writers. Perhaps the earliest allusion is in Dekker and Rowley's *Fortune by Land and Sea* (written *c.* 1607–9), where Young Forest seems to echo Valentine's claim to the Outlaws that 'I killed a man, whose death I much repent, / But yet I slew him manfully in fight, / Without false vantage or base treachery' (4.1.27–9): 'I have kild a man, but fairly as I am a Gentleman, without all base advantage in even trial of both our desperate fortunes' (*SAB*, 2.40).[1] There may also be an echo of Proteus's 'Say that upon the altar of her beauty / You sacrifice your tears, your sighs, your heart' (3.2.72–3) in Castabella's plea in *The Atheist's Tragedy* (1611): 'be not displeased if on / The altar of his tomb I sacrifice / My tears. They are the jewels of my love / Dissolved into grief' (3.1.57–60). A closer echo, of the Second Outlaw's 'To make a virtue of necessity' (4.1.61), can be heard in Richard Brathwait's *A Strappado for the Devil* (1615): 'No cure he finds to heale this malady, / But makes a vertue of necessity' (*SAB*, 1.256), but the proverbial nature of the phrase undermines any certainty here (see 4.1.61n.). These echoes are far from definite, but Cotgrave's *The English Treasury of Wit and Language* (1655) features dozens of quotations from Shakespeare's plays (and a few incorrectly attributed to him), including *Two Gentlemen*: 2.4.39–44 (under the rubric 'Of Eloquence, Garrulity, etc.', Cotgrave, 90–1), 5.4.79–81 ('Of Penitence, Repentance', Cotgrave, 216)[2] and 5.4.107–12 ('Of Inconstancy', Cotgrave, 143). The title of the play also shows up in lists of books or plays in 1656 (by T. Goff and by Edward Archer, *SAB*, 2.58–9), 1671 (by Francis Kirkman, *SAB*, 2.114), and others, and the song, 'Who is Silvia?', is quoted in 1671 in *The New Academy of Compliments* (*SAB*, 2.165).

The most important early references to the play, however, remain those of the play's editors. For Rowe, 'most of the Faults of this Play are Faults of Judgment more than Fancy'; '*Silvia* and the rest', he notes, do not behave themselves 'like Princes, Noblemen or the Sons and Daughters of such' (Rowe, 7.274, 275). Pope

---

1 When Anne asks 'And hand to hand?', Young Forest says 'In single opposition' – possibly echoing Hotspur's account of Mortimer's combat with Glendower in *1H4* 1.3.99: 'In single opposition, hand to hand' (*SAB*, 2.40).

2 George Eliot quotes Valentine's lines – 'Who by repentance is not satisfied / Is nor of heaven nor earth, for these are pleased' (5.4.79–80) – in letters dated 1846 (Eliot, 8.11) and 1859; in the latter, she astutely observes 'that doctrine is bad for the sinning, but good for those sinned against' (Eliot, 3.66). Elsewhere, the offer in the final scene, with 'Silvia standing by', Eliot claims, 'disgusted' her (Haight, 178).

describes the play's style as 'less figurative, and more natural and unaffected, than the greater Part of this Author's, though suppos'd to be one of the first he wrote', but he also criticizes its 'trifling conceits' at one point (Pope, 155, 157; see 1.1.70–141n.). Pope, moreover, seems to have been the first critic to focus on the play's most famous crux, the offer in the final scene: it is, he notes, 'very odd to give up his mistress thus at once' (Pope, 226). Theobald, 153, following Pope's edition a few years later, is more blunt: *Two Gentlemen* is 'One of his very worst' plays.

Samuel Johnson praises the play with faint damns when he speculates that the Folio text has 'escaped corruption, only because being seldom played, it was less exposed to the hazards of transcription', but he does assert, rather against the critical grain of the time, that

> When I read this play I cannot but think that I discover both in the serious and ludicrous scenes, the language and sentiments of Shakespear. It is not indeed one of his most powerful effusions, it has neither many diversities of character, nor striking delineations of life, but it abounds in [maxims] beyond most of his plays, and few have more lines or passages which, singly considered, are eminently beautiful.
>
> (Johnson, 179)

Johnson is also one of the first to point out some of the play's logical inconsistencies, and his comments are worth quoting in full because they typify, on the positive side, the early critical reactions to *Two Gentlemen*:

> In this play there is a strange mixture of knowledge and ignorance, of care and negligence. The versification is often excellent, the allusions are learned and just; but the author conveys his heroes by sea from one inland town to another in the same country; he places the Emperour at *Milan* and sends his young men to attend him, but never

mentions him more; he makes *Protheus*, after an interview with *Silvia*, say he has only seen her picture, and, if we may credit the old copies, he has by mistaking places, left his scenery inextricable. The reason of all this confusion seems to be, that he took his story from a novel which he sometimes followed, and sometimes forsook, sometimes remembered, and sometimes forgot.

(Johnson, 259)

Malone, in Boswell's edition of 1821, also defends the play as Shakespeare's from the doubt of Hanmer, among others, seeing it as among 'the first flights of a young poet', with a style not to be judged against that of the later plays; even the low comic parts, he claims, 'are as perfectly Shakspearian (I do not say as finished or as beautiful) as any of his other pieces' (Boswell–Malone, 5). He also specifically comments on the play's style, in response to Pope's comments: 'the conceits here objected to were not denominated by any person of Shakspeare's age low and trifling, but were very generally admired, and were considered pure and genuine wit' (Boswell–Malone, 6). In the end, the play's

> simplicity and unaffected elegance, and not its want of success, were, I conceive, the cause of its [the text] being less corrupted than some others. Its perspicuity rendered any attempt at alteration unnecessary. Who knows that it was not successful? For my own part, I have no doubt that it met with the highest applause.

(Boswell–Malone, 5)

Malone cannot defend the play's 'neglect of geography' by an appeal to youth, but noting that one of Shakespeare's 'latest productions [*The Winter's Tale*] is liable to the same objection', he concludes that Shakespeare had no interest in the unities; rather, 'he seems to have thought that the whole terraqueous globe was at his command' (Boswell–Malone, 7).

From the Restoration until the very early nineteenth century, *Two Gentlemen*, like many of Shakespeare's plays, was widely felt to be in need of improvement, particularly along the lines of the criticisms of Pope and Johnson, and Victor's adaptation was an early result: a reshuffling of scenes set in Verona or Milan to produce a more unified (if illogical) plot, the deletion of some inelegant or offensive passages, the addition of low comic scenes with Lance and Crab and a fairly drastic moral revision of the play's infamous offer and ending (see pp. 100–8).

The Romantics, more concerned with plays like *Hamlet*, showed relatively little interest in *Two Gentlemen*. Coleridge doubts the authorship at one point in 1809 – 'the Gent. Of Verona not a word of his' (Coleridge, *Fragments*, 252) – and in 1818 proposes as a lecture subject 'the reasons for doubting the two gentlemen of Verona, and a large proportion of the three parts of Henry the 6, and some scenes of Richard the Third, as Shakespear's' (Coleridge, *Lectures*, 34). Those who comment, like A.W. von Schlegel, stress the apparent youthfulness of the author: the play 'paints the irresolution of love, and its infidelity to friendship, pleasantly enough, but in some degree superficially, we might almost say with the levity of mind which a passion suddenly entertained, and as suddenly given up, presupposes'; the resolutions of the plot are 'as if the course of the world was obliged to accommodate itself to a transient youthful caprice, called love' (Bate, *Romantics*, 555). Keats seems hardly to have acknowledged the play, but a reference in a letter of 15 April 1817 – 'I saw . . . a little Wood with trees look you like Launce's Sister "as white as a Lilly and as small as a Wand"' (Keats, 17; cf. 2.3.19–20) – reveals a sharply specific memory of one of the comic scenes.

Hazlitt recognizes the play's lack of sophistication, but also defends it:

> This is little more than the first outlines of a comedy loosely sketched in. It is the story of a novel dramatised with very little labour or pretension; yet there are passages

of high poetical spirit, and of inimitable quaintness of humour, which are undoubtedly Shakespear's, and there is throughout the conduct of the fable a careless grace and felicity which marks it for his.

(Hazlitt, 318)

Hazlitt also notes Pope's inconsistent comments on the play's style (see p. 110):

It is strange that our fastidious critic should fall so soon from praising to reprobating. The style of the familiar parts of this comedy is indeed made up of conceits – low they may be for what we know, but then they are not poor, but rich ones. The scene of Launce with his dog (not that in the second, but that in the fourth act) is a perfect treat in the way of farcical drollery and invention; nor do we think Speed's manner of proving his master to be in love deficient in wit or sense, though the style may be criticised as not simple enough for the modern taste.

(Hazlitt, 318)

Hazlitt goes on to praise the scenes between Julia and Lucetta (1.2 and 2.7), especially Julia's speech at 2.7.24–38:

If Shakespear indeed had written only this and other passages in the *Two Gentlemen of Verona*, he would *almost* have deserved Milton's praise of him – 'And sweetest Shakespear, Fancy's child, / Warbles his native woodnotes wild' – But as it is, he deserves rather more praise than this.

(Hazlitt, 319)

Hazlitt does not mention the difficulties of the final scene, but in their *Tales from Shakespeare* (first printed in 1807), Charles and Mary Lamb smooth off the play's rough edges and inconsistencies, nowhere more clearly than in their account of the play's ending. Proteus rescues Silvia from the Outlaws but before he can renew 'his love suit', with 'his page (the forlorn Julia)' standing by 'fearing lest the great service which Proteus had just done to Silvia should win her to show him some favour, they were all strangely surprised with the sudden appearance of Valentine'. Proteus's shame comes as a result of 'being caught by his friend' 'courting Silvia'. The offer, unlike the attempted rape, however, is not shirked in Lamb:

> Proteus . . . was so much ashamed of being caught by his friend, that he was all at once seized with penitence and remorse; and he expressed such a lively sorrow for the injuries he had done to Valentine, that Valentine, whose nature was noble and generous, even to a romantic degree, not only forgave and restored him to his former place in his friendship, but in a sudden flight of heroism he said, 'I freely do forgive you; and all the interest I have in Silvia, I give it up to you.' Julia, who was standing beside her master as a page, hearing this strange offer, and fearing Proteus would not be able with this new-found virtue to refuse Silvia, fainted.
>
> (Lamb, 82–3)

The difficulties of the final scene were struggled with throughout the nineteenth century. Collier (1842), who dates the play around 1591, comments more technically and less judgementally on the play than previous editors, and proposes a somewhat unsatisfactory and implausible solution to the problem of the offer:

> if we suppose [Valentine] not to have overheard all that passed between Silvia and Proteus, and to draw a conclusion against her from finding her in the forest with him . . . It is very easy to imagine him to withdraw, in order to get out of the view of Silvia and Proteus, and to return to the scene, when he hears the exclamations of Silvia on the violence offered by Proteus. If he had overheard all that was said by them, he would have re-entered before, and no such attempt could have been made by Proteus.
>
> (Collier, 167)

Collier was hardly the first to seek some rationalization of this moment.

Few nineteenth-century editors or critics defend the play as strongly or as ably as Malone and Hazlitt – the defences are often positive (certain elements of the play are quite good) but still often apologetic (any problems are the result of a young, inexperienced author). Swinburne's comments (1879) are mixed. Placing *Two Gentlemen* between *Comedy of Errors* and *Love's Labour's Lost*, he remarks that

> in the *Two Gentlemen of Verona* rhyme has fallen seemingly into abeyance, and there are no passages of such elegiac beauty as in the former [i.e. *CE*], of such exalted eloquence as in the latter [i.e. *LLL*] of these plays; there is an even sweetness, a simple equality of grace in thought and language which keeps the whole poem in tune, written as it is in a subdued key of unambitious harmony . . . Slight and swift in execution as it is, few and simple as are the chords here struck of character and emotion, every shade of drawing and every note of sound is at one with the whole scheme of form and music.
>
> (Swinburne, 48–9)

Like most readers, Swinburne valued the play as much for what it foreshadowed in Shakespeare's career as for what it was in itself:

> Here too is the first dawn of that higher and more tender humour which was never given in such perfection to any man as ultimately to Shakespeare; one touch of the by-play of Launce and his immortal dog is worth all the bright fantastic interludes of Boyet and Adriano, Costard and Holofernes; worth even half the sallies of Mercutio, and half the dancing doggrel or broad-witted prose of either Dromio.
>
> (Swinburne, 49)

The twentieth century witnessed an enormous number of new editions of all of Shakespeare's plays, and *Two Gentlemen* has benefited greatly from these projects (especially from Ard[1], Ard[2] and Cam[2]).[1] Bond (xxxii) is disposed to regard *Two Gentlemen* as 'the earliest surviving romantic comedy of England, and almost of Europe', seeing only Robert Greene's *James IV* and *Friar Bacon and Friar Bungay* (with its courtship of Margaret) as rivals. In *Two Gentlemen*, he says,

> Shakespeare first opens the vein he worked so richly afterwards – the vein of crossed love; of flight and exile under the escort of the generous sentiments; of disguised heroines, and sufferings endured and virtues exhibited under their disguise; and of the Providence, kinder than life, that annuls the errors and forgives the sin: and here first he lays his scene in Italy.
>
> (Ard[1], xxxiv)

Later editors have built on the textual and annotative foundations of the earlier Arden editions of Bond and Leech – as I do in this edition – and Schlueter (Cam[2]) has been the first to provide a thorough stage history of *Two Gentlemen* in England up to 1981, usefully relating its performance history to the intellectual and textual issues the play presents.

TEXT AND DATE

The Two Gentlemen of Verona appears as the second play in the Folio of 1623, after *The Tempest* and before *The Merry Wives of Windsor*, occupying pages 20–38, or sigs B4ᵛ–D1ᵛ, of the volume. As Charlton Hinman has shown (Hinman, 2.353–71), it was the second play to be set by the compositors (five pages were set

---

1 Cam[1] adopted a theory of revision which was never accepted by other editions and was eventually withdrawn (1955) by Wilson. Still, Cam[1] was responsible for the most often quoted put-down of the play, in relation to Valentine's offer: 'one's impulse, upon this declaration, is to remark that there are, by this time, *no* gentlemen in Verona' (Cam[1], xiv).

concurrently with the last seven pages of *The Tempest*, as they appear in the same gathering; the last two pages, numbered 37 and 38, are in the gathering containing the first ten pages of *Merry Wives of Windsor*, which explains their incorrect running title, '*The Merry Wiues of Windsor*' (see Hinman, 1.175, and Fig. 21)). No quarto edition of the play is known to have existed.

Why was *Two Gentlemen* placed in such a prominent position in the Folio? Perhaps the most logical answer is that *Two Gentlemen* was grouped with *The Tempest*, *Merry Wives of Windsor* and the fourth play in the Folio, *Measure for Measure*, because all were set from scribal copies made in the early 1620s by the professional scribe Ralph Crane, who also prepared the text of *The Winter's Tale* (Honigmann, *Texts*, 59–76, has demonstrated that the text of *Othello* was also prepared by Crane, and strong arguments have been put forward that Crane also prepared *2 Henry IV* and *Cymbeline*).[1] Given how much Crane altered the texts he worked on, T.H. Howard-Hill has gone so far as to describe Crane as 'Shakespeare's earliest editor' (Howard-Hill, 'Editor'), an honour heretofore given to Nicholas Rowe, whose three editions in 1709 and 1714 did so much to establish the basic outlines of the edited Shakespearean text.

The identification of Crane by F.P. Wilson in 1926 (see Wilson, 'Crane') has led to a number of studies detailing the ways in which he usually worked, and hence how his transcriptions altered and transformed (some would say deformed) the manuscripts which he transcribed.[2] These studies now allow editors to identify and

---

1   Following more cautious ascriptions by some earlier editors (including Howard-Hill, *Crane*), Honigmann, *Texts*, 165–8, makes a convincing case for Crane's work on *2 Henry IV*; see also Shaaber, 512–14. On *Cymbeline*, see Nosworthy (xii–xiii), who asserts a 'professional scribe' without naming Crane; the first edition of the *Riverside* was cautious – 'the ascription [to Crane] remains at best a possibility' (*Riv*, 1561) – but in the second edition 'the copy behind the F1 text' is more confidently said to be 'a scribal transcript, probably by Ralph Crane, of a manuscript at one remove from Shakespeare's "foul papers"' (*Riv*, 1609). See also *TxC*, 604.

2   Major scholarship on Crane's work and influence since Wilson includes: Howard-Hill, *Crane*; Howard-Hill, 'Editor'; Honigmann, *Texts*; Roberts, 'Crane'; Taylor; and Werstine[5].

explain particular features of the Crane Folio texts. *Two Gentlemen*, for example, is one of three Crane plays in the Folio with so-called 'massed entries', in which every character who will appear in a given scene is listed in the initial stage direction, many of them long before his or her entry; the actual entry of the character, later in the scene, is rarely marked (an omission which the editors of the Second Folio of 1632 partly remedied). Crane's frequent but not universal employment of the massed entry has been attributed to the influence of the 1616 Ben Jonson Folio, 'the best literary model available to him' (Howard-Hill, 'Editor', 128). The consequence of Crane's practice in this case as well as others is that certain textual features of the manuscript from which he worked may have been obliterated and in most cases must remain unknowable. For *Two Gentlemen*, Crane's practice makes it more difficult to describe with any certainty the type of manuscript from which he was working – the author's so-called 'foul papers' (more or less a rough draft)[1] or 'promptbook', the text as used in the theatre, with characteristic stage directions and markings for actors. The massed entry format reflects neither authorial nor playhouse practice. Similarly, the absence of virtually all stage directions in F (assuming any existed) may also have been the result of Crane's transformation of his copy-text.[2]

In addition to the massed entries, many other characteristics attributed to Crane can be observed in *Two Gentlemen*. Like most of the other Crane plays, *Two Gentlemen* concludes with a list of dramatis personae[3] – 'The names of all the Actors' – arranged by

---

1 For opposing views of the very concept of 'foul papers', see Werstine[2, 3] and Honigmann, *Texts*, 150–1.

2 Taylor, 72, notes that the 'complete absence' of stage directions for offstage sounds in *Two Gentlemen* (as well as *Merry Wives of Windsor*, *Measure for Measure*, *Winter's Tale*, *Cymbeline*, *2 Henry IV* and *Othello*) 'must result from deliberate scribal excision: it testifies to the active intervention of a scribe, rather than his passive reflection of the manuscript he set out to copy'.

3 *The Tempest*, *Measure for Measure*, *Winter's Tale*, *2 Henry IV* and *Othello* all have such lists, but not *Merry Wives of Windsor* (which had no space available on its final page) or *Cymbeline* (where there was space; RP notes that the cast list would have

gender (male first); see Fig. 21. These lists are probably by Crane, or at least someone other than the author (see Vaughan, 127). In the list in *Two Gentlemen*, the description of Speed as '*a clownish seruant to Valentine*' does not seem accurate, since Lance – '*the like to Protheus*' in the list – is the traditional clown, probably played by Will Kemp (see p. 127).

The frequent occurrence of parentheses in some of the Folio texts has also been attributed to Crane's habits of punctuation. These parentheses often occur around marked parenthetical comments, where commas would have served, e.g. 'Then (liuing dully sluggardiz'd at home)' (1.1.7, TLN 10), 'But say *Lucetta* (now we are alone)' (1.2.1, TLN 152) and 'That (like a testie Babe) will scratch the Nurse' (1.2.58, TLN 212). The most common usage is around a form of address: either a proper name – '(*Iulia*)' (TLN 578), '(*Protheus*)' (TLN 819); or a more generic one – '(Madam)' (TLN 237, 251, 297, 499, 503, 523, etc.), '(my Lord)' (TLN 358, 1132, 1198, 1204, etc.), '(boy)' (TLN 443, 472, 485, 1257, etc.), '(sweet Lady)' (TLN 687). In most instances, parentheses are used around single words, but sometimes, two or three entire lines are included within them: TLN 721–2, 855–7, 1154–5, 1824–5, 2143–4. See Howard-Hill, *Crane*, 86–7. We cannot be sure that any particular use of parentheses in F is attributable to Crane, of course, but the unusually large number is characteristic of him.[1]

Crane also frequently employed hyphenated forms, e.g. 'bruzing-stones' (1.2.111, TLN 271), 'Corded-ladder' (3.1.40, TLN 1109) and 'foure gentleman-like-dogs' (4.4.17, TLN 1836); see Howard-Hill, *Crane*, 114. He also had a fondness for

---

been a long one, and its inclusion 'would have prevented the use of a final tail-piece ornament for the end of the volume and might consequently have reduced the prominence of the colophon'). A list of characters also follows *Timon of Athens* (which may also be linked to Crane; see Oliver, xix); Hinman, 1.38, argues that the lists for 2 *Henry IV* and *Timon of Athens* were printed merely to fill blank space (see Honigmann, *Texts*, 20–2).

1   See Thompson for the importance of parentheses in the Folio generally.

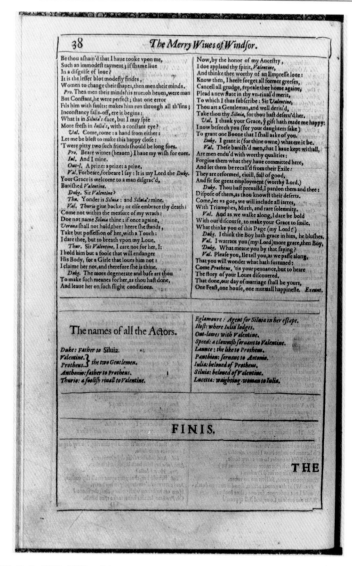

Be thou asham'd that I haue tooke vpon me,
Such an immodest rayment; if shame liue
In a disguise of loue?
It is the lesser blot modestly findes,
Women to change their shapes, then men their minds.
Pro. Then men their minds? is true: oh heuen, were man
But Constant, he were perfect; that one error
Fils him with faults: makes him run through all th'sins;
Inconstancy falls-off, ere it begins:
What is in *Siluia's* face, but I may spie
More fresh in *Iulia's*, with a constant eye?
Val. Come, come: a hand from either:
Let me be blest to make this happy close:
'T were pitty two such friends should be long foes.
Pro. Beare witnes (heauen) I haue my wish for euer.
Iul. And I mine.
Out-l. A prize: a prize: a prize.
Val. Forbeare, forbeare I say: It is my Lord the *Duke.*
Your Grace is welcome to a man disgrac'd,
Banished *Valentine.*
Duke. Sir *Valentine?*
Thu. Yonder is *Siluia*: and *Siluia's* mine.
Val. Thurio giue backe; or else embrace thy death:
Come not within the measure of my wrath:
Doe not name *Siluia* thine: if once againe,
Verona shall not hold thee: heere she stands,
Take but possession of her, with a Touch:
I dare thee, but to breath vpon my Loue.
Thur. Sir *Valentine,* I care not for her, I:
I hold him but a foole that will endanger
His Body, for a Girle that loues him not:
I claime her not, and therefore she is thine.
Duke. The more degenerate and base art thou
To make such meanes for her, as thou hast done,
And leaue her on such slight conditions.

Now, by the honor of my Ancestry,
I doe applaud thy spirit, *Valentine,*
And thinke thee worthy of an Empresse loue:
Know then, I heere forget all former greefes,
Cancell all grudge, repeale thee home againe,
Plead a new state in thy vn-riuall'd merit,
To which I thus subscribe: Sir *Valentine,*
Thou art a Genleman, and well deriu'd,
Take thou thy *Siluia,* for thou hast deseru'd her.
Val. I thank your Grace, § gift hath made me happy:
I now beseech you (for your daughters sake)
To grant one Boone that I shall aske of you.
Duke. I grant it (for thine owne) what ere it be.
Val. These banish'd men, that I haue kept withall,
Are men endu'd with worthy qualities:
Forgiue them what they haue committed here,
And let them be recall'd from their Exile:
They are reformed, ciuill, full of good,
And fit for great employment (worthy Lord.)
Duke. Thou hast preuaild, I pardon them and thee:
Dispose of them, as thou know'st their deserts.
Come, let vs goe, we will include all iarres,
With Triumphes, Mirth, and rare solemnity.
Val. And as we walke along, I dare be bold
With our discourse, to make your Grace to smile.
What thinke you of this Page (my Lord?)
Duke. I thinke the Boy hath grace in him, he blushes.
Val. I warrant you (my Lord) more grace, then Boy,
Duke. What meane you by that saying?
Val. Please you, Ile tell you, as we passe along,
That you will wonder what hath fortuned:
Come *Protheus,* 'tis your pennance, but to heare
The story of your Loues discouered.
That done, our day of marriage shall be yours,
One Feast, one house, one mutuall happinesse. *Exeunt.*

The names of all the Actors.

Duke: Father to Siluia.
Valentine. } the two Gentlemen.
Protheus. }
Anthonio: father to Protheus.
Thurio: a foolish riuall to Valentine.

Eglamoure: Agent for Siluia in her escape.
Host: where Iulia lodges.
Out-lawes with Valentine.
Speed: a clownish seruant to Valentine.
Launce: the like to Protheus.
Panthion: seruant to Antonio.
Iulia: beloued of Protheus.
Siluia: beloued of Valentine.
Lucetta: waighting-woman to Iulia.

FINIS.

THE

---

21 F sig. D1ᵛ, 1623 – this page and the previous one have the incorrect running
title, '*The Merry Wiues of Windsor*'; some of Ralph Crane's scribal habits are
evident on this page, such as the listing of 'The names of all the Actors' as
well as the frequent use of parentheses and hyphenation

unnecessary apostrophes, e.g. 'hap'ly' (1.1.12, TLN 15, etc.), 'answer's' (1.3.91, TLN 393), 'it's' (2.1.3, TLN 400, etc.) and 'do'st' (2.1.39, TLN 436, etc.). Howard-Hill, *Crane*, 100–2, and others have also identified some of Crane's habitual spellings, such as 'guift' for 'gift' (4.4.56, TLN 1875) and 'guifts' for 'gifts' (4.2.6, TLN 1628), 'extreame' (2.7.22, TLN 997), 'sirha' (2.5.9, TLN 881, etc.), 'wilbe' (2.7.54, TLN 1029) and 'ceazed' for 'seized' (5.4.33, TLN 2152); although spelling was not yet regularized in the period, these spellings are unique to the Crane plays, occur on pages set by different compositors and are found nowhere else in the Folio. Not every unusual spelling, hyphenation or parenthesis was necessarily made by Crane during his transcription, but it is the overwhelming number of them that leads to the identification of Crane.[1] In the end, it seems reasonable to say that Crane's intervention in the text from which he was copying was probably pervasive and often merely a matter of personal taste and style. Crane was an opinionated if not entirely consistent editor.[2] See Fig. 22.

Yet Crane was presumably not responsible for all of the textual anomalies and inconsistencies in *Two Gentlemen*. The text of the play, for one thing, was set by at least two, possibly three, different compositors. In 1963, Hinman proposed a division of the First Folio between five identifiable compositors, whom he designated A, B, C, D, E. He divided the nineteen pages of *Two Gentlemen* between A (who set nine) and C (who set ten). In 1973, Howard-Hill, 'Compositors', reassigned Compositor A's nine pages to a sixth, new, compositor, F. Compositor F, however, has not stood the test of time. Progressive study by John S. O'Connor, Jeanne

---

1   Many of these forms are collated in the textual notes.
2   After reviewing Crane's work on Middleton's *A Game at Chess*, Honigmann, *Texts*, 75, remarks: 'In brief, Crane was neither humble nor faithful; he "improved" his transcripts, as he would see it, a creative or destructive role, depending on one's point of view.'

34   *The two Gentlemen of Verona.*

Pro. I likewise heare that *Valentine* is dead.

Sil. And so suppose am I; for in her graue
Assure thy selfe, my loue is buried.

Pro. Sweet Lady, let me rake it from the earth.

Sil. Goe to thy Ladies graue and call hers thence,
Or at the least, in hers, sepulcher thine.

Iul. He heard not that.

Pro. Madam: if your heart be so obdurate:
Vouchsafe me yet your Picture for my loue,
The Picture that is hanging in your chamber:
To that ile speake, to that ile sigh and weepe:
For since the substance of your perfect selfe
Is else deuoted, I am but a shadow:
And to your shadow, will I make true loue.

Iul. If't weere a substance you would sure deceiue it,
And make it but a shadow, as I am.

Sil. I am very loath to be your Idoll Sir;
But, since your falshood shall become you well
To worship shadowes, and adore false shapes,
Send to me in the morning, and ile send it:
And so, good rest.

Pro. As wretches haue ore-night
That wait for execution in the morne.

Iul. Host, will you goe?

Ho. By my hallidome, I was fast asleepe.

Iul. Pray you, where lies Sir *Protheus*?

Ho. Marry, at my house:

Trust me, I thinke 'tis almost day.

Iul. Not so: but it hath bin the longest night
That ere I watch'd, and the most heauiest.

Scæna Tertia.

Enter Eglamore, Siluia.

Eg. This is the houre that Madam *Siluia*
Entreated me to call, and know her minde:
Ther's some great matter she'ld employ me in.
Madam, Madam.

Sil. Who cals?

Eg. Your seruant, and your friend;
One that attends your Ladiships command.

Sil. Sir *Eglamore*, a thousand times good morrow.

Eg. As many (worthy Lady) to your selfe:
According to your Ladiships impose,
I am thus early come, to know what seruice
It is your pleasure to command me in.

Sil. Oh *Eglamoure*, thou art a Gentleman:
Thinke not I flatter (for I sweare I doe not)
Valiant, wise, remorse-full, well accomplish'd.
Thou art not ignorant what deere good will
I beare vnto the banish'd *Valentine*:
Nor how my father would enforce me marry
Vaine *Thurio* (whom my very soule abhor'd.)
Thy selfe hast lou'd, and I haue heard thee say
No griefe did euer come so neere thy heart,
As when thy Lady, and thy true-loue dide,
Vpon whose Graue thou vow'dst pure chastitie:
Sir *Eglamoure*: I would to *Valentine*
To *Mantua*, where I heare, he makes aboad;
And for the waies are dangerous to passe,
I doe desire thy worthy company,

Vpon whose faith and honor, I repose.
Vrge not my fathers anger (*Eglamoure*)
But thinke vpon my griefe (a Ladies griefe)
And on the iustice of my flying hence,
To keepe me from a most vnholy match,
Which heauen and fortune still rewards with plagues,
I doe desire thee, euen from a heart
As full of sorrowes, as the Sea of sands,
To beare me company, and goe with me:
If not, to hide what I haue saidto thee,
That I may venture to depart alone.

Egl. Madam, I pitty much your grieuances,
Which, since I know they vertuously are plac'd,
I giue consent to goe along with you,
Wreaking as little what betideth me,
As much, I wish all good befortune you.
When will you goe?

Sil. This euening comming.

Eg. Where shall I meete you?

Sil. At Frier *Patricks* Cell,
Where I intend holy Confession.

Eg. I will not faile your Ladiship:
Good morrow (gentle Lady.)

Sil. Good morrow, kinde Sir *Eglamoure*.   *Exeunt.*

Scena Quarta.

Enter Launce, Protheus, Iulia, Siluia.

Lau. When a mans seruant shall play the Curre with him (looke you) it goes hard: one that I brought vp of a puppy: one that I sau'd from drowning, when three or foure of his blinde brothers and sisters went to it: I haue taught him (euen as one would say precisely, thus I would teach a dog) I was sent to deliuer him, as a present to Mistris *Siluia*, from my Master; and I came no sooner into the dyning-chamber, but he steps me to her Trencher, and steales her Capons-leg: O, 'tis a foule thing, when a Cur cannot keepe himselfe in all companies: I would haue (as one should say) one that takes vpon him to be a dog indeede, to be, as it were, a dog at all things. If I had not had more wit then he, to take a fault vpon me that he did, I thinke verily hee had bin hang'd for't: sure as I liue he had suffer'd for't: you shall iudge: Hee thrusts me himselfe into the company of three or foure gentleman-like-dogs, vnder the Dukes table: hee had not bin there (blesse the marke) a pissing while, but all the chamber smelt him: out with the dog (saies one) what cur is that (saies another) whip him out (saies the third) hang him vp (saies the Duke.) I hauing bin acquainted with the smell before, knew it was Crab; and goes me to the fellow that whips the dogges: friend (quoth I) you meane to whip the dog: I marry doe I (quoth he) you doe him the more wrong (quoth I) 'twas I did the thing you wot of: he makes me no more adoe, but whips me out of the chamber: how many Masters would doe this for his Seruant? nay, ile be sworne I haue sat in the stockes, for puddings he hath stolne, otherwise he had bin executed: I haue stood on the Pillorie for Geese he hath kil'd, otherwise he had suffer'd for't: thou think'st not of this now: nay, I remember the tricke you seru'd me, when I tooke my leaue of Madam *Siluia*: did

not

22 F sig. C5ᵛ, 1623; some of Ralph Crane's scribal habits are evident on this page, such as the massed entry for '*Scena Quarta*' (i.e. 4.4) as well as the frequent use of parentheses and hyphenation

122

Addison Roberts and Paul Werstine has led to the reassignment of the nine pages to Compositor D.[1]

Each compositor who worked on the Folio introduced his own typographical features into the text, sometimes as a matter of habit (particular spellings), sometimes as a result of mistakes and sometimes as a matter of necessity; in the latter case, for example, the contracted forms 'yᵘ' (2.7.15, TLN 990), 'yᵗ' (3.1.214, TLN 1285) and 'wᶜ' (5.4.88, TLN 2213) were undoubtedly employed (in each case, by Compositor C) in order to save space in a line which was in danger of overrunning the measure. Such clearly identifiable indications of compositorial practice are few in the absence of any parallel text for comparison. However, evidence for correction of two pages at press does survive in the form of verbal variation between copies of F, and this provides a glimpse of the compositors at work. Sigs B4ᵛ (1.1.1–93, TLN 1–99) and C4ʳ (3.1.287–3.2.38, TLN 1358–1483) reveal a number of small corrections of typical compositorial errors (e.g. 'nought' for 'naught', 1.1.68, TLN 72; 'try' for 'thy', 3.1.290, TLN 1361; 'follow' for 'followes', 3.1.313, TLN 1383; 'loue' for 'lone', 3.1.331, TLN 1402). More significantly, 'that last' for 'that' (3.1.345, TLN 1416) clarifies which specific 'article' Lance means, and later the speech prefix '*Pro.*' was inserted at 3.2.13, TLN 1458. A more difficult issue is raised by the correction of 'heauily' to 'grieuously' at 3.2.14, TLN 1459, which F4 returned to 'heauily'.

Past editors of *Two Gentlemen* have attempted, with little success, to identify the nature of the text from which Crane prepared his transcription. A theory was advanced in Cam¹ of an 'assembled text', which was 'made up by stringing together players' parts and arranging them in acts and scenes by the aid of a "plot" [a sheet on

---

1   C set B6ʳ⁻ᵛ, C1ʳ–3ᵛ and D1ʳ⁻ᵛ; D set B4ᵛ–5ᵛ and C4ʳ–6ᵛ. Interestingly, Roberts questioned the existence of Compositor F in part because the spellings used as evidence to distinguish between D and F were overwhelmingly to be found in plays set from Crane transcripts. See Roberts, 'Crane'; Werstine⁵ convincingly supports Roberts's position.

which were written the characters' names for each scene and the actors playing them]', but it was later withdrawn (Cam[1], 77–82; see p. 116, n. 99). Other editors, relying on the traditional distinction between 'foul papers' and 'promptbook' (but see Werstine[2, 3]), have come down on both sides of the question. Gary Taylor suggests that, while F 'yields no clue to the nature of the text which Crane was copying', still, 'on the basis of Crane's other Folio plays and other extant manuscripts, we may assume that what Crane copied in this instance had itself already been expurgated, and may have been a prompt-book' (Taylor, 89).[1] In *Riv*, on the other hand, the conclusion reached is that 'There is nothing in the F1 text to suggest that the copy behind Crane's transcript was a prompt-book', arguing that the confusions in F 'would probably have been cleared up in any copy associated with the stage' (*Riv*, 172). Leech concludes that Crane's copy 'was in all probability Shakespeare's "foul papers"' (Ard[2], xxxi). Schlueter notes 'the complete lack of all positive indications' of promptbook origin (Cam[2], 150), and, avoiding the term 'foul papers' with its implications of authorial intention, states simply that Crane must have worked from 'an early draft . . . an unfinished draft version of the play', noting that 'because of Crane's intervention', the usual signs of 'foul papers' are 'not visible' (Cam[2], 151). Stanley Wells regards the question as unanswered: 'We cannot be sure of the precise nature of the script that [Crane] was copying' (*TxC*, 166).

Various textual anomalies in F have fuelled much of the preceding analysis. The geographical confusion, for example, has perplexed editors. References to Verona, Milan, Padua and Mantua at times seem to be crossed, as at 2.5.1, TLN 873, where

---

1   Taylor, 78–84, argues that *Two Gentlemen* was, like *Merry Wives of Windsor* and *Measure for Measure*, a 'purged text' (80) – that is, a text purged of profanity in obedience to the Act to Restrain Abuses of Players, passed by Parliament in May 1606. The expurgation of *Merry Wives of Windsor* can be demonstrated by comparing Q and F texts, but since there is no quarto of *Two Gentlemen*, it cannot be determined whether the expurgation was done by Crane, or had already been done to the manuscript he transcribed. Taylor supports his conclusion that it 'may have been a prompt-book' with the less than convincing statement, 'At least, nothing contradicts this assumption' (Taylor, 89).

Speed welcomes Lance to '*Padua*', when everything else in the play indicates that they are in fact in Milan, or 3.1.81, TLN 1150, where the Duke tells Valentine about 'a Lady in *Verona* heere', when they are, evidently, still in Milan. Similarly troubling are the different references to Silvia's father as a 'Duke' or an 'Emperor', the question of whether or not Julia has a father and Proteus's use of Valentine's servant Speed to take his letter to Julia in 1.1, even though he has his own servant, Lance, who does not appear in the play until 2.3.[1] Leech (xv–xxi) assembles two lists, totalling forty-one items, of plot contradictions or anomalies, which taken together indicate, he concludes, the relatively unfinished nature of the play. However, several of Leech's instances, as he himself notes, can easily be explained away, or are of kinds commonly found in other plays in the Shakespeare canon. At 3.1.220–34, for example, Proteus describes Silvia begging her father to reverse his banishment of Valentine, but as the Duke had exited a mere fifty lines earlier, there could not have been time for this action to occur; this instance, like the passing of an 'hour' in the final scene of Marlowe's *Doctor Faustus*, seems simply a case of the difference between stage time and real time. Yet Leech maintains, in view of the number of inconsistencies and anomalies, that '*Two Gentlemen* takes these things to extremes' (Ard[2], xv). Editors have assumed, therefore, that the extent of the textual problems in F suggests that the copy Crane transcribed is unlikely to have been the prompt-book, as such problems would presumably have been ironed out before performance. Yet there are indications that Crane's copy was not 'foul papers' – for example, characteristic variability of speech prefixes is not a feature of F. In the end, we cannot know, on the basis of present evidence, the exact nature of the text which Crane prepared for the Folio compositors, but it seems unlikely that it was any kind of promptbook or theatrical manuscript. Whether Crane's copy was an authorial holograph cannot be determined.

---

1 See notes on List of Roles, 1; 1.3.27, 38; 2.5.1; 2.7.86–7; 3.1.81.

One feature of Leech's theory of the play's origin invites further comment. Leech (xxx) conjectures that there had been 'four stages in the play's composition'. Stage one begins with Valentine in love with Silvia, in Verona. Proteus comes on a visit and tries to take Silvia away. Julia, having followed Proteus to Verona, enters his service. In the course of composition a father is invented for Silvia but his rank, though elevated, remains undefined. The play ends in the forest. In stage two 'The first three scenes and II. ii, vii of the extant play are added, involving a change in the place of the main part of the action, a change not consistently carried through.' In stage three 'A new character, Launce, is introduced'; scenes are written for him, and some of Speed's lines in 3.1 transferred to him, but some details (e.g. Lance taking his own dog to Silvia) 'are never properly managed'. Finally, in stage four, 'A new soliloquy for Proteus (II. vi) is inserted after a new (Launce) scene and, ironically, immediately before II. vii, where we see Julia planning to follow Proteus.' Leech stresses that his is 'not a "revision-theory" in the customary sense of the term . . . I do not think two or more complete versions successively existed: the play was not regarded as "finished" until it reached the form in which we now have it' (Ard[2], xxx–xxxi). Leech's theory of composition explains much – too much, it might seem – and is plausible though impossible to prove. His scheme is accompanied by a conjecture about the play's date as well: 'We may guess (and it is only a guess) at 1592 for the first phase (*not* version), and late 1593 for the putting of the play into its present shape' (Ard[2], xxxv). Leech's assumption, then, is that the manuscript from which Crane made his transcription was 'Shakespeare's composite draft (consisting of fragments from each phase of composition)'.

Leech's conjecture can be neither proven nor disproven; it seems over-elaborate, but it could also seem congruous with the informal, even untidy, way writers work. Perhaps the most persuasive of his stages is the third, namely that the part of Lance was interpolated into the play after much of the romantic plot was completed. For Leech, this argument addresses several of the plot contradictions he notes. His claim is that Lance's part seems more or less detachable from the rest of the play, especially as he does not appear until 2.3. Some aspects of his character, moreover, are not an exact fit in the play: for example, in 2.5 his language seems far too witty – in fact he outwits Speed. The motive for adding this new part could have been that Shakespeare, at some point in the compositional process, needed to write a clown's part for Will Kemp.[1] Kemp had certainly joined the Chamberlain's Men in 1594 (see Gurr, *Stage*, 34 and 36). Therefore, according to this theory, which assumes that Shakespeare had written the play more or less as we have it before working with Kemp (Lance being added later for him), a possible date for composition could be in the early 1590s, and possibly prior to the closing of the theatres in 1592 because of plague. Whether the play was actually performed by 1592 is not known. With the reopening of the theatres in June 1594, or perhaps somewhat earlier in preparation for the reopening, Shakespeare found he had a talented comic actor ready for action. Therefore, the part of Lance was added,[2] with additional, larger roles for Kemp – Costard in *Love's Labour's Lost*, Bottom in *A Midsummer Night's Dream*, Dogberry in *Much Ado About Nothing* – to follow in the next few years. Complicating this theory, however, is the fact that the Lance–Crab episodes are so expertly crafted to reflect, parody or subvert the values and pretensions of the major characters and their actions, right down to the verbal echo of individual words in different scenes (e.g. 'tide' at 2.2.14 and 'tied' at 2.3.35–8).[3] There is no reason, in any event, to doubt that the play as we have it was completed prior to 1598.

---

1 See Wiles, 73–4; Gurr, *Playgoing*, 152; and Campbell, 'Actors'.

2 It has been argued that the part of Peter in *Romeo and Juliet* was probably added for Kemp as well (Wiles, 83–92; Gurr, *Playgoing*, 152).

3 RP notes as well that 'it is barely thinkable that Proteus's two soliloquies in 2.4 and 2.6 which define the two distinct and separate stages in his move towards infidelity are not intrinsic to the play's design – and if this is so, something must separate them to make them psychologically plausible. That something can't be a plot scene as the plot now hinges on Proteus, which must explain the use of a scene for Lance and Speed in 2.5.'

The preceding analysis moves toward establishing a *terminus a quo* for the play. *Two Gentlemen* has been felt by most commentators to be an early, indeed very early, play. Chambers, *WS*, 1.330, places it in the 1594–5 theatrical season, but Honigmann, *Impact*, 88, pushes it back as early as 1588, and Schlueter concurs, 'it is not impossible that the creation of our play must be sought in the late 1580s' (Cam², 2). In *TxC*, 109, the date proposed is 1590–1. John Tobin, however, citing supposed borrowings from Nashe's *Have With You to Saffron Walden* (published in 1596, but circulated in manuscript before publication), argues that 'parts, if not all of the drama must be dated no earlier than the middle of 1595' (Tobin, 'Nashe', 122). Virtually all editors have regarded the likely date of composition as falling between 1588 and 1595. Among the factors which complicate this framework are Shakespeare's use of George of Montemayor's romance, *Diana*, printed in 1542 and translated into French in 1578. The first English translation, by Bartholomew Yonge, was not printed until 1598. It was, however, finished in 1582 and therefore we need not conclude that *Two Gentlemen* was begun in 1598 or later, since Shakespeare could have seen Yonge's translation in manuscript (see Bullough, 1.206, and Ard², xli–xlii). Moreover, a now lost play, 'Felix & Philiomena', was performed at court by the Queen's Men in 1585 (Chambers, *WS*, 1.331), which might also have relied on the same story in *Diana* that Shakespeare used in *Two Gentlemen*. Other allusions – 1.1.21–2, possibly to Marlowe's *Hero and Leander* (entered in the Stationers' Register in 1593, not published until 1598), and 2.1.19, 'the pestilence' (possibly alluding to the plague of 1592) – are inconclusive as evidence in for an early date. Shakespeare's indebtedness to and borrowings from the work of John Lyly, however, are more certain; the works in question date primarily from the 1580s and early 1590s (e.g. *Euphues*, 1578; *Campaspe* and *Sapho and Phao*, both 1584; *Endymion*, 1588; *Midas*, 1592).

Internal features – such as frequency of rhyme, word-usage and so on – do not provide significant evidence for dating. For most editors, readers and audiences, the play feels very early, in part because of the often undistinguished verse, in part because of the relatively underdeveloped characterization of the central characters. The contradictions and anomalies in the plot have also been judged to be signs of 'apprentice' work, while the prevalence of 'duets' (Beckerman's term; see 1.1.70–141n.) and the relative infrequency and clumsiness of scenes involving more than two characters seem the marks of an inexperienced playwright. These are all assumptions about what characterizes writing as early, but even if they are accepted, there is the further underlying assumption that once Shakespeare showed that he could write more complex characters, he could never fall back on 'earlier' habits. This line of reasoning produces a narrative of Shakespeare's inevitable improvement from play to play that reinforces prevailing ideas about Shakespeare's career as a writer, but – *pace* metrical and other technical 'tests' – no evidence supports it.

The single tangible piece of external evidence relating to the play's date occurs in Francis Meres's *Palladis Tamia: Wit's Treasury*, dedicated 19 October 1598, entered in the Stationers' Register on 7 September of that year. In a 'comparative discourse of our English Poets', Meres lists twelve of Shakespeare's plays:

> As *Plautus* and *Seneca* are accounted the best for Comedy and Tragedy among the Latines: so *Shakespeare* among the English is the most excellent in both kinds for the stage; for Comedy, witnes his *Gentlemen of Verona*, his *Errors*, his *Love labors lost*, his *Love labours wonne*, his *Midsummers night dreame*, & his *Merchant of Venice*.
>
> (Chambers, *WS*, 2.194)

The only comedy missing from this list that is known to have existed prior to 1598 is *The Taming of the Shrew*; the reference to '*Love labours wonne*' is notorious in its own right (see Woudhuysen, 78–81). Meres establishes what most editors have taken to be the *terminus ad quem* for composition of the play. Certainly some version of the play was in existence by 1598, and it was most likely the version we now have. There is no further explicit reference to the play until its appearance in the 1623 Folio. Meres's list also tantalizingly suggests an order of composition of the comedies; since the latter five were probably produced in the order listed, by implication, '*Gentlemen of Verona*' would have been the first.[1] Yet this speculation cannot be confirmed by any clear evidence. Meres's mention of the play also raises the question of how he knew about the play, since there is no record of its performance; apparently living in London at the time, however, Meres demonstrates a daunting knowledge of the literary scene, with references to dozens of writers in all genres.[2]

To conclude: only two facts about the date of *Two Gentlemen* can be considered absolute – that it was published in 1623 and that Francis Meres lists its title in 1598. Two additional hypotheses are supported by compelling evidence, rising to near certainty: that Ralph Crane transcribed some version of the play for inclusion in the 1623 Folio; and that Will Kemp performed the part of Lance, in which case at least those parts of the play with Lance in them presumably post-date 1593. Whether the manuscript that Crane transcribed was an authorial holograph cannot be known, but whatever its nature, some of its own features have undoubtedly been obscured or erased by Crane's interventionist habits of transcription. The text of *Two Gentlemen* is often said to be 'in many ways a good one' (Ard², xv), and so it is, certainly in comparison with some of the other plays in the Folio, but even such a 'good' text must be recognized to be heavily mediated.

---

1 Meres's list of the tragedies, however, is not chronological: '*Richard the* 2. *Richard the* 3. *Henry the* 4. *King John, Titus Andronicus* and his *Romeo* and *Juliet*' (Chambers, *WS*, 2.194).

2 Meres also mentions Shakespeare as one of those who has 'mightily enriched, and gorgeouslie invested in rare ornaments and resplendent abiliments' the 'English tongue', as one linked several times with Ovid ('the sweete wittie soule of *Ovid* lives in mellifluous & hony-tongued *Shakespeare*, witnes his *Venus* and *Adonis*, his *Lucrece*, his sugred Sonnets among his private friends, &c.'), as among the best 'Lyrick Poets' (Chambers, *WS*, 2.194) and as among 'the most passionate among us to bewaile and bemoane the perplexities of Love' (Chambers, *WS*, 2.195), a category of particular interest in relation to *Two Gentlemen*.

THE TWO
GENTLEMEN
OF VERONA

THE NAMES OF ALL THE ACTORS

DUKE	*father to Silvia*	
VALENTINE PROTEUS	*the two gentlemen*	
ANTONIO	*father to Proteus*	
TURIO	*a foolish rival to Valentine*	5
EGLAMOUR	*agent for Silvia in her escape*	
HOST	*where Julia lodges*	
OUTLAWS	*with Valentine*	
SPEED	*a clownish servant to Valentine*	
LANCE	*the like to Proteus*	10
PANTINO	*servant to Antonio*	
JULIA	*beloved of Proteus*	
SILVIA	*beloved of Valentine*	
LUCETTA	*waiting-woman to Julia*	
[SERVANT	*to the Duke*]	15

[Attendants and Musicians]

LIST OF ROLES This list appears at the end of the text in F; as argued on p. 118–9, it was probably compiled by the scrivener Ralph Crane. The list is generally accurate, but it does mischaracterize Speed as '*a clownish seruant*' and misspells (through a misreading of whatever manuscript served as source) Pantino's name (see List of Roles, 11n.). It also omits reference to the musicians (*these*, 4.2.36) who help perform the song, to Silvia's servant, Ursula, who retrieves the portrait at 4.4.115, and possibly to an unnamed servant at 2.4.113.1 (see n.). The order in which the names are listed reflects early modern hierarchical formulae: male characters first, then female.

1 DUKE Entry SDs ('*Duke*') and SPs throughout ('*Duk.*', '*Duke.*' or '*Du.*') agree, yet at some points in the play, the character is an 'Emperour' (see 1.3.27n.). Bond, 18, suggests that Shakespeare was simply casual with titles, and was perhaps influenced by Lyly's *Euphues*, in which the Emperor holds court at Naples. Brooks (Ard[2], xxxi) suggests that Shakespeare may have been thinking of the princess, Augusta Caesarina, in Montemayor's *Diana*, a source for *TGV*, when he twice used the phrase *empress' love*, at 2.4.74 and 5.4.139 (although Proteus's counterpart, Don Felix, doesn't fall in love with her); this imperial association then extended itself from Silvia to the Duke. Schlueter tentatively suggests a link to the Spanish Emperor Charles V, who inherited the duchy of Milan. Leech sees this apparent confusion as evidence of a process of revision; see p. 125. As is the case with Duke Senior in *AYL* or the Duke of Venice in *MV*, no proper name is given.

2 VALENTINE The name suggests he is the very type of a 'lover' (*OED sb.* 2); see 3.1.191–2n. The name could refer to God (*OED sb.* 2b); see p. 26. 'Valentine' is also the name of Orsino's attendant in *TN* and the name of one of the principals in *Valentine and*

Orson, a French romance translated into English in about 1550 (though little else in this romance is relevant to *TGV*).

3 PROTEUS His name derives from the classical sea god who could change his shape at will; the myth had an enormously rich tradition from Ovid through to the Middle Ages (see *Met.*, 2.9, *Art*, 1.755–7, Giamatti and Greene), much of it negative. Proteus became an emblem of deceit and fickleness; cf. Gloucester's boast in *3H6* 3.2.191–3: 'I can add colours to the chameleon, / Change shapes with Proteus for advantages, / And set the murderous Machiavel to school.' For Bacon (*Wisdom of the Ancients*) and other writers, 'Proteus' was the mythological name for primordial matter 'in its infinite receptivity to form, especially generable form' (Nohrnberg, 586; see his entire discussion, 579–86). Shakespeare's audience would not have been surprised to find a character so named suddenly change in some way. The 'th' in F's '*Protheus*' represented a stop rather than a fricative, hence it was pronounced as 't'; the modernized form has been adopted.

4 ANTONIO The name is among the more frequently used in Shakespeare: there are Antonios in *MV*, *MA*, *TN* and *Tem*, Antony in *JC* and *AC* and Anthony in *R3* (Anthony Woodville) and *RJ* (a Capulet servant). The majority form of the name in F is '*Antonio*'; only once does it appear as '*Anthonio*' and that is in 'The names of all the Actors'. As in the case of 'Proteus', therefore, the 'h' has been dropped.

5 TURIO The origins of this name are unclear. Schlueter speculates that the name may derive from the Latin *centurio*, by way of the generic *capitano* figure of the commedia dell'arte, though there is little other evidence to support the idea. There is a 'Curio' in Lyly's *Euphues*. RP notes that there is a 'Turia', an allegorical old man representing 'the principall river' of

Valencia, in Gil Polo's *Enamoured Diana* (*Diana*, 341). The name is '*Thurio*' in F; as in the case of 'Proteus', the 'h' has been dropped throughout.

6 EGLAMOUR His name embodies romantic associations ('amour'; he is a *knight*). At 1.2.9, an *Eglamour* is described as a rival suitor to Julia, along with *Mercatio* and *Proteus*, but it seems unlikely that this is the same figure who offers his *service* to Silvia, is described in chivalric terms later in the play (4.3.9, 18–21) and is in 'The names of all the Actors' as an '*Agent for Siluia in her escape*' to Valentine. This is one of the textual 'oddities' that Leech, xviii, believes indicates different stages of revision; see p. 125. Leech, 11, also suggests that the name may have acquired a burlesque significance, citing Dekker's *Satiromastix*, 4.1.169–70: 'Adew, Sir Eglamour; adew Lutestringe, Curtin-rod, Goose-quill' (Dekker, 1.352). A metrical romance, *Sir Eglamour of Artois*, was printed in 1500 and reprinted at least three times in the sixteenth century.

8 OUTLAWS Three Outlaws are identified in F; some are claimed to be *gentlemen* (4.1.43), but none is given a proper name. Two of their offstage comrades are *Moses* and *Valerius* (see notes on 5.3.8).

9 SPEED Speed is surprisingly identified by F as '*a clownish seruant to Valentine*', when he is actually a *page* (1.2.38) to Valentine; his part derives from the tricky servant in Plautine comedy, perhaps by way of Lyly's quick-witted pages. The character might have been performed by one of the company's boy actors (he is frequently called *boy* in the play) or, more likely, by the second clown–actor in the company, Thomas Pope (Baldwin, *Company*, 231–5). His name reflects his quick wit, though not necessarily the speed with which he delivers messages.

10 LANCE probably an abbreviated form of 'Lancelot' ('Launcelot' and 'Launce' were variant spellings), the most famous of King Arthur's knights;

in spite of his heroic virtues, Lancelot was unable to achieve the Grail adventure. As a '*seruant*', Lance reflects a comic decline in the chivalric ideal. A 'lance' was also a weapon, 'consisting of a long wooden shaft and an iron or steel head' (*OED sb.*[1] 1), and figuratively, a phallus; as a verb, 'to lance' meant 'To pierce . . . to cut, gash, slit' (*OED v.* II 6) or 'to make an incision' (*OED v.* II 7), as in surgery. In his parody of various actions in the play (see p. 127), Lance fits all these definitions. F's designation of Speed as '*clownish seruant*' and Lance as '*the like*' conceals the contrast between them; Lance's is the traditional clown's part, probably performed by Will Kemp (see p. 127).

11 PANTINO The name appears six times in F: twice as '*Panthino*' (1.3.0.1, 1.3.1); once as '*Panthmo*' (1.3.76), a misreading of 'm' for 'in' which is corrected in F2; and three times as '*Panthion*' (in the massed entry SDs for 2.2 and 2.3, and in 'The names of all the Actors'). The name has traditionally been given as 'Panthino' on the grounds that 'Panthion' occurs only in material originating with the scrivener Ralph Crane (see p. 117) – though in the entry SD for 1.3 the name is '*Panthino*'. As in the case of 'Proteus', the 'h' has been dropped throughout. Bond asserts, with little evidence, that 'Shakespeare was probably Italianising the name Pandion in Lyly's *Sapho and Phao*', while Schlueter speculates that the name 'developed from the word "pantler", meaning a sort of butler, with the addition of an Italian diminutive' (Schlueter, 53). RP suggests a possible glance at the French *pantin* = puppet.

12 JULIA Shakespeare employs the name 'Julia' only in *TGV*, but there are Juliets in *Romeus* and of course *RJ*, as well as in *MM*. 'Julia' is an extremely common name for one's mistress in Renaissance love poetry.

13 SILVIA Her name clearly associates her with the forest, from the Latin *silva*; cf. the male character Silvius in *AYL*. In

contrast to that love-sick young shepherd, however, Silvia is mature and self-possessed. Her name seems to anticipate her rescue in the forest in 5.4; see p. 66.

14 LUCETTA Her name is the Italianate diminutive form of 'Luce' or 'Lucy'. Shakespeare plays with the name elsewhere: as the huge (though offstage) kitchen wench Luce (loose) in *CE*; as 'luces' (heraldic designation of the pike), at *MW* 1.1.14, deformed by a pun into 'louses' (lice) at *MW* 1.1.16; and, in the male form, as the ironically named Lucio (light) in *MM*. Her role in this play is comparable to, but not as fully developed as, Celia's in *AYL*.

THE TWO
GENTLEMEN
OF VERONA

1.1   *[Enter]* VALENTINE *[and]* PROTEUS.

VALENTINE
Cease to persuade, my loving Proteus;
Home-keeping youth have ever homely wits.
Were't not affection chains thy tender days
To the sweet glances of thy honoured love,
I rather would entreat thy company   5
To see the wonders of the world abroad

1.1 The play's title implies that the opening action is set in Verona, although the first reference to Verona is only at 3.1.81. There is no clear indication whether this scene is indoors or outdoors, but many editors have nonetheless indulged their imaginations – e.g. '*Verona: a street near Julia's house; trees and a seat*' (Cam[1]). Shakespeare's stage was, in any case, generally unlocalized and had little if any scenery.

1 **Proteus** usually disyllabic, but pronounced here with three syllables; see also 1.2.14, 97, 113; 1.3.3, 12, 88; 2.4.65, 182; 2.7.7, 71; 5.4.39, 54, 68.

2 **Home-keeping** that keeps or stays at home
ever always
homely dull

3 **affection** passion, desire (stronger than modern usage)

tender young

5–8 Valentine's speech reflects a common theme for young men in the early modern period: to form themselves by encountering the world of action, rather than becoming *shapeless* through *idleness* (which was particularly to be avoided). Petruchio tells Hortensio that he has come to Padua for similar reasons: 'Such wind as scatters young men through the world / To seek their fortunes farther than at home, / Where small experience grows' (*TS* 1.2.49–51). Cf. Dent, N274. Similar themes are present in two of Shakespeare's sources for *TGV*, *Diana* and *Romeus*. Contrast also the opening scene of *LLL*, where the men seek to retreat from the world into their 'little academe' (1.1.13).

6 **abroad** away from home

1.1] *Actus primus, Scena prima. F*   0.1] *Rowe; Valentine: Protheus,* and *Speed. F*   2 Home-keeping youth] *(*Home-keeping-youth*)*

Than, living dully sluggardized at home,
Wear out thy youth with shapeless idleness.
But since thou lov'st, love still, and thrive therein,
Even as I would when I to love begin.   10

PROTEUS

Wilt thou be gone? Sweet Valentine, adieu.
Think on thy Proteus when thou haply seest
Some rare noteworthy object in thy travel.
Wish me partaker in thy happiness
When thou dost meet good hap; and in thy danger,   15
If ever danger do environ thee,
Commend thy grievance to my holy prayers,
For I will be thy beadsman, Valentine.

VALENTINE

And on a love-book pray for my success?

PROTEUS

Upon some book I love I'll pray for thee.   20

VALENTINE

That's on some shallow story of deep love –
How young Leander crossed the Hellespont.

---

7 **sluggardized** made idle or lazy
9 **still** constantly
   thrive succeed
12 **haply** by chance; as you may
13 **object** sight
15 **hap** fortune
16 **environ** 'surround with hostile intention . . . beset' (*OED v.* 2b)
17 **Commend** entrust
   grievance distress, suffering
18 **beadsman** one hired to say prayers
   for another, by telling the beads on a
   rosary; Proteus remains behind
   because of his love for Julia, but here
   wittily pretends he will lead a solitary
   religious life praying for Valentine's
   safety. Valentine's reference to a *love-
   book* in 19 shows his amused scepti-
   cism about Proteus's claim to piety.

21–6 The *deep love* of Hero and Leander
was one of the staples of romantic
mythology, most notably treated by
Marlowe in his poem *Hero and Leander*.
Probably written in the 1580s while
Marlowe was at Cambridge, the poem
circulated in manuscript; it was entered
in the Stationers' Register in 1593, but
not published until 1598. Leander's
attempt to swim the Hellespont to
reach his beloved Hero, confined to a
tower, ends tragically in his drowning.
Shakespeare invokes the story in part
for its melodramatic excess; see
Rosalind's mockery in *AYL* 4.1.95–100.
Proteus and Valentine trade jokes on
how *deep* Leander was, in love and in
the Hellespont. When Valentine alludes
to the legend again at 3.1.119–20, it is

12, 32 haply] *(hap'ly)*   13 noteworthy] *(note-worthy)*   15, 92 dost] *(do'st)*   18 beadsman]
(beades-man)

PROTEUS

> That's a deep story of a deeper love,
> For he was more than over-shoes in love.

VALENTINE

> 'Tis true; for you are over-boots in love   25
> And yet you never swam the Hellespont.

PROTEUS

> Over the boots? Nay, give me not the boots.

VALENTINE

> No, I will not, for it boots thee not.

PROTEUS   What?

VALENTINE

> To be in love, where scorn is bought with groans,
> Coy looks with heart-sore sighs, one fading
>   moment's mirth   30
> With twenty watchful, weary, tedious nights.
> If haply won, perhaps a hapless gain;
> If lost, why then a grievous labour won;
> However, but a folly bought with wit,
> Or else a wit by folly vanquished.   35

---

without condescension, as he finds himself there in *bold Leander*'s position, ready to 'scale another Hero's tower' himself. Valentine's reversal of position, which parallels Proteus's changes, is one of many in the play.

24 **over-shoes** 'so deep as to cover the shoes – shoe-deep . . . e.g. in water' (*OED* over-shoes *phr.*)

25 **over-boots** completes the proverb 'over shoes over boots' (Dent, S379). Valentine implies that Proteus is in love even more deeply than Leander was.

27 **give . . . boots** an idiomatic expression for 'don't mock me' (cf. Dent, B537). The 'boots' was also an instrument of

torture (*OED sb.*[3] 3), which crushed the bones of the foot and leg.

28 **boots** profits

30 alexandrine starting with two stressed syllables. Ard[1] (xiii, n. 2) lists all such extrametrical lines. Cf. 2.1.99, 2.4.60, 3.1.204 and 5.4.120.
Coy not responding readily to familiar advances

31 **watchful** sleepless

32 **haply . . . hapless** by chance . . . unfortunate

34 **However** in either case
but only
wit intellect

35 **wit** one who possesses intellect
vanquished vanquishèd

26 swam] *(swom)*; swum *Cam*

139

PROTEUS

So, by your circumstance, you call me fool.

VALENTINE

So, by your circumstance, I fear you'll prove.

PROTEUS

'Tis Love you cavil at. I am not Love.

VALENTINE

Love is your master, for he masters you;
And he that is so yoked by a fool   40
Methinks should not be chronicled for wise.

PROTEUS

Yet writers say, as in the sweetest bud
The eating canker dwells, so doting love
Inhabits in the finest wits of all.

VALENTINE

And writers say, as the most forward bud   45

---

36 **circumstance** deduction, argument; the language of logic continues in Valentine's *prove* in the next line. Cf. 82n.
   you Proteus shifts from *thee* to the more formal *you* as the argument becomes slightly more serious in tone. See 51n. on *thee* and Abbott, 231.

37 **circumstance** state of affairs

38–9 In trying to avoid ridicule, Proteus personifies *Love*. In characterizing *Love* as Proteus's *master*, however, Valentine maintains the upper hand throughout this battle of wits. Cf. 2.6.6–8n.

40–1 Ruled by love's folly, Proteus becomes foolish himself; there is proleptic irony in Valentine's sceptical position.

40 **yoked** yokèd; placed in a yoke or harness, like cattle or oxen

41 **Methinks** it seems to me
   chronicled for recorded as (as in a chronicle history)

42–4 a literary commonplace (see Dent, C56). Cf. *Son* 35.4: 'And loathsome

canker lives in sweetest bud', and *Son* 70.7: 'For canker vice the sweetest buds doth love.'

43, 46 **canker** canker-worm, destructive caterpillar; 'an eating, spreading sore or ulcer; a gangrene' (*OED sb.* 1); and, figuratively, 'Anything that frets, corrodes, corrupts, or consumes slowly and secretly' (*OED sb.* 6)

43–4 **doting . . . all** Cf. Dent, W576: 'The finest wits are soonest subject to love.'

43 *****doting** This emendation has merit (see Wells, *Re-Editing*, 43). The repetition of *eating* (echoed again in *eaten*, 46) seems unlikely, since *Inhabits* already conveys its penetration. Moreover, the opposition is to the concept of *finest wits* (44).

45–50 Cf. *Ham* 1.3.39–40: 'The canker galls the infants of the spring / Too oft before their buttons be disclosed.' Valentine turns the literary commonplace back against Proteus.

45 **most forward** earliest

43 doting] *Oxf*; eating *F*

Is eaten by the canker ere it blow,
Even so by love the young and tender wit
Is turned to folly, blasting in the bud,
Losing his verdure, even in the prime,
And all the fair effects of future hopes.   50
But wherefore waste I time to counsel thee
That art a votary to fond desire?
Once more, adieu. My father at the road
Expects my coming, there to see me shipped.

PROTEUS
And thither will I bring thee, Valentine.   55

VALENTINE
Sweet Proteus, no. Now let us take our leave.
To Milan let me hear from thee by letters
Of thy success in love, and what news else
Betideth here in absence of thy friend;

---

46 **ere** before
blow blossom
48 **blasting** withered; an unusual grammatical effect, a present participle used in the passive sense (Abbott, 372)
49 **verdure** greenness, i.e. youth
prime springtime of life (*OED sb.*¹ 8)
50 **effects** fulfilment, manifestation
51 **counsel** advise; for other references to *counsel* in the play, see 68, 1.2.2, 1.3.34, 2.4.183, 2.6.35 and 2.7.1
thee Valentine returns to the informal usage (see 36n. on *you*), as he moves the conversation toward his parting from Proteus; but note that at 62 the more formal *you* recurs (either as he distances himself from Verona or possibly because *you* is plural there, referring generally to his friends).
52 **votary** one who has sworn a (religious) oath. Valentine plays off Proteus's *beadsman* (18) one last time. Cf. 3.2.58 and the frequent use in *LLL*: 'Who are the votaries . . . ?' (2.1.37); 'this Berowne is one of the votaries' (4.2.135); 'I am a

votary' (5.2.870–1).
fond foolish
53 **road** roadstead, where ships ride at anchor (*OED sb.*¹ 3a); cf. 2.4.185n.
54 **Expects my coming** is waiting for me
shipped Valentine is travelling from Verona to Milan by ship, as Proteus will in 2.2; Verona and Milan are both, however, inland. Shakespearean geography is often inaccurate. Prospero tells Miranda of their departure from Milan, 'they hurried us aboard a bark, / Bore us some leagues to sea' (*Tem* 1.2.144–5). Whether it was possible to travel from Verona to Milan by water (other than by sea) is another question. An extensive system of waterways between the cities did exist from Roman times, but the play's references are inconsistent (cf. *tide*, 2.2.14, and *river*, 2.3.49). See pp. 76–7, and Gurr, 'Localities'.
57 'write to me in Milan'
57, 61, 71 **Milan** stressed on first syllable
58 **success** fortune, whether good or bad
59 **Betideth** happens

And I likewise will visit thee with mine.   60

PROTEUS

All happiness bechance to thee in Milan.

VALENTINE

As much to you at home, and so farewell.   *Exit.*

PROTEUS

He after honour hunts, I after love:
He leaves his friends to dignify them more;
I leave myself, my friends and all, for love.   65
Thou, Julia, thou hast metamorphosed me:
Made me neglect my studies, lose my time,
War with good counsel, set the world at naught;
Made wit with musing weak, heart sick with thought.

[*Enter* SPEED.]

SPEED

Sir Proteus, 'save you. Saw you my master?   70

60 **mine** i.e. the *news* in my *letters*
61 **bechance to** befall
62 **you** See 51n. on *thee.*
63 Cf. *LLL* 1.1.1–11, where Navarre assumes a similar opposition between *honour* and *love*. Navarre and his friends, like Valentine, will find *love* while in pursuit of *honour*, but, like Proteus, they will violate codes of *honour* (breaking their oaths) in pursuit of *love*.
64, 65 **friends** This term could also include relatives.
64 **dignify them more** bring increased honour to them
66 **metamorphosed** the first of many references in the play to the energies of metamorphosis; see pp. 54–9.
67–9 The effects of falling in love that Proteus enumerates were highly

conventional.
67 **lose** waste
68 **good counsel** may have the force of a personification, as in moral interludes (RP); see Carroll, '*Romeo*', 61–4, on a similar use of 'good counsel' in *RJ*. For other occurrences of *counsel*, see 51n.
  set . . . naught neglect my business
  world as opposed to the flesh
69 **musing** meditating, pondering
70–141 Earlier commentators criticized this dialogue (e.g. Pope: 'the lowest and most trifling conceits'), but Beckerman argues that this and similar 'duets' in the play 'display an elemental mastery of the presentational art'; such 'binary structure', he concludes, 'is the basis of all dramatic presentation' (Beckerman, 6, 17).
70 **'save** God save

65 leave] *Pope;* loue *F*   all,] *Dyce;* all *F*   66 metamorphosed] *(*metamorphis'd*)*   68 naught] *Fu;* nought *Fc*   69.1] *Rowe*

PROTEUS

But now he parted hence to embark for Milan.

SPEED

Twenty to one, then, he is shipped already,

And I have played the sheep in losing him.

PROTEUS

Indeed, a sheep doth very often stray,

An if the shepherd be awhile away.   75

SPEED

You conclude that my master is a shepherd then, and I
    a sheep?

PROTEUS   I do.

SPEED

Why then, my horns are his horns, whether I wake or
    sleep.

PROTEUS   A silly answer, and fitting well a sheep.

SPEED   This proves me still a sheep.   80

PROTEUS   True, and thy master a shepherd.

SPEED   Nay, that I can deny by a circumstance.

---

71 **parted hence** left here
72–3 **shipped . . . sheep** The *sheep* jokes
  in the ensuing dialogue are launched
  by Speed's deliberate shift from *ship*
  to its homophone *sheep*. Cf. *LLL*
  2.1.217–20: '*Boyet* I was as willing to
  grapple as he was to board. / *Katherine*
  Two hot sheeps, marry! *Boyet* And
  wherefore not 'ships'? / No sheep,
  sweet lamb, unless we feed on your
  lips. / *Katherine* You sheep, and I pasture', and *CE* 4.1.93–4: 'Why, thou
  peevish sheep, / What ship . . . ?'
74–5 Cf. Dent, S312.
75 **An if** if
76, 78 doggerel; cf. 106–7n. and 132–6n.
78 **my . . . horns** As a servant, Speed is
  owned by his master; Speed's *horns* –
  those of an animal but also of a cuck-
  old – will therefore be his master's.

wake or sleep an allusion to the familiar nursery rhyme 'Little Boy Blue'
  ('Little Boy Blue, come blow your
  horn. / The sheep's in the meadow,
  the cow's in the corn. / But where is
  the boy who looks after the sheep? /
  He's under the haycock, fast asleep',
  cited in Penguin); cf. *KL* 3.6.41:
  'Sleepest or wakest thou, jolly shepherd?'
79 **silly** simple
80 **proves me still** confirms that I am
  sheep i.e. fool
82 **circumstance** logical argument, as at
  36. This term introduces a parody of
  logical argument up to and including
  90, with formal terminology – *deny*
  (82), *circumstance* (82), *prove* (83),
  Therefore (86) – employed with specious logic to continue the wit-game.

75 An] *(And)*   76 a sheep] *F2;* Sheepe *F*

PROTEUS   It shall go hard but I'll prove it by another.

SPEED   The shepherd seeks the sheep, and not the sheep
the shepherd; but I seek my master, and my master   85
seeks not me. Therefore I am no sheep.

PROTEUS   The sheep for fodder follow the shepherd, the
shepherd for food follows not the sheep; thou for wages
followest thy master, thy master for wages follows not
thee. Therefore thou art a sheep.   90

SPEED   Such another proof will make me cry 'baa'.

PROTEUS   But dost thou hear? Gav'st thou my letter to
Julia?

SPEED   Ay, sir. I, a lost mutton, gave your letter to her, a
laced mutton, and she, a laced mutton, gave me, a lost   95
mutton, nothing for my labour.

PROTEUS   Here's too small a pasture for such store of
muttons.

SPEED   If the ground be overcharged, you were best stick
her.   100

PROTEUS   Nay, in that you are astray; 'twere best pound
you.

83 **It . . . I'll** I'll really be out of luck if I
fail to

91 **'baa'** This bleat seems to prove Speed
a sheep after all, but it might also be
heard as contempt – 'bah!' – for
Proteus's logic. Cf. *LLL* 5.1.44–7:
'*Moth* What is a, b, spelt backward
with the horn on his head? *Holofernes*
Ba, *pueritia*, with a horn added. *Moth*
Ba, most silly sheep with a horn.'

92 **dost . . . hear** pay attention

92–3 **Gav'st . . . Julia** It has been noted
that Proteus asks Speed, Valentine's
servant, rather than Lance, his own
servant, to carry his message to Julia;
see p. 125.

95 **laced mutton** slang for a loose
woman or prostitute (*OED sb.*[1] 4;
Dent, M1338), 'Probably with reference to a laced bodice, and perhaps to

a Bridewell lacing' (Williams, 212),
although it is applied to Julia – or perhaps Speed means Lucetta (see
1.2.38n.). Proteus wants to change
rhetorical direction, in asking about his
letter to Julia, but Speed continues the
sheep jokes, now with the upper hand.

97 **store** provision, quantity

99 **overcharged** over-full, burdened. Cf.
Mac 1.2.37: 'cannons overcharged
with double cracks'.
stick stab – i.e. slaughter the excess
sheep. But *stick* also carries a bawdy
meaning, implying that Proteus should
penetrate Julia sexually.

101–2 Proteus rejects Speed's sexual suggestion, implying he should be beaten
(*pound*), while also completing, at last,
the line of *sheep* jokes, as a 'stray' sheep
would be im*pound*ed.

91 baa] *(baâ)*   94, 95–6 lost mutton] *(lost-Mutton)*   95 laced mutton] *(lac'd-Mutton)*

SPEED   Nay, sir, less than a pound shall serve me for
          carrying your letter.

PROTEUS   You mistake; I mean the pound – a pinfold.   105

SPEED

          From a pound to a pin? Fold it over and over,
          'Tis threefold too little for carrying a letter to your
              lover.

PROTEUS   But what said she?

SPEED [*Nods his head.*]   Ay.

PROTEUS   Nod-ay – why, that's 'noddy'.   110

SPEED   You mistook, sir. I say she did nod, and you ask me
          if she did nod, and I say 'Ay'.

PROTEUS   And that set together is 'noddy'.

SPEED   Now you have taken the pains to set it together,
          take it for your pains.   115

PROTEUS   No, no, you shall have it for bearing the letter.

SPEED   Well, I perceive I must be fain to bear with you.

---

103 **pound** Speed squeezes a third mean-
     ing out of this word, as a sum of
     money – the tip he is hoping to receive.
105 **pinfold** Proteus here turns *pound* back
     to the sense of an enclosure for stray
     cattle or sheep, or *pinfold*; cf. *KL* 2.2.9.
106–7 These alliterative rhyming lines
     are verse in F, in the middle of a long
     prose section, and most editions retain
     them as such, on the grounds that they
     are 'Doggerel verse' (Cam²; cf. 76, 78
     and 2.1.125–30) – another of Speed's
     comic delays frustrating Proteus's
     desire to learn about his letter. Cf.
     132–6n.
106 **pin** i.e. something virtually worth-
     less; cf. 2.7.55, *Ham* 1.4.65: 'I do not
     set my life at a pin's fee' and Dent,
     P334: 'Not worth a pin'.
     Fold i.e. multiply; Speed now picks up
     fold from *pinfold* to pun on.

108–13 The verbal–visual joking here is
     clear enough onstage, but editors have
     reasonably introduced SDs and quota-
     tion marks to clarify it on the page (see
     109 t.n.).
110 **'noddy'** fool, simpleton (*OED sb.*[1] 1);
     'a card-game resembling cribbage'
     (*OED sb.*[2]). There is also a sexual
     implication: cf. Middleton's *Blurt,
     Master-Constable*, 3.2: 'she'll sit up till
     you come, because she'll have you play
     a game at noddy' (Middleton, 1.58),
     and Marston's *Insatiate Countess*: 'O
     partner, I am with child of laughter,
     and none but you can be my midwife.
     Was there ever such a game at noddy?'
     (Marston, 3.3.1–2).
114, 115, 120 **pains** care, effort
116 **bearing** carrying
117 **fain** willing, ready
117, 118 **bear with** put up with

---

108 she?] she; did she nod? *Theobald*   109 SD] *Theobald subst.; Speed nods. Proteus looks at* Speed *in
question. / Sisson;*   Ay] She nodded and said, I. *Pope*   110 Nod-ay] *(*Nod-I*)*   111–12] *Capell; F
lines* ¹nod; / I. /

PROTEUS   Why, sir, how do you bear with me?

SPEED   Marry, sir, the letter, very orderly, having nothing
but the word 'noddy' for my pains.   120

PROTEUS   Beshrew me, but you have a quick wit.

SPEED   And yet it cannot overtake your slow purse.

PROTEUS   Come, come, open the matter; in brief, what
said she?

SPEED   Open your purse, that the money and the matter   125
may be both at once delivered.

PROTEUS   [*Gives him a coin.*]   Well, sir, here is for your
pains. What said she?

SPEED   [*Examines coin.*]   Truly, sir, I think you'll hardly
win her.   130

PROTEUS   Why? Couldst thou perceive so much from her?

SPEED

Sir, I could perceive nothing at all from her;

No, not so much as a ducat for delivering your letter.

And being so hard to me that brought your mind,

I fear she'll prove as hard to you in telling your mind.   135

---

119 **Marry . . . orderly** Speed literalizes
bear with as 'carry'.
  Marry a mild oath, from the Virgin
  Mary's name
  orderly i.e. as my duty required
121 **Beshrew me** mild oath
123 **open the matter** tell me what happened
125 **matter** possibly a pun on the Latin
  mater (= mother), who could be *delivered* (126) of a child as the *purse* (frequently a metaphor of the womb; see
  Parker, 95) could be *delivered* of *money*
126 **delivered** a metaphor of childbirth,
  perhaps also reaching as far back as
  bear (118) and ahead to *pains* (128)
127 SD *It would seem to be a single,
  inadequate coin, a testern or tester
  (see 139n.). Speed has been angling

for a very large tip, certainly more
than he receives here (cf. *pound*, 103).
132–6 These lines are arranged as verse in
  F, again interrupting a long prose
  exchange. The same logic applies here
  as at 106–7 (see n.) – Speed's bad sing-
  song verse frustrates Proteus's impatient demands. Many editions, however,
  such as Ard², *Riv* and Oxf, follow
  Capell in relining as prose. Yet in contrast to 111–12 and 138–40, which
  Capell also relines, these lines (like
  106–7) rhyme in F, badly but appropriately for Speed.
133 **ducat** a gold coin, worth considerably more than the tester Speed actually receives. See 139n.
135 **in . . . mind** i.e. when you speak to
  her in person

119–20] Capell; F *lines* orderly, / paines. /   123 matter; in brief] *this edn (RP)*; matter in brief; F
127 SD] *Collier² subst.*   129 SD] *Folg²*; *eyeing the coin with contempt Cam¹*

Give her no token but stones, for she's as hard as steel.
PROTEUS   What said she, nothing?
SPEED   No, not so much as 'Take this for thy pains.' To
testify your bounty, I thank you, you have testerned
me; in requital whereof, henceforth carry your letters   140
yourself. And so, sir, I'll commend you to my master.   [*Exit.*]
PROTEUS

Go, go, begone, to save your ship from wreck,
Which cannot perish having thee aboard,
Being destined to a drier death on shore.
I must go send some better messenger.   145
I fear my Julia would not deign my lines,
Receiving them from such a worthless post.   *Exit.*

1.2   *Enter* JULIA *and* LUCETTA.

JULIA

But say, Lucetta, now we are alone,
Wouldst thou then counsel me to fall in love?

---

136 RP suggests that Speed 'seems to be juggling proverbs here' (see Dent, S839: 'As hard (stiff, strong, tough) as steel', and S878: 'As hard as a stone (flint, rock)'). Speed puns on *stones* meaning 'precious jewels' (i.e. nothing less will win over Julia) and 'testicles'. He then continues the bawdy joke in describing Julia as *hard as steel*, virtually mannish, in rejecting him without a tip.

137 Alternative suggestions for punctuating this line are plausible (see t.n.), but F makes sense.

139 *testerned* F's 'cestern'd' seems a simple compositor's error or misreading of *t* as *c*. A testern or tester was an Elizabethan sixpence (*OED* tester *sb.*[3]), worth much less than the *ducat* or *pound* Speed has so hopefully insinuated before; there is perhaps also a punning echo of *testify*. Servants in come-

dy are traditionally dissatisfied with their tips.

142–4 Proteus alludes to the proverbial saying, 'He that is born to be hanged (drowned) shall never be drowned (hanged)', Dent, B139. Cf. *Tem* 1.1.28–9: 'Methinks he hath no drowning mark upon him – his complexion is perfect gallows.'

146 **deign** i.e. condescend to accept

147 **post** messenger, but also alluding to Dent, P490: 'as deaf (dumb) as a post'. Cf. *AYL* 4.1.8–9: '*Jaques* Why, 'tis good to be sad and say nothing. *Rosalind* Why then, 'tis good to be a post.'

1.2 The action appears to shift to the house of Julia's *father* (130), probably outdoors (*stones*, 111; *wind*, 118), near *dinner-time* (67) – in Julia's garden, according to Cam[2] – but the references are vague.

2 **counsel** advise; see 1.1.51n.

137] What, said she nothing? *Pope;* What said she? nothing? *Cam*   138–40 *Capell; F lines* pains: /
me; /   139 testerned] *F2;* cestern'd *F*   141 SD] *Capell*   1.2] *Scoena Secunda. F*

147

LUCETTA

Ay, madam, so you stumble not unheedfully.

JULIA

Of all the fair resort of gentlemen

That every day with parle encounter me,   5

In thy opinion which is worthiest love?

LUCETTA

Please you repeat their names, I'll show my mind

According to my shallow simple skill.

JULIA

What think'st thou of the fair Sir Eglamour?

LUCETTA

As of a knight well-spoken, neat and fine;   10

But, were I you, he never should be mine.

JULIA

What think'st thou of the rich Mercatio?

LUCETTA

Well of his wealth; but of himself, so-so.

JULIA

What think'st thou of the gentle Proteus?

LUCETTA

Lord, Lord, to see what folly reigns in us!   15

---

3   **so** provided that
    stumble i.e. commit any (sexual)
    impropriety
    unheedfully carelessly
4–33   A young woman and her maid assess
    the former's prospective suitors: this is
    a stock scene in romance. Shakespeare
    employs the device elsewhere, e.g.
    Portia and Nerissa in *MV* 1.2.
4   **resort** company
5   **parle** conversation
    encounter Along with *parle*, the
    idiom here is military (RP).
7   **Please** if it please
    mind opinion; preference
8   **shallow** Cf. Valentine's *shallow*
    (1.1.21).

9   **Eglamour** See List of Roles, 6n.
10 **neat** elegant
12 **Mercatio** His name embodies mer-
    cantile associations (Italian *mercato* =
    merchant). He is *rich* but personally
    unappealing, while Eglamour by con-
    trast is a bit of a dandy, *neat and fine*
    (10). *Gentle* (14) Proteus appears clear-
    ly superior to both. Leech speculates
    that his name might have been
    prompted by, or perhaps be an error
    for, the 'Mercutio' in Brooke's *Romeus*.
14 **gentle** well-born
14, 97, 113 **Proteus** trisyllabic; see 1.1.1n.
15 **reigns in** rules, controls

---

5 parle] *(par'le)*   13 so-so] *(so, so)*

JULIA

How now? What means this passion at his name?

LUCETTA

Pardon, dear madam, 'tis a passing shame

That I, unworthy body as I am,

Should censure thus on lovely gentlemen.

JULIA

Why not on Proteus, as of all the rest?   20

LUCETTA

Then thus: of many good, I think him best.

JULIA

Your reason?

LUCETTA

I have no other but a woman's reason:

I think him so because I think him so.

JULIA

And wouldst thou have me cast my love on him?   25

LUCETTA

Ay, if you thought your love not cast away.

JULIA

Why, he of all the rest hath never moved me.

LUCETTA

Yet he of all the rest I think best loves ye.

JULIA

His little speaking shows his love but small.

LUCETTA

Fire that's closest kept burns most of all.   30

16 **passion** strong emotion
17 **passing** surpassing, exceeding
19 **censure** pass judgement
23 **a woman's reason** proverbial (Dent, B179); cf. *TC* 1.1.102: 'Because not there. This woman's answer sorts.'
25 **cast** bestow (*OED v.* 7b)
26 **cast away** thrown away, wasted; RP suggests 'castaway' (cf. *AC* 3.6.41), in a possible ironic premonition of Proteus's desertion.

27 **moved** proposed marriage to; aroused my interest
29 **little speaking** i.e. not saying much to me
30 proverbial; cf. Guazzo, *Civil Conversation*, 1.18: 'as hidden flames by force kept downe are most ardent' (cited under Dent, F265), and *MA* 3.1.77–8: 'let Benedick, like covered fire, / Consume away in sighs, waste inwardly'. Cf. also 2.7.21–3.

JULIA

They do not love that do not show their love.

LUCETTA

O, they love least that let men know their love.

JULIA

I would I knew his mind.

LUCETTA

Peruse this paper, madam.   [*Gives her a letter.*]

JULIA

To Julia. Say, from whom?   35

LUCETTA

That the contents will show.

JULIA

Say, say, who gave it thee?

LUCETTA

Sir Valentine's page; and sent, I think, from Proteus.
He would have given it you, but I, being in the way,
Did in your name receive it. Pardon the fault, I pray.   40

JULIA

Now, by my modesty, a goodly broker!
Dare you presume to harbour wanton lines?

---

32 proverbial (Dent, L165); cf. 2.2.16–
18n. and Marlowe, *Hero*, 1.186: 'True
love is mute.'

33 **mind** feelings, intentions

34 SD *Lucetta gives a *paper*, Proteus's
letter, to Julia. The letter is passed
back and forth, dropped, torn into
pieces and partly reassembled: so
much is evident from the text, but the
nature and exact placement of appropriate SDs have been a source of con-
troversy among editors (see 46n. and
69 SDn.). On the thematics of letters
in the play, see p. 59–67.

36 **contents** probably stressed 'contènts'

38 Speed had implied that he delivered
the letter directly to Julia (1.1.94–6).

Lucetta's line is cited by Leech (xviii)
as one of the textual anomalies in support of a theory of authorial revision;
he suggests that Lance's part could not
yet have existed and was added later, as
he should be the servant doing
Proteus's bidding (see p. 126). But
why then would Shakespeare self-
consciously call attention to the use of
Speed? On Speed's role as *page*, see
List of Roles, 9n.

41 **goodly** fine (ironic)
broker go-between, with suggestions
of pandering

42 **harbour** shelter; receive. Cf. 3.1.140
and 149.
wanton amorous

34 SD] *Dyce*

To whisper and conspire against my youth?
Now trust me, 'tis an office of great worth,
And you an officer fit for the place.   45
There, take the paper. See it be returned,
Or else return no more into my sight.

LUCETTA
To plead for love deserves more fee than hate.

JULIA
Will ye be gone?

LUCETTA   That you may ruminate.   *Exit.*

JULIA
And yet I would I had o'erlooked the letter;   50
It were a shame to call her back again
And pray her to a fault for which I chid her.
What fool is she, that knows I am a maid
And would not force the letter to my view,
Since maids in modesty say 'No' to that   55
Which they would have the profferer construe 'Ay'.
Fie, fie, how wayward is this foolish love
That, like a testy babe, will scratch the nurse

---

46 **There . . . paper** Julia returns the letter to Lucetta, but it is unclear, in the
light of stage business suggested at 70
and 73, whether Lucetta drops the letter before she exits at 49 or takes it off
with her and drops it later when she
re-enters. Although both options have
been made to work onstage, the latter
seems preferable. See 69 SDn.
49 **That** so that
   ruminate think about it
50 **would** wish
   o'erlooked read over, examined; cf.
   Son 82.2.
52 **to a fault** to commit a fault
   chid scolded
53 **What . . . she** what a fool she is
   maid virgin, unmarried girl
55–6 proverbial   (Dent,   W660);   cf.

3.1.100–1 and n. A nastier version of
this sentiment is evident in Bucking-
ham's advice to Richard on how he
should accept the crown: 'be not easily
won to our requests. / Play the maid's
part: still answer nay and take it' (*R3*
3.7.50–1).
56 **construe** cònstrue; interpret as
57 **Fie, fie** expression of strong disapproval
   wayward disobedient, self-willed (as of
   a *babe*, 58); with possible further implied
   sense of 'perverse' (cf. F 'weyward' =
   perverse in *Mac* F TLN 130, 355 and
   596, habitually emended to 'weird')
58–9 proverbial (Dent, R156); cf. *R2*
   5.1.31–2: 'wilt thou, pupil-like, / Take
   the correction mildly, kiss the rod . . . ?'
58 **testy** peevish

53 fool] (*'foole*)   57 wayward] (*way-ward*)

And presently, all humbled, kiss the rod!
How churlishly I chid Lucetta hence,   60
When willingly I would have had her here!
How angerly I taught my brow to frown,
When inward joy enforced my heart to smile!
My penance is to call Lucetta back
And ask remission for my folly past.   65
What ho! Lucetta!

[*Enter* LUCETTA.]

LUCETTA   What would your ladyship?
JULIA

Is't near dinner-time?

LUCETTA   I would it were,
That you might kill your stomach on your meat
And not upon your maid.
        [*Drops and picks up the letter.*]
JULIA

What is't that you took up so gingerly?   70
LUCETTA   Nothing.
JULIA

Why didst thou stoop then?
LUCETTA

To take a paper up that I let fall.

---

59 **presently** immediately
62 **angerly** angrily (*OED* 2); see Abbott, 447.
65 **remission** pardon
68 **kill** satisfy
    stomach appetite; anger. The stomach was thought to be the seat of anger. Cf. Dent, M187: 'A hungry man an angry man'.
68–9 **meat . . . maid** a near pun: *meat* would have been pronounced 'mate'.

69 **maid** maidservant
69 SD *Lucetta drops a *paper* (73), the letter, and picks it up again, perhaps to draw it to Julia's attention. Leech has Lucetta drop the letter at 48 and leave it there until she picks it up again here. Most editors conclude, given Julia's monologue (50–65), that Lucetta does take the letter away with her at 49.
70 **gingerly** with extreme caution, so as to avoid making a noise (*OED* A b)

66 SD] *Rowe subst.*   67 dinner-time] *(dinner time)*   69 SD] *Collier*[2] *subst.*   70] *Collier; F lines* you / gingerly? /

JULIA

And is that paper nothing?

LUCETTA

Nothing concerning me.   75

JULIA

Then let it lie for those that it concerns.

LUCETTA

Madam, it will not lie where it concerns,

Unless it have a false interpreter.

JULIA

Some love of yours hath writ to you in rhyme.

LUCETTA

That I might sing it, madam, to a tune.   80

Give me a note, your ladyship can set –

JULIA

As little by such toys as may be possible.

Best sing it to the tune of 'Light o'love'.

LUCETTA

It is too heavy for so light a tune.

76–7 **lie . . . lie** remain lying on the ground . . . speak falsely
78 i.e. unless you deliberately misread it
80 **That** so that
81 **note** a musical note
*set – F has no punctuation at the end of this line, which seems to be the beginning of a sentence by Lucetta, interrupted dismissively by Julia (82). In *set*, Lucetta may be asking Julia to start a tune (*OED v.*[1] B 54c), to put the words to a tune (*OED v.*[1] B 73a) or to choose the pitch (*OED v.*[1] B 26c). Julia then twists the meaning from the musical to a put-down (*set as little* = value so little).
82 **toys** trifles
83 **'Light o'love'** fickle; also the title of a

well-known popular tune. Cf. *MA* 3.4.41–3: '*Margaret* Clap 's into "Light o' love." That goes without a burden; do you sing it, and I'll dance it. *Beatrice* Ye light o' love with your heels!', and *TNK* 5.2.54: 'gallops to the tune of "Light o' love"'. Simpson, 447–8, notes that 'At least four ballads were sung to the tune, though there must have been others that have not survived', and cites other allusions in *The Glass of Man's Folly*, 1595, and Fletcher's *The Wild Goose Chase*. Julia therefore implies that the writer of the letter is fickle or unfaithful (*light* = unstable, wanton).

84, 85 **heavy** sad, serious

81 set –] *Penguin;* set *F;* set. *F2*   83 Light o'love] *Theobald; Light O, Loue F; Light O Loue / Rowe*

JULIA

Heavy? Belike it hath some burden then?   85

LUCETTA

Ay, and melodious were it, would you sing it.

JULIA

And why not you?

LUCETTA   I cannot reach so high.

JULIA

Let's see your song.   [*Takes the letter.*]
                 How now, minion!

LUCETTA

Keep tune there still, so you will sing it out.
And yet methinks I do not like this tune.   90

JULIA

You do not?

LUCETTA   No, madam, 'tis too sharp.

JULIA

You, minion, are too saucy.

---

85 **Belike** perhaps; no doubt
   burden the bass line of a song (*OED
   sb.* 9); something heavy to carry; possibly a sexual allusion to the weight of a
   man's body during intercourse
86 **melodious . . . you** it would be melodious if you would
87 **high** high in the musical register; high
   in social rank
88 SD *Several possibilities of stage
   action have been suggested here: Julia
   snatches the supposed *song*, discover-
   ing it to be the letter again; or Julia
   tries to take the letter but Lucetta
   withholds it. Clearly, Julia possesses
   the letter by 99, when she tears it into
   pieces.
88 **minion** hussy; possibly a pun on
   'minim', a half-note in music (Bantam)
89–97 a series of puns (*tune, sharp, flat,
   descant, mean, bass*): as musical terms;

as social behaviour. Lucetta in effect
tells Julia that her responses are inappropriate, *too sharp* (i.e. too bitter,
aggressive) or *too flat* and *harsh* (i.e.
too blunt and strident), and that she is
spoiling the potential *concord* of their
relationship. Julia lacks a *mean* – a
middle or alto voice, i.e. Proteus, but
also moderated behaviour – to make
her song harmonious. See also notes
on 89, 94 and 96.
89–90 Some editors have prescribed stage
action to provoke Lucetta's lines:
Hanmer, followed substantially by
Ard[2], proposes '*a box on the ear*' from
Julia, after 89, and Schlueter inserts
the SD '*Threatens her*' before.
89 **Keep tune** stay in tune; keep your
   temper
92 **saucy** insolent

88] Hanmer; F lines Song: / Minion? /   SD] Dyce subst.

LUCETTA

Nay, now you are too flat,

And mar the concord with too harsh a descant.

There wanteth but a mean to fill your song.   95

JULIA

The mean is drowned with your unruly bass.

LUCETTA

Indeed, I bid the base for Proteus.

JULIA

This babble shall not henceforth trouble me;

Here is a coil with protestation.   [*Tears the letter.*]

Go, get you gone, and let the papers lie.   100

You would be fingering them to anger me.

---

94 **descant** an extemporaneous melodic
line higher in pitch than the tune
(*OED sb.* I 1); cf. *R3* 1.1.27: 'descant on
mine own deformity'.

95 **wanteth but** is lacking only

96 *****your unruly bass** F2 makes sense,
semantically and metrically, but it is
possible that F is correct (as
Tannenbaum, 7, argues), and that it is
a direct address to Lucetta (i.e. 'the
mean [= middle part] is drowned with
[= by] you, unruly bass').
bass lowest voice in music; dishon-
ourable action (= 'base')

97 **bid . . . for** 'challenge on behalf of',
from the game 'Prisoner's base', in
which a member of one team challenges the players on the other team to
pursue him/her, thus leaving the prisoner at the *base* free to escape. Lucetta
is putting herself forward as Proteus's
champion. Cf. *VA* 303: 'To bid the
wind a base he now prepares', and
Marlowe, *Edward II*, 4.2.65–6: 'We
will finde comfort, money, men, and
friends / Ere long, to bid the English

king a base' (Marlowe, 2.65).

98 **babble** confusion of words, idle talk;
also possibly a pun on 'bauble' (= phallus, as in *RJ* 2.4.91: 'hide his bauble in
a hole'). The letter is an eroticized
symbol for Proteus's phallus throughout this scene: it is 'took up so gingerly' (70), then *let fall* (73), and Julia
complains that Lucetta is *fingering*
(101) the letter's pieces. Cf. 128–9n.

99 **coil** disturbance
protestation pronounced with five
syllables; declaration of love (possibly a
self-revealing slip for Proteus/tation).
Cf. 4.4.127.

99 SD *****Julia** tears the letter into pieces.
A similar but imaginary scene,
designed to gull Benedick, is described
in *MA* 2.3.138–46, while Berowne
tears up his own letter in *LLL* 4.3.195
SD and Troilus tears up Cressida's last
letter in *TC* 5.3.108 SD.

100 **and . . . lie** Lucetta may be picking
up the pieces (*fingering them*), and Julia
doesn't want her to see them.

---

96 your] *F2;* you *F*   bass] *(*base*)*   98 babble] bauble *Cam¹*   99 SD] *Pope subst.*   101 fingering]
*(*fingring*)*

LUCETTA

She makes it strange, but she would be best pleased
To be so angered with another letter.   [*Exit.*]

JULIA

Nay, would I were so angered with the same.
O hateful hands, to tear such loving words!   105
Injurious wasps, to feed on such sweet honey
And kill the bees that yield it with your stings!
I'll kiss each several paper for amends.
Look, here is writ *kind Julia*. Unkind Julia!
As in revenge of thy ingratitude,   110
I throw thy name against the bruising stones,
Trampling contemptuously on thy disdain.
And here is writ *love-wounded Proteus*.
Poor wounded name, my bosom as a bed
Shall lodge thee till thy wound be throughly healed;   115
And thus I search it with a sovereign kiss.
But twice or thrice was *Proteus* written down.
Be calm, good wind, blow not a word away
Till I have found each letter in the letter,
Except mine own name. That, some whirlwind bear   120

102–3 Some editions (Penguin, Cam², Oxf) mark this speech as an aside, and therefore heard only by the audience, but Julia's echoing of *angered* suggests that she hears Lucetta's comment. Believing these lines an aside, Staunton also transfers 104 to Lucetta.
102 **makes it strange** pretends to be indifferent
105 Here Julia apparently picks up scraps of the torn letter and comments on them throughout her monologue.
106–7 Wasps were known as enemies of bees: 'The waspe doth much more hurt then the hornet: for the hornet now and then killeth a Bee, but the waspe wasteth the hony, whereby many whole

stalles doe perish' (Butler, H6ᵛ).
106 **wasps** i.e. her fingers
108 **several paper** i.e. the separate fragments of the torn letter
109 **Unkind** unnatural
110 **As** as if
114–15 See 128–9n., 3.1.144n. and 248.
115 **throughly** thoroughly
116 **search** probe (the wound)
     sovereign healing
118 As RP suggests, this line may reflect the reality of open-air performances, which can often be affected by wind.
120–2 **That . . . sea** Julia's melodramatic language here is both a sign of the power of her passion and a moment of comic excess.

---

103 SD] *F2* 109 *kind . . .* Julia!] *Bantam;* kinde *Iulia*: vnkinde *Iulia, F* 111 bruising stones] *(*bruzing-stones*)* 113 *love-wounded*] *(Loue wounded)* 120 whirlwind] *(*whirle-winde*)*

Unto a ragged, fearful, hanging rock,
And throw it thence into the raging sea.
Lo, here in one line is his name twice writ,
Poor forlorn Proteus, passionate Proteus,
To the sweet Julia – that I'll tear away;   125
And yet I will not, sith so prettily
He couples it to his complaining names.
Thus will I fold them, one upon another;
Now kiss, embrace, contend, do what you will.

[*Enter* LUCETTA.]

LUCETTA

Madam, dinner is ready, and your father stays.   130

JULIA

Well, let us go.

LUCETTA

What, shall these papers lie like tell-tales here?

JULIA

If you respect them, best to take them up.

LUCETTA

Nay, I was taken up for laying them down.
Yet here they shall not lie, for catching cold.   135
[*Picks up pieces of the letter.*]

125 **that** i.e. her own name
126 **sith** since
127 **couples** joins together, with a strong
sexual implication amplified in the
next two lines
complaining lamenting
128–9 By folding the paper, Julia brings
the two names – hers and Proteus's –
one upon another, in a comic mimicry of
sexual intercourse, anticipated at
114–15, where Julia speaks of lodging
Proteus's *wounded name* in her 'bosom
as a bed'.
129 Cf. the suggestive rhythm of this line

with *Oth* 4.1.34: '*Iago* Lie. *Othello*
With her? *Iago* With her, on her, what
you will.'
130 **father** Julia's father (never seen) is
referred to again at 1.3.48; but see
2.7.86–7n. and p. 38.
stays is waiting
133 **respect** value, esteem (*OED* 4b); cf.
Son 149.9.
best it would be best
134 **taken up** reprimanded
135 **for** for fear of. This line implies that
Lucetta, perhaps also with Julia, picks
up the scattered pieces of the letter.

121 fearful, hanging] fearful-hanging *Delius*   129.1] *Rowe; Enter. F2*   135 SD] *Cam¹ subst.*

JULIA

    I see you have a month's mind to them.

LUCETTA

    Ay, madam, you may say what sights you see;

    I see things too, although you judge I wink.

JULIA

    Come, come, will't please you go?   *Exeunt.*

1.3   *Enter* ANTONIO *and* PANTINO.

ANTONIO

    Tell me, Pantino, what sad talk was that

    Wherewith my brother held you in the cloister?

PANTINO

    'Twas of his nephew, Proteus your son.

ANTONIO

    Why? What of him?

PANTINO   He wondered that your lordship

    Would suffer him to spend his youth at home   5

    While other men, of slender reputation,

---

136 **month's mind to** liking for, inclination toward; proverbial (Dent, M1109). Leech, following Ard[1], notes that the phrase originally referred to 'a religious commemoration of a deceased person on a day one month after his death', exemplified by Nashe in *Martin's Month's Mind* (1589); eventually the phrase acquired 'the sense of a "longing" such as that experienced by a pregnant woman in the last month of pregnancy' (Ard[2]).

138 **I wink** I have my eyes shut

1.3 The location of this scene has been given as the house of Proteus's father,

Antonio (Ard[1]), or a public place of encounter or business.

1 **Pantino** See List of Roles, 11n.
    sad serious

3 ***nephew, Proteus** RP argues that F's placement of the comma after rather than before *Proteus* implausibly implies that Antonio needs 'to be reminded that Proteus is his son, whereas Proteus need not be his brother's only nephew'. *Proteus* is trisyllabic (see 1.1.1n.).

5 **suffer** allow

6 **of slender reputation** i.e. of lower status than you

139 will't] *Rowe³*; wilt *F*   1.3] *Scoena Tertia. F*   0.1] *Rowe (Enter* Anthonio *and* Panthion.*); Enter* Antonio *and* Panthino. *Protheus. F*   1 Pantino] *(Panthino); Panthion F3*   3 nephew, Proteus your] *this edn (RP);* Nephew *Protheus,* your *F*

Put forth their sons to seek preferment out –
Some to the wars to try their fortune there;
Some to discover islands far away;
Some to the studious universities.   10
For any or for all these exercises
He said that Proteus your son was meet,
And did request me to importune you
To let him spend his time no more at home,
Which would be great impeachment to his age   15
In having known no travel in his youth.

ANTONIO

Nor need'st thou much importune me to that
Whereon this month I have been hammering.
I have considered well his loss of time,

---

7 echoes Valentine's comments at
1.1.5–8 and Proteus's at 1.1.63–4
Put . . . sons i.e. send their sons out
into the world
preferment advancement, promotion
out abroad; elsewhere. Cf. *KL* 1.1.31:
'He hath been out nine years.'
8–10 typical means of advancement for a
young man: as a soldier, explorer or
scholar. Cf. Ophelia's description of
Hamlet: 'The courtier's, soldier's,
scholar's, eye, tongue, sword, / . . .
The glass of fashion and the mould
of form' (*Ham* 3.1.154–6). Among
Shakespeare's contemporaries, Sir
Philip Sidney and John Donne (in his
earlier career) exemplified this striving
for an active engagement with the
world and the intellectual life. Noting
the use of anaphora in these lines,
Elam observes that 'Virtually all the
speakers in *TG* employ the anaphoric
mode in at least one speech, and over
the widest possible range of topics, so
that it comes to represent part of an
overall rather than individual stylistic
idiolect in the play'; cf. Valentine at
2.4.129–30 and Julia at 2.7.75–8. Elam
contrasts these uses of the figure,

which represent 'coincidence and inte-
gration . . . the harmonious dramatic
situation in the comedy's early scenes'
with the seemingly similar but very
different effects in Proteus's soliloquy
of betrayal in 2.6 (Elam, 246).
8 **fortune** luck
11 **exercises** activities
12, 88 **Proteus** trisyllabic; see 1.1.1n.
12 **meet** suitable (*OED* A 3)
13, 17 **importune** impòrtune; urge
15 **impeachment** detriment, injury
(*OED* 2)
16 **travel** Cf. Bacon, 'Of Travel': '*Travaile*, in the younger Sort, is a Part of
Education; In the Elder, a Part of
Experience . . . The Things to be seene
and observed are: The Courts of
Princes, specially when they give
Audience to Ambassadours: The
Courts of Justice . . . Consistories
Ecclesiasticke . . . The Wals and
Fortifications of Cities and Townes . . .
Antiquities, and Ruines' (Bacon, 56).
Cf. the activities proposed at 30–3.
18 **hammering** pondering, thinking over
19 **loss of time** advancing years; waste of
opportunity

And how he cannot be a perfect man   20
Not being tried and tutored in the world.
Experience is by industry achieved
And perfected by the swift course of time.
Then tell me, whither were I best to send him?

PANTINO

I think your lordship is not ignorant   25
How his companion, youthful Valentine,
Attends the Emperor in his royal court.

ANTONIO

I know it well.

PANTINO

'Twere good, I think, your lordship sent him thither.
There shall he practise tilts and tournaments,   30
Hear sweet discourse, converse with noblemen
And be in eye of every exercise

---

20 **perfect** complete, having all the essential qualities (*OED* B 3); cf. *perfected* (23). Cf. Lindenbaum on the thematic significance of the concept of the 'perfect' man in the play. 'Perfection' was one of the eight categories – along with Youth, Recreation, Disposition, Acquaintance, Education, Moderation and Vocation – that Richard Brathwait analysed as constitutive of 'The English Gentleman'; true perfection could only be found 'farre above the Sphere of Mortality', and the gentleman could only aspire to perfection 'by assistance of Gods Spirit, and a desire in man to second that assistance by an assiduall endevour' (Brathwait, 373–4; see Fig.1).

21 **tried** tested

23 **perfected** made complete; probably stressed on the first syllable (Kökeritz, 335)

27 **Emperor** Throughout this scene (38, 41, 58, 67), it is suggested that Valentine is at the court of the *Emperor*

(see notes on List of Roles, 1, 2.3.4, 2.4.74–5 and 5.4.139). Elsewhere in the play Silvia's father is *Duke* of Milan.

30 **tilts and tournaments** Such chivalric military displays – found in Montemayor's *Diana*, among many other texts of the period – demonstrated a young man's heroic and romantic powers. Queen Elizabeth regularly enjoyed such festivities, and Jonson wrote a court masque employing tilt and barriers for Prince Henry. These activities and the others listed – observing and associating *with noblemen* (31) – reflect the courtly values articulated in Castiglione's *The Courtier*, among many other works. For an overview of the social and ethical aspects of such an honour-based culture, see James.

31 **sweet** pleasing (*OED* A 5c)
converse with associate with (*OED v.* 2); speak with

32 **be . . . of** witness

---

31 noblemen] *(*Noble-men*)*

Worthy his youth and nobleness of birth.

ANTONIO

I like thy counsel; well hast thou advised.
And that thou mayst perceive how well I like it,   35
The execution of it shall make known;
Even with the speediest expedition
I will dispatch him to the Emperor's court.

PANTINO

Tomorrow, may it please you, Don Alfonso
With other gentlemen of good esteem   40
Are journeying to salute the Emperor
And to commend their service to his will.

ANTONIO

Good company – with them shall Proteus go.

[*Enter* PROTEUS *reading a letter.*]

And in good time! Now will we break with him.

PROTEUS

Sweet love, sweet lines, sweet life!   45
Here is her hand, the agent of her heart;
Here is her oath for love, her honour's pawn.

---

34 **counsel** advice; see 1.1.51n.
35–6 'a conflation of two constructions: (1) how well I like it the execution of it shall make known; (2) in order that thou mayst perceive how well I like it, the execution of it shall make it known' (Ard²)
37 **expedition** urgency
39 **Don Alfonso** suggests a Spaniard; cf. 2.4.52. 'Don' is elsewhere used as a title only in *LLL* (Don Armado) and *MA* (Don Pedro, Don John, even 'Don Worm, his conscience', 5.2.79).
40 **esteem** reputation
41 **salute** greet
43.1 *Julia's letter here parallels Proteus's

in the previous scene and anticipates Valentine's letter to Silvia in 3.1; for discussion of letters, see pp. 59–67.
44 **in good time** at the right moment
break speak; broach the matter. Cf. 3.1.59.
45–50 Antonio and Pantino evidently do not overhear Proteus's rapturous lines. Penguin adds the SD '*aside*', Bantam offers '*To himself*' and RP suggests '*apart*'; most directors have placed Proteus to one side of the stage, physically away from his father.
46 **hand** handwriting
47 **pawn** pledge

---

39 Alfonso] (*Alphonso*)   43.1 *Enter* PROTEUS] *F2 (Enter Pro.) after 44   reading a letter*] *Capell subst.*

O, that our fathers would applaud our loves
To seal our happiness with their consents.
O heavenly Julia!   50

ANTONIO

How now? What letter are you reading there?

PROTEUS

May't please your lordship, 'tis a word or two
Of commendations sent from Valentine,
Delivered by a friend that came from him.

ANTONIO

Lend me the letter. Let me see what news.   55

PROTEUS

There is no news, my lord, but that he writes
How happily he lives, how well beloved
And daily graced by the Emperor,
Wishing me with him, partner of his fortune.

ANTONIO

And how stand you affected to his wish?   60

PROTEUS

As one relying on your lordship's will,
And not depending on his friendly wish.

ANTONIO

My will is something sorted with his wish.
Muse not that I thus suddenly proceed,

---

48 **fathers** See 1.2.130n. on *father*.
52–3 Proteus's lie to his father about Julia's letter is understandable, but it backfires in helping produce exactly the reverse of the result desired.
53 **commendations** greetings
58 **graced** gracèd; favoured
59 **fortune** success, prosperity
60 And what is your desire regarding his wish?
61 i.e. I will do whatever pleases you

62 **his friendly wish** the wish of my friend
63 **something sorted** somewhat in agreement
64–71 The assertive, *peremptory* (71) father is a typical figure in Shakespearean comedy and tragedy; old Capulet in *RJ*, Egeus in *MND* and, to reach further, King Lear, all block their children's happiness, though in most cases it is a daughter being constrained.
64 **Muse not** don't be surprised

50 O] *F2; Pro.* Oh *F*

For what I will, I will, and there an end.   65
I am resolved that thou shalt spend some time
With Valentinus in the Emperor's court.
What maintenance he from his friends receives,
Like exhibition thou shalt have from me.
Tomorrow be in readiness to go.   70
Excuse it not, for I am peremptory.

PROTEUS

My lord, I cannot be so soon provided;
Please you deliberate a day or two.

ANTONIO

Look what thou want'st shall be sent after thee.
No more of stay: tomorrow thou must go.   75
Come on, Pantino, you shall be employed
To hasten on his expedition.   [*Exeunt Antonio and Pantino.*]

PROTEUS

Thus have I shunned the fire for fear of burning
And drenched me in the sea where I am drowned.
I feared to show my father Julia's letter   80
Lest he should take exceptions to my love,
And with the vantage of mine own excuse
Hath he excepted most against my love.
O, how this spring of love resembleth

---

65 **there an end** there is no more to say
(*OED sb.* 23); cf. 2.1.149; Dent,
E113.1; and *R2* 5.1.69.
68 **What maintenance** whatever subsidy
friends family
69 **Like exhibition** the same allowance
71 **peremptory** completely resolved;
insistent on compliance or obedience
(*OED* I 5)
72 **provided** equipped
74 **Look . . . want'st** whatever you need
75 **stay** delay
77 **expedition** journey; pronounced with
five syllables

79 **drenched** submerged
81 **take exceptions** object
82–3 i.e. my own excuse has given him
the opportunity to do the most harm
to my love
84–7 a conventional simile; cf. *Son*
33.9–12: 'Even so my sun one early
morn did shine / With all triumphant
splendour on my brow; / But out
alack, he was but one hour mine, /
The region cloud hath masked him
from me now.'
84 **resembleth** perhaps pronounced with
four syllables

67 Valentinus] *Valentino F2; Valentine / Warburton*   76 Pantino] *F2 (Panthino); Panthmo F*
77 SD] *Rowe subst.*

The uncertain glory of an April day,   85
Which now shows all the beauty of the sun,
And by and by a cloud takes all away.

[*Enter* PANTINO.]

PANTINO
    Sir Proteus, your father calls for you.
    He is in haste, therefore I pray you go.
PROTEUS
    Why this it is: my heart accords thereto,   90
    And yet a thousand times it answers 'No'.   *Exeunt.*

2.1   *Enter* VALENTINE [*and*] SPEED.

SPEED
    Sir, your glove.
VALENTINE   Not mine – my gloves are on.
SPEED
    Why then, this may be yours, for this is but one.
VALENTINE
    Ha? Let me see. Ay, give it me, it's mine.

---

87 **by and by** instantly
88 ***father calls** Tannenbaum, 8, argues
   for the F reading, but has found little
   support.
91 ***it answers** As 'it' could sometimes
   be used meaning 'its' as the possessive,
   Tannenbaum, 8, argues for the F reading (i.e. construing 'answer's' as
   'answer is'; see Abbott, 228). However,
   use of 'it', and, indeed, of 'its', as the
   possessive was extremely rare in the
   period, the regular form being 'his'
   (see 3.2.8n.). Moreover, *it answers*
   would only have been heard as subject
   and verb. Crane had a habit of intro-

ducing superfluous apostrophes,
which could explain F's reading (see
p. 121).
2.1 The location shifts to Milan, according to the earlier descriptions of
   Valentine's destination, but there are
   no references in the scene to a specific
   place.
1 Speed apparently picks up Silvia's
   glove; directors have often engineered
   some stage business, such as Silvia
   passing across the stage and dropping
   the glove, sometimes deliberately.
2 **one** a homophone echoing *on* in the
   previous line (see Kökeritz, 232)

87.1] *Rowe subst.; Enter. F2*   88 father calls] *F4;* Fathers call's *F;* Father call's *F2*   91 answers]
*(*answer's*)*   SD] *Rowe; Exeunt. Finis. F*   **2.1**] *Actus secundus: Scoena Prima. F*   0.1] *Rowe; Enter
Valentine, Speed, Siluia. F*

Sweet ornament that decks a thing divine.
Ah, Silvia, Silvia!   5
SPEED [*Calls.*]   Madam Silvia! Madam Silvia!
VALENTINE   How now, sirrah?
SPEED   She is not within hearing, sir.
VALENTINE   Why sir, who bade you call her?
SPEED   Your worship, sir, or else I mistook.   10
VALENTINE   Well, you'll still be too forward.
SPEED   And yet I was last chidden for being too slow.
VALENTINE   Go to, sir. Tell me, do you know Madam Silvia?
SPEED   She that your worship loves?
VALENTINE   Why, how know you that I am in love?   15
SPEED   Marry, by these special marks: first, you have
         learned, like Sir Proteus, to wreathe your arms, like a
         malcontent; to relish a love-song, like a robin redbreast;

---

4   **decks** covers
7   **sirrah** form of address to a social in-
    ferior
11 **you'll still be** i.e. you are always
    forward presumptuous
12 **chidden** rebuked
13 **Go to** expression of impatience
16–29 The *special marks* of the lover are
    conventional in early modern comedy.
    Cf. Rosalind's description of the marks
    Orlando lacks in *AYL* 3.2.364–72: 'A
    lean cheek . . . a blue eye and sunken
    . . . an unquestionable spirit . . . a beard
    neglected . . . your hose should be
    ungartered, your bonnet unbanded,
    your sleeve unbuttoned, your shoe
    untied, and everything about you
    demonstrating a careless desolation'.
16, 55 **Marry** See 1.1.119n.
17 **wreathe your arms** the typical pose of
    a melancholy lover; cf. three instances in
    LLL: 'your arms crossed on your thin-
    belly doublet' (3.1.16–17); 'Dan Cupid,
    / Regent of love-rhymes, lord of folded
    arms' (3.1.175–6); and 'Longaville /

Did . . . never lay his wreathed arms
athwart / His loving bosom to keep
down his heart' (4.3.130–3). The well-
known Newbattle Abbey portrait of
John Donne represents him as a melancholy lover with folded arms. This pose
was not restricted to lovers, but could
designate sad or melancholy thought
more generally: Brutus is described as
'Musing, and sighing, with [his] arms
across' (*JC* 2.1.239) and Ferdinand,
after the shipwreck, is left 'sitting, /
His arms in this sad knot' (*Tem*
1.2.223–4).
18 **malcontent** This character type,
    of a man suffering from melancholy
    and/or frustrated in love, became
    popular in the late 1590s and into the
    seventeenth century: cf. Jaques in
    AYL, Malvolio in *TN*, Hamlet, and
    Malevole in John Marston's *The
    Malcontent* (1603).
    relish sing with pleasure (*OED v.*²); cf.
    Luc 1126: 'Relish your nimble notes to
    pleasing ears.'

---

4 divine.] *Rowe;* diuine, *F*   6 SD] *Dyce*   18 malcontent] *(*Male-content*)*   robin redbreast]
(Robin-redbreast*)*

to walk alone, like one that had the pestilence; to sigh,
like a schoolboy that had lost his *A B C*; to weep, like a   20
young wench that had buried her grandam; to fast, like
one that takes diet; to watch, like one that fears
robbing; to speak puling, like a beggar at Hallowmas.
You were wont, when you laughed, to crow like a cock;
when you walked, to walk like one of the lions; when   25
you fasted, it was presently after dinner; when you
looked sadly, it was for want of money. And now you
are metamorphosed with a mistress, that when I look
on you, I can hardly think you my master.

VALENTINE   Are all these things perceived in me?   30

SPEED   They are all perceived without ye.

VALENTINE   Without me? They cannot.

SPEED   Without you? Nay, that's certain, for without you
were so simple, none else would. But you are so without
these follies, that these follies are within you, and shine   35

---

19 **pestilence** plague (anyone with signs
of the plague would be avoided)
20 *A B C* primer, spelling book (*OED sb*.
3)
21 **grandam** grandmother
22 **takes** keeps to a
watch stay awake
23 **puling** whining, feebly wailing
Hallowmas the feast of All Saints'
Day, 1 November; beggars traditionally sought alms on this date.
24, 67 **wont** accustomed
25 **one . . . lions** The Tower of London
kept and bred lions (Stow, *Annals*,
895); cf. Webster, *White Devil*, 5.6.266:
'to be like the lions i' th' Tower'.
25–6 **when . . . dinner** proverbial (see
Dent, B289: 'The belly that is full may
well fast.')
26 **presently** immediately

27 **sadly** serious
want lack
28 **with** by
that so that
31 **without ye** i.e. on your outside
32 Valentine takes Speed to mean 'in my
absence'.
33 **Without . . . without** beyond . . .
unless
34 **none else would** perhaps 'none else
would perceive them' (Ard[1])
35–8 **shine . . . malady** Early modern
physicians would diagnose diseases on
the basis of the clarity of the urine; cf.
2H4 1.2.1–2, where Falstaff asks 'what
says the doctor to my water?' Here,
Valentine's symptoms of love are like
the symptoms of a real *malady*; for many
early modern writers, romantic love
could indeed be thought of as a sickness.

---

19 had] hath *Collier²*   20 schoolboy] *(Schoole-boy)*   21 buried] lost *F2*   23 Hallowmas]
(Hallow-Masse)   28 are] are so *Collier²*   metamorphosed] *(Metamorphis'd)*   31 ye] you *Capell*

through you like the water in an urinal, that not an eye that sees you but is a physician to comment on your malady.

VALENTINE   But tell me, dost thou know my lady Silvia?

SPEED   She that you gaze on so, as she sits at supper?   40

VALENTINE   Hast thou observed that? Even she I mean.

SPEED   Why sir, I know her not.

VALENTINE   Dost thou know her by my gazing on her, and yet knowst her not?

SPEED   Is she not hard-favoured, sir?   45

VALENTINE   Not so fair, boy, as well-favoured.

SPEED   Sir, I know that well enough.

VALENTINE   What dost thou know?

SPEED   That she is not so fair as – of you – well favoured.

VALENTINE   I mean that her beauty is exquisite but her   50
favour infinite.

SPEED   That's because the one is painted and the other out of all count.

VALENTINE   How painted? And how out of count?

SPEED   Marry, sir, so painted to make her fair that no man   55
counts of her beauty.

VALENTINE   How esteem'st thou me? I account of her beauty.

SPEED   You never saw her since she was deformed.

VALENTINE   How long hath she been deformed?   60

---

36 **urinal** glass vessel which holds urine;
cf. Evans in *MW* 3.1.13: 'I will knog
his urinals.'

36–7 **not . . . but** everyone that sees you

42 **know** Speed puns on *know* in the sexual sense.

45 **hard-favoured** ugly

46, 49 **fair** beautiful

46 **well-favoured** attractive, charming

49 **of** by
  well favoured highly regarded; i.e.
  your infatuation with her makes her

seem attractive

51 **favour** charm, graciousness (*OED sb*. 2)

52–6 female beauty is often said to be the
false product of cosmetics. Cf. *Ham*
5.1.193: 'let her paint an inch thick'.

53 **out . . . count** beyond calculation; cf.
5.4.70 and Dent, C704.1.

56 **counts of** values, appreciates

59–61 Valentine's love for Silvia has
deformed her because he now sees her
as more beautiful than she actually is.

39, 43 dost] *(do'st)*   50–1] *Capell; F lines* exquisite, / infinite. /

SPEED   Ever since you loved her.

VALENTINE   I have loved her ever since I saw her, and still
I see her beautiful.

SPEED   If you love her, you cannot see her.

VALENTINE   Why?   65

SPEED   Because Love is blind. O, that you had mine eyes,
or your own eyes had the lights they were wont to have
when you chid at Sir Proteus for going ungartered.

VALENTINE   What should I see then?

SPEED   Your own present folly and her passing deformity;   70
for he, being in love, could not see to garter his hose;
and you, being in love, cannot see to put on your hose.

VALENTINE   Belike, boy, then you are in love, for last
morning you could not see to wipe my shoes.

SPEED   True, sir, I was in love with my bed. I thank you,   75
you swinged me for my love, which makes me the
bolder to chide you for yours.

VALENTINE   In conclusion, I stand affected to her.

SPEED   I would you were set, so your affection would cease.

---

62 **still** always
66 **Love is blind** proverbial (Dent, L506);
cf. 2.4.94. The standard personification
of Love, as Cupid, shows him blindfolded: 'This wimpled, whining, pur-
blind, wayward boy' (*LLL* 3.1.174).
Cupid's 'love shaft' (*MND* 2.1.159), the
arrow of desire he shoots, thus strikes
arbitrarily. So Love is blind, and so too
are those in love. Cf. *Son* 137.1–4:
'Thou blind fool love, what dost thou to
mine eyes, / That they behold, and see
not what they see? / They know what
beauty is, see where it lies, / Yet what
the best is, take the worst to be.'
67 **lights** power of vision
68 **chid at** rebuked
   ungartered another sign of the lover
   (garters kept stockings from falling
   down); cf. *AYL* 3.2.369: 'Then your

hose should be ungartered'.
70 **passing** surpassing, exceeding
72 **put . . . hose** Several unnecessary
emendations have been suggested in
Cam[1] – 'put on your shoes', 'beyond
your nose', 'put on your clothes' – but
the F reading sufficiently conveys
Speed's mockery of Valentine, the latter being in an even worse state than
Proteus, whom Valentine had formerly
rebuked for being in love in 1.1.
73 **Belike** See 1.2.85n.
76 **swinged** beat; cf. 3.1.369.
78 **stand affected to** am in love with
79 **set** seated, in contrast to Valentine's
   stand (78); a bawdy response to
   Valentine's unwitting pun on *stand* as
   an erection. Cf. 4.1.3–4.
   affection passion

62–3] *Capell; F lines* [2]her, / beautifull. /   73–4] *Rowe; F lines* morning / shooes. /

VALENTINE   Last night she enjoined me to write some   80
lines to one she loves.

SPEED   And have you?

VALENTINE   I have.

SPEED   Are they not lamely writ?

VALENTINE   No, boy, but as well as I can do them.   85

[*Enter* SILVIA.]

Peace, here she comes.

SPEED [*aside*]   O excellent motion! O exceeding puppet!
Now will he interpret to her.

VALENTINE

Madam and mistress, a thousand good-morrows.

SPEED [*aside*]   O, give ye good e'en! Here's a million of   90
manners.

SILVIA

Sir Valentine and servant, to you two thousand.

SPEED [*aside*]   He should give her interest, and she gives it
him.

80, 95 **enjoined** required

84 **lamely** Verse lines have metrical 'feet', hence the familiar joke; cf. *MA* 5.4.86: 'halting sonnet'.

87–8 Silvia is Valentine's *puppet*, since she has used him as an interpreter of her love (to himself). Cf. *Ham* 3.2.244–5: 'I could interpret between you and your love, if I could see the puppets dallying'; see Shershow for the rich cultural connotations of puppets. *OED* defines *motion* in this instance as 'puppet' (*sb.* 13b); however, 'puppet-show' (*sb.* 13a) seems more relevant. This passage contains three distinct elements: the show itself, the puppet and the interpreter.

88 **interpret** act like a chorus, in

describing a puppet's actions; cf. Jonson's *Bartholomew Fair*, 3.4.124: 'when you hear him interpret Master Littlewit's motion' (Jonson, 4.60).

90 **give ye** God give you

92 **servant** one dedicated to serve a lady – a term from the courtly love tradition (*OED sb.* 4b)

93–4 This speech can be interpreted in two ways: 'He should show romantic *interest* in her if (*and* = an) she has, by doubling his greeting from *a thousand* to *two thousand*, given him financial *interest*'; 'He ought to give her *interest* (romantic/financial) as he loves her, but instead (*and* implying "yet") she is giving it to him.'

80–1] *Pope; F lines* me, / loues. /   85–6] *Oxf; F lines* them: / comes. /   85.1] *Rowe*   87, 90, 93 SDs] *Victor*   87–8] *Theobald; F lines* Puppet: / her. /   90 give] ('giue)   ye good e'en] (ye-good-eu'n)

VALENTINE

> As you enjoined me, I have writ your letter   95
> Unto the secret, nameless friend of yours,
> Which I was much unwilling to proceed in
> But for my duty to your ladyship.   [*Gives her a letter.*]

SILVIA

> I thank you, gentle servant, 'tis very clerkly done.

VALENTINE

> Now trust me, madam, it came hardly off,   100
> For being ignorant to whom it goes
> I writ at random, very doubtfully.

SILVIA

> Perchance you think too much of so much pains?

VALENTINE

> No, madam; so it stead you, I will write,
> Please you command, a thousand times as much.   105
> And yet –

SILVIA

> A pretty period. Well, I guess the sequel;
> And yet I will not name it. And yet I care not.
> And yet take this again.   [*Offers him the letter.*]
>   And yet I thank you,
> Meaning henceforth to trouble you no more.   110

---

99 alexandrine; see 1.1.30n.
  clerkly written like a clerk or scholar
100 **it . . . off** it was very difficult
102 **very doubtfully** full of uncertainty
103 Perhaps you think the effort too great?
104 **so** provided that
  stead be of use to, assist (*OED v.* I 1a)
106 **And yet** – The dash is in F. Valentine presumably stops short of expressing in full his unwillingness to write any

more but in doing so expresses it anyway.
107 **period** end of a sentence (*OED sb.* 11). Silvia is being ironic in response to Valentine's loaded pause.
  sequel i.e. what he was going to say after *And yet*
108, 109, 111 **And yet** The repetitions of *And yet*, no doubt with pauses or emphases, mockingly echo Valentine's hesitation.

98 SD] *Capell subst.*   100 hardly off] *(*hardly-off*)*   104 stead] *(*steed*)*   107 guess] *(*ghesse*)*
109 SD] *Cam¹*

SPEED [*aside*]

   And yet you will, and yet another 'yet'!

VALENTINE

   What means your ladyship? Do you not like it?

SILVIA

   Yes, yes, the lines are very quaintly writ,

   But, since unwillingly, take them again.

   [*Offers the letter again.*]

   Nay, take them.

VALENTINE   Madam, they are for you.   115

SILVIA

   Ay, ay, you writ them, sir, at my request,

   But I will none of them. They are for you.

   I would have had them writ more movingly.

VALENTINE

   Please you, I'll write your ladyship another.

SILVIA

   And when it's writ, for my sake read it over,   120

   And if it please you, so. If not, why, so.

VALENTINE

   If it please me, madam? What then?

SILVIA

   Why, if it please you, take it for your labour.

   And so, good morrow, servant.   *Exit.*

SPEED [*aside*]

   O jest unseen, inscrutable, invisible   125

---

113 **quaintly** skilfully, elegantly; cf.
   3.1.117. For discussion of the play's
   letters, see pp. 59–67.
125–30 more of Speed's doggerel verse,
   as at 1.1.76, 78, 106–7 and 132–6

125–6 **invisible . . . face** proverbial: 'As
   plain (seen) as the nose on a man's face'
   (Dent, N215). Cf. *TN* 4.1.8: 'nor this
   is not my nose, neither. Nothing that is
   so is so.'

111 SD] *Rowe*   112] *Pope; F lines* Ladiship? / it? /   114 SD] *Cam¹ subst.*   121 so. . . . so.] *Oxf;* so:
if not: why so: *F*   124 good morrow] *(good-morrow)*   SD] *(Exit. Sil.)*   125 SD] *Penguin*
125–6] *as prose Pope*

As a nose on a man's face, or a weathercock on a
    steeple!
My master sues to her, and she hath taught her suitor,
He being her pupil, to become her tutor.
O excellent device, was there ever heard a better?
That my master, being scribe, to himself should write
    the letter?   130

VALENTINE   How now, sir? What, are you reasoning with
    yourself?

SPEED   Nay, I was rhyming; 'tis you that have the reason.

VALENTINE   To do what?

SPEED   To be a spokesman from Madam Silvia.   135

VALENTINE   To whom?

SPEED   To yourself. Why, she woos you by a figure.

VALENTINE   What figure?

SPEED   By a letter, I should say.

VALENTINE   Why, she hath not writ to me.   140

SPEED   What need she, when she hath made you write to
    yourself? Why, do you not perceive the jest?

VALENTINE   No, believe me.

SPEED   No believing you indeed, sir. But did you perceive
    her earnest?   145

VALENTINE   She gave me none, except an angry word.

SPEED   Why, she hath given you a letter.

---

127 **sues** pleads, appeals
130 **scribe** one who writes (i.e. her secre-
    tary)
131–3 **reasoning . . . rhyming** Speed
    plays on the proverbial 'rhyme and
    reason' (Dent, R98.1). Cf. *LLL*:
    '*Dumaine* In reason nothing. *Berowne*
    Something then in rhyme' (1.1.99) and

'A dangerous rhyme, master, against
the reason of white and red'
(1.2.102–3).
137 **a figure** a device, indirect means (the
    letter, 139); rhetorical trope; number,
    digit
145 **earnest** serious intention; initial
    down payment on a contract

130] *Pope; F lines* scribe, / Letter? /   131–2] *Pope; F lines* Sir? / selfe? /   131 What, are] *Collier;*
What are *F*   135 spokesman] *(Spokes-man)*   140 me.] *Rowe;* me? *F*   141–2] *Capell; F lines* ¹she,
/ selfe? / iest? /   144–5] *Pope; F lines* sir: / earnest? /

VALENTINE   That's the letter I writ to her friend.

SPEED   And that letter hath she delivered, and there an end.

VALENTINE   I would it were no worse.   150

SPEED   I'll warrant you, 'tis as well.

For often have you writ to her, and she, in modesty
Or else for want of idle time, could not again reply,
Or fearing else some messenger that might her mind
    discover,
Herself hath taught her love himself to write unto her
    lover.   155
All this I speak in print, for in print I found it. Why
    muse you, sir? 'Tis dinner-time.

VALENTINE   I have dined.

SPEED   Ay, but hearken, sir: though the chameleon Love
    can feed on the air, I am one that am nourished by my   160
    victuals, and would fain have meat. O, be not like your
    mistress – be moved, be moved!   *Exeunt.*

---

148 **friend** lover
149 **there an end** See 1.3.65n.
152–5 These rhyming lines (known as 'fourteeners') have seven metrical feet.
153 **want** lack
    idle time leisure
154 **fearing else** else fearing
    discover reveal
156 **All . . . it** Speed may be claiming to quote these four lines of verse from a book; they are sometimes printed in quotation marks. Cf. *AYL* 5.4.89: 'we quarrel in print, by the book'.
    speak in print recite accurately; cf. *LLL* 3.1.167: 'I will do it, sir, in print.'
156–7 **Why muse you** Why are you dreaming?
159–60 **chameleon . . . air** The

chameleon's reputed ability to feed itself on air was proverbial (Dent, M226). Cf. 2.4.25–7; also *Ham* 3.2.92–3, where Hamlet, when asked how he 'fares', replies: 'of the chameleon's dish: I eat the air, promise-crammed'. This ability to live on nothing was linked with the power of love: cf. Lyly, *Endymion*, 3.4.129, 'Love is a Camelion, which draweth nothing into the mouth but aire' (Lyly, 3.50). Valentine has presumably *dined* (158) on love; cf. 2.4.139–40.
161 **fain** gladly (*OED* B)
    meat food
162 **be moved** have compassion; go to dinner

156–7] *Dyce; F lines* it. / time. /   157 dinner-time] *(dinner time)*

173

2.2   *Enter* PROTEUS [*and*] JULIA.

PROTEUS

Have patience, gentle Julia.

JULIA

I must, where is no remedy.

PROTEUS

When possibly I can, I will return.

JULIA

If you turn not, you will return the sooner.

Keep this remembrance for thy Julia's sake.   5

[*Gives him a ring.*]

PROTEUS

Why then, we'll make exchange: here, take you this.

[*Gives her a ring.*]

JULIA

And seal the bargain with a holy kiss.   [*They kiss.*]

PROTEUS

Here is my hand for my true constancy.

And when that hour o'erslips me in the day

Wherein I sigh not, Julia, for thy sake,   10

2.2 The action shifts back to Verona. Cam[1] places the lovers '*on a seat beneath the trees*', but again, there is no specific reference to a location in the scene.

1–2 proverbial (Dent, R71 and R71.1); cf. *Mac* 3.2.13–14: 'Things without all remedy / Should be without regard.'

2   where is where there is

4   turn not remain constant; do not change

5–6 A familiar device of comedy, the lovers' exchange of rings will be central to the plot resolutions of the final scene, as in *MV* and *AW*; cf. 4.4.69–71.

7   holy kiss Cf. *RJ* 1.5.96–7: 'My lips, two blushing pilgrims, ready stand / To smooth that rough touch with a tender kiss.' This scene represents a spousal ceremony, with exchange of rings, kiss and handclasp, though the language does not quite say it and there are no witnesses. See Cook, 204, on this subject. Julia's taking the initiative here (she is without *patience*, 1) anticipates her pursuit of Proteus later. Cf. 2.4.177 where Valentine is also *betrothed*, echoed by Silvia at 4.2.107.

9   o'erslips passes by

2.2] *Scoena secunda. F*   0.1] *Rowe; Enter Protheus, Iulia, Panthion. F*   5 SD] *Rowe subst.*   6] *Pope; F lines* exchange; / this. /   SD] *Dyce subst.*   7 SD] *Bantam*

The next ensuing hour some foul mischance
Torment me for my love's forgetfulness.
My father stays my coming; answer not.
The tide is now – nay, not thy tide of tears,
That tide will stay me longer than I should.   15
Julia, farewell.   [*Exit Julia.*]
              What, gone without a word?
Ay, so true love should do: it cannot speak,
For truth hath better deeds than words to grace it.

[*Enter* PANTINO.]

PANTINO
  Sir Proteus, you are stayed for.
PROTEUS   Go, I come, I come.   19
  Alas, this parting strikes poor lovers dumb.   *Exeunt.*

13 **stays** is waiting for
14–15 Parodying these lines, Lance will pun on *tide* = *tied* at 2.3.35–6; Lance will later seem to have witnessed this scene between Proteus and Julia (see 2.5.11–12n.).
14 **The tide** i.e. the high tide for the departure of a ship. See 1.1.54n. on *shipped*.
15 **stay** delay
16–18 **What . . . it** proverbial (Dent, L165). Cf. 1.2.32n.; *MND* 5.1.104–5: 'Love, therefore, and tongue-tied simplicity / In least speak most'; and *KL* 1.1.62: 'Love, and be silent.' In *Diana*, 87, Felix (= Proteus) is so sad that he leaves without ever seeing Felismena (= Julia).

18 **deeds than words** proverbial (Dent, W820); cf. *1H6* 3.2.48: 'let no words, but deeds, revenge' and *H8* 3.2.154: 'words are no deeds'.
   grace adorn
19 **you . . . for** 'They are waiting for you.'
   I . . . come The second *I come* has sometimes been taken for a compositor's erroneous repetition; its deletion would regularize the metre, as would elision of *you are* to *you're* (RP). Either adjustment would render the rhyming couplet clearer. The F reading is retained because the repetition and excess indicate Proteus's anxiety, and the rhyme will be heard in any case.

16 SD] *Rowe opp. 15*   18.1] *Rowe subst.*   19 I . . . come] I come *Pope*

2.3 *Enter* LANCE [*with his dog Crab*].

LANCE Nay, 'twill be this hour ere I have done weeping; all
the kind of the Lances have this very fault. I have
received my proportion, like the prodigious son, and am
going with Sir Proteus to the Imperial's court. I think
Crab my dog be the sourest-natured dog that lives: my   5
mother weeping, my father wailing, my sister crying,
our maid howling, our cat wringing her hands and all
our house in a great perplexity, yet did not this

2.3 The setting remains Verona. This
scene mirrors the previous one, especially Lance's *weeping* and Julia's *tide of
tears* (2.2.14). See p. 127, for this
scene's place in the play's composition.

0.1 **Crab* The dog's name suggests the
crab-apple, known as bitter, as in *sourest-
natured* (5) (cf. *TS* 2.1.228–9), and thus
his disposition, as ill-tempered; the
dog's manner of walking may resemble
a crab's (e.g. a bulldog?). Shakespeare's
patterns of imagery were said to reveal a
dislike of dogs (Spurgeon, 195–9),
though it does not seem evident here.
Beadle, 18, notes that in one of *Tarlton's
Jests*, Richard Tarlton, one of Kemp's
predecessors in the clown tradition, is
said 'in his travaile [to have] had a
Dogge of fine qualities'; in another
of the jests, Tarlton is described as
kneeling to his father and asking his
blessing, in response to which the
father throws an apple at him. Tarlton
then jests, 'But as for an Apple he hath
cast a Crab, / So in stead of an honest
woman God hath sent me a Drab'
(Beadle, 19–20). See pp. 67–75.

1–30 Lance's speeches throughout the
play are entirely in prose.

1 **ere** before

2 **kind** family, kin

2–3 **I . . . son** Lance alludes to the parable
of the Prodigal Son (Luke, 15.11–32)
but his reference may be ironically self-

condemning, as the Prodigal Son wastes
his inheritance but is welcomed home
and forgiven by his father. The issue of
forgiveness introduced here through the
Prodigal Son parable returns in 5.4, as
Proteus, Valentine and the Outlaws are
all forgiven. Noble, 277, notes that the
Prodigal Son is 'the most frequently
mentioned Parable of the Gospels in
[Shakespeare's] plays'. See pp. 35–41.

3 **proportion** malapropism for 'portion',
inheritance; but possibly also with
sense of equity: 'Due relation of one
part to another' (*OED sb.* 4)
prodigious malapropism for 'prodigal'; 'Of extraordinarily large size'
(*OED a.* 4). Campbell, 'Actors', 181,
suggests this may be a comic reference
to the actor's size, as Kemp, who may
have played Lance, 'was large and
slow', in obvious contrast here to
Speed (see List of Roles, 10n.). The
word usually connoted something
'ominous, portentous' (*OED a.* 1; cf.
MND 5.1.407: 'Nor mark prodigious')
or 'Causing wonder or amazement;
marvellous, amazing; (in a bad sense)
monstrous' (*OED a.* 3).

4 **Imperial's** malapropism for 'Emperor's'; see List of Roles, 1n., and
1.3.27n.

5 **be** is; Abbott, 299, suggests that this
form 'is used with some notion of
doubt, question, thought'.

2.3] *Scoena Tertia.* F 0.1 *Enter* LANCE] *Rowe; Enter Launce, Panthion.* F *with . . . Crab*] *Pope*
5 sourest-natured] *(sowrest natured)*

cruel-hearted cur shed one tear. He is a stone, a very
pebblestone, and has no more pity in him than a dog. A   10
Jew would have wept to have seen our parting. Why, my
grandam, having no eyes, look you, wept herself blind at
my parting. Nay, I'll show you the manner of it. This
shoe is my father. No, this left shoe is my father. No, no,
this left shoe is my mother. Nay, that cannot be so   15
neither. Yes, it is so, it is so: it hath the worser sole. This
shoe with the hole in it is my mother, and this my father.
A vengeance on't – there 'tis. Now, sir, this staff is my
sister; for, look you, she is as white as a lily and as small
as a wand. This hat is Nan, our maid. I am the dog. No,   20
the dog is himself, and I am the dog. O, the dog is me,
and I am myself. Ay, so, so. Now come I to my father:
'Father, your blessing.' Now should not the shoe speak

10 **no . . . dog** proverbial (Dent, D510.1:
'To have as much pity as a dog'). Crab
shows no apparent response or
sympathy (though stage dogs have
been known to engage in all kinds of
doggy behaviour). Skura, 161, notes
that Crab here is '"dog" as *symbol* or
sign of cruelty . . . [as well as] more
immediately "dog" as dog or *referent*'.
See States.
11 **Jew** Jews were proverbially hard-
hearted (Dent, J50.1: 'It would make a
Jew rue'); perhaps also a link to *MV*
and Lancelot Gobbo. Lance displaces
his resentments here and at 2.5.45–7
onto the most marginalized of social
subgroups.
12 **grandam** grandmother
   having no eyes i.e. blind
13–28 **This . . . down** Lance presumably
takes his shoes off during the speech,
as he gives both a *kiss* (24, 26).
16 **worser sole** It belongs to the mother
because the female has the inferior 'soul'
to the male, according to misogynistic

tradition.
17 **hole** i.e. female genitals. Lance's
bawdy is as unintentional here as his
malapropisms, but the clown's comic
function is traditionally to exemplify
the lower world of the body through
obscenity and blasphemy; see Bakhtin.
Simmons, 860, observes that this reference is to 'the only mother in the
play', and that the sole/soul pun establishes 'the theological justification of
female inferiority and the more important physical reality of "the hole" that
gives the play space for its preoccupation with male subjectivity'.
19 **white . . . lily** proverbial (Dent, L296)
   small slender
20 **wand** stick
   Nan The *maid*'s race was specified in
Victor's adaptation (followed by
Kemble and others) – 'This hat is Nan
– ay, black Nan, our maid' (Victor, 21)
– perhaps because of the proliferation
of black servants in eighteenth-
century London.

10 pebblestone] *(pibble stone)*

a word for weeping. Now should I kiss my father – well,
he weeps on. Now come I to my mother: O, that she   25
could speak now, like a wood woman! Well, I kiss her.
Why there 'tis – here's my mother's breath up and
down. Now come I to my sister: mark the moan she
makes. Now the dog all this while sheds not a tear nor
speaks a word; but see how I lay the dust with my tears.   30

[*Enter* PANTINO.]

PANTINO   Lance, away, away! Aboard! Thy master is
shipped, and thou art to post after with oars. What's the
matter? Why weep'st thou, man? Away, ass, you'll lose
the tide if you tarry any longer.

26 *a wood woman** a mad (or furious) woman. Some editors have argued that this meaning is 'inappropriate in the context' (Penguin). Others have been reluctant to drop the 'l' in 'would' because it was sometimes still pronounced at the time and so it seemed an unlikely compositorial error for 'wood'. Plenty of evidence exists, however, to suggest that 'would' and 'wood' were already potential homophones (see Kökeritz, 311, n. 4). Indeed, elsewhere in Shakespeare, the spellings 'would' and 'wood' are used interchangeably (see *MW* Q 2.2.178, 'Would you wood helpe me to beare it', cited Kökeritz, 312). Several emendations have been proposed: Pope's 'an old' (which assumes an F misprint of 'a nould'); 'wold', an obsolete (already in Shakespeare's time) form of the word 'old' (Folg²; see Werstine⁴); and 'moved', the result of a misreading (Oxf; see Wells, *Re-Editing*, 36). But Theobald's emendation still seems the most reasonable. Shakespeare uses

'wood' in the same sense – as 'mad' (*OED a.* 1) or 'enraged, furious' (*OED a.* 3b) – in *MND* 2.1.192: 'here am I, and wood within this wood'. Bond suggests 'a pun on the material of which his shoes are made'.

27–8 **my . . . down** Sanders thinks that 'Launce makes the shoe representing his mother give out a squeaking sound *up and down* like an asthmatic old woman', but surely Lance is smelling the shoe, identifying it with his mother's bad *breath* (*up and down* = 'in every respect; entirely, thoroughly' (*OED adv.* 6a)).

28 **mark** listen to
    moan lamentation

30 **lay . . . tears** Cf. *R2* 3.3.43: 'lay the summer's dust with showers of blood' and *KL* 4.6.192–3: 'To use his eyes for garden water-pots. / Ay, and laying autumn's dust'.

32 **shipped** Cf. 49n. and see 1.1.54n.
    post hurry
    with oars in a rowing boat

33 **lose** miss

26 a wood woman] *Theobald;* a would-woman *F;* an ould woman *Pope;* a moved woman *Oxf;* a wold woman *Folg²*   30.1] *Rowe subst.*   31 Aboard] *(*a Boord*)*

LANCE   It is no matter if the tied were lost, for it is the   35
    unkindest tied that ever any man tied.
PANTINO   What's the unkindest tide?
LANCE   Why, he that's tied here, Crab, my dog.
PANTINO   Tut, man, I mean thou'lt lose the flood, and in
    losing the flood, lose thy voyage, and in losing thy   40
    voyage, lose thy master, and in losing thy master, lose
    thy service, and in losing thy service – why dost thou
    stop my mouth?
LANCE   For fear thou shouldst lose thy tongue.
PANTINO   Where should I lose my tongue?   45
LANCE   In thy tale.
PANTINO   In thy tail!
LANCE   Lose the tide, and the voyage, and the master, and
    the service, and the tied? Why, man, if the river were
    dry, I am able to fill it with my tears; if the wind were   50
    down, I could drive the boat with my sighs.
PANTINO   Come, come away, man. I was sent to call thee.
LANCE   Sir, call me what thou dar'st.
PANTINO   Wilt thou go?   54
LANCE   Well, I will go.   *Exeunt.*

---

36 **unkindest** most unnatural; cf. *JC*
3.2.181: 'the most unkindest cut of all'.
39 **flood** the favourable tide
42 **service** place as a servant
45–7 Lance's obscenity here is presumably unintentional, as at *hole* (17), but
Pantino certainly hears it; cf. *TS*
2.1.218: 'What, with my tongue in
your tail?' Hanmer's emendation (see
t.n.) is 'anatomically difficult' (*TxC*,
167). Pantino may repeat Lance's line
in confusion, as a question, as a witty
response or in exasperation, perhaps
emphasizing *thy* with a kick in his rear

(as suggested in Cam[2] SD). RP notes a
parallel in Peele's *The Old Wife's Tale*,
l. 117: 'Nay either heare my tale, or
kisse my taile' (Peele, 391).
49 **river** The *river* in Verona, the Adige,
seems to have a *tide*; see 1.1.54n.,
2.2.14n.
50–1 **tears . . . sighs** clichés of
Petrarchan love poetry, mirroring the
lovers' parting in 2.2; cf. Romeo 'With
tears augmenting the fresh morning's
dew, / Adding to clouds more clouds
with his deep sighs' (*RJ* 1.1.132–3).
52 **call** summon

35–6 tied . . . ¹tied] *Theobald* (ty'd . . . ty'd); tide . . . Tide *F*   36 ²tied] *Rowe* (ty'd); tide *F*   38
tied] *Rowe* (ty'd); tide *F*   47 thy] my *Hanmer*   48 tide] flood *Pope*   49 tied] *Singer²*; tide *F*

2.4   *Enter* VALENTINE, SILVIA, TURIO [*and*] SPEED.

SILVIA   Servant!

VALENTINE   Mistress?

SPEED   Master, Sir Turio frowns on you.

VALENTINE   Ay, boy, it's for love.

SPEED   Not of you.   5

VALENTINE   Of my mistress then.

SPEED   'Twere good you knocked him.   [*Exit.*]

SILVIA   Servant, you are sad.

VALENTINE   Indeed, madam, I seem so.

TURIO   Seem you that you are not?   10

VALENTINE   Haply I do.

TURIO   So do counterfeits.

VALENTINE   So do you.

TURIO   What seem I that I am not?

VALENTINE   Wise.   15

TURIO   What instance of the contrary?

VALENTINE   Your folly.

TURIO   And how quote you my folly?

VALENTINE   I quote it in your jerkin.

2.4 The action is set in Milan, usually located in the Duke's palace.

3 Presumably Turio is jealous because Silvia addresses Valentine rather than himself.

7 **knocked** struck

7 SD *Speed has no further lines to speak in this scene, it therefore seems appropriate that he exit here. Some editors allow him to remain onstage, on the grounds that 'as Valentine's page, he could remain in silent attendance' (Wells, *Re-Editing*, 74–5), but he still must be given an exit (absent entirely in Oxf) somewhere in the scene.

11 **Haply** perhaps

12 **counterfeits** deceivers

16 **instance** proof; cf. *MW* 2.2.235–6: 'my desires had instance and argument to commend themselves' and *AYL* 3.2.49: 'Instance, briefly; come, instance.'

18 **how quote you** in what do you observe

19 As *quote* and 'coat' were homophones (see Kökeritz, 99), Valentine is punning here, hence *jerkin*.
   jerkin a short coat or jacket worn over or instead of a doublet

---

2.4] *Scena Quarta. F* 0.1] *Rowe; Enter Valentine, Siluia, Thurio, Speed, Duke, Protheus. F* 1 Servant!] *Staunton;* Seruant. *F;* Servant, – *Theobald* 2 Mistress?] *Theobald;* Mistris. *F* 7 SD] *Cam* 11 Haply] *(Hap'ly)*

TURIO My jerkin is a doublet. 20

VALENTINE Well, then, I'll double your folly.

TURIO How!

SILVIA What, angry, Sir Turio? Do you change colour?

VALENTINE Give him leave, madam, he is a kind of chameleon. 25

TURIO That hath more mind to feed on your blood than live in your air.

VALENTINE You have said, sir.

TURIO Ay, sir, and done too, for this time.

VALENTINE I know it well, sir. You always end ere you 30 begin.

SILVIA A fine volley of words, gentlemen, and quickly shot off.

VALENTINE 'Tis indeed, madam, we thank the giver.

SILVIA Who is that, servant? 35

VALENTINE Yourself, sweet lady, for you gave the fire. Sir Turio borrows his wit from your ladyship's looks, and spends what he borrows kindly in your company.

TURIO Sir, if you spend word for word with me, I shall make your wit bankrupt. 40

VALENTINE I know it well, sir. You have an exchequer of words and, I think, no other treasure to give your

---

20 **doublet** a short and loose coat-like garment
21 **double** punning on *doublet* in previous line
24–7 **he . . . air** See 2.1.159–60n.
28–9 echoing the proverbial 'no sooner said than done' (see Dent, S117); cf. *TS* 1.2.184: 'So said, so done.'
30–3 **You . . . off** Valentine jokes that Turio stops before he comes to an actual duel; has little wit, ending

before he can begin; and (possibly) suffers from premature ejaculation, and is thus incapable of satisfying a woman (perhaps mockingly echoed in Silvia's *quickly shot off*).
30 **ere** before
36 **fire** the spark that ignited the *volley*; Valentine continues Silvia's metaphor of firearms (32–3).
38 **kindly** naturally; properly
41 **exchequer** treasury

36–8] *Pope; F lines* fire, / lookes, / company. /   41–4] *Pope; F lines* words, / followers: / Liueries / words. /

181

followers, for it appears by their bare liveries that they
live by your bare words.

[*Enter* DUKE.]

SILVIA   No more, gentlemen, no more. Here comes my   45
father.

DUKE

Now, daughter Silvia, you are hard beset.
Sir Valentine, your father is in good health;
What say you to a letter from your friends
Of much good news?

VALENTINE   My lord, I will be thankful   50
To any happy messenger from thence.

DUKE

Know ye Don Antonio, your countryman?

VALENTINE

Ay, my good lord, I know the gentleman
To be of worth, and worthy estimation,
And not without desert so well reputed.   55

DUKE

Hath he not a son?

VALENTINE

Ay, my good lord, a son that well deserves
The honour and regard of such a father.

DUKE

You know him well?

43–4 it . . . **words** Valentine accuses
Turio of meanness in letting his servants be poorly dressed (cf. 173, where
Valentine says that Turio's 'possessions are so huge').
44 **bare words** worthless words; words
alone
47 **hard beset** strongly besieged (by

suitors)
49 **What say you** what would you say
51 **happy messenger** bringer of good
news
52 **Don** suggests a Spaniard; see 1.3.39n.
54 **worthy estimation** good reputation
55 **desert** deserving

44.1] *Rowe after 46*   45–6] *Pope; F lines* more: / father. /   52 ye] you *Cam¹*   54 worth] wealth
Collier²

VALENTINE

I knew him as myself, for from our infancy   60
We have conversed and spent our hours together.
And though myself have been an idle truant,
Omitting the sweet benefit of time
To clothe mine age with angel-like perfection,
Yet hath Sir Proteus, for that's his name,   65
Made use and fair advantage of his days:
His years but young, but his experience old;
His head unmellowed, but his judgement ripe;
And in a word, for far behind his worth
Comes all the praises that I now bestow,   70
He is complete in feature and in mind,
With all good grace to grace a gentleman.

DUKE

Beshrew me, sir, but if he make this good,
He is as worthy for an empress' love,
As meet to be an emperor's counsellor.   75
Well, sir, this gentleman is come to me
With commendation from great potentates,
And here he means to spend his time awhile.
I think 'tis no unwelcome news to you.

---

60 alexandrine; see 1.1.30n.
   knew Hanmer's present tense 'know' has frequently been accepted, but the past tense in this context was a common usage (see Abbott, 347); cf. *AC* 1.4.85: 'I knew it for my bond.'
61 **conversed** been companions; talked
62–72 Valentine ironically believes that Proteus exceeds him in all ways, when in fact Proteus will have much more to learn about himself.
63 **Omitting** neglecting
65, 182 **Proteus** trisyllabic; see 1.1.1n.
68 **unmellowed** i.e. without grey hair
70 **Comes** the singular form of the verb

preceding a plural subject (Abbott, 335)
71 **complete** perfect
   feature body, appearance
73 **Beshrew me** mild oath
   make this good prove equal to this description
74–5 **empress' ... emperor's** Although the imperial titles are generic, the Duke may be implicitly referring to his own status and that of his daughter; cf. *potentates* (77), another indirect boosting of personal status. See notes on List of Roles, 1, 1.3.27, and p. 125.
75 **meet** suitable

60 knew] know *Hanmer*   70 Comes] Come *Rowe*   75 counsellor] *(Councellor)*

VALENTINE

    Should I have wished a thing, it had been he.   80

DUKE

    Welcome him then according to his worth.

    Silvia, I speak to you, and you, Sir Turio;

    For Valentine, I need not cite him to it.

    I will send him hither to you presently.   *[Exit.]*

VALENTINE

    This is the gentleman I told your ladyship   85

    Had come along with me, but that his mistress

    Did hold his eyes locked in her crystal looks.

SILVIA

    Belike that now she hath enfranchised them

    Upon some other pawn for fealty.

VALENTINE

    Nay, sure, I think she holds them prisoners still.   90

SILVIA

    Nay, then he should be blind, and being blind

    How could he see his way to seek out you?

VALENTINE

    Why, lady, Love hath twenty pair of eyes.

TURIO

    They say that Love hath not an eye at all.

VALENTINE

    To see such lovers, Turio, as yourself;   95

---

83 **cite** incite; urge
84 **presently** immediately
86 **Had** would have
87 **crystal looks** a cliché of Petrarchan poetry; cf. *VA* 633: 'thy soft hands, sweet lips, and crystal eyne'.
88 **Belike that** perhaps
88–9 **enfranchised . . . fealty** set his eyes free in exchange for some other token of loyalty. The vocabulary is chivalric, as *fealty* describes a feudal obligation between a tenant or vassal and his lord (*OED* 1).
90 Valentine misinterprets Silvia to mean that Julia has accepted a pledge from some other lover and that she and Proteus are no longer together, which he immediately repudiates.
93–4 See 2.1.66n.

84 SD] *Rowe*

184

Upon a homely object, Love can wink.

[Enter PROTEUS.]

SILVIA

Have done, have done. Here comes the gentleman.

VALENTINE

Welcome, dear Proteus! Mistress, I beseech you

Confirm his welcome with some special favour.

SILVIA

His worth is warrant for his welcome hither,   100

If this be he you oft have wished to hear from.

VALENTINE

Mistress, it is. Sweet lady, entertain him

To be my fellow-servant to your ladyship.

SILVIA

Too low a mistress for so high a servant.

PROTEUS

Not so, sweet lady, but too mean a servant   105

To have a look of such a worthy mistress.

VALENTINE

Leave off discourse of disability.

Sweet lady, entertain him for your servant.

PROTEUS

My duty will I boast of, nothing else.

SILVIA

And duty never yet did want his meed.   110

Servant, you are welcome to a worthless mistress.

---

96 **homely** plain
  wink close its eyes
102–3 **entertain . . . ladyship** chivalric
  terminology meaning 'take him into
  your service'; cf. *KL* 3.6.75–6: 'You,
  sir, I entertain you for one of my hundred.'

104 **Too low** in social terms (though
  Silvia is daughter of a duke); in height
105 **mean** lowly, humble
106 **of** from
107 **disability** unworthiness
108 **entertain** See 102–3n.
110 **want his meed** lack its reward

96.1] *Rowe; Enter. F2*   97 gentleman.] gentleman. *Exit Thurio / Collier*   106 worthy] *F2;* worthy a *F*

PROTEUS

    I'll die on him that says so but yourself.

SILVIA

    That you are welcome?

PROTEUS   That you are worthless.

[Enter Servant.]

SERVANT

    Madam, my lord your father would speak with you.

SILVIA

    I wait upon his pleasure.   *[Exit Servant.]*

                – Come, Sir Turio,   115

    Go with me. – Once more, new servant, welcome.

    I'll leave you to confer of home affairs;

    When you have done, we look to hear from you.

PROTEUS

    We'll both attend upon your ladyship.

                [Exeunt Silvia and Turio.]

VALENTINE

    Now tell me: how do all from whence you came?   120

PROTEUS

    Your friends are well and have them much
      commended.

112–13 Proteus's chivalric hyperbole anticipates the betrayal which will become clear in his soliloquy at 189–211.

112 **die on** die fighting against

113.1–114 SP *Theobald's introduction of a servant here, and his transfer of the speech from Turio to the servant, still seems justified. Some editors have the servant enter and whisper to Turio, thus permitting him to speak 114. Collier has Turio exit at 97 as Proteus

enters, then re-enter here (rather than the servant); but then Turio must still exit again at 119.

117 **confer** talk, converse
    home affairs i.e. news from Verona

119 SD *The servant's exit has occasionally been placed here, along with that of Silvia and Turio. Most editors who do not have Speed exit at 7 include him too in this exit SD.

121 **have . . . commended** send their kind regards

113.1] *Theobald; Enter Thurio / Collier*   114 SP] *Theobald; Thur. F*   115 SD] *Theobald*   116 new servant] my new servant *Pope*   118 to] *(too)*   119 SD] *Rowe; Exeunt Silvia, Thurio, Speed and Att. / Capell; Exeunt Silvia,Thurio, and Speed. / Malone*

VALENTINE

  And how do yours?

PROTEUS   I left them all in health.

VALENTINE

  How does your lady? And how thrives your love?

PROTEUS

  My tales of love were wont to weary you;

  I know you joy not in a love-discourse.   125

VALENTINE

  Ay, Proteus, but that life is altered now.

  I have done penance for contemning Love,

  Whose high imperious thoughts have punished me

  With bitter fasts, with penitential groans,

  With nightly tears and daily heart-sore sighs;   130

  For in revenge of my contempt of love,

  Love hath chased sleep from my enthralled eyes,

  And made them watchers of mine own heart's sorrow.

  O gentle Proteus, Love's a mighty lord,

  And hath so humbled me as I confess   135

  There is no woe to his correction,

  Nor to his service no such joy on earth.

  Now, no discourse, except it be of love;

  Now can I break my fast, dine, sup and sleep

  Upon the very naked name of love.   140

---

124 **were wont** used

127 **contemning** disdaining, scorning

128 **imperious** lofty, dominating; *Love* is the *mighty lord* (134) to whose *service* (137) Valentine pledges himself.

129–33 Valentine describes his love agony in stereotypical terms.

132 **enthralled** enthrallèd; captivated, enslaved. Cf. *MND* 3.1.134: 'So is mine eye enthrallèd to thy shape'.

133 **watchers** observers

134 **mighty lord** Cf. 1.1.38–9n. and 2.6.6–8n.

135 **as** that

136 **to his correction** i.e. compared to the punishment love inflicts; *correction* is pronounced with four syllables.

137 i.e. nor any joy on earth compared to being love's servant

139–40 Cf. 2.1.159–60n.

140 **very naked** mere

PROTEUS

    Enough; I read your fortune in your eye.

    Was this the idol that you worship so?

VALENTINE

    Even she; and is she not a heavenly saint?

PROTEUS

    No, but she is an earthly paragon.

VALENTINE

    Call her divine.

PROTEUS   I will not flatter her.   145

VALENTINE

    O, flatter me, for love delights in praises.

PROTEUS

    When I was sick, you gave me bitter pills,

    And I must minister the like to you.

VALENTINE

    Then speak the truth by her; if not divine,

    Yet let her be a principality,   150

    Sovereign to all the creatures on the earth.

PROTEUS

    Except my mistress.

VALENTINE   Sweet, except not any,

    Except thou wilt except against my love.

---

141 **your fortune** 'how things have turned out for you'

142–5 Proteus's word *idol* (142) indicates he believes Valentine is over-idealizing his love; cf. 4.2.125n. Valentine's responses – *heavenly saint* (143), *divine* (145) – prove Proteus correct; cf. *Son* 105.1–2: 'Let not my love be called idolatry, / Nor my beloved as an idol show.' In *TNK* 2.2.163–5, Arcite rebukes Palamon's idolatry: 'I will not as you do, to worship her / As she is heavenly and a blessed goddess. / I love her as a woman, to enjoy her'; as Potter, 192, points out in her note on these lines, *TNK* is very close to its source, Chaucer's *Knight's Tale*, here.

144 **earthly paragon** Cf. *Cym* 3.6.42–3: 'By Jupiter, an angel! Or, if not, / An earthly paragon!'

147–8 the metaphor of love as a disease; cf. 2.1.35–8n. and *MM* 4.6.7–8: ''tis a physic / That's bitter to sweet end'. Proteus's words again foreshadow his betrayal.

149 **by** about

150–1 **principality . . . earth** i.e. celestial being; member of one of the nine orders of angels (*OED* principality *sb.* 4)

152 **Except . . . except** excluding . . . exclude

153 **Except . . . against** unless you will take exception to

PROTEUS

    Have I not reason to prefer mine own?

VALENTINE

    And I will help thee to prefer her too: 155

    She shall be dignified with this high honour,

    To bear my lady's train, lest the base earth

    Should from her vesture chance to steal a kiss,

    And of so great a favour growing proud

    Disdain to root the summer-swelling flower   160

    And make rough winter everlastingly.

PROTEUS

    Why, Valentine, what braggartism is this?

VALENTINE

    Pardon me, Proteus, all I can is nothing

    To her, whose worth makes other worthies nothing;

    She is alone.

PROTEUS   Then let her alone.   165

VALENTINE

    Not for the world! Why, man, she is mine own,

    And I as rich in having such a jewel

    As twenty seas, if all their sand were pearl,

154–5 **prefer . . . prefer** like better . . . advance, promote
156–61 Valentine retorts that Proteus's beloved will be *dignified* and elevated by serving Silvia and holding her *train* ('elongated part of a . . . skirt trailing behind on the ground; commonly worn . . . by sovereigns', *OED sb.*[1] II 5) off the ground. The danger, he says, in an elaborate, hyperbolic personification (characterized by Proteus as *braggartism*, 162), is that should the *base earth* happen to *steal a kiss* (i.e. if the garment touches the ground), it would grow so *proud* that it would neglect its usual duties, such as rooting the flowers of summer, and hence bring in the catastrophe of an everlasting *rough winter*.
163 **can** can say
164 **To** compared to
    worthies qualities of excellence; worthy women
165 'She is unique. Then let her be.'
166–9 Valentine's claim to Silvia is both poetic and patriarchically possessive.

155 too] *(to)*   162 braggartism] *(Bragadisme)*   164 makes] *F2;* make *F*   165 Then] Why then *Hanmer*

The water nectar and the rocks pure gold.
Forgive me that I do not dream on thee,   170
Because thou seest me dote upon my love.
My foolish rival, that her father likes
Only for his possessions are so huge,
Is gone with her along, and I must after;
For love, thou knowst, is full of jealousy.   175

PROTEUS

But she loves you?

VALENTINE

Ay, and we are betrothed; nay more, our marriage
    hour,
With all the cunning manner of our flight,
Determined of: how I must climb her window,
The ladder made of cords, and all the means   180
Plotted and 'greed on for my happiness.

The word *jewel* (cf. 3.1.90, 4.4.46n.) stands for Silvia's value (*rich*) but also, in the drama of the period, for her sexuality – literally, her maidenhead (cf. *TNK* 5.4.119: 'your stol'n jewel' and Williams, 173). Similar references lead, in tragedy, to disaster, as in those of Leantio to his wife, Bianca, in Middleton, *Women Beware*: 'a most matchless jewel' (1.1.162) and 'The jewel is cased up from all men's eyes' (1.1.170).

170 **I . . . thee** i.e. '[I] seem careless in my welcome' (Ard[1]) or 'you are no longer my sole occupation' (RP). Valentine reveals here, before Proteus's confession at 189–211, that friendship for him is now subordinated to love.

172–3 Cf. 3.1.63–6 and n.

173 **for** because
    possessions . . . huge as well as a reference to his wealth, perhaps a comic glance at Turio's physical attributes. Cf. 43–4n.

175 **love . . . jealousy** proverbial (Dent, L510)

177 **betrothed** Valentine and Silvia have secretly exchanged troth-plight and are *betrothed* (cf. 4.2.105–7), committed to marry each other, even though Silvia's father prefers Turio. Cf. Proteus and Julia's spousal ceremony, 2.2.5–7 (see 2.2.7n.).

178 **our flight** Shakespeare anticipates here the flight of Hermia and Lysander in *MND*.

179–80 **how . . . cords** The plot with the ladder is found in *Romeus*, ll. 775–6: 'Of corde I will bespeake, a ladder by that time, / By which, this night, . . . I will your window clime'; climbing a tower to a prohibited lover is a common motif. Cf. Middleton, *The Family of Love*, 1.2.136–7: 'I prithee, love, attempt not to ascend / My chamber-window by a ladder'd rope' (Middleton, 3.19).

180 **cords** rope

181 **'greed** agreed

Good Proteus, go with me to my chamber
In these affairs to aid me with thy counsel.

PROTEUS

Go on before; I shall enquire you forth.
I must unto the road to disembark   185
Some necessaries that I needs must use,
And then I'll presently attend you.

VALENTINE

Will you make haste?

PROTEUS   I will.   *Exit* [*Valentine*].

Even as one heat another heat expels,
Or as one nail by strength drives out another,   190
So the remembrance of my former love
Is by a newer object quite forgotten.
Is it mine eye, or Valentine's praise,
Her true perfection, or my false transgression
That makes me reasonless to reason thus?   195

---

182 Valentine proposes to go to his *chamber*, but at 174 he intended to follow Silvia and Turio.
183 **counsel** advice; see 1.1.51n.
184 **enquire you forth** ask after you
185 **road** harbour; cf. 1.1.53n.
187 **presently** right away
189–211 Proteus's soliloquy, in its surrender to passion and self-conflict, is an important step in complicating his character; it anticipates Angelo's soliloquy in *MM* at the end of 2.2. Some actors (e.g. Mark Rylance (Shepherd)) have implied the beginning of a sense of shame or guilt even here, when Proteus accepts the need to betray his friend.
189–92 proverbial (see Dent, F277); cf. *Cor* 4.7.54: 'One fire drives out one fire; one nail, one nail.' Possibly echoing *Romeus*, ll. 206–10: 'The proverbe

saith, unminded oft are they that are unseene / And as out of a planke a naile a naile doth drive, / So novell love out of the minde the auncient love doth rive. / This sodain kindled fire in time is wox so great, / That onely death and both their blouds might quench the fiery heate.'
192 **by** because of
193 ***Is . . . eye** The F2 correction recognizes the problem here, and Theobald's insertion of *eye* (= sight of her) is justified on grounds both of metre and of sense.
   Valentine's The variations in Valentine's name which have been suggested are attempts to bring the line to an even ten syllables.
195 **reasonless** without justification; irrational

---

188 SD *Exit*] *Rowe; opp.* haste? *F; om. F2–4   Valentine*] *Rowe   193 Is it*] *F2; It is F   mine eye,*] *Theobald; mine, F; mine then, F2   Valentine's*] *Valentineans F2; Valentino's / Rowe; Valentinus' Malone*

She is fair; and so is Julia that I love –
That I did love, for now my love is thawed,
Which like a waxen image 'gainst a fire
Bears no impression of the thing it was.
Methinks my zeal to Valentine is cold,   200
And that I love him not as I was wont.
O, but I love his lady too too much,
And that's the reason I love him so little.
How shall I dote on her with more advice
That thus without advice begin to love her?   205
'Tis but her picture I have yet beheld,
And that hath dazzled my reason's light;
But when I look on her perfections,
There is no reason but I shall be blind.
If I can check my erring love, I will;   210
If not, to compass her I'll use my skill.   *Exit.*

196 **fair** beautiful
197–9 **my . . . was** simile of metamor-
    phosis and iconoclasm; see p. 54–9.
198 **'gainst** i.e. near, exposed to
199 **impression** resemblance (implying
    the stamp of a seal or signet ring)
200 **Methinks** it seems to me
    zeal affection
201 **was wont** used to
204–5 possibly an echo of *Romeus*, ll.
    601–2: 'Advise is banishd quite from
    those that followe love, / Except
    advise to what they like their bending
    minde do move.'
204 **advice** consideration; cf. 205, 3.1.73
    and 4.4.120.
205 **without advice** recklessly
206 **picture** external appearance. Some
    editors have taken *picture* to mean an
    actual portrait, anticipating the action
    in 4.4, when Silvia gives Julia the por-
    trait that Proteus had requested earlier
    ('The picture that is hanging in your

chamber', 4.2.118). This is obviously
mistaken as Proteus has seen Silvia,
but confusion has arisen from the
seeming inconsistency with 208, which
editors have taken to mean 'when I
actually see her'. Yet *perfections* presumably means 'inner qualities'.
Kiernander, 37, citing Julia's reference
to a *sun-expelling mask* (4.4.151) typi-
cally worn by ladies, speculates that
Silvia might have been masked during
her first meeting with Proteus; if so,
then he 'has fallen desperately and
duplicitously in love . . . with nothing
but her representation'.
207 **dazzled** probably pronounced with
    three syllables: 'dazzelèd'
208 **perfections** pronounced with four
    syllables
209 **no reason but** no doubt that
210 **check** restrain
211 **compass** obtain, win

202 too too] *(too-too)*   207 dazzled] *(dazel'd)*; dazel'd so *F2*   211 SD] *F2; Exeunt. F*

192

2.5   *Enter* SPEED, *and* LANCE [*with his dog Crab*].

SPEED   Lance, by mine honesty, welcome to Milan.

LANCE   Forswear not thyself, sweet youth, for I am not
welcome. I reckon this always, that a man is never
undone till he be hanged, nor never welcome to a place
till some certain shot be paid and the hostess say   5
'Welcome'.

SPEED   Come on, you madcap. I'll to the alehouse with
you presently, where, for one shot of fivepence, thou
shalt have five thousand welcomes. But, sirrah, how did
thy master part with Madam Julia?   10

LANCE   Marry, after they closed in earnest, they parted
very fairly in jest.

SPEED   But shall she marry him?

2.5 The location is clearly Milan despite
F's reference to '*Padua*'. See 1n.

0.1 **with . . . Crab* Editors have in the
past been reluctant to include Crab in
the entry SD, even though his presence is clearly indicated by *Ask my dog*
(31) and the following line; Cam¹
seems to have been the first ('*SPEED
meeting LAUNCE and his dog*'), with
more recent editors following suit,
Bantam being the first to name Crab.
Adapters of the play, however, have
long included Crab in the entry to this
scene. Victor's adaptation, for example,
ran together 2.3 and 2.5 with Crab present throughout, as did Kemble's,
while Kean offered the SD, '*Launce
has the dog with him, his staff, and several packages*' (Kean, 28). Most productions seem to have included Crab,
given his popularity with audiences, as
witness the several new scenes added
by Victor and Kemble (see pp. 86–8).

1   **Milan** F's '*Padua*' is one of several
geographic errors in the play; see pp.

75–80. Maurer questions Pope's emendation to 'Milan' on the grounds that as
a piece of 'incidental nonsense' it anticipates the illogic of the ending:
'Figuratively, what Launce does with
Speed's line at 2.5.1 is what Proteus does
with Valentine's offer of Silvia' (Maurer,
405). Some productions have retained
'*Padua*' and turned it into a joke.

2   **Forswear** perjure

4   **undone** ruined

5   **shot** payment, tavern account; cf. *1H4*
5.3.30–1: 'Though I could scape shot-
free at London, I fear the shot here.'

8   **presently** at once

10   **part with** take leave of

11–12 Lance seems to have personally
witnessed the parting of Proteus and
Julia in 2.2, though he is not present in
the text of that scene.

11   **closed** embraced; came to terms
in earnest seriously; as a promise of
future marriage

12   **in jest** light-heartedly; possibly, 'in-
sincerely'

2.5] *Scena Quinta. F; Scaena Quarta. F2*   0.1 *with his dog]* Cam¹ *subst.*   *Crab]* Bantam   1 Milan]
Pope; Padua F   4 be] is *Rowe*   7 Come on] (Come-on)   madcap] (mad-cap)   alehouse] (Alehouse)

LANCE	No.	
SPEED	How then? Shall he marry her?	15
LANCE	No, neither.	
SPEED	What, are they broken?	
LANCE	No, they are both as whole as a fish.	
SPEED	Why then, how stands the matter with them?	
LANCE	Marry, thus: when it stands well with him, it stands well with her.	20
SPEED	What an ass art thou! I understand thee not.	
LANCE	What a block art thou that thou canst not! My staff understands me.	
SPEED	What thou sayst?	25
LANCE	Ay, and what I do too. Look thee, I'll but lean, and my staff understands me.	
SPEED	It stands under thee indeed.	
LANCE	Why, stand-under and under-stand is all one.	
SPEED	But tell me true, will't be a match?	30
LANCE	Ask my dog. If he say 'Ay', it will; if he say 'No', it will; if he shake his tail and say nothing, it will.	
SPEED	The conclusion is, then, that it will.	
LANCE	Thou shalt never get such a secret from me but by a parable.	35
SPEED	'Tis well that I get it so. But Lance, how sayst thou that my master is become a notable lover?	

---

17 **broken** separated, fallen out; cf. *Cor* 4.6.50–1: 'It cannot be / The Volsces dare break with us.'

18 **as . . . fish** proverbial, meaning 'entirely sound' (Dent, F301). Lance misinterprets *broken* (17) as 'wounded'.

19 **how . . . matter** i.e. what is the state of things

20 **Marry** See 1.1.119n.

20, 21 **stands well** is agreeable; at 20, Lance also puns sexually (*stands* = is, or grows, erect).

23 **block** blockhead, fool

23–9 **My . . . one** Playing off his pun on *stands* (20), Lance pursues a series of jokes on multiple meanings of *understand*: to comprehend; to support or prop up; to come from below sexually, with *staff* = phallus, *stand* = erection. Cf. *LLL* 1.1.253: '*sweet understanding*' (RP).

34–5 **by a parable** in a hidden or allegorical form; indirectly

23–4] *Capell; F lines* not? / me? / 37 that] *F2;* that that *F*

LANCE   I never knew him otherwise.

SPEED   Than how?

LANCE   A notable lubber, as thou reportest him to be.   40

SPEED   Why, thou whoreson ass, thou mistak'st me.

LANCE   Why, fool, I meant not thee, I meant thy master.

SPEED   I tell thee, my master is become a hot lover.

LANCE   Why, I tell thee, I care not, though he burn himself
    in love. If thou wilt, go with me to the alehouse; if not,   45
    thou art an Hebrew, a Jew, and not worth the name of a
    Christian.

SPEED   Why?

LANCE   Because thou hast not so much charity in thee as
    to go to the ale with a Christian. Wilt thou go?   50

SPEED   At thy service.   *Exeunt.*

2.6   *Enter* PROTEUS *alone.*

PROTEUS
    To leave my Julia shall I be forsworn;

---

40 **lubber** clumsy, stupid man; punning on *lover* (37). Leech notes similar puns in Puttenham, 203, and *Damon and Pythias*, l. 1226.

41 **thou mistak'st me** i.e. you misunderstand my meaning

42 Lance twists Speed's reply to mean 'you are giving me the wrong character'.

44 **burn himself** i.e. by contracting a venereal disease, a symptom of which is a burning sensation; Lance picks up on Speed's *hot lover* (43).

45 *****wilt**, Knight's simple insertion of a comma here is an elegant solution to F's apparently incomplete sentence. F2 adds 'so' after *alehouse*; Cam² omits the comma but inserts a SD, '*Makes an inviting gesture*'.

46–50 **thou . . . Christian** The basic sense is that only a miserly, hard-hearted Jew would not join a Christian in his drinking. See 2.3.11n. Some editors gloss *ale* as short for 'alehouse'; however, 'go to the ale' may imply that the drinking was to take place at a church *ale*, a recurrent church festivity (hence a place only for a Christian). In printing 'go to the ale' in quotation marks, this meaning is implied by Cam¹ and accepted by later editors, although not all follow this typography.

2.6 The location remains Milan, more or less in continuation of 2.4.

1–43 Proteus's soliloquy resembles one by Lyly's Euphues on his treachery to his friend: 'Shall I not then hazarde my life to obtaine my love? and deceive

---

45 wilt,] *Knight²*; wilt *F*   alehouse] *(Ale- / house)*; Alehouse, so *F2*   50 ale] Ale-house *Rowe*   **2.6]** *Scoena Sexta. F*   0.1 *alone*] *Folg²*; *solus F*   1 Julia] *Oxf*; *Iulia*; *F*; Julia, *Theobald*   1, 2 forsworn;] *Theobald*; forsworne? *F*

195

To love fair Silvia shall I be forsworn;
To wrong my friend, I shall be much forsworn.
And e'en that power which gave me first my oath
Provokes me to this threefold perjury.   5
Love bade me swear, and Love bids me forswear.
O sweet-suggesting Love, if thou hast sinned,
Teach me, thy tempted subject, to excuse it.
At first I did adore a twinkling star,
But now I worship a celestial sun.   10
Unheedful vows may heedfully be broken,

Philautus to receive *Lucilla*? Yes *Euphues*, where love beareth sway, friendshippe can have no shew: As *Philautus* brought me for his shadowe the last supper, so will I use him for my shadow til I have gained his Saint' (*Euphues*, ll. 30–4; Lyly, 1.209), and, more generally, one by Elyot's Titus in *The Boke Named the Governour*: 'neither the study of Philosophie, neither the remembraunce of his dere frende Gysippus, who so moche loved and trusted him, coulde any thinge withdrawe him from that unkinde appetite, but that of force he must love inordinately that lady, whom his saide frende had determined to mary' (Elyot, 136). Cf. also *Son* 42.6–10, with its painful analysis: 'Thou dost love her, because thou knowst I love her . . . If I lose thee, my loss is my love's gain, / And losing her, my friend hath found that loss' and Arcite's words to Palamon in *TNK* 2.2.176–98, including: 'I love her with my soul: / If that will lose ye, farewell, Palamon' (*TNK* 2.2.178–9). Suffice it to say that Proteus's speech reflects a crucial if typical moment in the male friendship tradition, when the pressures of heterosexual desire begin to fracture the homosocial bond between male friends; see Adelman. Elam links the heavy use of anaphora and epistrophe in Proteus's speech

to earlier uses in the play (see 1.3.8–10n.): where those were 'conjunctive', Proteus's here are 'disjunctive', and hence 'an evident index of the sophistry of Proteus's reasoning'. Citing Julia's speech at 4.4.88–105 ('Because he loves her, he despiseth me; / Because I love him, I must pity him', 4.4.93–4) on the conflicts in her role, Elam argues that disjunction becomes 'the dominant anaphoric function' in the rest of the play (Elam, 246–7).

1, 2, 3 **forsworn** guilty of perjury
5 **threefold** i.e. against Julia, Silvia and Valentine
6–8 This personification is a displacement of responsibility, as Proteus struggles to rationalize his betrayal. Cf. 1.1.38–9n.
6 **forswear** renounce my oath
7 **sweet-suggesting** sweetly tempting or seductive; cf. *suggested* (3.1.34) and *Son* 144.1–2: 'Two loves I have, of comfort and despair, / Which, like two spirits, do suggest me still.'
8 **excuse** justify
9–10 a conventional conceit of romantic love; cf. *Romeus*, ll. 227–8: 'He in her sight did seeme to passe the rest as farre / As Phoebus shining beames do passe the brightnes of a starre.'
11 **Unheedful** ill-considered
  heedfully upon consideration

2 Silvia] *Oxf; Siluia; F;* Silvia, *Theobald*   5 threefold] *(three-fold)*   7 thou hast] I have *Warburton*

And he wants wit that wants resolved will
To learn his wit t'exchange the bad for better.
Fie, fie, unreverent tongue, to call her bad
Whose sovereignty so oft thou hast preferred   15
With twenty thousand soul-confirming oaths.
I cannot leave to love, and yet I do;
But there I leave to love where I should love.
Julia I lose, and Valentine I lose;
If I keep them, I needs must lose myself.   20
If I lose them, thus find I by their loss,
For Valentine, myself, for Julia, Silvia.
I to myself am dearer than a friend,
For love is still most precious in itself,
And Silvia – witness heaven that made her fair –   25
Shows Julia but a swarthy Ethiope.

---

12 **wants** lacks
resolved resolvèd; determined
13 **learn** teach; cf. *Have learned me*
(5.3.4).
t'exchange . . . better proverbial
(Dent, B26)
14 **unreverent** irreverent
15 **sovereignty** Valentine had described
Silvia as 'Sovereign to all the creatures
on the earth' (2.4.151); Proteus's echo
of that term here, in reference to Julia,
links the pairs of lovers together. The
metaphor places the male lover as a
subject to the sovereign power, but in
practice Proteus is the aggressor.
preferred recommended, urged
17, 18 **leave** cease
19–20 Proteus reverses the usual lover's
conceit of losing oneself in love, as he
imagines that he will *lose* himself if he
does not abandon Julia and Valentine.
Cf. the similar notion in Browne's
speech urging his friends to love in
LLL 4.3.335–6: 'Let us once lose our

oaths to find ourselves, / Or else we
lose ourselves to keep our oaths.'
Hallett, 169, describes this soliloquy as
a 'symphony of 180-degree reversals'.
23 Here Proteus violates one of the central tenets of male friendship theory,
placing his own desires before any consideration of his friend. Cf.
Bodenham, 96: 'No man should love
himselfe more than his friend.'
24 **still** always
26 **Shows Julia but** shows Julia up as
only
swarthy Ethiope frequently used in
comparison with stereotypical white
European female beauty to signify its
African opposite. Cf. *LLL* 4.3.114–15:
'Thou for whom Jove would swear /
Juno but an Ethiop were'; *RJ* 1.5.46–7:
'It seems she hangs upon the cheek of
night / As a rich jewel in an Ethiop's
ear'; and *MA* 5.4.37: 'I'll hold my
mind, were she an Ethiope.' Cf.
3.1.103n., 4.4.154 and 5.2.10.

---

14 unreverent] *(vnreuerend)*   16 soul-confirming] Soul-confirmed *Rowe³*   24 most] more
Steevens   itself] *(it selfe); its self Theobald*

I will forget that Julia is alive,
Remembering that my love to her is dead.
And Valentine I'll hold an enemy,
Aiming at Silvia as a sweeter friend.   30
I cannot now prove constant to myself
Without some treachery used to Valentine.
This night he meaneth with a corded ladder
To climb celestial Silvia's chamber-window,
Myself in counsel, his competitor.   35
Now presently I'll give her father notice
Of their disguising and pretended flight,
Who, all enraged, will banish Valentine,
For Turio he intends shall wed his daughter.
But Valentine being gone, I'll quickly cross   40
By some sly trick blunt Turio's dull proceeding.
Love, lend me wings to make my purpose swift,
As thou hast lent me wit to plot this drift.   *Exit.*

---

30 **friend** Here the key concept of male friendship theory slides into a term also meaning 'A lover or paramour' (*OED sb.* 4); the pressure of romantic desire cannot be resisted. 'Friend' and 'lover', key terms in the discourses of friendship and romantic love, may only appear to be in opposition, as here they coincide; see Masten, 41.
32 **to** i.e. against
33 **corded** rope
35 **Myself in counsel** i.e. as his confidant; for other occurrences of *counsel*, see 1.1.51n.
   ***counsel,** Capell inserted the comma here, presumably to distinguish Proteus as helper (*counsel*) and as rival

(*competitor*). RP notes, however, that *competitor* can also mean 'associate' (*OED* 2, citing this passage), in which case the comma would not be necessary. It is likely that the word carries both meanings at the same time, hence the adoption of the comma here.
   competitor rival; associate
36 **presently** at once
37 **pretended** intended; cf. *pretence*, 3.1.47.
40 **cross** block, thwart
41 **blunt** stupid
42 **wings** Cf. 2.7.11.
43 **drift** plan, scheme; cf. 3.1.18 and 4.2.80.

28 Remembering] *(Remembring)*   33 corded ladder] *(Corded-ladder)*   34 chamber-window] *(chamber window)*   35 counsel,] *Capell;* counsaile *F*   42 Love,] *Theobald; Loue F*

2.7　　　　　　*Enter* JULIA *and* LUCETTA.

JULIA

　Counsel, Lucetta; gentle girl, assist me,
　And e'en in kind love I do conjure thee,
　Who art the table wherein all my thoughts
　Are visibly charactered and engraved,
　To lesson me and tell me some good mean　　　　　5
　How with my honour I may undertake
　A journey to my loving Proteus.

LUCETTA

　Alas, the way is wearisome and long.

JULIA

　A true-devoted pilgrim is not weary
　To measure kingdoms with his feeble steps;　　　　10
　Much less shall she that hath Love's wings to fly,
　And when the flight is made to one so dear,
　Of such divine perfection as Sir Proteus.

2.7 The location is Verona.

1　**Counsel** Julia's need for *Counsel* echoes Proteus's planned betrayal of *counsel* (2.6.35) as well as other instances in the play (see 1.1.51n.). In *RJ*, Juliet bids the Nurse 'Comfort me, counsel me' (3.5.210) when Romeo has been banished to Mantua.

3–4 **table . . . engraved** i.e. the other person is the surface on which the speaker's thoughts are written;

3　**table** slate or ivory tablet on which to write or engrave

4　**charactered** written down; stressed on second syllable

5　**lesson** teach (transitive; see Abbott, 290)
　mean singular form of 'means', i.e. method; cf. 3.1.38, 4.4.106 and *WT* 4.4.89–90: 'Yet nature is made better by

no mean / But nature makes that mean.'

6　**with** i.e. preserving

7, 71　**Proteus** trisyllabic; see 1.1.1n.

9　**pilgrim** a standard stereotype of romantic love poetry; cf. 1.1.52, where Valentine speaks of Proteus as 'a votary to fond desire'. The first encounter of Romeo and Juliet culminates in the famous sonnet where they address each other as respectively saint and pilgrim (*RJ* 1.5.94–107). Hunt, 14, sees the language in *TGV* as intimating the idea of charitable love, as opposed to self love, and argues that Julia's 'martyr-like loss of self in her role as her betrayer's faithful servant illustrates her charity'.

10　**measure** traverse, journey across

11　**Love's wings** Cf. Proteus's request at 2.6.42.

2.7] *Scoena septima. F*　5 mean] means *Bantam*

LUCETTA

  Better forbear till Proteus make return.

JULIA

  O, knowst thou not his looks are my soul's food?   15
  Pity the dearth that I have pined in
  By longing for that food so long a time.
  Didst thou but know the inly touch of love
  Thou wouldst as soon go kindle fire with snow
  As seek to quench the fire of love with words.   20

LUCETTA

  I do not seek to quench your love's hot fire,
  But qualify the fire's extreme rage,
  Lest it should burn above the bounds of reason.

JULIA

  The more thou damm'st it up, the more it burns.
  The current that with gentle murmur glides,   25

---

16 **dearth** famine
  pined pinèd; starved
18 **inly** inward; *OED* cites this passage
  and Drayton, *Poly-olbion* (1612): 'Ever
  for those inly heats which through
  your loves they felt' (6.88).
  touch Cf. 3.2.78, 5.4.60 and 128; see
  pp. 28–29.
19–20 proverbial (Dent, F284); cf. *MV*
  3.2.30–1: 'There may as well be amity
  and life / 'Tween snow and fire, as
  treason and my love.'
22 **qualify** moderate
  fire's disyllabic
24 **damm'st** Here the metaphor begins
  to shift, in a characteristically Shakespearean move, from fire to water;
  some editors have objected to the shift.
  But *damm'st* could also mean to bank a
  fire with more fuel (Penguin); cf.
  1.2.30n.; *VA* 331–2: 'An oven that is
  stopped, or river stayed, / Burneth
  more hotly, swelleth with more rage';
  and *MM* 3.1.242–5: 'his unjust un-
  kindness, that in all reason should have

quenched her love, hath, like an
impediment in the current, made it
more violent and unruly'.
25–32 This narrative of the *current* (of
love) flowing to the *wild ocean* (32) may
recall the story of Orpheus, whose
severed head and lyre 'downe the
streame they swam, / His Harp did
yeeld a moorning sound: his liveless
toong did make / A certeine lamentable
noise as though it still yit spake, / And
bothe the banks in moorning wise made
answer to the same. / At length adowne
their country streame to open sea they
came' (Golding, 274–5). Cf. *Diana*, 229:
'But the faire Shepherdesse leaving that
place and citie on the right hand, went
softly on by a path hard by the river
towards that part, where the Cristalline
waters with a gentle and pleasant noise
runne smoothly into the Ocean.'
25–6 Cf. *Luc* 1118–19: 'Deep woes roll
forward like a gentle flood, / Who,
being stopped, the bounding banks
o'erflows.'

Thou knowst, being stopped, impatiently doth rage;
But when his fair course is not hindered,
He makes sweet music with th'enamelled stones,
Giving a gentle kiss to every sedge
He overtaketh in his pilgrimage;   30
And so by many winding nooks he strays
With willing sport to the wild ocean.
Then let me go and hinder not my course,
I'll be as patient as a gentle stream
And make a pastime of each weary step   35
Till the last step have brought me to my love,
And there I'll rest as after much turmoil
A blessed soul doth in Elysium.

LUCETTA
But in what habit will you go along?

---

27 **hindered** hinderèd
28 **enamelled** polished; variegated
29 Cf. *TS* Induction 2.51–3: 'And Cytherea all in sedges hid, / Which seem to move and wanton with her breath, / Even as the waving sedges play wi' th' wind.'
sedge grassy plant
31 **nooks** corners
32 **wild** Collier's emendation once found some support, but 'wild' meaning 'open, unenclosed' makes good sense; cf. *CE* 2.1.21: 'the wide world and wild watery seas' and *TC* 1.1.98: 'the wild and wand'ring flood'.
ocean trisyllabic
33 A comma rather than full stop has been placed at the end of this line, on the grounds that *let me go* can mean 'if you let me go' – an imperative expressing a condition – and that 'the statement could therefore be stating the condition on which what follows will happen' (RP).
38 **Elysium** in Greek mythology, the home of the blessed after death

39 **habit** clothing
40–3 This is the first instance in Shakespeare's plays of a female character putting on the costume of a man: Julia will be succeeded by Portia and Jessica in *MV*, Rosalind in *AYL*, Viola in *TN* and Imogen in *Cym*. Disguise is a standard device in romance generally; cf. *Romeus*, l. 1620: 'What letteth, but in other weede I may my selfe disguise?' In *Diana*, Felismena says, 'I determined to adventure that, which I thinke never any woman imagined: which was, to apparell my selfe in the habit of a man, and to hie me to the Court to see him, in whose sight al my hope and content remained: which determination, I no sooner thought of, then I put in practise, love blinding my eyes and minde with an inconsiderate regarde of mine owne estate and condition . . . for, being furnished with the helpe of one of my approoved friends, and treasouresse of my secrets, who bought me such apparell, as I willed

32 wild] wide *Collier²*

JULIA

    Not like a woman, for I would prevent   40
    The loose encounters of lascivious men.
    Gentle Lucetta, fit me with such weeds
    As may beseem some well-reputed page.

LUCETTA

    Why then, your ladyship must cut your hair.

JULIA

    No, girl, I'll knit it up in silken strings   45
    With twenty odd-conceited true-love knots.
    To be fantastic may become a youth
    Of greater time than I shall show to be.

LUCETTA

    What fashion, madam, shall I make your breeches?

JULIA

    That fits as well as 'Tell me, good my lord,   50
    What compass will you wear your farthingale?'
    Why, e'en what fashion thou best likes, Lucetta.

LUCETTA

    You must needs have them with a codpiece, madam.

JULIA

    Out, out, Lucetta, that will be ill-favoured.

---

her, and a good horse for my journey, I went not onely out of my countrie but out of my deere reputation (which I thinke) I shall never recover againe)' (*Diana*, 87). See pp. 44–54 and Shapiro, *Gender*, for a useful survey of the tradition of the cross-dressed woman.

40–1 **prevent . . . encounters** forestall the immoral advances

42 **weeds** garments

43 **beseem** be appropriate to

46 **odd-conceited** strangely imagined
true-love knots 'A kind of knot, of a complicated and ornamental form . . . used as a symbol of true love' (*OED*);

related to the 'virgin knot'. Cf. *Per* 4.2.147, *Tem* 4.1.15 and Carroll, 'Virgin'.

47 **fantastic** fanciful

48 **greater time** older years
show appear

51 **compass** circumference
farthingale hooped petticoat

53 **must needs** must
codpiece appendage like a small bag or flap at the crotch of men's breeches; often a euphemism for the phallus, as in *MM* 3.2.111–12: 'the rebellion of a codpiece'

54 **ill-favoured** unbecoming

53, 56 codpiece] *(cod-peece)*

LUCETTA

    A round hose, madam, now's not worth a pin   55
    Unless you have a codpiece to stick pins on.

JULIA

    Lucetta, as thou lov'st me, let me have
    What thou think'st meet and is most mannerly.
    But tell me, wench, how will the world repute me
    For undertaking so unstaid a journey?   60
    I fear me it will make me scandalized.

LUCETTA

    If you think so, then stay at home and go not.

JULIA

    Nay, that I will not.

LUCETTA

    Then never dream on infamy, but go.
    If Proteus like your journey when you come,   65
    No matter who's displeased when you are gone.
    I fear me he will scarce be pleased withal.

JULIA

    That is the least, Lucetta, of my fear.
    A thousand oaths, an ocean of his tears,
    And instances of infinite of love   70

---

55 **round hose** 'the close-fitting part of the hose or breeches extended farther up the leg, giving a greater bulge and roundness to the remaining portion' (Ard[1])

    not . . . pin i.e. worthless; cf. 1.1.106.

56 **codpiece . . . pins** Codpieces were often decorated with pins; cf. Webster, *White Devil*, 5.3.100–1: 'Look you his codpiece is stuck full of pins / With pearls o'th' head of them.' It is ironic that Julia's assumed name, *Sebastian* (4.4.39), is that of the saint shot full of arrows.

58 **meet** appropriate
    mannerly respectable, modest

60 **unstaid** immodest; reckless

61 **scandalized** the subject of scandal

66 **No matter** it does not matter

69 **ocean . . . tears** still a classic cliché of grief; cf. *2H6* 3.2.142–3: 'to drain / Upon his face an ocean of salt tears' and Kyd, *The Spanish Tragedy*, 2.5.23: 'to drown thee with an ocean of my tears'.

70 **of infinite** of an infinite quantity; F2's emendation is rational but unnecessary. Bond suggested but did not adopt 'infinity'.

67 withal] *(with all)*   70 ¹of] as *F2;* of the *Boswell–Malone*

Warrant me welcome to my Proteus.

LUCETTA

All these are servants to deceitful men.

JULIA

Base men, that use them to so base effect!
But truer stars did govern Proteus' birth.
His words are bonds, his oaths are oracles,   75
His love sincere, his thoughts immaculate,
His tears pure messengers sent from his heart,
His heart as far from fraud as heaven from earth.

LUCETTA

Pray heaven he prove so when you come to him.

JULIA

Now, as thou lov'st me, do him not that wrong   80
To bear a hard opinion of his truth.
Only deserve my love by loving him,
And presently go with me to my chamber
To take a note of what I stand in need of
To furnish me upon my longing journey.   85
All that is mine I leave at thy dispose,
My goods, my lands, my reputation;
Only, in lieu thereof, dispatch me hence.

---

71 **Warrant** guarantee
74 a common astrological notion
75 Julia's confidence in the absoluteness
of Proteus's language is naive; see
pp. 64–5. Cf. *TN* 3.1.21: 'words are
very rascals since bonds disgraced
them', and Dent, M458.
79 **prove so** turns out to be
81 **hard** bad, negative
83, 89 **presently** immediately
85 **longing** prompted by longing
86–7 These lines seem to suggest Julia is
an orphan, in charge of her own estate
and destiny; but cf. 1.2.130 where
Julia's father is apparently alive and

well offstage. Presumably the main
point is that Lucetta is Julia's only
confidante and her father mustn't
know about her plans.
86 **All . . . mine** Julia's expression of
trust in Lucetta anticipates that of
Valentine when he offers Silvia to
Proteus ('All that was mine in Silvia I
give thee', 5.4.83).
at thy dispose at your disposal; cf.
4.1.75.
87 **reputation** pronounced as five syllables
88 **in lieu thereof** i.e. in exchange for
this favour (of giving Lucetta control)

79 heaven] *(heau'n)*

Come, answer not, but to it presently;   89
I am impatient of my tarriance.   *Exeunt.*

3.1   *Enter* DUKE, TURIO [*and*] PROTEUS.

DUKE

Sir Turio, give us leave, I pray, awhile;
We have some secrets to confer about.   [*Exit Turio.*]
Now tell me, Proteus, what's your will with me?

PROTEUS

My gracious lord, that which I would discover
The law of friendship bids me to conceal,   5
But when I call to mind your gracious favours
Done to me, undeserving as I am,
My duty pricks me on to utter that
Which else no worldly good should draw from me.
Know, worthy prince, Sir Valentine my friend   10
This night intends to steal away your daughter;
Myself am one made privy to the plot.
I know you have determined to bestow her
On Turio, whom your gentle daughter hates,
And should she thus be stol'n away from you,   15
It would be much vexation to your age.
Thus, for my duty's sake, I rather chose
To cross my friend in his intended drift
Than, by concealing it, heap on your head
A pack of sorrows which would press you down,   20

---

90 **tarriance** delay
3.1 The location shifts back to Milan.
2 **confer** talk, converse
2 SD *Turio's almost immediate exit
here, added by Rowe, has been taken
as evidence of some revision of F; see
Leech, xv-xxi.
4–9 Proteus, by protesting too much,

highlights his insincerity here.
4 **discover** reveal
8 **pricks** urges
12 **made privy to** confided in concerning
18 **cross** oppose, thwart
drift plan, scheme; cf. 2.6.43 and
4.2.80.

3.1] *Actus Tertius, Scena Prima.* F   0.1] *Rowe; Enter Duke, Thurio, Protheus, Valentine, Launce, Speed.*
F   2 SD] *Rowe*

Being unprevented, to your timeless grave.
DUKE

    Proteus, I thank thee for thine honest care,
    Which to requite command me while I live.
    This love of theirs myself have often seen,
    Haply when they have judged me fast asleep,   25
    And oftentimes have purposed to forbid
    Sir Valentine her company and my court.
    But fearing lest my jealous aim might err
    And so unworthily disgrace the man –
    A rashness that I ever yet have shunned –   30
    I gave him gentle looks, thereby to find
    That which thyself hast now disclosed to me.
    And that thou mayst perceive my fear of this,
    Knowing that tender youth is soon suggested,
    I nightly lodge her in an upper tower,   35
    The key whereof myself have ever kept;
    And thence she cannot be conveyed away.
PROTEUS

    Know, noble lord, they have devised a mean
    How he her chamber-window will ascend
    And with a corded ladder fetch her down;   40
    For which the youthful lover now is gone,
    And this way comes he with it presently,
    Where, if it please you, you may intercept him.
    But, good my lord, do it so cunningly

---

21 **Being unprevented** if they were not prevented
timeless untimely; cf. *RJ* 5.3.162: 'timeless end'.
25 **Haply** by chance
28 **jealous . . . err** suspicion might be wrong
aim conjecture, guess; cf. *JC* 1.2.162: 'What you would work me to, I have some aim.'

34 **suggested** tempted; cf. 2.6.7: *sweet-suggesting*.
35 as Hero was; see 1.1.21–6n.
37 **conveyed** escorted; stolen. Cf. 128, 250 and *R2* 4.1.317: '"Convey"! Conveyers are you all.'
38 **mean** See 2.7.5n.
40 **corded** rope
42 **presently** directly

40 corded ladder] *(Corded-ladder)*   42 presently,] *Ard²;* presently. *F*

That my discovery be not aimed at;   45
For love of you, not hate unto my friend,
Hath made me publisher of this pretence.

DUKE
Upon mine honour, he shall never know
That I had any light from thee of this.   49

[*Enter* VALENTINE.]

PROTEUS
Adieu, my lord, Sir Valentine is coming.   [*Exit.*]

DUKE
Sir Valentine, whither away so fast?

VALENTINE
Please it your grace, there is a messenger
That stays to bear my letters to my friends,
And I am going to deliver them.

DUKE
Be they of much import?   55

VALENTINE
The tenor of them doth but signify
My health and happy being at your court.

DUKE
Nay then, no matter. Stay with me awhile;

---

45 **discovery** disclosure
   aimed at aimèd; i.e. suspected
47 **pretence** purpose; cf. 2.6.37 and *Mac*
   2.3.133–4: 'the undivulged pretence . . .
   Of treasonous malice'.
49 **light** i.e. information
52 **Please . . . grace** if it please your
   grace; a conventionally polite form of
   address to a superior
53 **stays** is waiting
   letters Directors have often had
   Valentine enter with letters in hand,

though the Duke seems, at 137, to discover the single *letter* to Silvia
concealed under or in the *cloak* (136).
The plural form, however, could carry
singular meaning: RP cites *Oth*
4.1.275: 'did the letters work upon his
blood . . . ?'
55 **import** gravity; significance
56 i.e. they only report
57 **My . . . being** i.e. that I am well and
   happy

49.1] *Rowe after 50; Enter. F2.*   50 SD] *Rowe*   56 tenor] *Theobald;* tenure *F*

I am to break with thee of some affairs
That touch me near, wherein thou must be secret.   60
'Tis not unknown to thee that I have sought
To match my friend Sir Turio to my daughter.

VALENTINE

I know it well, my lord, and sure the match
Were rich and honourable. Besides, the gentleman
Is full of virtue, bounty, worth and qualities   65
Beseeming such a wife as your fair daughter.
Cannot your grace win her to fancy him?

DUKE

No, trust me, she is peevish, sullen, froward,
Proud, disobedient, stubborn, lacking duty,
Neither regarding that she is my child   70
Nor fearing me as if I were her father.
And, may I say to thee, this pride of hers,
Upon advice, hath drawn my love from her,
And where I thought the remnant of mine age
Should have been cherished by her childlike duty,   75
I now am full resolved to take a wife
And turn her out to who will take her in.
Then let her beauty be her wedding dower,
For me and my possessions she esteems not.

---

59 **break with** confide in; cf. 1.3.44, and
   1H4 3.1.140: 'Break with your wives of
   your departure hence.'
60 **touch me near** concern me closely
63–6 Valentine's praise here is transpar-
   ently false and usually gains a laugh
   onstage.
64 **Were** would be
   rich Cf. 2.4.43–4n. and 172–3.
66 **Beseeming** appropriate to
68 **froward** rebellious; perverse
70 **regarding** concerned; cf. *Regard*
   (254).
73 **advice** consideration; see 2.4.204n.

74–8 Cf. *KL*: Lear, disowning Cordelia,
   says 'Thy truth then be thy dower'
   (1.1.109), stating that he had 'thought
   to set [his] rest / On [Cordelia's] kind
   nursery' (1.1.123–4) – a desire turned
   against him later, as the Fool points
   out, when he makes his other 'daughters [his] mothers' (1.4.164). The
   Duke's lines, and his anger with
   Valentine and Silvia, cast him as the
   senex iratus figure of classical comedy.
74 **where** whereas
   remnant . . . age remainder of my life
77 **who** whomever

VALENTINE

What would your grace have me to do in this?   80

DUKE

There is a lady of Verona here
Whom I affect, but she is nice and coy,
And naught esteems my aged eloquence.
Now therefore would I have thee to my tutor –
For long agone I have forgot to court;   85
Besides, the fashion of the time is changed –
How and which way I may bestow myself
To be regarded in her sun-bright eye.

---

81 *of Verona As this scene is clearly
still in Milan, F's reading is confusing.
Halliwell's emendation is sufficient.
Bond (citing White as his source) notes
that the choice of *Verona* is 'appropriate to the Duke's appeal to the
Veronese Valentine'.

82 affect love
   nice shy

85 agone ago
   forgot i.e. forgotten how

86 fashion . . . changed perhaps a specific reference to a changing court culture, like the allusions to taste and
fashion in *LLL*, but also a typical com-
plaint of an older generation

87 bestow conduct

88 regarded held in respect
   sun-bright Cf. Marlowe, *1 Tambur-
laine*, 2.3.22: 'our Sun-bright armour'
(Marlowe, 1.98).

89–105 Valentine's advice to the Duke
might be termed anti-Petrarchan: the
actions of the haughty, distant mistress
who will not return the appeals of the
male lover must be read as actually
welcoming such gifts. The fact that
these lines, beginning at 90, are
rhymed, however, also suggests
Valentine's artificiality. His final two
lines, a comic self-betrayal, are ironically prophetic, as Proteus will be

unable to *win* (105) Silvia, even with
moving words (5.4.55). Bond notes
extensive borrowings throughout from
Lyly (see notes on 93–5, 100–1 and
102–5).

89–91 This sentiment has a long history,
probably beginning in Ovid's advice in
Book 2 of *The Art of Love*, which is
reflected in Thynne, 58: 'Trust Ovid
then, whoe spake what he did knowe: it
shewes great witt, large giftes for to
bestowe' (cited in Dent, W704). Cf.
Marlowe, *Hero*, 2.225–6: ''Tis wisdom
to give much, a gift prevails / When
deep persuading oratory fails'; also
Lyly's *Sapho and Phao*, 2.4.105: 'He
hath wit ynough, that can give ynough.
Dumbe men are eloquent, if they be
liberall. Beleeve me great gifts are little
Gods' (Lyly, 2.391). In *Ham*, the
Ghost complains 'O wicked wit and
gifts, that have the power / So to
seduce!' (1.5.45–6) and in the play-
within-the-play the '*Poisoner woos the
Queen with gifts; she seems harsh
awhile, but in the end accepts love*'
(3.2.133.13–15). RP points out that
these sentiments are not exclusively
misogynistic, as the previous examples
might suggest, citing Olivia's words
about Cesario (Viola) at *TN* 3.4.3: 'For
youth is bought more oft than begged

VALENTINE

> Win her with gifts if she respect not words;
> Dumb jewels often in their silent kind   90
> More than quick words do move a woman's mind.

DUKE

> But she did scorn a present that I sent her.

VALENTINE

> A woman sometime scorns what best contents her.
> Send her another; never give her o'er,
> For scorn at first makes after-love the more.   95
> If she do frown, 'tis not in hate of you,
> But rather to beget more love in you.
> If she do chide, 'tis not to have you gone,
> Forwhy the fools are mad if left alone.
> Take no repulse, whatever she doth say,   100
> For 'Get you gone' she doth not mean 'Away!'
> Flatter and praise, commend, extol their graces;

---

or borrowed' and Livia's cynical wooing of Leantio in Middleton's *Women
Beware Women*.

89 **respect not** disregards
90 **Dumb** mute
   jewels disyllabic; cf. 2.4.166–9n. and
   4.4.46n.
   kind nature
91 **quick** lively
93–5 Cf. *Sapho and Phao*, 2.4.92: 'If she
   seeme at the first cruell, be not dis-
   couraged. I tell the[e] a straung thing,
   womenne strive, because they would
   be overcome: force they call it, but
   such a welcome force they account it,
   that continually they study to be
   enforced' (Lyly, 2.390–1).
94 **give her o'er** stop pursuing her
99 **Forwhy** because (*OED* B 1); cf. *Luc*
   1222: 'Forwhy her face wore sorrow's
   livery'.
100–1 Cf. *Sapho and Phao*, 1.4.43–7:
   'Wee are madde wenches, if men

marke our wordes: for when I say, I
would none cared for love more then I,
what meane I, but I woulde none loved
but I? where we cry "away," doe we not
presently say, "go too"? & when men
strive for kisses, we exclaime, "let us
alone," as though we would fall to that
our selves' (Lyly, 2.379–80). Although
Valentine states that women actually
mean the opposite of what they say
(echoing Julia at 1.2.55–6; see n.), it is
only Proteus, when he attempts to
force himself on Silvia, who really acts
on this assumption.
101 **For** by
102–5 Cf. *Sapho and Phao*, 2.4.60–7:
   'Flatter, I meane lie; litle things catch
   light mindes . . . It is unpossible for the
   brittle mettall of women to withstand
   the flattering attemptes of men . . . Be
   prodigall in praises and promises,
   bewtie must have a trumpet, & pride a
   gifte' (Lyly, 2.390).

93 sometime] sometimes *F3*

Though ne'er so black, say they have angels' faces.
That man that hath a tongue, I say, is no man
If with his tongue he cannot win a woman.   105

DUKE

But she I mean is promised by her friends
Unto a youthful gentleman of worth,
And kept severely from resort of men,
That no man hath access by day to her.

VALENTINE

Why then, I would resort to her by night.   110

DUKE

Ay, but the doors be locked and keys kept safe,
That no man hath recourse to her by night.

VALENTINE

What lets but one may enter at her window?

DUKE

Her chamber is aloft, far from the ground,
And built so shelving that one cannot climb it   115
Without apparent hazard of his life.

VALENTINE

Why then, a ladder quaintly made of cords
To cast up, with a pair of anchoring hooks,

---

103 A fair complexion was considered beautiful, not a *black* or dark one; cf. 2.6.26n. on *swarthy Ethiope*, 4.4.154 and 5.2.10.
104–5 These lines ironically anticipate Proteus's inability to win Silvia in the final scene, when he justifies his attempted rape; see 5.4.55–7.
104 **That . . . tongue** i.e. any man
106 **friends** family
108–11 These lines are full of potential sexual innuendo: *resort* (as noun = 'brothel'; cf. *MM* 1.2.101: 'houses of resort'), *access* (= sexual entry; cf. *MM*

2.4.18, *Mac* 1.5.44) and *doors . . . safe* (= protecting the locked doors of virginity from the phallic keys; see Rubinstein, 3, 219).
108 **severely** strictly
109, 112 **That** so that
109 **access** stressed on second syllable
113 **lets . . . enter** prevents anyone from entering
115 **shelving** projecting
116 **apparent** obvious
117 **quaintly** skilfully, elegantly; cf. 2.1.113.
    cords rope

Would serve to scale another Hero's tower,
So bold Leander would adventure it.   120

DUKE

Now, as thou art a gentleman of blood,
Advise me where I may have such a ladder.

VALENTINE

When would you use it? Pray, sir, tell me that.

DUKE

This very night; for Love is like a child
That longs for everything that he can come by.   125

VALENTINE

By seven o'clock I'll get you such a ladder.

DUKE

But hark thee: I will go to her alone.
How shall I best convey the ladder thither?

VALENTINE

It will be light, my lord, that you may bear it
Under a cloak that is of any length.   130

DUKE

A cloak as long as thine will serve the turn?

VALENTINE

Ay, my good lord.

DUKE   Then let me see thy cloak;
I'll get me one of such another length.

VALENTINE

Why, any cloak will serve the turn, my lord.

DUKE

How shall I fashion me to wear a cloak?   135
I pray thee let me feel thy cloak upon me.

119–20 See 1.1.21–6n.
120 **So** if; provided that
    adventure venture, risk
121 **blood** good parentage; passion
128 **convey** carry; see 37n.

129 **that** so that
130 **of any length** fairly long
131, 134 **turn** occasion
133 **such another** i.e. the same

[*Takes Valentine's cloak and finds a letter and a rope
ladder concealed under it.*]
What letter is this same? What's here? *To Silvia?*
And here an engine fit for my proceeding.
I'll be so bold to break the seal for once.
[*Reads.*] *My thoughts do harbour with my Silvia nightly,*   140
And slaves they are to me that send them flying.
O, could their master come and go as lightly,
Himself would lodge where, senseless, they are lying.
My herald thoughts in thy pure bosom rest them,
While I, their king, that thither them importune,   145
Do curse the grace that with such grace hath blessed them,
Because myself do want my servants' fortune.
　I curse myself for they are sent by me,
　That they should harbour where their lord should be.

137 **letter** Noting the *ladder* and *letter*
homophones, Simmons, 867–8, ob-
serves that the ladder connotes 'the
heroic lover successfully mounting the
balcony', while the letter 'intimates the
consequences of the notorious text
that tragically fails to reach its destination'.
138 **engine** device
139 **seal** the wax which seals the letter
140–9 Valentine's conceit here rests on
the idea that he, the *master/king/lord*
of his thoughts (the *slaves/herald/ser-
vants*), is actually powerless, whereas
his *thoughts* freely enjoy being with
Silvia; his *thoughts* are also a metonymy
for himself. The master–servant relation is frequently overturned in the
play. Cf. *Son* 27.5–6: 'my thoughts,
from far where I abide, / Intend a zeal-
ous pilgrimage to thee' and the beginning of a sonnet in *Diana*, 57: '*Goe now
my thoughts, where one day you were
going, / When neither fortune, nor my
love did lower.*' Valentine's lines equal a
regular Shakespearean sonnet minus

the first quatrain, like Orlando's in
AYL 3.2.1–10.
140, 149 *harbour* reside; cf. 1.2.42.
142 *lightly* easily
143 *senseless* insensible
144 *herald thoughts* thoughts preceding
me; thoughts carrying my message
in . . . bosom Bond, citing Steevens as
his source, suggests a reference to 'the
pocket formerly worn by women in the
front of their stays between the
breasts, in which they carried not only
love letters and tokens but even money
and needlework materials'; Malone
cites Surrey's *Sonnets* (1557): 'My
song . . . When she hath read . . .
Between her brests she shall thee put'
(see Ard¹). Cf. 248 and 1.2.114–15.
145 *importune* command; stressed on
second syllable
146 *grace . . . grace* good fortune . . .
favour
147 *want* lack
fortune luck
148 *for* because

136 SD] *Ard² subst.; Pulls off his cloak / Hanmer*
140 SD] *Rowe subst.*   144 *rest them*] (*rest-them*)   149 ²*should*] *would F2*

213

What's here?   150
    Silvia, this night I will enfranchise thee.
'Tis so; and here's the ladder for the purpose.
Why, Phaëton, for thou art Merops' son,
Wilt thou aspire to guide the heavenly car,
And with thy daring folly burn the world?   155
Wilt thou reach stars because they shine on thee?
Go, base intruder, overweening slave,
Bestow thy fawning smiles on equal mates,
And think my patience, more than thy desert,
Is privilege for thy departure hence.   160
Thank me for this more than for all the favours
Which, all too much, I have bestowed on thee.
But if thou linger in my territories
Longer than swiftest expedition
Will give thee time to leave our royal court,   165
By heaven, my wrath shall far exceed the love
I ever bore my daughter or thyself.

151 *enfranchise* liberate
153–6 Phaëton was the *son* of Phoebus, the sun god, who fathered him on Merops' wife, Clymene. Phaëton drove Phoebus's chariot, the *heavenly car*, too close to the earth, setting much of it on fire; he was destroyed by a thunderbolt from Jove. Ovid tells the story in *Met.*, 2.1–332. Shakespeare invokes the story of Phaëton in other early plays: cf. *3H6* 1.4.33–4, 2.6.11–13 and *R2* 3.3.178.
153 **Merops'** perhaps a pun on 'ropes' here (Cam¹)
156 proverbial: 'One may point (look) at a star but not pull (reach) at it' (Dent, S825). Cf. *AW* 1.1.87–9: ''Twere all one / That I should love a bright par-

ticular star / And think to wed it, he is so above me.'
    reach reach for
157 **overweening** presumptuous
158 **equal mates** i.e. your social equals (as opposed to a duke)
159 **desert** deserving
160 **Is privilege for** i.e. grants the privilege of, as in a royal patent or licence
163–9 The sovereign's impetuous banishment of a subject is common in Shakespeare: e.g. Prince Escalus in *RJ* 3.1.185–94; Richard II in *R2* 1.3.125–43; Duke Frederick in *AYL* 1.3.41–3; and King Lear in *KL* 1.1.168–80, among others.
164 **expedition** haste; pronounced with five syllables

150–1] *Malone; one line F*   162 too much] *(too-much)*

Begone, I will not hear thy vain excuse,
But, as thou lov'st thy life, make speed from hence.   [*Exit.*]

VALENTINE

And why not death, rather than living torment?   170
To die is to be banished from myself,
And Silvia is myself; banished from her
Is self from self – a deadly banishment.
What light is light, if Silvia be not seen?
What joy is joy, if Silvia be not by?   175
Unless it be to think that she is by
And feed upon the shadow of perfection.
Except I be by Silvia in the night,
There is no music in the nightingale.
Unless I look on Silvia in the day,   180
There is no day for me to look upon.
She is my essence, and I leave to be
If I be not by her fair influence
Fostered, illumined, cherished, kept alive.
I fly not death to fly his deadly doom: 185

170–87 Valentine's soliloquy here recalls Romeo's reaction to his banishment at *RJ* 3.3.17–46 and Suffolk's upon his at *2H6* 3.2.388–402.

171–3 The loved one is equated with one's own self; cf. Portia in *JC* 2.1.270–4: 'I charm you . . . / By all your vows of love, and that great vow / Which did incorporate and make us one, / That you unfold to me, your self, your half, / Why you are heavy.' Cf. 2.6.20–3.

177 **shadow** Cf. 4.2.120–4 (and 123–4n.), 4.4.115–18 and 195n. The *shadow* is the insubstantial counterpart of *substance* (4.2.120). This opposition figures in many of Shakespeare's plays

and sonnets, as in *Son* 37.10: 'this shadow doth such substance give' and *Son* 53.1–2: 'What is your substance, whereof are you made, / That millions of strange shadows on you tend?' Cf. also Lyly's *Love's Metamorphosis*, 3.1.20: 'men honour shadowes for substance, because they are men' (Lyly, 3.310).

178 **Except** unless

179 **nightingale** See 5.4.5n.

182 **leave** cease; cf. 2.6.17–18.

183 **influence** astrological term: her *influence*, like that of the stars, determines his life.

185 **his** i.e. the Duke's
doom sentence, i.e. of banishment

Tarry I here, I but attend on death,
But fly I hence, I fly away from life.

[*Enter* PROTEUS *and* LANCE.]

PROTEUS   Run, boy, run, run and seek him out.

LANCE   So-ho, so-ho!

PROTEUS   What seest thou?   190

LANCE   Him we go to find. There's not a hair on's head
    but 'tis a Valentine.

PROTEUS   Valentine?

VALENTINE   No.

PROTEUS   Who then? His spirit?   195

VALENTINE   Neither.

PROTEUS   What then?

VALENTINE   Nothing.

LANCE   Can nothing speak? Master, shall I strike?

PROTEUS   Who wouldst thou strike?   200

LANCE   Nothing.

PROTEUS   Villain, forbear.

LANCE   Why, sir, I'll strike nothing. I pray you –

PROTEUS

    Sirrah, I say forbear. Friend Valentine, a word.

---

186 **Tarry I** if I tarry
    but attend on merely wait for
187 **fly I** if I fly
188 **boy** i.e. Lance; cf. King Lear and the
    Fool (*KL* 3.2.68). There is no indica-
    tion that Crab is onstage with Lance in
    this scene, though some directors have
    nevertheless brought him on.
189 a hunting cry announcing that the
    quarry has been sighted; this might
    also suggest a pun on *hair* (191) = hare.
191–2 **There's . . . Valentine** i.e.

Valentine is a lover in every detail; *a
Valentine* = a lover (*OED sb.* 2)
199 **Can nothing speak** Cf. *KL* 1.1.90:
    'How, nothing will come of nothing.
    Speak again.'
202 **Villain** i.e. a social inferior (from
    'villein' = 'one of the class of serfs in
    the feudal system', *OED*)
    forbear Lance is apparently about to
    strike Valentine, who is now *nothing*
    (198, 201).
204 alexandrine; see 1.1.30n.

187.1] *F2 (Enter Pro. and Launs.)*   189 So-ho, so-ho!] *Theobald;* So-hough, Soa hough – *F*   191–2]
Capell; F lines finde, / *Valentine. /*   192 'tis] (t'is)   200 Who] Whom *F2*   203 you –] *Theobald;*
you. *F*

VALENTINE

    My ears are stopped and cannot hear good news,   205

    So much of bad already hath possessed them.

PROTEUS

    Then in dumb silence will I bury mine,

    For they are harsh, untuneable and bad.

VALENTINE

    Is Silvia dead?

PROTEUS   No, Valentine.

VALENTINE

    No Valentine indeed for sacred Silvia.   210

    Hath she forsworn me?

PROTEUS   No, Valentine.

VALENTINE

    No Valentine, if Silvia have forsworn me.

    What is your news?

LANCE   Sir, there is a proclamation that you are vanished.

PROTEUS

    That thou art banished – O, that's the news –   215

    From hence, from Silvia, and from me thy friend.

VALENTINE

    O, I have fed upon this woe already,

    And now excess of it will make me surfeit.

    Doth Silvia know that I am banished?

---

208 **they** the *news* (205)
  untuneable discordant
211, 212 **forsworn** repudiated
214 **vanished** apparently one of Lance's
  malapropisms (for 'banished'), but perhaps also a clever echo of Valentine's
  Nothing (198); as nothing, without his
  essence (182), Valentine – the 'lover' –

has disappeared.
215, 219 **banished** banishèd
218 **excess . . . surfeit** Malone notes the
  parallel with *TN* 1.1.2–3: 'Give me
  excess of it, that surfeiting, / The
  appetite may sicken and so die'; Bond
  also notes *MV* 3.2.112–14: 'scant this
  excess . . . For fear I surfeit'.

215, 219 banished] *(*banish'd*)*   215–16 O . . . From] *Val.* Oh, that's the news! / *Pro.* From *(Cam)*

217

PROTEUS

> Ay, ay; and she hath offered to the doom,   220
> Which unreversed stands in effectual force,
> A sea of melting pearl, which some call tears;
> Those at her father's churlish feet she tendered,
> With them, upon her knees, her humble self,
> Wringing her hands, whose whiteness so became them   225
> As if but now they waxed pale for woe.
> But neither bended knees, pure hands held up,
> Sad sighs, deep groans, nor silver-shedding tears
> Could penetrate her uncompassionate sire,
> But Valentine, if he be ta'en, must die.   230
> Besides, her intercession chafed him so,
> When she for thy repeal was suppliant,
> That to close prison he commanded her,
> With many bitter threats of biding there.

VALENTINE

> No more, unless the next word that thou speak'st   235
> Have some malignant power upon my life;
> If so, I pray thee breathe it in mine ear,
> As ending anthem of my endless dolour.

220–34 As Bond notes, Silvia's actions would have had to occur between 169 SD (the Duke's exit) and 187.1 (Proteus's entrance). Some editors, however, have taken this compression as a sign of a deleted scene or other revision; see p. 125.

220 **doom** sentence

221 which if unrevoked is binding; which has not been revoked and therefore is binding

223 **tendered** offered; cf. *Ham* 1.3. 100–1: 'tenders / Of his affection'.

226 **waxed** waxèd

228 **silver-shedding** 'that flow like silver streams' (Norton)

231 **chafed** irritated
him i.e. the Duke

232 **repeal** i.e. repeal from banishment; cf. 5.4.141.

234 **biding** remaining

236 **power . . . life** i.e. power to end my life

238 **anthem** song of mourning; Leech cites *PT* 21–2: 'Here the anthem doth commence. / Love and constancy is dead.' *OED*, however, gives this instance (incorrectly, it would seem) as an example of 'A song, as of praise or gladness' (*OED sb.* 3).

224 them,] *Rowe³*; them *F*   230 ta'en] *(tane)*   238 anthem] amen *(Singer²)*

PROTEUS

> Cease to lament for that thou canst not help
> And study help for that which thou lament'st.   240
> Time is the nurse and breeder of all good.
> Here if thou stay, thou canst not see thy love;
> Besides, thy staying will abridge thy life.
> Hope is a lover's staff; walk hence with that
> And manage it against despairing thoughts.   245
> Thy letters may be here, though thou art hence,
> Which, being writ to me, shall be delivered
> Even in the milk-white bosom of thy love.
> The time now serves not to expostulate.
> Come, I'll convey thee through the city-gate,   250
> And ere I part with thee confer at large
> Of all that may concern thy love affairs.
> As thou lov'st Silvia, though not for thyself,
> Regard thy danger and along with me.

VALENTINE

> I pray thee, Lance, an if thou seest my boy,   255
> Bid him make haste and meet me at the North Gate.

PROTEUS

> Go, sirrah, find him out. Come, Valentine.

VALENTINE

> O, my dear Silvia! Hapless Valentine!

> *[Exeunt Valentine and Proteus.]*

---

239 **that** that which
243 **abridge** shorten
244 **staff** walking stick; figuratively, support
245 **manage** employ; wield
248 **milk-white bosom** See 144n. and Dent, M931.1.
249 **expostulate** talk at length; cf. *Ham* 2.2.86–7: 'to expostulate / What majesty should be'.

250 **convey** escort; see 37n.
251 **ere** before
     confer at large talk at length; cf. 3.2.61.
253 **though** even if
254 **Regard** take account of, pay attention to; cf. *regarding* (70).
     along come along
255 **an if** if
     boy i.e. Speed

252 love affairs] *(*Loue-affaires*)* 255 an] *(*and*)* 256 North Gate] *(*North-gate*)* 258 SD] *Warburton; Exeunt. F2*

LANCE   I am but a fool, look you, and yet I have the wit to
think my master is a kind of a knave; but that's all one,   260
if he be but one knave. He lives not now that knows me
to be in love, yet I am in love, but a team of horse shall
not pluck that from me, nor who 'tis I love; and yet 'tis
a woman, but what woman I will not tell myself; and yet
'tis a milkmaid; yet 'tis not a maid, for she hath had   265
gossips; yet 'tis a maid, for she is her master's maid and
serves for wages. She hath more qualities than a
water-spaniel, which is much in a bare Christian. [*Pulls
out a paper.*] Here is the cate-log of her condition.

259–74 Lance's direct address to the
audience here has a different force
than Speed's witty one-line asides; see
Weimann, 40, on Lance's role in helping 'to define and to control, though
not necessarily to belittle, the main
theme of love and friendship'. Lance's
profession of love for the unnamed
woman parallels and parodies the
similar declarations by Proteus and
Valentine earlier in the play, and his
frequent use of the *and yet* locution
specifically recalls its occurrence at
2.1.106–11, where Speed comments,
'and yet another "yet" ' (2.1.111).

260 **but . . . one** but it makes no difference
261 **but one knave** only one knave, playing on *but* and *one* from 260. Editors
have proposed that Lance refers to the
proverb, 'Two false knaves need no
broker', hence Proteus being *but one
knave* needs his broker, Lance (Cam¹);
or that the sense is of 'single moderate
knavery as contrasted with double'
(Ard²). Cf. *Damon and Pythias*, l. 109:
'You lose Money by him if you sel him
for one knave, for he serves for twaine'
and *Mucedorus*, B3ᵛ and B4ʳ: 'captain
treble knave'.

He . . . now there's no one living
262 **horse** perhaps punning on 'whores'

265 **maid** virgin
266 **gossips** women who attend a child's
baptism or a pregnant woman's lying-
in, i.e. she is no virgin because she has
had a child. Cf. Middleton, *Chaste
Maid*, 2.3.57.1–2: '*Enter* Midwife *with
the child . . . and the* Gossips *to the
Kursning.*'
maid servant, i.e. *milkmaid* (265)
268 **water-spaniel** Bond, referring to
Fleming, links this reference to the
hunting dog which retrieves duck or
other fowl from the water. Elsewhere,
Shakespeare is not fond of spaniels: cf.
4.2.14–15: 'Yet, spaniel-like, the more
she spurns my love, / The more
it grows and fawneth on her still';
JC 3.1.43: 'base spaniel fawning';
and *MND* 2.1.205: 'Use me but as
your spaniel.' Lyly reveals the same
attitude in *Euphues*, ll. 7–8: 'Wilt thou
resemble the kinde Spaniell, which the
more he is beaten the fonder he is . . .
?' (Lyly, 1.249). Cf. Dent, S704 and
S705.
bare mere; naked
269–355 **Here . . . gracious** This comic
blazon resembles the elaborately comic
description of Nell in *CE* 3.2.90–145,
and a similar one in Lyly's *Midas*,
1.2.20–87 (Lyly, 3.120–1).

261 one knave] one kind of knave *Hanmer;* one kind *Warburton*   265 milkmaid] *(Milke-maid)*   268–9
SD] *Rowe subst., after* cate-log   269 cate-log] Cat-log *Rowe³;* catalogue *Cam¹*   condition] conditions *F4*

[*Reads.*] *Inprimis, she can fetch and carry.* Why, a horse   270
can do no more; nay, a horse cannot fetch but only
carry, therefore is she better than a jade. *Item, she can
milk.* Look you, a sweet virtue in a maid with clean
hands.

[*Enter* SPEED.]

SPEED   How now, Signior Lance? What news with your   275
mastership?

LANCE   With my master's ship? Why, it is at sea.

SPEED   Well, your old vice still: mistake the word. What
news, then, in your paper?

LANCE   The blackest news that ever thou heard'st.   280

SPEED   Why, man? How black?

LANCE   Why, as black as ink.

---

269 **cate-log** To modernize this ('cata-log') is to lose the joke on *cate*, a delicacy or treat, and 'Kate', possibly the woman's name, and hence a loose woman (see 266n.). Cam[1] explicitly rejects this argument. But cf. Petruchio in *TS* 2.1.189: 'For dainties are all Kates.'

270 **Inprimis** possibly another malapropism of Latin '*imprimis*' ('in the first place'), or possibly a minim misreading of *n* for *m*; cf. Q 'Imprimis' and F 'Inprimis' in *2H6* 1.1.43.

270–2 **she . . . jade** With the pun on *horse* (see 262n.) and the reference to a *jade* (tired mare; loose woman), Lance's language again veers toward the sexual; to *fetch* can also be an erotic activity (i.e. to draw forth, bring to ejaculation) which his *milkmaid* can accomplish but his *horse* cannot.

272 *Item* Latin term (meaning 'also') used to designate each new entry on a list

277 **at sea** on the ocean; lost, confused

278 **old vice** This is perhaps the earliest of Shakespeare's explicit references to the Vice figure of the Morality play tradition; cf. *R3* 3.1.82, *1H4* 2.4.441 and *TN* 4.2.125. Yet Lance is not really a Vice figure – his verbal mistakings, unlike those of the Vice, are usually inadvertent rather than self-conscious; see Spivack, 202–4. Weimann, 39, does note that 'the dramatic function of his laughter and audience awareness are . . . indebted to the farcical-allegorical anti-hero of the morality plays'. Friedman, 42, argues that Shakespeare splits 'the traits of the Vice figure between two characters, Launce and his master Proteus'.

282 **as . . . ink** proverbial (Dent, 173); cf. *Cym* 3.2.19–20: 'O damned paper, / Black as the ink that's on thee!'

---

270 SD] *Dyce*   270, 293 *Inprimis*] Imprimis *Rowe*   274.1] *F2*   277 master's ship] *Theobald;* Mastership *F*   280 blackest] *(*black'st*)*

SPEED   Let me read them.

LANCE   Fie on thee, jolt-head, thou canst not read.

SPEED   Thou liest: I can.   285

LANCE   I will try thee. Tell me this: who begot thee?

SPEED   Marry, the son of my grandfather.

LANCE   O illiterate loiterer! It was the son of thy grandmother. This proves that thou canst not read.

SPEED   Come, fool, come; try me in thy paper.   290

LANCE   [*Gives him the paper.*] There, and Saint Nicholas be thy speed.

SPEED   *Inprimis, she can milk.*

LANCE   Ay, that she can.

SPEED   *Item, she brews good ale.*   295

LANCE   And thereof comes the proverb, 'Blessing of your heart, you brew good ale.'

SPEED   *Item, she can sew.*

LANCE   That's as much as to say, 'Can she so?'

SPEED   *Item, she can knit.*   300

---

283 **them** the *news* (280); cf. 208 (*they*).

284 **jolt-head** blockhead (*OED* 2); cf. *TS* 4.1.154: 'You heedless jolt-heads.'

286, 290 **try** test

287–9 Cf. Dent, C309: 'It is a wise child that knows its own father.'

288 **loiterer** idler

291 **Saint Nicholas** as Warburton notes, the patron saint of scholars

292 **be thy speed** assist you; pun on Speed's name

293 *Inprimis* Speed unaccountably reads *Inprimis* (rather than *Item*) for this, the second example in the list (see 270).
milk There are multiple comic possibilities, in addition to the obvious skill of the *milkmaid* (265): to 'entice by wiles' (Cam[1]); to drain financially (Ard[2], citing Lyly's *Endymion*, 3.3.23–4: 'love hath as it were milkt my thoughts, and drained

from my hart the very substance of my accustomed courage', Lyly, 3.43); to give milk, or suckle, herself (Ard[2]); to masturbate (cf. Jonson's *The Alchemist*, 3.3.22: 'For she must milk his epididymis', Jonson, 3.292). The basic sexual implication is that she may milk but she's no maid.

296–7 The *proverb* is given by Dent, B450.

299 **so** As well as interpreting *sew* (298) as 'do so', Lance puns sexually on 'to sow'.

300 *knit* possibly implying a second sense, 'to conceive' (Cam[1], citing *OED* v. 5d); but it seems more vulgarly sexual (cf. Vindice in *Revenger's Tragedy*, 2.2.66–8: 'you shall have one woman knit more in a hour than any man can ravel again in seven and twenty year').

---

287 grandfather] *(Grand-father)*   289 grandmother] *Fc* (Grand-mother*)*; Grand-wother *Fu*   290 try] *Fc;* thy *Fu*   291 SD] *Cam[1]*   Saint] *(S.)*   298 sew] *Steevens;* sowe *F*   299 so?] *Fc;* so. *Fu*

LANCE   What need a man care for a stock with a wench,
when she can knit him a stock?

SPEED   *Item, she can wash and scour.*

LANCE   A special virtue, for then she need not be washed
and scoured.   305

SPEED   *Item, she can spin.*

LANCE   Then may I set the world on wheels, when she can
spin for her living.

SPEED   *Item, she hath many nameless virtues.*

LANCE   That's as much as to say 'bastard virtues', that   310
indeed know not their fathers, and therefore have no
names.

SPEED   Here follow her vices.

LANCE   Close at the heels of her virtues.

SPEED   *Item, she is not to be kissed fasting in respect of her*   315
breath.

LANCE   Well, that fault may be mended with a breakfast.
Read on.

SPEED   *Item, she hath a sweet mouth.*

---

301 **stock** dowry
302 **stock** stocking
304–5 **washed and scoured** 'knocked down and beaten' (Cam¹). Lance is punning on *wash* (= swash) and *scour* (= scourge, beat). *Scour* can also mean 'Purge the bowels, with the aid of a clyster' and one can 'Be scoured clean in the process of the VD cure' (Rubinstein, 231).
307 **set . . . wheels** i.e. take it easy; cf. Dent, W893.
308 **spin** to spin flax on a distaff, but also with a sexual connotation; cf. *TN* 1.3.100–2: 'I hope to see a huswife take thee between her legs and spin it off.'
309 *nameless* too many to name; too trivial to have a name, i.e. unknown

313–14 i.e. it is difficult to distinguish between them; there may also be a glancing allusion to the 'vice' and 'virtue' characters in the Morality play tradition.
315 ***kissed*** Rowe's emendation seems correct. Dyce cites Webster, *Duchess*, 2.1.42–3: 'than kiss one of you fasting'. *fasting* i.e. while fasting
317 **breakfast** morning meal; a meal which breaks her fast
319 *hath . . . mouth* i.e. likes to eat sweets; is lecherous. For the latter, Bond cites *Euphues*, ll. 11–12: '*Adonis* hath a sweete tooth in his head, and who knoweth not what followeth?' (Lyly, 2.83); see also Rubinstein, 265.

301–2] *Pope; F lines* wench, / stocke? /   310 bastard virtues] *(Bastard-vertues)*   313 follow] *Fc;* followes *Fu*   315 *kissed fasting*] *Rowe;* fasting *F;* – fasting *Cam¹;* broken with fasting *Oxf*

LANCE	That makes amends for her sour breath.	320
SPEED	*Item, she doth talk in her sleep.*	
LANCE	It's no matter for that, so she sleep not in her talk.	
SPEED	*Item, she is slow in words.*	
LANCE	O villain, that set this down among her vices! To be slow in words is a woman's only virtue. I pray thee out with't, and place it for her chief virtue.	325
SPEED	*Item, she is proud.*	
LANCE	Out with that too; it was Eve's legacy and cannot be ta'en from her.	
SPEED	*Item, she hath no teeth.*	330
LANCE	I care not for that neither, because I love crusts.	
SPEED	*Item, she is curst.*	
LANCE	Well, the best is, she hath no teeth to bite.	
SPEED	*Item, she will often praise her liquor.*	
LANCE	If her liquor be good, she shall; if she will not, I will, for good things should be praised.	335
SPEED	*Item, she is too liberal.*	
LANCE	Of her tongue she cannot, for that's writ down she is slow of; of her purse, she shall not, for that I'll keep shut. Now, of another thing she may, and that	340

322 **sleep** There is probably a pun on 'slip' (see Kökeritz, 146), but Collier's emendation is unnecessary. Cf. 1.1.72–3n.

324–6 Overly verbal women might be condemned as shrewish or worse, given the patriarchal ideal that a woman should be chaste, silent and obedient. Lance's milkmaid, *slow in words* (323), only approximates the category of silence.

325 **only** unique, sole; Leech cites *1H6* 4.4.189: 'Is Talbot slain, the Frenchmen's only scourge . . . ?'

327 *proud* with secondary meaning of 'lascivious', as Lance understands it at 328–9; cf. *Luc* 712: 'The flesh being proud'.

328 **Eve's legacy** i.e. she has inherited her nature from Eve and pride was the original deadly sin.

332 *curst* shrewish

334 *praise* appraise, test

336 **praised** commended; Lance shifts the sense of *praise* (334).

337 *liberal* generous; licentious. Cf. *Ham* 4.7.171: 'liberal shepherds'.

340 **thing** sexual organs: here, vagina (cf. *Oth* 3.3.306 and *Son* 136.7); elsewhere, the phallus, as at *1H4* 3.3.115–18.

322 sleep] slip *Collier²*   talk] *Fc* (talke); take *Fu*   324–6] *Pope; F lines* vices; / vertue: / vertue. /
324 villain] *Fc* (villaine); villanie *Fu*   328–9] *Pope; F lines* too: / her. /   329 ta'en] (t'ane)   331
love] *Fc* (loue); lone *Fu*

cannot I help. Well, proceed.

SPEED   *Item, she hath more hair than wit, and more faults than hairs, and more wealth than faults.*

LANCE   Stop there; I'll have her. She was mine and not mine twice or thrice in that last article. Rehearse that   345
once more.

SPEED   *Item, she hath more hair than wit –*

LANCE   More hair than wit. It may be; I'll prove it: the cover of the salt hides the salt, and therefore it is more than the salt; the hair that covers the wit is more than   350
the wit, for the greater hides the less. What's next?

SPEED   *And more faults than hairs –*

LANCE   That's monstrous. O, that that were out!

SPEED   *And more wealth than faults.*

LANCE   Why, that word makes the faults gracious. Well,   355
I'll have her; and if it be a match, as nothing is impossible –

SPEED   What then?

LANCE   Why, then will I tell thee that thy master stays for thee at the North Gate.   360

SPEED   For me?

---

342 *more . . . wit* proverbial (Dent, B736); cf. *CE* 2.2.81–2: 'there's many a man hath more hair than wit'. In *Satiromastix*, 4.3.55–6, Dekker's reference is self-conscious: '*Haire?* It's the basest stubble; in scorne of it, / This Proverbe sprung, *he has more haire then wit*' (Dekker, 1.361).

345 **Rehearse** repeat; cf. 4.1.26.

349–52 The wordplay here moves from the simple pun on *salt* as 'pungent wit' (*OED sb.*[1] 3c) into obscenity: *salt* = licentious (*OED a.*[2] b; cf. *AC* 2.1.21, 'salt Cleopatra'); *wit* = female sexual organs covered by *hair* (cf. *The*

Alchemist, 2.3.259–60: 'No trick, to give a man a taste of her – wit – / Or so?', Jonson, 3.272); and *fault* = crack, cleft, i.e. female genitals (cf. *KL* 1.1.15: 'Do you smell a fault', and see Astington) as well as 'an unsound or damaged place' (*OED* 4).

349 **cover . . .** [1]**salt** i.e. lid of salt-cellar

351 **greater . . . less** proverbial (Dent, G437); cf. *Luc* 663: 'The lesser thing should not the greater hide.'

355 **gracious** full of grace, i.e. acceptable

356–7 **nothing is impossible** proverbial (Dent, N298.1)

359 **stays** is waiting

342 hair] *Fc* (haire*)*; haires *Fu*   345 mine] *Fu;* mine, *Fc*   that last] *Fc;* that *Fu*   348 be;] *Theobald;* be *F*   355] *Pope; F lines* gracious: /   357 impossible –] *Rowe;* impossible. *F*

LANCE   For thee? Ay, who art thou? He hath stayed for a
better man than thee.

SPEED   And must I go to him?

LANCE   Thou must run to him, for thou hast stayed so   365
long that going will scarce serve the turn.

SPEED   Why didst not tell me sooner? Pox of your love
letters!   *[Exit.]*

LANCE   Now will he be swinged for reading my letter; an
unmannerly slave, that will thrust himself into secrets.   370
I'll after, to rejoice in the boy's correction.   *Exit.*

3.2   *Enter* DUKE *[and]* TURIO.

DUKE

Sir Turio, fear not but that she will love you
Now Valentine is banished from her sight.

TURIO

Since his exile she hath despised me most,
Forsworn my company and railed at me,
That I am desperate of obtaining her.   5

DUKE

This weak impress of love is as a figure

---

362 **stayed** waited
365 **stayed** delayed
366 **going** walking
   serve the turn be appropriate
367 **Pox** a mild curse; venereal disease
367–8 **love letters** On the significance
   of letters in the play, see pp. 59–67.
369 **swinged** beaten; cf. 2.1.76.
370 **unmannerly** ill-mannered
371 **after** follow
   correction punishment
3.2 The location remains Milan.
1 **but . . . will** i.e. that she will not

3   **exile** stressed on second syllable
4   **Forsworn** rejected
   railed at been abusive to (*OED v.*[4])
5   **That** so that
6–9 a simile of transformation (as at
   2.4.197–9): Silvia's *love* for Valentine
   will soon *melt* and dissolve like *ice*. Cf.
   Romeus, l. 98: the lover 'melts awaye, as
   snow against the sonne', and *R2* 4.1.
   260–2: 'a mockery king of snow . . . To
   melt myself away in water-drops!'
6   **impress** impression

367 Pox] *('pox)*   368 SD] *Capell*   371 SD] *Capell; Exeunt. F*   **3.2**] *Scena Secunda. F*   0.1] *Rowe;
Enter Duke, Thurio, Protheus. F*

Trenched in ice, which with an hour's heat
Dissolves to water and doth lose his form.
A little time will melt her frozen thoughts,
And worthless Valentine shall be forgot.   10

[Enter PROTEUS.*]*

How now, Sir Proteus, is your countryman,
According to our proclamation, gone?

PROTEUS
Gone, my good lord.

DUKE
My daughter takes his going grievously.

PROTEUS
A little time, my lord, will kill that grief.   15

DUKE
So I believe, but Turio thinks not so.
Proteus, the good conceit I hold of thee –
For thou hast shown some sign of good desert –
Makes me the better to confer with thee.

PROTEUS
Longer than I prove loyal to your grace   20
Let me not live to look upon your grace.

DUKE
Thou knowst how willingly I would effect
The match between Sir Turio and my daughter?

PROTEUS
I do, my lord.

---

7 **Trenched** trenchèd; carved
   hour's disyllabic
8 **his** its
14 **grievously** The 'heauily' of Fu and
   F4 certainly makes sense, but Fc's
   'grieuously', answered by Proteus's
   grief in the next line, seems preferable.

15 proverbial (Dent, T322)
17 **conceit** opinion; cf. *H8* 2.3.74–5: 'the
   fair conceit / The King hath of you'.
18 **desert** deserving
19 **the better** i.e. the more ready
   confer consult

10.1] *Rowe*   13 SP] *Fc; not in Fu*   14 grievously.] *Capell;* grieuously? *Fc;* heauily? *Fu;* heauily. *F4*

227

DUKE

    And also, I think, thou art not ignorant   25
    How she opposes her against my will?

PROTEUS

    She did, my lord, when Valentine was here.

DUKE

    Ay, and perversely she persevers so.
    What might we do to make the girl forget
    The love of Valentine, and love Sir Turio?   30

PROTEUS

    The best way is to slander Valentine
    With falsehood, cowardice and poor descent,
    Three things that women highly hold in hate.

DUKE

    Ay, but she'll think that it is spoke in hate.

PROTEUS

    Ay, if his enemy deliver it.   35
    Therefore it must with circumstance be spoken
    By one whom she esteemeth as his friend.

DUKE

    Then you must undertake to slander him.

PROTEUS

    And that, my lord, I shall be loath to do;
    'Tis an ill office for a gentleman,   40
    Especially against his very friend.

---

25 **And** The *And* is superfluous as well as extrametrical.
26 **her** herself
28 **persevers** persèvers
32 **descent** family, ancestry
34 **spoke** spoken (past participle)
35 **deliver** report
36 **circumstance** details, i.e. evidence; Bond also suggests 'with circumlocu-

tion and hesitation', citing *Ham* 1.5.133–4: 'And so, without more circumstance at all, / I hold it fit that we shake hands and part.'
40 **ill** bad, evil (an ironically true comment on Proteus's betrayal)
40, 44 **office** duty
41 **very** special; cf. *MV* 3.2.223: 'my very friends and countrymen'.

25 I] I doe *F2*

DUKE

Where your good word cannot advantage him,
Your slander never can endamage him;
Therefore the office is indifferent,
Being entreated to it by your friend. 45

PROTEUS

You have prevailed, my lord. If I can do it
By aught that I can speak in his dispraise,
She shall not long continue love to him.
But say this weed her love from Valentine,
It follows not that she will love Sir Turio. 50

TURIO

Therefore, as you unwind her love from him,
Lest it should ravel and be good to none,
You must provide to bottom it on me,

42–5 The Duke's logic here is as specious and self-serving as anything in Proteus's self-justifications.

44 **indifferent** neither good nor bad; cf. *Ham* 2.2.227: 'indifferent children of the earth'.

49 **weed** remove. Arguing for *weed*, Bond holds that *from* must loosely mean 'of', 'Valentine being the weed that is to be plucked from her love', but the grammar dictates that it is *her love* that must be weeded; Bond also notes the possibility of 'wind', 'used of working a ship out of harbour, and figuratively of any devious practice', citing *Revenger's Tragedy*, 3.1.16–17: 'some trick and wile / To wind our younger brother out of prison'. Leech, adopting 'wind', argues that the image of a garden does not fit in the context, and suggests that 'wind' is supported by *unwind* (51). The garden metaphor is still the most likely; cf. *MM* 3.2.263: 'To weed my vice and let his grow!' and *2H4*

4.1.205: 'He cannot so precisely weed this land.' The garden metaphor might also be justified as reflecting either Proteus's cunning (Silvia's love can easily be transferred to another and, as a 'weed', is now unnatural, hence should be removed) or his lack of respect for or anxiety about women's fidelity. The unweeded garden metaphor, as seen in *Ham* 1.2.135–7, insinuates loose female sexuality.

51–3 a metaphor of thread being unwound and then rewound into a skein or ball of wool: to *unwind* her love from Valentine, it must not be allowed to *ravel* (tangle); Turio is the *bottom* (a harder material on which the skein was wound) on which the thread (of love) will be rewound. Cf. 3.1.308 and n.; *TS* 4.3.133: 'a bottom of brown thread'; *Mac* 2.2.41: 'the raveled sleave of care'; and the name 'Bottom', a 'weaver', in *MND*.

---

47 aught] *(ought)* 49 weed] wean *Rowe;* wind *Keightley (Marshall);* wend *(Cam¹);* woo *Sisson*

Which must be done by praising me as much
As you in worth dispraise Sir Valentine.   55
DUKE
        And, Proteus, we dare trust you in this kind
        Because we know, on Valentine's report,
        You are already Love's firm votary,
        And cannot soon revolt and change your mind.
        Upon this warrant shall you have access   60
        Where you with Silvia may confer at large –
        For she is lumpish, heavy, melancholy,
        And, for your friend's sake, will be glad of you –
        Where you may temper her by your persuasion
        To hate young Valentine and love my friend.   65
PROTEUS
        As much as I can do, I will effect.
        But you, Sir Turio, are not sharp enough.
        You must lay lime to tangle her desires
        By wailful sonnets, whose composed rhymes
        Should be full-fraught with serviceable vows.   70
DUKE
        Ay, much is the force of heaven-bred poesy.

56 **in this kind** for a task of this sort
58 **votary** See 1.1.52n.
60 **warrant** guarantee
   access stressed on second syllable
61 **confer at large** talk at length; cf.
   3.1.251.
62 **lumpish** low-spirited ('unique in
   Shakespeare', Ard²)
   heavy sad, serious
63–5 The improbably mechanical trans-
   ference of friendships proposed here
   by the Duke anticipates Valentine's
   behaviour in the final scene of the play
   (see 5.4.83).
64 **temper** soften, make flexible; Malone
   cites *2H4* 4.3.127–9: 'I have him

already tempering between my finger
and my thumb, and shortly will I seal
with him.'
68 **lay . . . tangle** as one traps a bird with
   lime; cf. *Ham* 3.3.68: 'O limèd soul . . .
   struggling to be free', and *TN* 3.4.76:
   'I have limed her.' Bond notes that
   tangle ('enmesh') produces a mixed
   metaphor of entrapment.
69 **sonnets** poems praising a mistress, not
   necessarily in sonnet form; cf. John
   Donne's *Songs and Sonnets*.
   composed composèd
70 **full-fraught** fully loaded
   serviceable vows vows of service

70 full-fraught] *(full fraught)*   71 Ay, much] Much *Pope*

230

PROTEUS

Say that upon the altar of her beauty
You sacrifice your tears, your sighs, your heart.
Write till your ink be dry, and with your tears
Moist it again, and frame some feeling line   75
That may discover such integrity;
For Orpheus' lute was strung with poets' sinews,
Whose golden touch could soften steel and stones,
Make tigers tame and huge leviathans
Forsake unsounded deeps to dance on sands.   80
After your dire-lamenting elegies,
Visit by night your lady's chamber-window

72–86 Proteus's poetic advice is inspiring and lyrical, but it is also deceitful and treacherous. It echoes some of the most profound exaltations of the power of poetry in the Renaissance, but in the service of betrayal. The speech goes far beyond practical advice to Turio; as Proteus becomes inspired, it demonstrates how Proteus has indeed been moved by the power of love – though his intentions are entirely insincere. D'Amico, 101, claims that Shakespeare here uses the scene 'to satirize the poetic pretensions of courtly lovers and to reduce the class-conscious Duke to something of a citizen-father tricked by the wily Proteus'.

76 **discover** reveal
   integrity single-mindedness, devotion
77–80 The power of Orpheus's lute is a familiar and important Shakespearean motif; cf. *MV* 5.1.79–82: 'Therefore the poet / Did feign that Orpheus drew trees, stones, and floods, / Since naught so stockish, hard, and full of rage / But music for the time doth change his nature.' Berowne's great speech at *LLL* 4.3.320–3 invokes the

same powers: 'Never durst poet touch a pen to write / Until his ink were tempered with Love's sighs. / O, then his lines would ravish savage ears / And plant in tyrants mild humility.' RP also cites *Mucedorus*, E2ᵛ: 'In time of yore when men like brutish beasts / Did lead their lives in loathsom celles and woodes / And wholy gave themselves to witlesse will . . . Behould one *Orpheus* came as poets tell, / And them from rudenes unto reason brought.' Ovid tells of Orpheus's powers in *Met.*, 10.93–116, and *Tristia*, 4.1.17–18.

77 **sinews** 'A tendon taken out of an animal body and used for some purpose, esp. for binding or tying with; . . . a string in a musical instrument' (*OED sb.* 1b)

78 **Whose** i.e. Orpheus's
   touch Cf. 2.7.18, 5.4.60 and 128; see p. 28, on the repetition of this word in the play.
79 **leviathans** whales
81 **elegies** love poems; cf. *AYL* 3.2.351–4: 'There is a man . . . hangs odes upon hawthorns and elegies on brambles.'

With some sweet consort; to their instruments
Tune a deploring dump. The night's dead silence
Will well become such sweet-complaining grievance.   85
This, or else nothing, will inherit her.

DUKE

This discipline shows thou hast been in love.

TURIO

And thy advice this night I'll put in practice.
Therefore, sweet Proteus, my direction-giver,
Let us into the city presently   90
To sort some gentlemen well skilled in music.
I have a sonnet that will serve the turn
To give the onset to thy good advice.

DUKE

About it, gentlemen!

PROTEUS

We'll wait upon your grace till after supper,   95
And afterward determine our proceedings.

DUKE

Even now about it. I will pardon you.   *Exeunt.*

---

83 **consort** group of musicians; Leech suggests it might instead refer to a 'piece of music', but this seems doubtful. Cf. *2H6* 3.2.327: 'And boding screech-owls make the consort full!' and *KL* 2.1.97: 'he was of that consort'. Cf. 4.1.63.

84 **Tune** sing
dump mournful melody. Leech cites Anthony Munday, *Two Italian Gentlemen*, l. 1096: 'the Consort sounds a sollemne Dump'. Cf. *Luc* 1127: 'Distress likes dumps.' Bond argues that *dump* was not always melancholy, citing *RJ* 4.5.105: 'some merry dump', though the context there does indicate mourning.

85 **grievance** lamenting

86 **inherit** win, obtain

87 **discipline** knowledge, learning; cf. *TC* 2.3.27–8: 'Heaven bless thee from a tutor, and discipline come not near thee!'

89 **direction-giver** 'one who directs an archer's aim' (Ard[2]); cf. 5.4.100n.

90 **presently** at once

91 **sort** choose

92–3 Turio, thinking he is clever at language, offers the *turn* (anagram) of *sonnet* into *onset*.

92 **turn** occasion

93 **give . . . to** set in motion

95 **wait upon** attend

97 **I . . . you** i.e. you have my permission to leave

---

85 sweet-complaining] *(sweet complaining)* 93 onset] *(on-set)* advice] *(aduise)*

4.1   *Enter* VALENTINE, SPEED *and certain* Outlaws.

1 OUTLAW
    Fellows, stand fast. I see a passenger.

2 OUTLAW
    If there be ten, shrink not, but down with 'em.

3 OUTLAW
    Stand, sir, and throw us that you have about ye.
    If not, we'll make you sit and rifle you.

SPEED
    Sir, we are undone; these are the villains   5
    That all the travellers do fear so much.

VALENTINE   My friends –

1 OUTLAW
    That's not so, sir. We are your enemies.

4.1 The location shifts to the *wilderness* (62) outside Milan (cf. *forest*, 5.2.36) – possibly on the way to *Verona* (17–19), the destination given the Outlaws by Valentine, but thought to be *Mantua* by Silvia (see 4.3.23). At 5.1.11, Eglamour says 'The forest is not three leagues off.' At 5.4.2, Valentine describes the scene as 'This shadowy desert, unfrequented woods'. Shakespeare's non-illusionist, essentially bare stage is here what Northrop Frye terms a 'green world', though the properties of the woods outside Athens in *MND* and the forest of Arden in *AYL* are more pronouncedly magical and restorative; see Barber and Roberts, *Wild*.

0.1 *Riv* is alone among earlier editions in following F rather than adopting Rowe's suggestion of placing the entry of Valentine and Speed after 4.1.2. But, as NB observes, 'Valentine needs to be visible to be seen', and RP notes that 'simultaneous entry by different doors' is a possible option.

Outlaws The Outlaws have been represented in many different ways, from comic-operatic figures to rustic thugs or underground urban vagrants. The number of Outlaws onstage grew, like Falstaff's assailants, at an alarming rate in eighteenth- and nineteenth-century adaptations: Victor adds a fourth, while Kemble produces seven (with banditti names: Ubaldo, Luigi, etc.). In his 1981 production, Barton offered nine (Warren[1], 143).

1, 71 **passenger** traveller; cf. 5.4.15.

4 **make** Johnson's conjectural 'take' was based on disapproval of *make*: 'This is not the language of a very cunning robber.'
    sit in verbal if not semantic antithesis to *Stand* (3) or 'halt'; cf. *friends* (7) and *enemies* (8).
    rifle search, rob ('unique in Shakespeare', Ard[2]); *OED* cites Rowlands, *Dr Merry-man*, 3: 'Unto a Wood hard by, they hale him in, / And rifle him unto his very skin.'

4.1] *Actus Quartus. Scoena Prima. F*   3–4] *as prose Pope*   3 about ye] *(*about'ye*)*   4 make] take *(Johnson)*   sit] sir *F3*   5–6] *as prose Pope*   7 friends –] *Pope;* friends. *F*

2 OUTLAW   Peace! We'll hear him.

3 OUTLAW   Ay, by my beard will we; for he is a proper man.   10

VALENTINE

  Then know that I have little wealth to lose.
  A man I am crossed with adversity;
  My riches are these poor habiliments,
  Of which if you should here disfurnish me,
  You take the sum and substance that I have.   15

2 OUTLAW   Whither travel you?

VALENTINE   To Verona.

1 OUTLAW   Whence came you?

VALENTINE   From Milan.

3 OUTLAW   Have you long sojourned there?   20

VALENTINE

  Some sixteen months, and longer might have stayed
  If crooked fortune had not thwarted me.

1 OUTLAW   What, were you banished thence?

VALENTINE   I was.

2 OUTLAW   For what offence?   25

VALENTINE

  For that which now torments me to rehearse:
  I killed a man, whose death I much repent,

---

10 Capell's emendation was an attempt to
   smooth out the metrical roughness of
   this line.
   by my beard a mild oath
   proper fine-looking, gentlemanly
12 **crossed with** thwarted by
13 **habiliments** clothes
14 **disfurnish** deprive
15 **sum and substance** 'essence (of anything)' (*OED* sum *sb.*¹ 11, citing this
   instance)
21 **sixteen months** This can hardly be
   the time-span of the play, since it
   would require fifteen months to

pass between 1.1 and 1.3; the reference
is either another of Valentine's false
claims (see 27n.) or a further instance of
Shakespearean double-time schemes.
See p. 125.
22 **crooked** not direct, i.e. evil
22, 42 **fortune** luck
23–5 RP notes the iambic movement of
these lines, possibly suggesting two
rhyming trimeter lines (*thence? /
offence?*).
26 **rehearse** repeat; cf. 3.1.345.
27 **killed a man** Valentine, the arch-
'lover', defensively fakes credentials

10 he is] he's *Capell*   19 Milan] *(Millaine)*

But yet I slew him manfully in fight,
Without false vantage or base treachery.

1 OUTLAW

Why, ne'er repent it, if it were done so.　　　　　　30
But were you banished for so small a fault?

VALENTINE

I was, and held me glad of such a doom.

2 OUTLAW

Have you the tongues?

VALENTINE

My youthful travel therein made me happy,
Or else I often had been miserable.　　　　　　　35

3 OUTLAW

By the bare scalp of Robin Hood's fat friar,

for the benefit of the Outlaws by claiming to have committed a suitably horrific crime; his invented claim is Romeus's real offence (killing Tybalt) in *Romeus*. Leech also suggests 'that he was under an obligation as a "courtly lover" to conceal his real reason for leaving'. Cf. Lucentio's explanation for his disguise in *TS* 1.1.231–2: 'For in a quarrel since I came ashore, / I killed a man'.

29 **false vantage** unfair advantage
31 **small a fault** Cf. *petty crimes* (51): presumably meant to be comic.
32 **doom** judgement, sentence
33 'Can you speak foreign languages?' Cf. *MA* 5.1.164–5: 'he hath the tongues'.
34 **travel** F's 'trauaile' (= 'labour' as well as 'travel') could refer to Valentine's study of languages rather than his travel to foreign lands, though 35 suggests he has had occasion to use these languages *often*. Yet, as Schlueter notes, 'when

Valentine sets out "to see the wonders of the world" in 1.1, no earlier travel is mentioned'. Presumably Valentine's claim is further evidence of his self-protective strategy of appearing more worldly-wise than he is (see 27n.).
happy proficient; fortunate
36 **fat friar** i.e Friar Tuck. Shakespeare invokes the legend of Robin Hood – a very English rather than Italian outlaw. Cf. also *AYL* 1.1.111–12: 'there they live like the old Robin Hood of England', and *2H4* 5.3.104: 'And Robin Hood, Scarlet, and John'. Bond suggests a possible knowledge of two Robin Hood plays, both by Anthony Munday and Henry Chettle, and written in 1598, *The Downfall* and *The Death of Robert, Earl of Huntingdon*, but the late date of these plays makes any influence implausible. There were many earlier ballads and plays about Robin Hood.

34 travel] *(*trauaile*)*　35 often had been] *F2;* often had beene often *F;* had been often *Collier*

This fellow were a king for our wild faction.

1 OUTLAW

We'll have him. Sirs, a word.   [*Outlaws talk apart.*]

SPEED   Master, be one of them.

It's an honourable kind of thievery.

VALENTINE   Peace, villain.   40

2 OUTLAW

Tell us this: have you anything to take to?

VALENTINE   Nothing but my fortune.

3 OUTLAW

Know then that some of us are gentlemen,
Such as the fury of ungoverned youth
Thrust from the company of awful men.   45
Myself was from Verona banished
For practising to steal away a lady,
An heir, and near allied unto the Duke.

---

37 **were** would be
    king Valentine is invited to be the Out-
laws' *king*, though at 60 they imagine
him as their *general*, at 64 it will be
captain and at 66 *commander* and *king*.
40 **villain** See 3.1.202n.
41 **have . . . take to** have you any
resources
43 **gentlemen** Cf. *AYL* 2.7, where
Orlando also encounters outlaws who
turn out to be gentlemen.
45 **awful men** men who command awe,
respect; cf. *R2* 3.3.75–6: 'how dare thy
joints forget / To pay their awful duty
to our presence?'
46–50 The Third Outlaw is guilty of
Valentine's exact transgression, while
Valentine has already claimed the same
crime as the Second Outlaw; these
unlikely coincidences have suggested
revision or carelessness to some read-

ers, but they may also be part of the
comedy.
46 **banished** banishèd
47 **practising** plotting; cf. *KL* 3.2.56–7:
'That . . . Has practised on man's life!'
48 **heir** heiress (could refer to either sex)
    *****near** Theobald's emendation solves
the problem of the redundancy of F's
'Neece'. Bond defends 'niece allied' as
'not two expressions, but a formal cer-
emonial term, or else as meaning
"niece by marriage"'. The converse
error ('neere' for 'neece') has been
observed in *KJ* 2.1.425 and TLN 739
(Ard[1], citing White as source).
    allied stressed on second syllable
(disyllabic)
    Duke Verona is supposedly ruled by a
duke, although at the time it was under
the rule of the Venetian Republic.

---

38 SD] *Cam[1] subst.*   45 awful] lawful *Steevens (Hawkins);* aweful *Riv*   48 An] *F3; And F*   heir,
and near] *Theobald;* heire and Neece, *F*

2 OUTLAW

And I from Mantua, for a gentleman
Who, in my mood, I stabbed unto the heart.   50

1 OUTLAW

And I for suchlike petty crimes as these.
But to the purpose, for we cite our faults
That they may hold excused our lawless lives;
And partly, seeing you are beautified
With goodly shape, and by your own report   55
A linguist, and a man of such perfection
As we do in our quality much want –

2 OUTLAW

Indeed because you are a banished man,
Therefore above the rest we parley to you.
Are you content to be our general?   60
To make a virtue of necessity
And live as we do in this wilderness?

3 OUTLAW

What sayst thou? Wilt thou be of our consort?
Say 'Ay', and be the captain of us all,

---

50 **mood** angry fit; cf. *R3* 1.2.244: 'my angry mood' and *Son* 93.8: 'in moods and frowns'.
53 **That** so that
54 **beautified** Cf. *Ham* 2.2.111–12: 'That's an ill phrase, a vile phrase; "beautified" is a vile phrase.' The use of the word here may comically reflect on the speaker, given Valentine's *poor habiliments* (13). Cf. Robert Greene's notorious use of the word: 'an upstart Crow, beautified with our feathers' (Chambers, *WS*, 2.188) (RP).
56 **perfection** completeness; see 1.3.20n.
57 **quality** profession; status
   *****want** – lack; Theobald's insertion of a dash in place of F's full stop has been

adopted by most editors because the First Outlaw does not speak a complete sentence and the Second Outlaw seems to interrupt.
59 **above the rest** i.e. more than for any other reason
   parley to negotiate with, make an offer to
61 proverbial (Dent, V73); cf. *R2* 1.3.278: 'There is no virtue like necessity.'
63–75 The shift from *you* to *thou* forms in the speeches of the Outlaws, indicating a more relaxed or familiar dialogue relation, implies that the death threat (67) is not to be taken too seriously (RP).
63 **consort** company; cf. 3.2.83.

50 Who] Whom *Pope*   51 suchlike] *(such like)*   57 want –] *Theobald;* want. *F*   62 this] the *F2*

We'll do thee homage and be ruled by thee,   65
Love thee as our commander and our king.

1 OUTLAW

But if thou scorn our courtesy, thou diest.

2 OUTLAW

Thou shalt not live to brag what we have offered.

VALENTINE

I take your offer and will live with you,
Provided that you do no outrages   70
On silly women or poor passengers.

3 OUTLAW

No, we detest such vile base practices.
Come, go with us. We'll bring thee to our crews
And show thee all the treasure we have got,   74
Which, with ourselves, all rest at thy dispose.   *Exeunt.*

4.2   *Enter* PROTEUS.

PROTEUS

Already have I been false to Valentine,
And now I must be as unjust to Turio.
Under the colour of commending him
I have access my own love to prefer.
But Silvia is too fair, too true, too holy   5
To be corrupted with my worthless gifts.

---

67 This melodramatic threat underscores the comic absurdity of the Outlaws.
71 **silly** simple, innocent
73 **crews** bands. F's plural has been challenged – how could there be multiple gangs of outlaws? It could be, however, a use of the plural form with the singular meaning (see 3.1.53n. on *letters*).
75 **dispose** disposal; cf. 2.7.86.

4.2 The location returns to Milan, near Silvia's *window* (16).
3 **colour** pretext
4 **access** stressed on second syllable
  prefer advance
5 **too . . . holy** formulaic praise; cf. 40: 'Holy, fair and wise'.
6 **with** by

73 crews] cave *Collier²;* caves *Singer;* crew *Cam¹*   75 all] shall *Rowe³*   **4.2**] *Scoena Secunda. F*   0.1] *Rowe; Enter Protheus, Thurio, Iulia, Host, Musitian, Siluia. F*   6 gifts] *(guifts)*

When I protest true loyalty to her,
She twits me with my falsehood to my friend;
When to her beauty I commend my vows,
She bids me think how I have been forsworn   10
In breaking faith with Julia, whom I loved.
And notwithstanding all her sudden quips,
The least whereof would quell a lover's hope,
Yet, spaniel-like, the more she spurns my love,
The more it grows and fawneth on her still.   15

[*Enter* TURIO *and Musicians.*]

But here comes Turio. Now must we to her window,
And give some evening music to her ear.

TURIO
How now, Sir Proteus, are you crept before us?

PROTEUS
Ay, gentle Turio, for you know that love
Will creep in service where it cannot go.   20

TURIO
Ay, but I hope, sir, that you love not here.

PROTEUS
Sir, but I do, or else I would be hence.

7–15 This passage indicates a number of efforts by Proteus to court Silvia, none of which the play has shown.
8   **twits** reproves
9   **commend** address
10 **have been forsworn** have perjured myself
12 **quips** retorts, sarcastic utterances
13 **quell** kill
14–15 **spaniel-like . . . fawneth** See 3.1.268n. Proteus's simile not only

links him to Crab (see 4.4.28–9n.) but also reflects how the power of desire is transforming him.
15 **still** continually
18 **are you crept** have you moved in unnoticed or stealthily (*OED* 2); cf. *AYL* 1.2.146–7: 'Are you crept hither to see the wrestling?'
20 **creep** crawl (*OED* 1; a rejoinder to Turio's *crept*, 18)
    go walk

15.1] *Rowe after 17*

TURIO

    Who? Silvia?

PROTEUS   Ay, Silvia – for your sake.

TURIO

    I thank you for your own. Now, gentlemen,

    Let's tune, and to it lustily awhile.   25

[Enter Host, *and* JULIA *in boy's clothes, as Sebastian.]*

HOST   Now, my young guest, methinks you're allicholy.
    I pray you, why is it?

JULIA   Marry, mine host, because I cannot be merry.

HOST   Come, we'll have you merry. I'll bring you where
    you shall hear music, and see the gentleman that you   30
    asked for.

JULIA   But shall I hear him speak?

HOST   Ay, that you shall.

JULIA   That will be music.   *[Music plays.]*

HOST   Hark, hark!   35

JULIA   Is he among these?

HOST   Ay; but peace, let's hear 'em.

---

23 **Ay ... sake** Proteus's *Ay, Silvia* could be performed either as a momentary lapse revealing his true feelings (from which he has quickly to recover) or as a calculated attempt to unsettle Turio (which he then jokingly redresses).

25–78 The musical interlude begins with instruments alone (*Let's tune*, 25), then the song (38), then an additional instrumental section (perhaps played by Proteus) *on the strings* (58). The Host and Julia presumably stay to one side so as not to be heard.

26–8 proverbial: see Dent, S14: 'I am sad because I cannot be glad.'

26 **methinks** it seems to me

allicholy the Host's version of 'melancholy'; the same mistake is made by Mistress Quickly in *MW* 1.4.142: 'she is given too much to allicholy and musing'. Cf. the QF form 'mallicholie' at *LLL* 4.3.12, 13.

28 **Marry** See 1.1.119n.

29–31 Cf. *Diana*, 88: 'But midnight being a little past, mine host called at my chamber doore, and tolde me if I was desirous to heare some brave musicke, I should arise quickly, and open a window towards the street. The which I did by and by . . . And then began a voice to sing, the sweetest (in my opinion) that ever I heard.'

---

23 Who] Whom *F2*   25 to] *(too)*   25.1] *Rowe subst.*   26 you're] *(your')*   allicholy] *(allycholly)*
34 SD] *Capell*   37 hear 'em] *(heare'm)*

SONG

Who is Silvia? What is she,
That all our swains commend her?
Holy, fair and wise is she;   40
The heaven such grace did lend her,
    That she might admired be.

Is she kind as she is fair?
For beauty lives with kindness.
Love doth to her eyes repair   45
To help him of his blindness,
    And, being helped, inhabits there.

Then to Silvia let us sing,
That Silvia is excelling;
She excels each mortal thing   50
Upon the dull earth dwelling.
    To her let us garlands bring.

38–52 Neither F nor most editions offer a SP at 38, but the song is probably sung by Proteus, as Julia's subsequent comments suggest (e.g. *He plays false*, 57). Some productions, such as that of Edward Hall in 1998, have one of the musicians sing it. Earlier commentators, such as Long, argue that the musicians must be offstage during the song, on the grounds that simultaneous stage action would be too demanding on an audience; countless productions of the play have disproved this argument. Proteus may both play and sing, then, accompanied by Turio and at least one musician (*gentlemen*, 24, could refer to Proteus and one other). Schlueter claims that the song is 'almost certainly' Turio's *sonnet* (3.2.92), which – given the song's beauty – seems unlikely. The song has been set to music many times, most notably by Schubert.

39 **swains** country youth (diction reflecting the pastoral tradition)
40 Cf. 5 and n.
42 **That** in order that
    admired admirèd; wondered at
45–7 Blindfolded (hence *blindness*) Cupid (see Dent, L506) resides in her eyes, so that he may see; cf. Sidney, *Astrophil and Stella*, 65.7–8: Love 'being blind / By Nature borne, I gave to thee mine eyes' (Sidney, 198).
45 **repair** resort
46 **help** cure
49 **excelling** absolute usage; cf. *excels*, 50, 80

SD SONG] SONG Proteus *Folg²*; SONG Musician *Bantam*   41 heaven] heav'ns *Johnson*

HOST   How now, are you sadder than you were before?
           How do you, man? The music likes you not.

JULIA   You mistake; the musician likes me not.   55

HOST   Why, my pretty youth?

JULIA   He plays false, father.

HOST   How, out of tune on the strings?

JULIA   Not so; but yet so false that he grieves my very
           heart-strings.   60

HOST   You have a quick ear.

JULIA   Ay, I would I were deaf; it makes me have a slow
           heart.

HOST   I perceive you delight not in music.

JULIA   Not a whit, when it jars so.   65

HOST   Hark, what fine change is in the music!

JULIA   Ay, that change is the spite.

HOST   You would have them always play but one thing?

JULIA

           I would always have one play but one thing.

54 **likes** pleases
55 **likes** Julia's response takes up the
Host's sense of the word, but she also
means 'loves'.
57 **He plays false** Julia plays on a double
sense of *false*: the ethical and the musical; cf. the similar use of musical terms
at 1.2.89–97 (see n.).
   father a generic reference to an older
man
58 The Host understands Julia's *false* to
mean *out of tune* musically.
60 **heart-strings** 'The tendons or nerves
supposed to brace and sustain the
heart' (*OED sb. pl.* 1), but also – as
appropriate to this scene – 'with allusion to stringed instruments of music'
(*OED sb. pl.* 2c). Thus *grieves* (59)
means both 'give grief to' and 'press

heavily on' (as if he were playing her
heart-strings).
61 **quick** perceptive; keen
62 **deaf** Julia takes the Host's *quick* also
to mean 'alive', hence her desire for a
deaf, i.e. 'dead', ear.
   slow heavy
65 **Not a whit** not at all
   jars grates
66–7 **change . . . change** musical variation . . . mutability, fickleness
67 **spite** injury, harm
69 Julia's desire for constancy, like her
belief in the stability of language (see
2.7.75n.), is utopian; there may also be
a sexual implication in *play* and/or
thing (see 3.1.340n.). Cf. Proteus's
recognition at 5.4.109–11.

53–4] *Pope; F lines* before; / not. /   59–60] *Pope; F lines* yet / heart-strings. /   68 would] would
then *Boswell–Malone*   always play] play always *F4*   thing?] *Pope; thing. F*

242

But, host, doth this Sir Proteus that we talk on   70
Often resort unto this gentlewoman?

HOST   I tell you what Lance, his man, told me: he loved
her out of all nick.

JULIA   Where is Lance?

HOST   Gone to seek his dog, which tomorrow, by his   75
master's command, he must carry for a present to his
lady.

JULIA   Peace, stand aside; the company parts.

PROTEUS

Sir Turio, fear not you; I will so plead
That you shall say my cunning drift excels.   80

TURIO

Where meet we?

PROTEUS   At Saint Gregory's well.

TURIO   Farewell.

[*Exeunt Turio and Musicians.*]

[*Enter* SILVIA *above.*]

---

70 **talk on** speak of
71 **resort unto** frequent
73 **out . . . nick** beyond all reckoning; Bond, citing Warburton as his source, glosses: 'the Host's characteristic metaphor from the keeping of a score by nicks or notches on a stick or tally' (though the Host is supposedly quoting Lance here).
75–7 The Host anticipates Lance's story about Crab and the gift dog for Silvia (4.4.6–7). For Leech, xx, both references are 'palpably absurd' in the light of 4.4.44–56 and hence are seen as further evidence of textual anomaly pointing to revision;
78 **parts** separates; is leaving
80 **drift** plan, scheme; cf. 2.6.43, 3.1.18.

81 **Saint Gregory's well** Bond identifies this as 'an actual well near Milan'.
Farewell perhaps another example of Turio's weak wit, echoing Proteus's *well*; cf. 3.2.92–3n.
81.1 *above That it is night (see 3.2.82–3), that the Duke is keeping Silvia *nightly* in an *upper tower* (3.1.35–7) and the reference to *window* (16) together sufficiently justify Rowe's '*above*'. The dialogue further suggests that Silvia is so positioned as to be unable to see the speaker clearly (see 84) – a device used for the same effect at 4.3.4, where again she enters '*above*' in the very early morning before anyone but Eglamour is yet up (4.3.9).

72–3] *Pope; F lines* me, / nicke. /   81 SD] *Rowe subst.*   81.1] *Rowe; Silvia, above, at her Window / Theobald*

243

PROTEUS

Madam, good even to your ladyship.

SILVIA

I thank you for your music, gentlemen.

Who is that that spake?

PROTEUS

One, lady, if you knew his pure heart's truth,   85

You would quickly learn to know him by his voice.

SILVIA

Sir Proteus, as I take it.

PROTEUS

Sir Proteus, gentle lady, and your servant.

SILVIA

What's your will?

PROTEUS   That I may compass yours.

SILVIA

You have your wish. My will is even this,   90

That presently you hie you home to bed.

Thou subtle, perjured, false, disloyal man,

Think'st thou I am so shallow, so conceitless,

To be seduced by thy flattery

That hast deceived so many with thy vows?   95

Return, return, and make thy love amends.

For me – by this pale queen of night I swear –

---

89 **compass** achieve, obtain; Proteus
suggestively responds to Silvia's polite
question, taking *will* to mean 'sexual
desire'.
91 **presently** immediately
hie hasten
92 Leech notes the shift from *you* (83–6)
to *Thou* at the beginning of Silvia's
denunciation (92), perhaps marking
her contempt; she returns to *you* usage
at 125.

subtle cunning
93 **conceitless** without perception; wit-
less
94 **seduced** seducèd
95 **so many** Presumably this reference is
to Proteus's friends and family, rather
than to numerous female victims.
96 **thy love** i.e. Julia
97 **pale queen** i.e. the moon as Diana,
goddess of chastity – an appropriate
figure for Silvia to invoke here

82 even] *(eu'n)*   89 What's] What is *Pope*   95 hast] *(has't)*

I am so far from granting thy request
That I despise thee for thy wrongful suit,
And by and by intend to chide myself   100
Even for this time I spend in talking to thee.

PROTEUS

I grant, sweet love, that I did love a lady,
But she is dead.

JULIA [*aside*]   'Twere false, if I should speak it,
For I am sure she is not buried.

SILVIA

Say that she be; yet Valentine thy friend   105
Survives, to whom, thyself art witness,
I am betrothed. And art thou not ashamed
To wrong him with thy importunacy?

PROTEUS

I likewise hear that Valentine is dead.

SILVIA

And so suppose am I, for in his grave   110
Assure thyself, my love is buried.

PROTEUS

Sweet lady, let me rake it from the earth.

SILVIA

Go to thy lady's grave and call hers thence,
Or, at the least, in hers sepulchre thine.

JULIA [*aside*]   He heard not that.   115

---

100 **by and by** soon, immediately
103 **if** even if
104 **buried** burièd
107 **betrothed** See 2.4.177n.
108 **importunacy** importunity, i.e. urging your suit
109 'This excuse is so feeble that it reflects from the incompetence of Proteus to that of the dramatist' (Ard²); the outrageousness of the

claim, however, may be just the point, as it is when Richard tries out a similar lie on Lady Anne, *R3* 1.2.89: 'Say that I slew him not?'
111 **buried** burièd
113 **hers** i.e. her love
114 **hers** i.e. her grave
    sepulchre bury; stressed on second syllable
115 i.e. he won't want to listen to that

103, 115, 123 SDs] *Pope*   106 thyself] even thy self *Hanmer*   110 his] *F2;* her *F*

PROTEUS

Madam, if your heart be so obdurate,
Vouchsafe me yet your picture for my love,
The picture that is hanging in your chamber.
To that I'll speak, to that I'll sigh and weep;
For since the substance of your perfect self   120
Is else devoted, I am but a shadow,
And to your shadow will I make true love.

JULIA [*aside*]

If 'twere a substance you would sure deceive it
And make it but a shadow, as I am.

SILVIA

I am very loath to be your idol, sir.   125
But, since your falsehood shall become you well
To worship shadows and adore false shapes,
Send to me in the morning, and I'll send it.
And so, good rest.   [*Exit.*]

PROTEUS   As wretches have o'ernight   129

---

116 **obdurate** hard
117 **picture** her actual portrait, in contrast to *picture*, her appearance, at 2.4.206
120–4 See 3.1.177n.
120 **perfect** complete; see 1.3.20n.
121 **else** elsewhere
 devoted vowed, dedicated
 shadow nothing
122 **shadow** her *picture* (117); cf. 4.4.115–18 and Lyly's *Campaspe*, 1.2.71–2: 'to shadow a Ladies face' (Lyly, 2.321).
123–4 Julia is a mere *shadow* of herself without Proteus's love, even as he has claimed, in the identical words (121), to be a *shadow* of himself without Silvia's love; moreover, if the picture itself were the real thing (a *substance*), Proteus would *deceive it* as well and turn it into a *shadow*. See 3.1.177n.

125 **idol** object of false worship. Her *picture* (117) will become the object of his *worship* (127). This metaphor of idolatry echoes earlier language of love as a religion (cf. 1.1.52n. on *votary* and 2.4.142–5n.).
128 **I'll send it** Silvia's promise is a practical plot necessity, preparing for Julia's encounter with Silvia in 4.4, but commentators adept at character analysis have wondered why Silvia would agree even to this – is it a 'touch of coquetry' (Ard[1])? Leech, rejecting this reading on the grounds that 'Silvia is not a suitable character for psychological probing', goes on to cite (but not accept) Harold Brooks's suggestion (Ard[2]) that the gift is a 'stinging rebuke' to Proteus. Schlueter sees the line as Silvia 'merely ratifying his defeat'.

126 your falsehood] you're false, it (*Johnson*)   129 SD] *Cam[1] subst.*

That wait for execution in the morn.   [*Exit.*]

JULIA   Host, will you go?

HOST   By my halidom, I was fast asleep.

JULIA   Pray you, where lies Sir Proteus?

HOST   Marry, at my house. Trust me, I think 'tis almost day.

JULIA

Not so; but it hath been the longest night   135

That e'er I watched, and the most heaviest.   [*Exeunt.*]

4.3   *Enter* EGLAMOUR.

EGLAMOUR

This is the hour that Madam Silvia

Entreated me to call and know her mind;

There's some great matter she'd employ me in.

Madam, madam!

[*Enter* SILVIA *above.*]

SILVIA   Who calls?

EGLAMOUR   Your servant and your friend;

129, 130 SDs *Separate exits for Proteus and Silvia are indicated in place of F2's general '*Exeunt*' since they obviously do not go off together. Ard¹ gives '*Exeunt Pro. and Sil. severally*', while Cam¹, remembering that Silvia is '*above*', offers the pragmatic '*she shuts her window*' (Proteus then supposedly '*closes the postern and passes down the lane*').

132 The Host evidently has fallen asleep during the dialogue between Proteus and Silvia, leaving Julia alone in her pain, and ensuring that he does not witness the Proteus–Silvia exchange.
By my halidom i.e. bless me; up to the end of the sixteenth century

halidom meant 'A holy thing, a holy relic; anything regarded as sacred' (*OED* 3).

133 **lies** lodges; cf. *R3* 5.3.7: 'Here will I lie tonight.'

135 **Not so** Julia denies the Host's hope of dawn.

136 **watched** stayed awake
most heaviest a double superlative (see Abbott, 11)

4.3 The scene is more or less a continuation of the previous scene, presumably *early* (9) the next morning. It appears that Silvia's escape was planned prior to her encounter with Proteus in 4.2.

4   SD *above* See 4.2.81.1n.

---

130 SD] *Cam¹ subst.; Exeunt. F2; Exeunt Proteus and Silvia. / Rowe*   134] *Pope; F lines* house: / day. /
136 SD] *F2*   **4.3**] *Scoena Tertia. F*   0.1] *Rowe; Enter Eglamore, Siluia. F*   4   Madam, madam]
Madam *Hanmer*   SD] *Rowe*

> One that attends your ladyship's command.   5

SILVIA

> Sir Eglamour, a thousand times good morrow.

EGLAMOUR

> As many, worthy lady, to yourself.
> According to your ladyship's impose,
> I am thus early come to know what service
> It is your pleasure to command me in.   10

SILVIA

> O Eglamour, thou art a gentleman –
> Think not I flatter, for I swear I do not –
> Valiant, wise, remorseful, well accomplished.
> Thou art not ignorant what dear good will
> I bear unto the banished Valentine,   15
> Nor how my father would enforce me marry
> Vain Turio, whom my very soul abhorred.
> Thyself hast loved, and I have heard thee say
> No grief did ever come so near thy heart
> As when thy lady and thy true love died,   20
> Upon whose grave thou vowed'st pure chastity.
> Sir Eglamour, I would to Valentine,

---

8 **impose** order, command
13 **remorseful** compassionate
16 **would** wished to
17 **Vain** empty
   abhorred Hanmer's emendation has
   seemed acceptable to many editors, but
   F's past tense makes sense if Turio is
   seen as totally in the past for Silvia,
   now that she has met (and is running
   off to join) Valentine. The *would* (16)
   also suggests an event in the past, for
   Silvia if not for her father.
18 **Thyself hast loved** Eglamour, as
   befits his name, is given a romantic

past; that his one *true love* has *died*
(20), and that he has thereafter taken a
pledge of *pure chastity* on her *grave*
(21), makes him both a paradigm of
the faithful lover (his chastity the
opposite of Proteus's attempted rape
in 5.4) and an utterly safe travelling
companion for Silvia (but see 5.3.6n.).
The *Eglamour* of 1.2.9–11, an erst-
while suitor of Julia, is presumably a
different character from the one here;
see List of Roles, 6n.
22 **would to** i.e. wish to go to

---

17 abhorred] *(abhor'd)*; abhors *Hanmer*   20 true love] *(true-loue)*

To Mantua, where I hear he makes abode;
And for the ways are dangerous to pass
I do desire thy worthy company,   25
Upon whose faith and honour I repose.
Urge not my father's anger, Eglamour,
But think upon my grief, a lady's grief,
And on the justice of my flying hence
To keep me from a most unholy match,   30
Which heaven and fortune still rewards with plagues.
I do desire thee, even from a heart
As full of sorrows as the sea of sands,
To bear me company and go with me;
If not, to hide what I have said to thee,   35
That I may venture to depart alone.

EGLAMOUR

Madam, I pity much your grievances,

23 **Mantua** This reference may be another instance of the play's geographical confusion, as Valentine tells the Outlaws at 4.1.17 that he is going to Verona. Mantua is, however, repeated at 5.2.45 and is also the place of exile in both *Romeus* and *RJ*.
makes abode is living
24 **for** because
pass travel
26 **repose** rely
29–31 Silvia's father *would enforce* (16) her to marry without her consent; she justifies her flight on the grounds that enforced marriages usually come to disastrous ends (*plagues*; in *RJ* 5.2.8–12 a plague quarantine prevents the Friar's message from reaching Romeo). In the next two decades, the theme of enforced marriage would become an even more popular subject on the stage, as reflected in the title of George Wilkins's play of 1607, *The Miseries of*

Enforced Marriage. A marriage to Turio would be *unholy* in Silvia's eyes as she sees herself as already *betrothed* to Valentine (4.2.105–7). This is possibly a reminiscence of the proposed marriage of the already married Juliet to Paris in *Romeus*, ll. 1971–82. The term *unholy* also inverts the play's love-as-religion language. Cf. the enforced marriage of Bertram in *AW* 2.3.105–83.
31 **fortune** chance
still always
rewards i.e. reward (two singular subjects with a singular verb; see Abbott, 336)
33 Cf. Dent, S90.1: 'As many (thick) as the sands (gravel) of the sea'.
37 **grievances** sufferings, distresses; cf. 1.1.17. Sanders believes this definition is impossible, given the following line, and supports Johnson's suggestion, 'sorrowful affections', citing 3.2.85.

37–8 grievances, / Which] grievances / And sympathize with your affections, / Which *(Keightley)*

Which, since I know they virtuously are placed,
I give consent to go along with you,
Recking as little what betideth me   40
As much I wish all good befortune you.
When will you go?

SILVIA   This evening coming.

EGLAMOUR
Where shall I meet you?

SILVIA   At Friar Patrick's cell,
Where I intend holy confession.

EGLAMOUR
I will not fail your ladyship: 45
Good morrow, gentle lady.

SILVIA
Good morrow, kind Sir Eglamour.   *Exeunt.*

4.4   *Enter* LANCE [*with his dog Crab*].

LANCE   When a man's servant shall play the cur with him,
look you, it goes hard: one that I brought up of a

---

38 **virtuously are placed** AT suggests
'her *grievances* (sufferings) are on
account of her *virtuous* love, *placed* on
Valentine'. The exact meaning is
obscure, but the general sense is that
Silvia's difficult circumstances are not
caused by any action of her own, since
she is virtuous.
40 **Recking** caring, heeding
betideth happens to
41 **As much** as much as
befortune befall, happen to; *OED*
cites this instance as the only known
example prior to a second one in 1855.
43 **Friar Patrick's cell** This whole scene
echoes *Romeus*: the refuge in *Mantua*

(23) of the banished lover, the threat of
marriage to an unwanted man (16–17)
and the rendezvous at a Friar's cell.
44 **confession** pronounced as four syllables
4.4 The location continues in Milan, still
near Silvia's *chamber* (see 84n.).
1 **play the cur** As applied to Crab,
cur means 'a worthless, low-bred, or
snappish dog' (*OED* 1), but *play the
cur*, in relation to a *man's servant*, also
suggests the negative, figurative sense,
'a surly, ill-bred, low, or cowardly
fellow' (*OED* 1b). Cf. *MND* 3.2.65:
'Out, dog! Out, cur!'
2 **of** i.e. from when he was

---

38 placed] *caused (Staunton)*   40 Recking] *Pope;* Wreaking *F;* Reaking *Riv*   42 evening coming]
evening coming on *Capell;* coming evening *Cam (anon)*   45–7] *Riv lines* ¹morrow, / Eglamour. /
45–6] *as prose Cam*   4.4] *Scena Quarta.* F   0.1 Enter LANCE] *Rowe;* Enter Launce, Protheus, Iulia,
Siluia. F   *with his dog*] *Pope*   Crab] *White*

puppy; one that I saved from drowning when three or
four of his blind brothers and sisters went to it. I have
taught him even as one would say precisely, 'Thus I   5
would teach a dog.' I was sent to deliver him as a
present to Mistress Silvia from my master, and I came
no sooner into the dining-chamber but he steps me to
her trencher and steals her capon's leg. O, 'tis a foul
thing when a cur cannot keep himself in all companies!   10
I would have, as one should say, one that takes upon
him to be a dog indeed, to be, as it were, a dog at all
things. If I had not had more wit than he, to take a fault
upon me that he did, I think verily he had been hanged
for't; sure as I live, he had suffered for't. You shall   15
judge. He thrusts me himself into the company of
three or four gentleman-like dogs under the Duke's

4 **blind** i.e. so young that their eyes had
not yet opened
went to it euphemism for 'died'; cf.
Ham 5.2.56: 'So Guildenstern and
Rosencrantz go to 't.'
5–6 **even . . . dog** just as one would teach
a dog; 'by the book'. Bond's emendation (see 5 t.n.) is unnecessary.
6–7 **I . . . master** See 4.2.75–7n.
8 **steps me** equivalent to the ethical
dative form in Latin; cf. *thrusts me* (16),
goes me (23) and *makes me* (27). See
Abbott, 220.
9 **trencher** wooden plate
foul with a pun on 'fowl' (glancing
back at *capon's*)
10 **keep** restrain
12–13 **dog at . . . things** i.e. adept at; cf.
Dent, D506: 'To be (old) dog at it',
and *TN* 2.3.60–1: 'I am dog at a catch.'
13 **fault** offence
14, 15 **had** would have
14, 21 **hanged** Dogs could be hanged for
stealing or other offences. Caius

reported that Henry VII commanded
mastiffs 'should be hanged, being
deepely displeased, and conceaving
great disdaine that an ill favred rascall
curre should with such violent villany,
assault the valiaunt Lion king of all
beastes. An example for all subjects
worthy remembraunce, to admonishe
them that it is no advantage to them to
rebell against the regiment of their
ruler, but to keep them within the limits of loyaltie' (Fleming, 26). Thomas,
102, notes that working dogs 'were
generally hanged or drowned when
they had outlived their usefulness'.
16–18 **He . . . table** Among the many
ways in which this speech anticipates
Proteus's actions (see 28–9n.) is the
image of crude social climbing, as
Proteus will seek to take Valentine's
place among the *gentlemen* of the
Duke's table.
17, 22 **Duke's** See List of Roles, 1n., and
1.3.27n.

5 say precisely, 'Thus] say, 'precisely thus *Ard¹*   6 was sent] went *Theobald*   9 capon's leg]
(Capons-leg)   17 gentleman-like dogs] (gentleman-like-dogs)

table. He had not been there – bless the mark! – a
pissing-while but all the chamber smelt him. 'Out with
the dog', says one; 'What cur is that?' says another;   20
'Whip him out', says the third; 'Hang him up', says the
Duke. I, having been acquainted with the smell before,
knew it was Crab, and goes me to the fellow that whips
the dogs. 'Friend,' quoth I, 'you mean to whip the dog?'
'Ay, marry do I', quoth he. 'You do him the more   25
wrong,' quoth I, ' 'twas I did the thing you wot of.' He
makes me no more ado but whips me out of the
chamber. How many masters would do this for his
servant? Nay, I'll be sworn I have sat in the stocks for
puddings he hath stolen, otherwise he had been   30

18 **bless the mark** 'originally an ejaculatory invocation of the Cross, familiar as a *mark* on coins and elsewhere; and so of similar intent and effect as crossing oneself' (Ard[1]), used parenthetically when something unpleasant is said; cf. Dent, G179.1, and *MV* 2.2.22: 'God bless the mark.'

19 **pissing-while** figuratively, a very short while, but also meant literally

23–4 **fellow . . . dogs** an actual bureaucratic position: for 'dog-whipper', *OED* gives 'An official formerly employed to whip dogs out of a church or chapel'; Bond cites *Mucedorus*, E1[r]: 'ile proove mine office good, for looke sir when . . . a dog chance to blow his nose backewarde, then with a whip I give him the good time of the day'. Cf. also *The First Part of the Return from Parnassus*, ll. 1235–9, 'youe are too proude to whipp they doggs out . . . the parish doggs have not bene ashamed to beraye mine owne pue' (Leishman, 194), and *Piers Penniless*, l. 25, 'the dog whipper in *Paules*' (Nashe, 1.239). RP also cites *Knack*, A4[r]: '*Wil* the whipper of the dogs'.

25, 44, 47 **marry** See 1.1.119n.

26 **the . . . of** RP notes that this phrase was 'an evasive euphemism for something unmentionable' (*wot* = know).

28–9 **How . . . servant** Cf. Julia at 88: 'How many women would do such a message?' As this parallel suggests, Lance's monologue here foreshadows the rest of the scene: his loyalty to and sacrifice for his *servant* (1), or dog, parallels Julia's loyalty to Proteus. Crab's betrayal is verbally linked to that of Proteus by the term *servant* (implying 'courtly lover' in relation to Proteus at 2.4.102–6) and both shall *play the cur* (1). Brooks, 99, notes that 'As a present for Silvia, Crab resembles the love that Proteus proffers her.'

29–31 **stocks . . . pillory** instruments of punishment; the *stocks* imprisoned the feet, the *pillory* usually the hands and neck (in a standing position).

30 **puddings** animal guts, usually the stomach or intestines with a stuffing of meat, spices, etc.; cf. *MW* 2.1.26: 'as sure as his guts are made of puddings'.

19 pissing-while] *(pissing while)*   24 dog?] *Rowe*; dog: F

executed. I have stood on the pillory for geese he hath
killed, otherwise he had suffered for't. [*to Crab*] Thou
think'st not of this now. Nay, I remember the trick you
served me when I took my leave of Madam Silvia. Did
not I bid thee still mark me, and do as I do? When didst   35
thou see me heave up my leg and make water against a
gentlewoman's farthingale? Didst thou ever see me do
such a trick?

[*Enter* PROTEUS, *and* JULIA *as Sebastian.*]

PROTEUS
    Sebastian is thy name? I like thee well,
    And will employ thee in some service presently.   40
JULIA
    In what you please; I'll do what I can.
PROTEUS
    I hope thou wilt. [*to Lance*] How now, you whoreson
        peasant,
    Where have you been these two days loitering?

35 **mark** pay attention to
36 **make water** urinate; Beadle, 29, notes
'the dog's outbreak of feral behaviour
upon coming into Silvia's presence'
and the 'overtly sexual significance . . .
in urinating upon Silvia's clothing'.
The comic emphasis of the speech on
'lower' bodily functions, displaced
onto Crab, can usefully be read in
terms of Bakhtin's analysis of carnival.
As Jardine, 15, notes, John Rainoldes,
in *The Overthrow of Stage Plays* (1599),
says that a male prostitute can be
termed a 'dogge'.

37 **farthingale** hooped petticoat; cf. 2.7.51.
37–8 **Didst . . . trick** Lance, who was
probably played by Will Kemp,
protests that he is more responsible
than Crab. See p. 127.
39, 61 **Sebastian** Shakespeare uses this
name again for Viola's brother in *TN*.
40, 69 **presently** at once
41 F2's addition was designed to smooth
out the metre, which could also be
accomplished by expanding *I'll* to 'I
will'.
42 **whoreson** bastard; sometimes used in
a rough but affectionate way

32 SD] *Cam²*   34 Silvia] Julia *Warburton*   38.1] *Rowe subst.*   39 name?] *Rowe;* name: *F*   41 I'll
do] ile doe Sir *F2*   42] *Pope; F lines* wilt. / pezant, /   SD] *Johnson*   whoreson] *(*whor-son*)*

LANCE   Marry, sir, I carried Mistress Silvia the dog you
   bade me.   45

PROTEUS   And what says she to my little jewel?

LANCE   Marry, she says your dog was a cur, and tells you
   currish thanks is good enough for such a present.

PROTEUS   But she received my dog?

LANCE   No, indeed, did she not. Here have I brought him   50
   back again.

PROTEUS   What, didst thou offer her this from me?

LANCE   Ay, sir, the other squirrel was stolen from me by
   the hangman's boys in the market-place, and then I
   offered her mine own, who is a dog as big as ten of   55
   yours, and therefore the gift the greater.

PROTEUS

   Go, get thee hence, and find my dog again,
   Or ne'er return again into my sight.

---

46 **jewel** i.e. the dog itself, not its name,
as some editors have suggested (on the
grounds that the word is capitalized in
F). Cf. Valentine's description of
Silvia as a *jewel* (2.4.166–9; see n.).
Beadle, 29, describes the 'ancient
motif' of 'a go-between with a dog', in
which the dog represents 'to the victim
the retributive consequences of a failure to co-operate with [the] agent's
plans for sexual conquest'; the *jewel*
has been *stolen* (53), in an ominous
phrase, 'by the hangman's boys' (53–4;
cf. 14n. on *hanged*).

48 **currish** mean-spirited

52 **this** i.e. Crab

53 **squirrel** not the name of the dog, as
some have believed (e.g. Victor, 42:
'your little dog Squirrel'), but suggesting that the other dog was tiny in
contrast to Crab ('as big as ten of
yours', 55–6); Bond also notes that

fashionable ladies sometimes carried
squirrels as pets, citing Lyly's
Endymion, 2.2.136–8: '*Top*. . . . What is
that the gentlewoman carrieth in a
chaine? *Epi*. Why it is a Squirrill'
(Lyly, 3.37).

54 ***the hangman's boys** The addition
in Var. 1803 of an apostrophe is gram-
matically necessary, but many editors
have dropped F's 's' altogether taking
'hangman' as an epithet of reproba-
tion, meaning 'fit for the hangman'
(Penguin), rather than as a person;
'hangman' was often used derogatively
(cf. *MA* 3.2.10–11: 'the little hangman
[Cupid] dare not shoot at him'). There
seems to be no justification, however,
for reducing F's 'boyes' to singular
'boy'.

55–6 **as big . . . yours** This phrase suggests Crab was a very large dog, but
directors have used dogs of all sizes.

50–1] *Pope; F lines* not: / againe. /   52 this] this cur *Collier²*   53–6] *Pope; F lines* me / place, / dog
/ greater. /   54 hangman's boys] *Var. 1803;* Hangmans boyes *F;* hangmans boy *F2;* hangman's boy
Rowe; hangman boys *Singer²*   market-place] *(market place)*   56 gift] *(guift)*

Away, I say! Stayest thou to vex me here?
A slave that still an end turns me to shame.   60

                    [Exit Lance with Crab.]

Sebastian, I have entertained thee
Partly that I have need of such a youth
That can with some discretion do my business –
For 'tis no trusting to yond foolish lout –
But chiefly for thy face and thy behaviour,   65
Which, if my augury deceive me not,
Witness good bringing-up, fortune and truth.
Therefore know thou, for this I entertain thee.
Go presently, and take this ring with thee,
Deliver it to Madam Silvia.   70
She loved me well delivered it to me.

JULIA

It seems you loved not her, to leave her token.
She is dead belike?

PROTEUS   Not so; I think she lives.

---

59 **Stayest thou** are you lingering;
  S*tayest* is monosyllabic.
60 **still an end** incessantly
  turns brings
61–71 The situation here anticipates
  Orsino's commission to Cesario
  (Viola) at *TN* 1.4.24–36.
61 **entertained** entertainèd; taken into
  service
62 **that** because
65 **behaviour** i.e. demeanour, rather than
  observed actions
66 **augury** prophetic skill; cf. *Ham*
  5.2.217: 'we defy augury'.
67 **fortune** prosperity
68 ***thou** Abbott, 212, notes that 'thee'
  often appears after imperatives as an
  uninflected 'thou'; Schlueter describes

F2's emendation as reflecting 'a
change of taste' in language.
entertain have taken into service
69 **this ring** i.e. the ring given to Proteus
  by Julia at 2.2.5 SD, here unwittingly
  given back (in order to be given to
  someone else). See 5.4.92n. The device
  of the ring is a staple of romance;
  Shakespeare will use the idea again in
  MV and *AW*.
71 **delivered** i.e. who delivered; see
  Abbott, 244.
72 **leave** part with; cf. similar phrasing
  used of the ring at *MV* 5.1.172: 'I dare
  be sworn for him he would not leave
  it.'
73 **belike** perhaps; Julia quotes Proteus's
  own lie (from 4.2.103) back at him.

---

60 an] on *Oxf* SD *Exit Lance*] *Rowe; Exit. F2 with Crab*] *Bantam* 67 bringing-up] (*bringing
vp*) 68 thou] *F2;* thee *F* 72 to leave] *F2;* not leaue *F;* nor love *Cam¹ (Johnson)* 73 belike?]
belike. *F2*

JULIA   Alas!

PROTEUS

Why dost thou cry 'Alas'?

JULIA   I cannot choose   75

But pity her.

PROTEUS   Wherefore shouldst thou pity her?

JULIA

Because methinks that she loved you as well

As you do love your lady Silvia.

She dreams on him that has forgot her love;

You dote on her that cares not for your love.   80

'Tis pity love should be so contrary;

And thinking on it makes me cry 'Alas'.

PROTEUS

Well, give her that ring, and therewithal

This letter. That's her chamber. Tell my lady

I claim the promise for her heavenly picture.   85

Your message done, hie home unto my chamber,

Where thou shalt find me sad and solitary.   [*Exit.*]

JULIA

How many women would do such a message?

---

76 **Wherefore** why
77 **methinks** it seems to me
83 **therewithal** with it
84 **her chamber** seen by some editors as
indicating a shift from an exterior to an
interior location. Otherwise, they pro-
pose, there is an apparent discrepancy
between this reference to Silvia's
chamber, which has previously been
'*above*' (see 4.2.81.1n.), and the ensuing dialogue, which suggests no difference of stage level between her and

Julia. This supposed discrepancy has
been taken as an additional sign of
revision or adaptation; see p. 125.
Cam[1] gives Silvia's entry as '*from the
postern*', arguing that the following dialogue 'clearly should take place in
Silvia's chamber, since . . . she bids
Ursula fetch the picture and without a
pause hands it to Julia'.
85 **promise** See 4.2.128n.
86 **hie** hurry
88 See 28–9n.

75, 140 dost] *(do'st)*   75–6 I . . . her.] *Hanmer; one line F*   87 SD] *F2*

Alas, poor Proteus, thou hast entertained
A fox to be the shepherd of thy lambs.   90
Alas, poor fool, why do I pity him
That with his very heart despiseth me?
Because he loves her, he despiseth me;
Because I love him, I must pity him.
This ring I gave him when he parted from me   95
To bind him to remember my good will.
And now am I, unhappy messenger,
To plead for that which I would not obtain,
To carry that which I would have refused,
To praise his faith which I would have dispraised.   100
I am my master's true confirmed love,
But cannot be true servant to my master
Unless I prove false traitor to myself.
Yet will I woo for him, but yet so coldly
As, heaven it knows, I would not have him speed.   105

[*Enter* SILVIA *attended.*]

89 **entertained** taken into service
90 proverbial (see Dent, W602); cf. *2H6*
3.1.252–3: 'were't not madness then /
To make the fox surveyor of the fold'.
91 **poor fool** i.e. herself
92–4 See end of 2.6.1–43n.
97–103 Julia's predicament is echoed by
Viola's in *TN* 1.4.41–2 and 2.2.36–7;
cf. Felismena in *Diana*, 97: 'I was
forced to make warre against mine
owne selfe, and to be the intercessour
of a thing so contrarie to mine owne
content.' Julia's 'false traitor to myself'
(103) ironically echoes Proteus (cf.
2.6.19–20n.).
97–8 Cf. Felismena in *Diana*, 100: 'O
thrise unfortunate *Felismena*, that with

thine owne weapons art constrained to
wounde thy ever-dying hart, and to
heape up favours for him, who made so
small account of thine.'
99, 100 **would have** wish to have
101 **confirmed** confirmèd
105 **heaven it knows** i.e. heaven knows
speed succeed
105.1 *Neither F nor F2 indicates attendants, but Silvia is accompanied at
least by *Ursula* (115), who retrieves the
picture. Whether or not there are several attendants, the dialogue between
Silvia and Julia eventually becomes
almost private, perhaps played out of
earshot of the other(s).

105.1 *Enter* SILVIA] *F2   attended*] *Malone*

Gentlewoman, good day. I pray you, be my mean
To bring me where to speak with Madam Silvia.

SILVIA

What would you with her, if that I be she?

JULIA

If you be she, I do entreat your patience
To hear me speak the message I am sent on.　　　　110

SILVIA　From whom?

JULIA　From my master, Sir Proteus, madam.

SILVIA　O, he sends you for a picture?

JULIA　Ay, madam.

SILVIA　Ursula, bring my picture there. [*She brings it.*]　　115
Go, give your master this. Tell him from me,
One Julia, that his changing thoughts forget,
Would better fit his chamber than this shadow.

JULIA

Madam, please you peruse this letter.
　　[*Gives her a letter.*]
Pardon me, madam, I have unadvised　　　　120
Delivered you a paper that I should not.

106–8 AT notes that the non-recognition
of Silvia is reproduced later in *TN*
1.5.162–81 (though Olivia wears a
'veil' there).
106 **mean** See 2.7.5n.
107 **where to speak** i.e. where I may
speak
118 **fit** suit
　shadow i.e. the *picture*; cf. 4.2.122.
119 Some editors have felt the need to
add to this line to regularize the metre.
120 **unadvised** unthinkingly; see 2.4.
204–5n. and 204n.
121 **a paper** evidently one of Proteus's

former letters to Julia, who will make a
similar mistake with the rings at
5.4.90–4; editors and directors have
debated whether Julia makes this mistake intentionally or unwittingly. In
some productions (e.g. Wager), Julia
still has Proteus's original torn letter,
now conspicuously and comically
taped back together. As Kiefer, 77,
notes, 'Seeing this letter together with
the letter to Sylvia, we cannot help
reflecting on what they contain: equally ardent professions of love written by
the same man to different women.'

106 Gentlewoman] Lady *Pope*　mean] means *Bantam*　115 SD] *Capell subst.*　119 please you
peruse] may't please you to peruse *Pope;* wilt please you to peruse *Capell*　SD] *Dyce*

This is the letter to your ladyship.

[*Takes back the letter and gives her another.*]

SILVIA

I pray thee let me look on that again.

JULIA

It may not be. Good madam, pardon me.

SILVIA   There, hold.   125

I will not look upon your master's lines.

I know they are stuffed with protestations

And full of new-found oaths, which he will break

As easily as I do tear his paper.   [*Tears the letter.*]

JULIA

Madam, he sends your ladyship this ring.   130

SILVIA

The more shame for him that he sends it me,

For I have heard him say a thousand times

His Julia gave it him at his departure.

Though his false finger have profaned the ring,

Mine shall not do his Julia so much wrong.   135

JULIA   She thanks you.

SILVIA   What sayst thou?

JULIA

I thank you, madam, that you tender her.

122–9 The stage action is slightly obscure, but Silvia returns the letter to Julia and then tears up the one addressed to her (echoing 1.2.99–100, when Julia tears up Proteus's letter). Silvia's *There, hold* (125) may suggest some additional stage action, such as handing over the portrait or offering '*to return the second letter which Julia refuses to take*' (Cam²).

127 **protestations** See 1.2.99n.

128 **new-found** i.e. newly created, hence affected, pretentiously fashionable; cf. *Son* 76.1–4: 'Why is my verse so bar-ren of new pride, / So far from varia-tion or quick change? / Why with the time do I not glance aside / To new-found methods and to compounds strange?'

132 **a thousand times** conventional exaggeration, as 'a hundred several times' (143)

134 **profaned** treated with contempt; desecrated (continuing the metaphori-cal linking of love with religion; cf. 1.1.52n. on *votary* and 4.2.125n.)

138 **tender** have concern for

122 SD] *Cam¹ subst.*   129 SD] *Dyce subst.*

Poor gentlewoman, my master wrongs her much.

SILVIA

Dost thou know her?   140

JULIA

Almost as well as I do know myself.

To think upon her woes I do protest

That I have wept a hundred several times.

SILVIA

Belike she thinks that Proteus hath forsook her?

JULIA

I think she doth, and that's her cause of sorrow.   145

SILVIA

Is she not passing fair?

JULIA

She hath been fairer, madam, than she is.

When she did think my master loved her well,

She, in my judgement, was as fair as you.

But since she did neglect her looking-glass   150

And threw her sun-expelling mask away,

The air hath starved the roses in her cheeks

And pinched the lily-tincture of her face,

141–70 Julia's self-description is an inevitable moment in the disguise tradition; cf. *Diana*, 99: 'Celia began in good earnest to aske me what manner of woman *Felismena* was; whom I answered, that touching her beautie, Some thought her to be very faire, but I was never of that opinion, bicause she hath many daies since wanted the chiefest thing, that is requisite for it. What is that said *Celia*? Content of minde, saide I.' Speaking allegedly of her 'sister', Viola will describe her own love for him to the unwitting Orsino at *TN* 2.4.105–18.

143 **several** separate

144 **Belike** perhaps

146 **passing** surpassingly, exceedingly

151 **sun-expelling mask** Fashionable women wore masks to protect their faces from sunburn or harsh weather, since a fair complexion was considered more beautiful than a darker one; cf. *Cym* 5.3.21–2: 'faces fit for masks, or rather fairer / Than those for preservation cased'.

152 **starved** withered; killed

153–4 **pinched . . . black** i.e. sunburned; cf. *AC* 1.5.28–9: 'me, / That am with Phoebus' amorous pinches black'. Warburton's suggestion of 'pitch'd' was based on the observation that a

153 pinched] pitch'd *Warburton*

That now she is become as black as I.

SILVIA

How tall was she?   155

JULIA

About my stature; for at Pentecost,
When all our pageants of delight were played,
Our youth got me to play the woman's part,
And I was trimmed in Madam Julia's gown,
Which served me as fit, by all men's judgements,   160
As if the garment had been made for me;
Therefore I know she is about my height.
And at that time I made her weep a-good,

---

skin which was 'pinched' did not turn black; rather, the sun's heat was indicated. This account seems overly technical. On the white–black distinction in terms of beauty, cf. 2.6.26n. on *swarthy Ethiope*, 3.1.103n. and 5.2.10. As part of her disguise, Julia may have 'smirch[ed]' her face with 'umber', as Celia does at *AYL* 1.3.110 (AT).

153 **tincture** colouring; cf. 'Tincture' at *WT* 3.2.205 and 'tinct' at *Cym* 2.2.23.

154 **That** so that

156–7 **Pentecost ... played** Julia cites the date of the religious festival of Pentecost, the seventh week after Easter, also known as Whitsuntide, which commemorated the events of Acts 2, when the Holy Spirit descended upon Jesus's apostles in Jerusalem, enabling them to 'speak in other tongues' to those present. Perdita, too, refers to this festival in *WT* 4.4.133–4: 'Methinks I play as I have seen them do / In Whitsun pastorals.' Performances of Mystery plays, *pageants of delight* (157) and other festive celebrations took place at this time. The mixture of secular *pageants* and mirth with a major holy day of the Christian year became

increasingly controversial in the early modern period; see Cressy.

158 **woman's part** This is one of the earliest instances in Shakespeare of metadramatic gender self-consciousness: a boy actor plays 'Julia' who pretends to be 'Sebastian' who claims to have worn woman's clothing and played a female role on the stage. Such metadramatic layering becomes even more complex in the cases of Rosalind, *AYL*, and Viola, *TN* (Orsino repeats the phrase 'a woman's part' at *TN* 1.4.34; the phrase also occurs at *Cym* 2.5.22, in a different context). In *TS*, the page Bartholomew is 'dressed in all suits like a lady' (*TS* Induction 1.105) as part of the trick played on the drunken Sly, who takes him for a woman.

159 **trimmed** dressed

Madam Julia's gown This detail suggests that the performance of the classical subject described at 165–6 was in contemporary Elizabethan rather than period costume.

160 **served** servèd
as fit as well

163 **a-good** in earnest

163 a-good] *(a good)*

For I did play a lamentable part.
Madam, 'twas Ariadne, passioning   165
For Theseus' perjury and unjust flight,
Which I so lively acted with my tears
That my poor mistress, moved therewithal,
Wept bitterly; and would I might be dead
If I in thought felt not her very sorrow.   170

SILVIA

She is beholding to thee, gentle youth.
Alas, poor lady, desolate and left!
I weep myself to think upon thy words.
Here, youth, there is my purse. I give thee this
For thy sweet mistress' sake, because thou lov'st her.   175
Farewell.   [*Exeunt Silvia and Attendants.*]

JULIA

And she shall thank you for't, if e'er you know her.
A virtuous gentlewoman, mild and beautiful.
I hope my master's suit will be but cold,
Since she respects my mistress' love so much.   180
Alas, how love can trifle with itself!
Here is her picture. Let me see, I think

---

164 **lamentable** 'The active and causative
  senses are both present' (Ard¹).
165–6 **Ariadne . . . flight** Ovid has
  Ariadne tell her own story in
  Heroides, Epistle 10; it is also given in
  Chaucer's *The Legend of Good Women*.
  Shakespeare evidently knew both.
  Theseus is a central figure in *MND*
  and in *TNK*, where the situation of
  the Jailer's Daughter broadly resembles that of Ariadne. Ariadne, abandoned by her lover on the island of
  Naxos, is a particularly apt and ironic
  part for Julia to claim to have played;
  Ovid's Ariadne anticipates Julia's forgiveness of Proteus at 5.4.118–19:
  'Though you do not deserve it, I love
  you' (*Heroides*, 10.141).
165 **passioning** passionately grieving; cf.
  VA 1059: 'Dumbly she passions.'
167 **lively** the adjectival form used as an
  adverb (Abbott, 1)
168 **moved** movèd
  therewithal by it
171 **beholding** beholden, obligated to
179 **cold** i.e. unsuccessful; cf. *MV* 2.7.73:
  'your suit is cold'.
180 **my mistress' love** i.e. her own; she
  has continued to speak as 'Sebastian'.

---

171 beholding] beholden *Oxf*   175–6] *F2; one line F*   176] *om. Pope*   SD] *Dyce opp. 177; Exit. F2*
180 my] his *Hanmer*

If I had such a tire, this face of mine
Were full as lovely as is this of hers;
And yet the painter flattered her a little,   185
Unless I flatter with myself too much.
Her hair is auburn, mine is perfect yellow;
If that be all the difference in his love,
I'll get me such a coloured periwig.
Her eyes are grey as glass, and so are mine.   190
Ay, but her forehead's low, and mine's as high.
What should it be that he respects in her
But I can make respective in myself,
If this fond Love were not a blinded god?
Come, shadow, come, and take this shadow up,   195
For 'tis thy rival.   [*Looks at the picture.*]
                O thou senseless form,
Thou shalt be worshipped, kissed, loved and adored;

---

183 **tire** head-dress; cf. *AC* 2.5.22: 'Then
put my tires and mantles on him'.
187 **auburn** The term meant 'nearly
white' or 'blond' at this time.
perfect yellow Bond claims that *yellow* was the 'natural colour of Queen
Elizabeth's [hair], and so the fashionable colour in her time'. Cf. Hayward,
7, on the young Elizabeth: 'her haire
was inclined to pale yellow'; also Lyly's
Campaspe, 3.4.89–90: 'For now, if the
haire of her eye browes be black, yet
must the haire of her head be yellowe'
(Lyly, 2.340). In *Diana*, Felismena's
hair is golden (see 189n.).
189 **periwig** wig; cf. *Ham* 3.2.9: 'a robustious periwig-pated fellow', and *Diana*,
138–9: 'a naturall crisped periwigge of
her owne haire, matching the brightest
golde in colour, which adorned either
side of her cristalline forehead'.
190 **grey as glass** Malone argues that
'the Elizabethans meant "blue" when

they said "grey eye"', but *OED* does
not support his reading; the inference
in any event is that *grey* is an admired
colour.
191 **forehead's . . . high** A high forehead
was considered more desirable (*RJ*
2.1.19: 'By her high forehead') than a
low one (*AC* 3.3.32–3: 'her forehead /
As low as she would wish it'). Hayward,
7, reports of Queen Elizabeth, 'her
foreheade large and faire, a seemeing
sete for princely grace'.
192 **respects** values, esteems
193 **make respective** render worthy of
respect; rate as highly
194 **fond** foolish
blinded god See 2.1.66n.
195 **shadow . . . shadow** herself . . . the
picture; cf. 3.1.177n. and 4.2.123–4n.
take . . . up 'with play on sense of hostile action or attitude' (Ard[1])
196 **senseless** insensible

---

187 auburn] (Aburne)   191 forehead's] (fore-head's)   196 SD] *Bantam*

And were there sense in his idolatry
My substance should be statue in thy stead.
I'll use thee kindly for thy mistress' sake   200
That used me so; or else, by Jove I vow,
I should have scratched out your unseeing eyes
To make my master out of love with thee.   *Exit.*

5.1   *Enter* EGLAMOUR.

EGLAMOUR

The sun begins to gild the western sky,
And now it is about the very hour
That Silvia at Friar Patrick's cell should meet me.
She will not fail, for lovers break not hours,
Unless it be to come before their time,   5
So much they spur their expedition.

[*Enter* SILVIA.]

See where she comes. Lady, a happy evening!
SILVIA

Amen, amen. Go on, good Eglamour,

---

198 **sense** reason
199 i.e. my self (*substance*), as opposed to
the mere *shadow* (195) of the portrait,
should be the object (*statue*) of his *idolatry* (198); cf. 4.2.125n.
202 **your** the shift to the more formal,
and here more hostile, form; contrast
the opposite movement from *you* to
Thou for similar effect at 4.2.92 (see
n.).
5.1 The location is *Friar Patrick's cell* (3)
at the *abbey* (9) – to show that Silvia
has escaped. This scene provides
another parallel to *RJ* (4.1), when
Juliet flees to the Friar's cell.

1 **gild** 'cover or tinge with a golden
colour or light (said esp. of the sun)'
(*OED* v^1. 4) – i.e. at sunset; cf. *Tit*
2.1.5–6: 'the golden sun . . . having gilt
the ocean with his beams'.
4 **break not hours** i.e. do not fail to
meet their appointed time; cf. *AYL*
4.1.42: 'Break an hour's promise in
love?'
5–6 i.e. unless they arrive early because
they're in such a hurry (with possible
sexual innuendo)
6 **expedition** progress; haste (pronounced with five syllables)

---

199 statue] sainted *Hanmer;* statued *Warburton*   203 SD] *F2; Exeunt. F*   **5.1]** *Actus Quintus. Scoena
Prima. F*   0.1] *Rowe; Enter Eglamoure, Siluia. F*   3 That Silvia] Silvia *Pope*   6.1] *Rowe after 7*

Out at the postern by the abbey wall;
I fear I am attended by some spies. 10

EGLAMOUR

Fear not. The forest is not three leagues off;
If we recover that, we are sure enough. *Exeunt.*

5.2 *Enter* TURIO, PROTEUS, [*and*] JULIA
[*as Sebastian*].

TURIO

Sir Proteus, what says Silvia to my suit?

PROTEUS

O, sir, I find her milder than she was,
And yet she takes exceptions at your person.

TURIO What? That my leg is too long?

PROTEUS No, that it is too little. 5

TURIO

I'll wear a boot, to make it somewhat rounder.

JULIA [*aside*]

But love will not be spurred to what it loathes.

TURIO What says she to my face?

---

9 **postern** small private gate or door

10 **attended** followed; watched

11 **three leagues** A 'league' was a measure of distance, 'varying in different countries, but usually estimated at about 3 miles; app. never in regular use in England, but often occurring in poetical or rhetorical statements of distance' (*OED sb.*[1]); *three leagues* would equal 9–10 miles – too far to imagine Eglamour and Silvia walking – but the effect here is simply to say 'it's not far away'.

12 **recover** reach
sure secure, safe

5.2 The location continues to be Milan.

3 **takes exceptions at** makes objections to; cf. 1.3.81, 83 and 2.4.153.

5 **little** i.e. thin; also with a possible sexual innuendo about Turio's insufficiency

7 SP *F*'s assignment of this line to '*Pro.*' is plainly wrong, in terms both of the line's meaning and of the following series of choric comments (marked as asides) by Julia in the scene.

7 **spurred** Julia plays on *boot* (as a riding-boot with spurs in the previous line.

8 **to** about

5.2] *Scoena Secunda. F* 0.1 *Enter . . . JULIA*] *Rowe; Enter Thurio, Protheus, Iulia, Duke. F* 0.2 *as Sebastian*] *Cam*[1] 7 SP] *Collier (Boswell–Malone); Pro. F* SD] *Collier (Boswell–Malone)*

PROTEUS   She says it is a fair one.

TURIO

    Nay then, the wanton lies; my face is black.   10

PROTEUS

    But pearls are fair; and the old saying is,

    'Black men are pearls in beauteous ladies' eyes.'

JULIA [*aside*]

    'Tis true, such pearls as put out ladies' eyes,

    For I had rather wink than look on them.

TURIO   How likes she my discourse?   15

PROTEUS   Ill, when you talk of war.

TURIO

    But well when I discourse of love and peace.

JULIA [*aside*]

    But better, indeed, when you hold your peace.

TURIO   What says she to my valour?

PROTEUS   O, sir, she makes no doubt of that.   20

JULIA [*aside*]

    She needs not when she knows it cowardice.

TURIO   What says she to my birth?

---

9   **fair** pale-complexioned, hence beautiful; but also with an insinuation of 'effeminate', as at *MA* 3.1.61–2: 'If fair-faced, / She would swear the gentleman should be her sister'.

10 **wanton** flirt; RP suggests Turio's tone here is 'of an inappropriately intimate attitude to Silvia'.
    black tan, sun-burned; cf. 2.6.26n. on *swarthy Ethiope*, 3.1.103n. and 4.4.153–4n.

11–12 The *old saying* is given by Dent at M79; Ard[1] and Ard[2] give numerous examples. The *saying* is conventionally used as flattery of a man who does not have a fair complexion. Cf. the reference to Aaron the Moor at *Tit* 5.1.42: 'This is the pearl that pleased your

empress' eye.'

13 SP *F's assignment of these lines to '*Thu.*' seems wrong on the same grounds that 7 SP is incorrect; Julia serves as a commentator on the Proteus–Turio dialogue until the Duke's entrance at 29.

13 Julia uses *pearls* here to mean 'cataracts' (*OED sb.*[1] II 4b).
    put out blind

14 **wink** shut my eyes

16 This line also suggests effeminacy (*Ill* = badly)

18 **hold your peace** are quiet

20 **makes . . . of** does not question; knows the true nature of (i.e. that he is a coward, as Julia concludes in 21).

---

13 SP] *Rowe; Thu. F*   SD] *Rowe*   18, 21, 24, 28 SDs] *Victor*   18 your] *F3;* you *F*

PROTEUS   That you are well derived.

JULIA *[aside]*   True, from a gentleman to a fool.

TURIO   Considers she my possessions?   25

PROTEUS   O, ay, and pities them.

TURIO   Wherefore?

JULIA *[aside]*   That such an ass should owe them.

PROTEUS

That they are out by lease.

[Enter DUKE.]

JULIA   Here comes the Duke.

DUKE

How now, Sir Proteus! How now, Turio!   30
Which of you saw Eglamour of late?

TURIO

Not I.

PROTEUS   Nor I.

DUKE   Saw you my daughter?

PROTEUS   Neither.

DUKE

Why then, she's fled unto that peasant Valentine,
And Eglamour is in her company.

---

23 **well derived** well descended, of good
   birth; cf. 5.4.144.
24 Julia plays on the idea of Turio's
   descent (from *derived*) in the sense of a
   decline in status.
25 **possessions** Some editors have suggested a more figurative sense of
   possessions as 'mental endowments'
   (Ard², citing Steevens) or 'being possessed by spirits' (Penguin), in relation
   to Proteus's responses at 26 and 29,
   but the sense of property is more likely, given the play's several references to
   Turio's finances (cf. 2.4.43–4n. and
   173n.).

26 **pities** is sorry for them; **considers**
   them pitiful
27 **Wherefore** why
28 **owe** own
29 **out by lease** further reference to
   Turio's miserliness; his generosity
   does not extend to giving but only to
   lending (presumably for interest). Cf.
   R2 2.1.59: 'Is now leased out'.
   Duke See List of Roles, 1n., and
   1.3.27n.
31 **of late** recently
33 **peasant** base person; the Duke raises
   the class issue only after he has been
   deceived by Valentine.

29 SD] *Rowe after 29*   31 saw] say saw Sir *F2–3;* saw Sir *F4*   33] *Capell; F lines* then / *Valentine;* /

267

'Tis true, for Friar Laurence met them both   35
As he in penance wandered through the forest.
Him he knew well, and guessed that it was she,
But, being masked, he was not sure of it.
Besides, she did intend confession
At Patrick's cell this even, and there she was not.   40
These likelihoods confirm her flight from hence.
Therefore, I pray you, stand not to discourse,
But mount you presently and meet with me
Upon the rising of the mountain foot
That leads toward Mantua, whither they are fled.   45
Dispatch, sweet gentlemen, and follow me.   [*Exit.*]

TURIO

Why, this it is to be a peevish girl
That flies her fortune when it follows her.
I'll after, more to be revenged on Eglamour   49
Than for the love of reckless Silvia.   [*Exit.*]

PROTEUS

And I will follow, more for Silvia's love
Than hate of Eglamour that goes with her.   [*Exit.*]

---

35 **Friar Laurence** also the name of the friar in *RJ*, but it may simply be a slip for Friar Patrick (cf. 40, 4.3.43 and 5.1.3)
36 **forest** See 4.1 headnote.
37 **Him** i.e. Eglamour
38 **being masked** because Silvia wore a mask; see 4.4.151n.
39 **confession** pronounced with four syllables
40 **even** evening
42 **stand** delay; cf. *JC* 5.3.43: 'Stand not to answer.'
    discourse stressed on second syllable
43 **mount** i.e. on horses

presently at once
44 **mountain foot** foothills
45 **Mantua** See 4.3.23n.; the Duke somehow knows their destination.
46 **Dispatch** make haste
47 **peevish** foolish; perverse
48 **fortune** good luck, i.e. to be wooed by Turio
50 **reckless** 'Having no care or consideration for oneself or another' (*OED* 1c)
50, 52, 54 SDs *Capell's numerous separate exits are preferred to F's mass '*Exeunt*' on the grounds that Turio does not hear Proteus's lines, nor Proteus Julia's.

42 you, stand] *Warburton;* you stand, *F*   46 SD] *Rowe*   50, 52 SDs] *Capell*

JULIA

> And I will follow, more to cross that love
> Than hate for Silvia, that is gone for love.   *Exit.*

5.3   [*Enter*] SILVIA [*and*] Outlaws.

1 OUTLAW   Come, come, be patient. We must bring you to
   our captain.

SILVIA

> A thousand more mischances than this one
> Have learned me how to brook this patiently.

2 OUTLAW   Come, bring her away.   5

1 OUTLAW

> Where is the gentleman that was with her?

3 OUTLAW

> Being nimble-footed, he hath outrun us.
> But Moses and Valerius follow him.
> Go thou with her to the west end of the wood;
> There is our captain. We'll follow him that's fled.   10
> The thicket is beset, he cannot scape.

                    [*Exeunt Second and Third Outlaws.*]

---

53 **cross** thwart, block
5.3 The location returns to the forest.
4 **learned** taught
   brook endure
6 **gentleman** i.e. Eglamour; he hardly
   seems to have acted like a gentleman,
   given that he *hath outrun* (7) the
   Outlaws and abandoned Silvia. Silvia's
   portrayal of him at 4.3.11–21 suggests
   a more heroic figure, but he eventually
   needs to disappear so that Silvia is
   alone in the final scene; the Friar in *RJ*

5.3.151–9 also runs away, abandoning
Juliet at her moment of crisis.
8 ***Moses** F's '*Moyses*' is an alternative
   Latin form of *Moses*.
   Valerius the name Felismena adopts
   when she disguises herself as a page in
   Diana, 91; also the name of a messenger in *TNK*
9 **west end** presumably suggesting a
   large forest
11 **beset** surrounded
   scape escape

54 SD] *Capell; Exeunt. F*   **5.3**] *Scena Tertia. F*   0.1] *Rowe; Siluia, Out-lawes. F*   1–2] *Pope; F lines patient: / Captaine. /*   7 nimble-footed] *(*nimble footed*)*   8 Moses] *(Moyses)*   11 SD] *Capell subst.*

1 OUTLAW

Come, I must bring you to our captain's cave.
Fear not, he bears an honourable mind
And will not use a woman lawlessly.   14

SILVIA

O Valentine, this I endure for thee!   *Exeunt.*

5.4   *Enter* VALENTINE.

VALENTINE

How use doth breed a habit in a man!
This shadowy desert, unfrequented woods,
I better brook than flourishing peopled towns.
Here can I sit alone, unseen of any,
And to the nightingale's complaining notes   5
Tune my distresses and record my woes.
O thou that dost inhabit in my breast,

---

15 Oxf unnecessarily marks Silvia's line
as an aside.
5.4 The location remains the forest.
1–6 The pastoral pose (*nymph, swain*,
12) is conventional; Leech suggests a
possible source in Seneca's *Hippolytus*,
where the hero praises life in the forest
and dispraises city life. This is a common sentiment, however, in virtually
every work in the pastoral tradition.
The Duke in *AYL* 2.1.1–17 offers a
classic statement of this idea.
1   **use** custom
2   **desert** 'any wild, uninhabited region,
including forest-land' (*OED sb.*[2] 1b);
cf. *AYL*: 'this desert place' (2.4.68)
and 'this desert inaccessible' (2.7.109).
3   **better brook** endure more easily; cf.
1H4 5.4.77: 'I better brook the loss of
brittle life.'
5   **nightingale's complaining notes**
Ovid tells the story of Tereus and
Philomela in *Met.*, 6, where Philomela
is transformed into a nightingale after

Tereus rapes her. Bond cites Lyly's
Campaspe, 5.1.32–3: 'What Bird so
sings, yet so dos waile? / O t'is the ravish'd Nightingale' (Lyly, 2.351).
Shakespeare invokes the myth frequently. In *Tit*, Lavinia is reduced to
the same plight as Philomela and
reveals her rape by pointing to the story
of Philomela in the *Metamorphoses* (*Tit*
4.1.41–9); at *Cym* 2.2.44–6 it is the
story of Philomela, whether or not in
Ovid, that Imogen falls asleep over
before Iachimo invades her bedcham-
ber. Cf. 3.1.179. Valentine's allusion to
this poetic cliché anticipates, in ways he
cannot imagine, Proteus's attempted
rape of Silvia at 58–9; Silvia's long
silence after the offer, to the end of the
play, may reflect Philomela's speech-
lessness.
6   **record** sing; cf. *Per* 4 Chorus 26–7:
'She sung, and made the night bird
[i.e. the nightingale] mute, / That still
records with moan.'

5.4] *Scoena Quarta*. F   0.1] *Rowe; Enter Valentine, Protheus, Siluia, Iulia, Duke, Thurio, Out-lawes.* F

Leave not the mansion so long tenantless,
Lest, growing ruinous, the building fall
And leave no memory of what it was.   10
Repair me with thy presence, Silvia;
Thou gentle nymph, cherish thy forlorn swain.

> [*Shouts within.*]

What hallowing and what stir is this today?
These are my mates, that make their wills their law,
Have some unhappy passenger in chase.   15
They love me well; yet I have much to do
To keep them from uncivil outrages.

> [*Enter* PROTEUS, SILVIA, *and* JULIA *as Sebastian.*]

Withdraw thee, Valentine.   [*Steps aside.*]
                              Who's this comes here?

PROTEUS

Madam, this service I have done for you
(Though you respect not aught your servant doth),   20
To hazard life and rescue you from him
That would have forced your honour and your love.

---

7 **thou** i.e. Silvia
8–9 **mansion . . . fall** The metaphor of
the lover's heart as a *mansion* may be
found in many texts of the period; cf.
RJ 3.2.26–7: 'O, I have bought the
mansion of a love / But not possessed
it.' Cf. also *Son* 146.5–6, referring to
the ageing body: 'Why so large cost,
having so short a lease, / Dost thou
upon thy fading mansion spend?'
11 **Repair** restore
13 **stir** activity
15 **Have** i.e. who have
   passenger traveller; cf. 4.1.1, 71.
17 **uncivil** Cf. 60.
19–22 Proteus invokes chivalric terms
(*service*, *servant*) to describe his *rescue*

of Silvia from those who would have
raped her (*forced your honour*), only to
cross over to the side of the *uncivil* (17,
60) himself. Lindenbaum, 238, argues
'it is reasonable to assume that Proteus,
in order to help his own suit, is over-
stating the danger Silvia was in'. The
rescue – conspicuously not shown by
Shakespeare – is added to the adaptations of Victor and Kemble (see pp.
100–3).
20 **respect** value, regard
21 These actions are his *service* (19).
21–2 **him . . . love** It appears that the
First Outlaw (*him*, 21) attempted to
rape Silvia; it has been argued that the
implausibility of this suggests a scene

12 SD] *Collier*²   17.1] *Rowe subst., after 18*   18 SD] *Johnson*

Vouchsafe me for my meed but one fair look;
A smaller boon than this I cannot beg,
And less than this, I am sure, you cannot give.   25
VALENTINE [*aside*]
How like a dream is this I see and hear!
Love, lend me patience to forbear awhile.
SILVIA
O miserable, unhappy that I am!
PROTEUS
Unhappy were you, madam, ere I came;
But by my coming I have made you happy.   30
SILVIA
By thy approach thou mak'st me most unhappy.
JULIA [*aside*]
And me, when he approacheth to your presence.
SILVIA
Had I been seized by a hungry lion
I would have been a breakfast to the beast
Rather than have false Proteus rescue me.   35
O heaven, be judge how I love Valentine,
Whose life's as tender to me as my soul!

is missing, possibly one in which
Proteus slanders Valentine's intentions, and that therefore *him* in 21 is a
reference to Valentine (see Ard²). This
line, however, may be better understood as Proteus's projection of his
own desires (see also 19–22n.). The
Duke's forgiveness at 156 suggests the
Outlaws have not done anything so
serious, but cf. 154n.
23 **meed** reward
24 **boon** gift, favour
27 Leech notes that Collier has Valentine
leave the stage after this line, returning

at 60, when he interrupts the attempted
rape; the logic of this suggestion is to
make more comprehensible Valentine's
eventual forgiveness of Proteus. It is at
this point in the scene that many editors
start to intervene in order to make
Valentine's forgiveness of Proteus more
psychologically plausible; see pp. 114–5.
29 **ere** before
31 **approach** in the sense of amorous
advance (and so understood by Julia)
33 **seized** seizèd
37 **tender** dear; cf. *Mac* 1.7.56: 'How tender 'tis to love the babe that milks me.'

26 SD] *Theobald*   this I see] *Hanmer;* this? I see *F;* this, I see *Theobald*   28 am!] *F4;* am. *F*   32
SD] *Rowe*   33 seized] *(ceazed)*   34 breakfast] *(break-fast)*

And full as much, for more there cannot be,
I do detest false perjured Proteus.
Therefore be gone, solicit me no more.   40

PROTEUS

What dangerous action, stood it next to death,
Would I not undergo for one calm look?
O, 'tis the curse in love, and still approved,
When women cannot love where they're beloved.

SILVIA

When Proteus cannot love where he's beloved.   45
Read over Julia's heart, thy first, best love,
For whose dear sake thou didst then rend thy faith
Into a thousand oaths, and all those oaths
Descended into perjury to love me.
Thou hast no faith left now, unless thou'dst two,   50
And that's far worse than none; better have none
Than plural faith, which is too much by one.
Thou counterfeit to thy true friend!

PROTEUS   In love

39, 54, 68 **Proteus** trisyllabic; see 1.1.1n.
41 **stood . . . death** however perilous
42 **calm** gentle, mild
43 **still** continually
   approved confirmed by experience;
   cf. *KL* 2.2.158: 'Good King, that must
   approve the common saw'.
47–9 **rend . . . me** F2's 'deceive' for *love*
   (49) reflects a common lack of 'entire
   confidence that F here is accurate'
   (Ard²), but these lines make sense
   without revision: fidelity to Julia has
   been torn (*rend*, 47) into a *thousand
   oaths* (48), which have degenerated
   into *perjury* as he declared his *love* for
   Silvia.
49 *****me**. RP defends F's comma here:
   'and, because you've perjured yourself

by swearing love to me, you now have
no faith'.
50 **unless thou'dst two** i.e. unless you
   can be faithful to both Julia and me at
   the same time
51–2 **better . . . one** i.e. true *faith* by definition serves only one, therefore to
   have more, *plural*, nullifies the whole
   idea of *faith*. The use of *faith* ties love
   to religion, as elsewhere in the play
   (see 1.1.52n. on *votary*, 2.4.142–5n.
   and 4.2.125n.)
53–4 **In . . . friend** Cf. Dent, L549. Bond
   cites Lyly's *Euphues*, 1. 32: 'where love
   beareth sway, friendshippe can have no
   shew' (Lyly, 1.209). Cf. also Lyly's
   Endymion, 3.4.110: 'Love knoweth neither friendshippe nor kindred' (Lyly,

---

49 love] deceive *F2*   me.] *Rowe;* me, *F*

Who respects friend?

SILVIA   All men but Proteus.

PROTEUS

Nay, if the gentle spirit of moving words   55
Can no way change you to a milder form,
I'll woo you like a soldier, at arms' end,
And love you 'gainst the nature of love – force ye.
    [*Seizes her.*]

SILVIA

O heaven!

PROTEUS   I'll force thee yield to my desire.

VALENTINE [*Comes forward.*]

Ruffian, let go that rude uncivil touch,   60

3.50); *MA* 2.1.169–70: 'Friendship is constant in all other things / Save in the office and affairs of love'; and see p. 11.

54 **respects** regards

57 **woo** F2 may have offered 'moue' on the grounds that *woo* dramatically misstates what Proteus is doing here; on the other hand, that he believes he can *woo* Silvia *like a soldier* reflects how much he has perverted the romantic ideal. Victor, 51, adopts the F2 reading.
like a soldier The *soldier* is the antithesis of the *servant*, in terms of dominance and submission; Proteus tries to justify rape by use of the Petrarchan metaphor of 'love as war'.
at arms' end i.e. at sword's point, with a sexual implication; Leech, printing 'arm's', notes that the usual meaning of the phrase is 'at a distance' (*OED* arm *sb.*[1] 2b), as at *AYL* 2.6.9: 'hold death awhile at the arm's end'.

58 The play's first adapter, Victor, altered and softened this line to three words: 'And force you' (51). Cf. Volpone's

attempt on Celia in *Volpone*, 3.7.264–5: 'I should have done the act, and then have parleyed. / Yield, or I'll force thee' (Jonson, 3.66).

58 SD *This assault is in many ways the key moment in Proteus's story; the relative violence of his attempt on Silvia varies enormously in different productions of the play. Victor, 51, first added a SD here. See pp. 95–9.

59 **I'll . . . desire** Victor, 51, deletes Proteus's line here, again softening the brutality of the moment; some early productions followed suit.
thee This is Proteus's first shift of pronoun since his entrance at 17.1 as he drops his last pretence of respect for Silvia.

60 **uncivil** Cf. 17.

60, 128 **touch** Cf. 2.7.18 and 3.2.78; on the significance of this word, see pp. 28.

61 Victor, 51, provides here a nine-line exchange between Valentine and Silvia, showing their coming together and breaking Silvia's silence in F.

57 woo] moue *F2*   arms'] *Var. 1803*; armes *F*; arm's *Capell*   58 SD] *Victor*   60 SD] *Collier*[2]

Thou friend of an ill fashion!

PROTEUS   Valentine!

VALENTINE

Thou common friend, that's without faith or love,
For such is a friend now! Treacherous man,
Thou hast beguiled my hopes. Naught but mine eye
Could have persuaded me. Now I dare not say   65
I have one friend alive; thou wouldst disprove me.
Who should be trusted, when one's right hand
Is perjured to the bosom? Proteus,
I am sorry I must never trust thee more,
But count the world a stranger for thy sake.   70
The private wound is deepest. O time most accurst,
'Mongst all foes that a friend should be the worst!

PROTEUS

My shame and guilt confounds me.
Forgive me, Valentine; if hearty sorrow
Be a sufficient ransom for offence,   75
I tender't here. I do as truly suffer

Thou Valentine addresses Proteus as *thou* throughout the scene until his final speech of reconciliation at 166–71.

ill fashion bad sort

62 **common** ordinary; degraded. Cf. *Ham* 1.2.68–74: '*Queen* . . . Thou know'st 'tis common, all that lives must die, / Passing through nature to eternity. / *Hamlet* Ay, madam, it is common.'

63 **Treacherous** trisyllabic; earlier editors added a syllable, following F2 in mistakenly supposing the line was metrically deficient (see t.n.).

67 Various editors have attempted to regularize the metre by adding 'now' or 'own' (see t.n.).

70 **count** account, consider; cf. 2.1.53.

71 **private wound** Proteus's betrayal as opposed to his own banishment; there may also be a glancing reference to Valentine's love for Silvia, the initial cause of his *wound* (cf. *MND* 2.1.166–7: 'a little western flower, / Before milk-white, now purple with love's wound').

73 **confounds** destroys (another singular verb after a double subject; see Abbott, 336)

75 **ransom** payment, i.e. in atonement; cf. *Son* 120.13–14: 'But that your trespass now becomes a fee; / Mine ransoms yours, and yours must ransom me'.

76 **tender't** offer it

---

63 Treacherous] Thou treacherous *F2*; Though treacherous *F3*; Tho treacherous *F4*; Tho', treacherous *Rowe*   64 Naught] *(nought)*   65 Now I] I *Pope*   67 trusted, when one's] trusted now, when one's *F2*; trusted now, when the *Pope*; trusted, when one's own *Johnson*   71 time most accurst,] *Ard¹*; time, most accurst: *F*; time, most curst *Johnson*

As e'er I did commit.

VALENTINE   Then I am paid,
And once again I do receive thee honest.
Who by repentance is not satisfied
Is nor of heaven nor earth, for these are pleased;   80
By penitence th'Eternal's wrath's appeased.
And that my love may appear plain and free,
All that was mine in Silvia I give thee.

---

77 **commit** i.e. commit sin; cf. *KL* 3.4.79–80: 'commit not with man's sworn spouse'.
paid satisfied
78 **receive** accept; consider
honest i.e. as honest, honourable
79–81 For most modern readers and audiences, Proteus's *repentance* can seem too brief to be convincing – just five lines – but his behaviour during Valentine's preceding speech, and how he delivers 73–7, can vary enormously (see pp. 103–4). Valentine's comment that *penitence* is sufficient in the eyes of God, moreover, is fundamental Protestant doctrine. On the early modern drama of 'forgiveness', see Hunter, *Comedy*, and Friedman. Lindenbaum, 240, argues that Valentine's act of forgiveness suggests to Proteus 'a frame of reference for judging human acts which is totally opposed to Proteus's earlier refusal to look any higher than mere self-interest'.
79 **Who** whoever
80 **nor . . . earth** neither divine nor human
82–3 Valentine's forgiveness of Proteus and his apparent offer of Silvia to him have occasioned more comment than any other elements of the play. Both strike many as objectionable on aesthetic grounds alone: the fact that lines 80–1 (*pleased*/*appeased*) and 82–3 (*free*/*thee*) rhyme seems to suggest that the offer is formulaic or superficial.

More urgently, though, the forgiveness and offer have been rejected on moral grounds and as psychologically impossible. Many editors, therefore, attempt to explain away the lines' apparent meaning. Bond (xxxvii) accepts Batteson's suggestion that the lines are deliberately ambiguous, meaning 'nothing more than "I give you my love as frankly and unreservedly as I gave it to Silvia: you shall have as much interest in my heart as she"'. Leech argues that 'Surely by now we can be in little doubt as to its intended effect', namely that Valentine has been shown to be credulous and captive to the code of friendship, thus 'his continued preoccupation with the demands of friendship makes him ready to hand over his love to the man who has just been trying to rape her. . . . never in the play has [Valentine] shown any recognition of his own folly or excess' (lxvii–lxviii). Schlueter simply glosses *love* (82) as 'amity' or friendship. Hunt, 19, denies that there is any offer at all: Valentine 'is merely extending his infinite affection to his friend. The words . . . do not refer to any rights of ownership, but to his love.' Several other possibilities are offered in Norton: 'All my claims to Silvia; all that was mine, in the person of Silvia; all the love I gave to Silvia'. Julia's faint, however, suggests that she takes Valentine's offer as not merely of friendship, but of Silvia herself. In the story of Titus and Gisippus

---

82–3] *transferred to end of Turio's speech, 133 Malone (Blackstone)*   83 mine in Silvia] *Pope*; mine, in Siluia, F

JULIA

O me unhappy! [*Faints.*]

PROTEUS   Look to the boy.

VALENTINE   Why, boy!

Why, wag! How now? What's the matter? Look up;   85
speak.

JULIA   O good sir, my master charged me to deliver a ring to
Madam Silvia, which out of my neglect was never done.

PROTEUS   Where is that ring, boy?

JULIA   Here 'tis; this is it. [*Gives him a ring.*]   90

in Elyot, 141–2, the offer to Titus by Gissipus is quite specifically that of the woman: 'Here I renounce to you clerely all my title and interest that I nowe have in that faire mayden', and Titus in fact marries her. Some adapters, unable to explain away the offer, have resorted to emendation or outright deletion of the line: Victor, 53, moves 77–83 to follow the speech at 115–17 (see n.) and alters the troublesome two lines to a single, clear expression: 'Thy Valentine, and Julia, both are thine.' See pp. 92–5.

84 SD *Julia apparently faints – or engages in some equivalent stage action – upon hearing Valentine's offer of Silvia to Proteus; whether her faint is deliberate (as Leech believes) or not is controversial. F has no SD indicating that Julia faints, just as F *Mac* (which, unlike *TGV*, has many SDs) has no SD for Lady Macbeth's fainting at 2.3.120. Some feminist critics, however, accept Pope's SD as fact (e.g. Belsey, 179: Julia's 'swoon . . . reaffirms her femininity'), but Shapiro, *Gender*, 78, questions the SD, noting that 'the text endows Julia with greater resiliency than the word *swoon* implies'. In Victor, 52, she faints because Proteus speaks a new line, 'I merit death', an idea extended in some productions (e.g. Langham) with 'a threat of suicide with a pistol by the repentant Proteus'

(Byrne, 471). In Kemble, she faints when '*The Outlaws are taking* PROTEUS *away*' at Valentine's stern order: 'Go, – bear him from my sight; – and in my cave / Await my further will' (Kemble, 69).

85–91 The scene briefly turns to prose; it may reflect 'compositorial corruption of the text' (Cam²), but is more likely a deliberate stylistic unsettling which reflects the emotional weight of the moment (and, if Julia really does faint, rather than pretending to, her emotional upheaval). RP proposes that 88, 'which out of my neglect was never done', may have been 'a verse line crowded in as prose to save a line in a tight column in F', since F's abbreviation of *which* ('wᶜ') 'suggests a desire to save space near the foot of D1ʳ (the last page of the final forme of the sheet, and therefore offering no latitude for rearrangement of page division)'.

85 **wag** mischievous boy

88 **never done** Is this a contradiction in the text, as some (such as Sanders) have argued? At 4.4.130–5, Julia attempts to deliver Proteus's ring to Silvia, but the implication there is that Silvia refuses to receive it, hence it has not been delivered.

90–2 Does Julia deliberately give Proteus the wrong ring? She should be giving

84 SD] *Pope (Swoons)*   90 SD] *Johnson subst.*

PROTEUS   How? Let me see.
          Why, this is the ring I gave to Julia.

JULIA

    O, cry you mercy, sir, I have mistook.
    This is the ring you sent to Silvia.
    [*Shows another ring.*]

PROTEUS

    But how cam'st thou by this ring? At my depart   95
    I gave this unto Julia.

JULIA

    And Julia herself did give it me –
    And Julia herself hath brought it hither.
    [*Reveals herself.*]

PROTEUS   How? Julia?

Proteus the ring she gave to him at 2.2.5, which Proteus at 4.4.69–70 told Julia/Sebastian to deliver to Silvia, and which Silvia refused to receive at 4.4.131–5. Some editors and directors have argued that Julia's repetition here of the mistake she made earlier with the letter (4.4.119–22) strains belief and have accordingly treated this moment as calculated. Overriding the question, however, is the fact that this mis-giving is a crucial device to prompt Julia's revelation of her true identity, and the memory of her earlier mistake adds a lightening, almost comic, tone here.

92 **ring** To his surprise, Proteus receives the *ring* he gave at 2.2.6 SD and so the exchange of rings is reversed, symbolically undoing the initial act of betrothal, but in a way that leads to revelation, forgiveness and restoration. See 4.4.69n.

93 **cry you mercy** I beg your pardon

95 **depart** departure

97–8 The mirroring syntax here frames,

between the lines, the transition from 'Sebastian' (*me*) to 'Julia' (*herself*); the brilliance of these lines stems in large part from the double duty that *herself* does, as first indicating another and then as reflexive. Julia reveals herself linguistically, then, before any physical gesture.

98 SD *Julia reveals herself here, possibly by taking off a hat and shaking her hair loose, as do heroines 'in narratives by Ariosto, Tasso, and Spenser' (Shapiro, *Gender*, 72), though long hair is of course not incompatible with male gender. Cf. 2.7.45–6 and 46n.; also Beaumont & Fletcher, *Philaster* (5.5.112), where Euphrasia, disguised as a male page, '*Kneels to Dion and discovers her haire*'. Certainly Proteus now recognizes her, and she announces herself in the typical language of revelation (*Behold her*, 100), but at the end of the scene, the Duke still sees her as a *boy* (163), as she is still in her page's costume. In Wager's production, to overcome this seeming discrepancy,

92 Why] *om. Pope*   94 SD] *Johnson subst.*   95 But] *om. Pope*   97 me –] *this edn (RP);* me, *F*   98 SD] *Collier² subst.*

JULIA

Behold her that gave aim to all thy oaths 100
And entertained 'em deeply in her heart.
How oft hast thou with perjury cleft the root!
O Proteus, let this habit make thee blush.
Be thou ashamed that I have took upon me
Such an immodest raiment, if shame live 105
In a disguise of love.
It is the lesser blot, modesty finds,
Women to change their shapes than men their minds.

the actress turned her back to the audience, faced Proteus and ripped open her blouse to reveal herself to him – thus undercutting the already inherent shame of simply being dressed as a boy (expressed by Julia at 104–5 (see 105n.)). It could be argued that Julia's lines (100–6) alone are enough to reveal her (especially as they are explicit about her disguise); this would then accommodate the fact that Proteus recognizes her while the Duke doesn't. Proteus's line at 99 would then be read as a simple questioning of Julia's previous lines rather than as a reaction to any visual revelation.

100–8 When this speech is delivered 'as a guilt-mongering whimper', Shapiro, *Gender*, 80, notes, 'Proteus's repentance seems motivated by a bad conscience', but with 'enough momentum behind it, the speech could also dazzle Proteus with Julia's presence and convince spectators that he truly does find her beauty no less than Silvia's'.

100 **gave aim to** was the aim of; guided the aim of (the language of archery). Cf. 3.2.89n. and Webster, *White Devil*, 3.2.24–5: 'I am at the mark sir, I'll give aim to you, / And tell you how near you shoot.'

101 **entertained** welcomed

102 **cleft the root** a term from archery:

'cleaving the pin' (of the target, i.e. her heart). Cf. *RJ* 2.4.15–16: 'the very pin of his heart cleft with the blind bow-boy's butt shaft' (cited *OED v.*[1] B 1e and Ard[1]).

103 **habit** clothing; cf. *Diana*, 239: 'in the habite of a base page I served thee (a thing more contrarie to my rest and reputation then I meane now to reherse)'.

105 **immodest raiment** Many scholars have suggested that Shakespeare drew this idea from Sidney's *Arcadia*, where Pyrocles speaks of Zelmane, 'whom unconsulting affection . . . had made borrowe so much of her naturall modestie, as to leave her more-decent rayments, and . . . had apparelled her selfe like a Page'; he goes on to describe the moment when, on her deathbed, she revealed how, for love of him, she had 'put off the apparell of a woman, & (if you judge not more mercifully) modestie' (Bullough, 1.254, 256). Given the cultural condemnation of transvestism, and accusations in particular against the theatre's use of male actors in female costume, it is surprising that so few characters in early modern drama express such anxiety. See Shapiro, *Gender*, and Orgel.

108 **shapes** appearances (with a theatrical overtone suggesting 'costumes')

106 love.] *Collier;* loue? *F*

PROTEUS

Than men their minds? 'Tis true. O heaven, were man
But constant, he were perfect. That one error   110
Fills him with faults, makes him run through all th' sins;
Inconstancy falls off ere it begins.
What is in Silvia's face but I may spy
More fresh in Julia's, with a constant eye?

VALENTINE

Come, come, a hand from either.   115
Let me be blest to make this happy close.

109–10 O . . . perfect These lines, echoing *perfect* once again (see 1.3.20n.), suggest a new recognition in Proteus of the potential for *faults* and *all th' sins* in humankind. Lindenbaum, 242, sees a 'radical change' in the play's definition of a 'perfect man' from a 'mere courtier [earlier] to, in effect, an unfallen being', hence the major characters have learned to see 'man, and particularly Proteus, for what he is as imperfect and fallen'. Cf. Calvin, 1.15.5, 8: 'Nothing is more inconstant than man. Contrary motions stir up and variously distract his soul . . . Adam could have stood if he wished, seeing that he fell solely by his own will. But it was because his will was capable of being bent to one side or the other, and was not given the constancy to persevere, that he fell so easily.'

111 th' sins The oddness of this elision has struck many editors. Pope's deletion of *th'* seems to have been because it was extrametrical.

112 *Riv* paraphrases: 'an inconstant man begins to be faithless even before he has declared his love'.
ere before

115–17 These lines have, in some editions and in some productions, been transferred from Valentine to Silvia. The logic is two-fold: first, Silvia's silence from 59 to the end of the play seems

both unrealistic and difficult to stage (what is she doing all this time?); second, by speaking the lines of reconciliation, she sanctions Valentine's actions and her motives are seen as love of Valentine and sympathy for Julia. In this scenario, *friends* (117) refers either to Valentine and Proteus or, since the speech follows Proteus's return to Julia, to Proteus and Julia (*friends* could also mean 'lovers'). The latter remains more likely in view of 118 and 119; thus, Silvia would restore their relationship, correcting the structural disequilibrium. Victor's SD at this point reads: Silvia '*joins the hands of* Protheus *and* Julia; *and then takes the hand of* Valentine *to give to* Protheus' (Victor, 53); many productions include some such stage action. As logical as the SP alteration may sound, however, there is no textual evidence to support it and, in any case, Silvia's silence during the reconciliation has frequently been used to advantage in production; see pp. 105–6. Friedman, 49, points out that Valentine here 'in a reconstitution of the betrothal ceremony performed earlier by Proteus and Julia, rejoins the hands of the two lovers'.

116 close union; 'the conclusion of a musical phrase, theme, or movement' (*OED sb.*[2] 2). Cf. *R2* 2.1.12: 'music at the close'.

---

111 th' sins] sins *Pope*   112 falls off] *(falls-off)*

'Twere pity two such friends should be long foes.

PROTEUS

Bear witness, heaven, I have my wish forever.

JULIA

And I mine.

[*Enter* Outlaws *with* DUKE *and* TURIO.]

OUTLAWS   A prize, a prize, a prize!

VALENTINE

Forbear, forbear, I say! It is my lord the Duke.   120
Your grace is welcome to a man disgraced,
Banished Valentine.

DUKE   Sir Valentine!

TURIO

Yonder is Silvia, and Silvia's mine.

VALENTINE

Turio, give back, or else embrace thy death;
Come not within the measure of my wrath.   125
Do not name Silvia thine; if once again,
Verona shall not hold thee. Here she stands;
Take but possession of her with a touch –
I dare thee but to breathe upon my love.

TURIO

Sir Valentine, I care not for her, I.   130

---

120 alexandrine; see 1.1.30n.
    Duke See List of Roles, 1n., and
    1.3.27n.
122 **Banished** banishèd
124 **give back** go back; yield
125 **measure** reach
127 **Verona** F's '*Verona*' seems to be
    incorrect, since Turio is a citizen of
    Milan, but it is just possible that
    Verona should be understood as fitting
    Valentine's frame of reference.

129 'Valentine's prompt and passionate
    assertion of his rights in Silvia suffi-
    ciently negatives his supposed surren-
    der of her at line 83' (Ard[1]).
130–3 Turio's comic cowardice here
    shifts the scene away from the disturb-
    ing elements earlier to more conven-
    tional moments of comic closure;
    moreover, Turio's cowardice provides
    an opening for the Duke to overcome
    his social objections to Valentine.

119 SD] *Rowe subst.*   126 if] but *Hanmer*   127 Verona] Milan *Theobald;* And Milan *Hanmer*   128
touch –] *Steevens;* Touch: F

I hold him but a fool that will endanger
His body for a girl that loves him not.
I claim her not, and therefore she is thine.
DUKE

The more degenerate and base art thou
To make such means for her as thou hast done,   135
And leave her on such slight conditions. –
Now, by the honour of my ancestry,
I do applaud thy spirit, Valentine,
And think thee worthy of an empress' love.
Know then, I here forget all former griefs,   140
Cancel all grudge, repeal thee home again,
Plead a new state in thy unrivalled merit,
To which I thus subscribe: Sir Valentine,
Thou art a gentleman, and well derived;
Take thou thy Silvia, for thou hast deserved her.   145

---

135 **means** efforts; approaches. Cf. *R3* 5.3.248: 'One that made means to come by what he hath'.
136 **on . . . conditions** so easily; *conditions* is pronounced with four syllables.
139 **empress'** could be taken as generic or indeed as a direct reference to Silvia (and may suggest that Silvia is the Duke's heir; cf. 2.4.74–5 (and n.), where the Duke uses the same phrase to Proteus. See List of Roles, 1n., and 1.3.27n.
141 **grudge** ill-will, resentment
repeal call back; cf. 3.1.232.
142 Bond suggests, but does not adopt, 'statute' as making more sense than *state* – a 'legal metaphor' suggesting a new 'order of things'; Bond also conjectures 'Plant' for *Plead*, for the sense of 'found my kingdom anew in you'. Sanders argues that 'Plead a new state' is a term 'from rhetoric, with *state* meaning "the point in question or debate between contending parties, as

it emerges from their pleadings". The Duke is saying that he takes up a new position (on the question of Valentine's merits).' Essentially the Duke, while restoring his good opinion of Valentine, is placing Valentine in the *new* position of *unrivalled* suitor to Silvia.
143 **To . . . subscribe** which I bear witness to, which I ratify with these words
144 **gentleman** This is an ideologically loaded term of praise. The Duke has overcome his sneering condescension at Valentine's position when he banished him (see 3.1.156–8). His conversion from the role of blocking father and impetuous sovereign (see 3.1.163–9n.) to that of magnanimous patron and generous father, in order not only to rehabilitate but elevate Valentine to the play's highest level of patriarchal order, seems contrived at this point.
well derived well descended, of good birth; cf. 5.2.23.

---

142 state] statute *(Ard¹)*   unrivalled] *(vn-riual'd)*; arrival'd *F2*

VALENTINE

    I thank your grace; the gift hath made me happy.
    I now beseech you, for your daughter's sake,
    To grant one boon that I shall ask of you.

DUKE

    I grant it for thine own, whate'er it be.

VALENTINE

    These banished men, that I have kept withal,   150
    Are men endued with worthy qualities.
    Forgive them what they have committed here,
    And let them be recalled from their exile.
    They are reformed, civil, full of good
    And fit for great employment, worthy lord.   155

DUKE

    Thou hast prevailed; I pardon them and thee.
    Dispose of them as thou knowst their deserts.
    Come, let us go. We will include all jars
    With triumphs, mirth and rare solemnity.

VALENTINE

    And as we walk along, I dare be bold   160

---

146 **gift** Valentine's language here conforms to the discourse of 'traffic in women' (Rubin) and is little different from his allusion to Silvia earlier as a *jewel* (see 2.4.166–9n.). Victor's SD is unambiguous: '*presenting* Silvia *to* Valentine' (Victor, 54). As RP notes, Anglican ritual assumed the woman's passive role as *gift*.

147 Here some early adapters, such as Victor, add a new scene, with Speed, Lance and Crab, in which Lance, believing they are in danger, offers to die for Crab (illustrating true friendship in contrast to Proteus), but is disabused and brought into the general reconciliation. See pp. 86–8.

148 **boon** gift, request; Valentine's selfless request contrasts with Proteus's desire for a *boon* (24) earlier.

150 **kept withal** lived with

153 **exile** stressed on second syllable

154 **reformed** reformèd; not according to Valentine's comments at 14–17, where he can hardly restrain their *uncivil outrages*

157 'Employ them according to your knowledge of what they deserve.'

158 **include** i.e. conclude
    jars conflicts; musical discord

159 **triumphs** pageants; cf. *R2* 5.2.52: 'Do these jousts and triumphs hold?'; *Per* 2.2.1: 'Are the knights ready to begin the triumph?'; and *Diana*, 242: 'There they were all married with great joy, feasts, and triumphes.'

---

151 enduded] endowed *Oxf*   158 include] conclude *Hanmer*

With our discourse to make your grace to smile.
What think you of this page, my lord?

DUKE

I think the boy hath grace in him; he blushes.

VALENTINE

I warrant you, my lord, more grace than boy.

DUKE

What mean you by that saying?   165

VALENTINE

Please you, I'll tell you as we pass along,
That you will wonder what hath fortuned.
Come, Proteus, 'tis your penance but to hear
The story of your loves discovered.
That done, our day of marriage shall be yours,   170
One feast, one house, one mutual happiness.   *Exeunt.*

---

163 proverbial (Dent, B480: 'Blushing (Bashfulness) is virtue's color (is a sign of grace)')

167 **That** so that
wonder be amazed
fortuned fortunèd; happened

169 **discovered** discoverèd; revealed

170–1 As Woudhuysen, 297, points out, only *TGV* among the early comedies ends with an unrhymed verse speech. Valentine's final lines speak of *marriage* and the joining together of the two couples in a *mutual happiness*, but the terms in the final line also reflect the rhetoric of the male friendship tradition: Damon and Pythias are 'All one in effect, all one in their going, / All one in their study, all one in their doing . . . but one heart between them!' (*Damon and Pythias*, ll. 235–6, 242); also, according to Walter Dorke, Scipio and Laelius were such close friends that 'one house served them both, one face, one joint study, one delight, one consent in all things: not onely in private affaires, but also in publique, in travailes, in voyages,

in sojourning, at home and abroad all were alike common: was not this a laudable kind of Friendship?' (Dorke, B2ᵛ). Valentine's lines suggest a communal celebration, now two marriages in *one house* in place of one soul in two bodies. These new unions are usually represented onstage visually by embraces and handclasps. See pp. 105–7.

171 After this line Victor, 55, adds a final moralistic couplet to be spoken by Proteus: 'A convert to this truth I stand confess'd, / That lovers must be faithful, to be bless'd.' Kemble, 73, goes further, with five additional lines to Victor's in which the sincerity of Proteus's return to Julia is confirmed: 'Thanks, generous Valentine: – and I myself / Will be the trumpet of my Julia's worth, / Her stedfast faith, her still-enduring love, / And of my own misdoings. – Pardon me, / Ye who have ever known what 't is to err! – / And be this truth by all the world confest, / That lovers must be faithful, to be blest.'

162 page] stripling page *Collier²*   165 saying?] saying, Valentine? *Collier²*

APPENDIX

CASTING CHART

Adult Actor	1.1	1.2	1.3	2.1	2.2	2.3	2.4	2.5	2.6	2.7
1	Pro		Pro		Pro		Pro		Pro	
2	Val			Val			Val			
3						Lance		Lance		
4			Ant				Serv			
5			Pant		Pant	Pant				
6							Turio			
7							Duke			
8	Speed			Speed			Speed	Speed		
Boy Actor										
1		Julia			Julia					Julia
2				Silvia			Silvia			
3		Lucet								Lucet

Adult Actor	3.1	3.2	4.1	4.2	4.3	4.4	5.1	5.2	5.3	5.4
1	Pro	Pro		Pro		Pro		Pro		Pro
2	Val		Val							Val
3	Lance					Lance				
4			Outlaw	Host			Egla		Outlaw	Outlaw
5			Outlaw		Egla				Outlaw	Outlaw
6	Turio	Turio		Turio				Turio		Turio
7	Duke	Duke						Duke		Duke
8	Speed		Speed							
Boy Actor										
1				Julia		Julia	Silvia	Julia		Julia
2				Silvia	Silvia	Silvia			Silvia	Silvia
3			Outlaw			Attend			Outlaw	Outlaw

The Outlaws, with relatively few lines to speak, might also simply have been hired from outside the main company for just these parts.

ABBREVIATIONS AND REFERENCES

Throughout this edition, quotations from the First Folio are reproduced as closely as possible to the original, except that the long 's' is reduced and 'th' substituted for thorn. For the reader's convenience, however, quotations from other early modern texts follow present-day usage of 'i' and 'u' as vowels and 'j' and 'v' as consonants, irrespective of their position within the word. Quotations and references to Shakespeare plays other than *The Two Gentlemen of Verona* are from *The Arden Shakespeare Third Series*, where they exist as of this date; other quotations are from *The Complete Works of Shakespeare*, ed. David Bevington, 4th edition (New York, 1992). In all references, place of publication is London unless otherwise stated.

ABBREVIATIONS

ABBREVIATIONS USED IN NOTES

c	corrected state
n.	note
n.d.	no date
n.p.	no place
n.s.	new series
om.	omitted in
opp.	opposite
Q	quarto
SD	stage direction
sig., sigs	signature, signatures
SP	speech prefix
subst.	substantially
this edn	a reading adopted for the first time in this edition
TLN	through line numbering in *The Norton Facsimile: The First Folio of Shakespeare*, prepared by Charlton Hinman (New York, 1968)
t.n.	textual note
u	uncorrected state

| ( ) | enclosing a reading in the textual notes indicates original spelling; enclosing an editor's or scholar's name indicates a conjectural reading |
| * | precedes commentary notes when they involve readings in this edn substantively altered from the original edition |

WORKS BY AND PARTLY BY SHAKESPEARE

AC	*Antony and Cleopatra*
AW	*All's Well That Ends Well*
AYL	*As You Like It*
Car	*The History of Cardenio*
CE	*The Comedy of Errors*
Cor	*Coriolanus*
Cym	*Cymbeline*
DF	Lewis Theobald, *Double Falsehood*
E3	*King Edward III*
Ham	*Hamlet*
1H4	*King Henry IV, Part 1*
2H4	*King Henry IV, Part 2*
H5	*King Henry V*
1H6	*King Henry VI, Part 1*
2H6	*King Henry VI, Part 2*
3H6	*King Henry VI, Part 3*
H8	*King Henry VIII*
JC	*Julius Caesar*
KJ	*King John*
KL	*King Lear*
LC	*A Lover's Complaint*
LLL	*Love's Labour's Lost*
Luc	*The Rape of Lucrece*
MA	*Much Ado About Nothing*
Mac	*Macbeth*
MM	*Measure for Measure*
MND	*A Midsummer Night's Dream*
MV	*The Merchant of Venice*
MW	*The Merry Wives of Windsor*
Oth	*Othello*
Per	*Pericles*
PP	*The Passionate Pilgrim*
PT	*The Phoenix and Turtle*
R2	*King Richard II*
R3	*King Richard III*
RJ	*Romeo and Juliet*
Son	*Sonnets*

STM	*The Book of Sir Thomas More*
TC	*Troilus and Cressida*
Tem	*The Tempest*
TGV	*The Two Gentlemen of Verona*
Tim	*Timon of Athens*
Tit	*Titus Andronicus*
TN	*Twelfth Night*
TNK	*The Two Noble Kinsmen*
TS	*The Taming of the Shrew*
VA	*Venus and Adonis*
WT	*The Winter's Tale*

REFERENCES

EDITIONS OF SHAKESPEARE COLLATED OR REFERRED TO

Ard¹	*The Two Gentlemen of Verona*, ed. R. Warwick Bond, The Arden Shakespeare (1906)
Ard²	*The Two Gentlemen of Verona*, ed. Clifford Leech, The Arden Shakespeare (1969)
Bantam	*The Two Gentlemen of Verona*, in *Three Early Comedies*, ed. David Bevington, The Bantam Shakespeare (1988)
Bevington	*Complete Works*, ed. David Bevington, 4th edn (New York, 1992)
Blackstone	See Malone
Bond	See Ard¹
Boswell–Malone	*Plays and Poems*, ed. James Boswell, 21 vols (1821)
Cam	*Works*, ed. W.G. Clark, John Glover and W.A. Wright, 9 vols (Cambridge, 1863–6)
Cam¹	*The Two Gentlemen of Verona*, ed. Arthur Quiller-Couch and John Dover Wilson (Cambridge, 1921)
Cam²	*The Two Gentlemen of Verona*, ed. Kurt Schlueter (Cambridge, 1990)
Capell	*Comedies, Histories, and Tragedies*, ed. Edward Capell, 10 vols (1767–8)
Collier	*Works*, ed. John Payne Collier, 8 vols (1842–4)
Collier²	*Comedies, Histories, Tragedies, and Poems*, ed. John Payne Collier, 6 vols (1858)
Delius	*Works* (*Werke*), ed. Nicolaus Delius, 7 vols (Elberfeld, 1854–61)
Dyce	*Works*, ed. Alexander Dyce, 6 vols (1857)
F, F1	*Comedies, Histories, and Tragedies*, The First Folio (1623)

F2	*Comedies, Histories, and Tragedies*, The Second Folio (1632)
F3	*Comedies, Histories, and Tragedies*, The Third Folio (1663)
F4	*Comedies, Histories, and Tragedies*, The Fourth Folio (1685)
Folg²	*The Two Gentlemen of Verona*, ed. Barbara A. Mowat and Paul Werstine, The New Folger Library Shakespeare (New York, 1999)
Halliwell	*Works*, ed. James O. Halliwell, 16 vols (1853–65)
Hanmer	*Works*, ed. Thomas Hanmer, 6 vols (Oxford, 1743–4)
Hawkins	See Steevens
Hudson	*Works*, ed. H.N. Hudson, 11 vols (Boston, Mass., 1864)
Johnson	*Plays*, ed. Samuel Johnson, 8 vols (1765)
Keightley	*Plays*, ed. Thomas Keightley, 6 vols (1864)
Kittredge	*Complete Works*, ed. G.L. Kittredge (New York, 1936)
Knight²	*Comedies, Histories, Tragedies, and Poems*, ed. Charles Knight, 8 vols (1842–4)
Leech	See Ard²
Malone	*Plays and Poems*, ed. Edmond Malone, 10 vols (1790)
Marshall	See Keightley
Norton	*The Norton Shakespeare: Based on the Oxford Edition*, ed. Stephen Greenblatt, Walter Cohen, Jean E. Howard and Katharine Eisaman Maus (New York, 1997)
Oxf	*Complete Works*, ed. Stanley Wells, Gary Taylor, John Jowett and William Montgomery (Oxford, 1986)
Penguin	*The Two Gentlemen of Verona*, ed. Norman Sanders (Harmondsworth, England, 1968)
Pope	*Works*, ed. Alexander Pope, 6 vols (1723–5)
Riv	*The Riverside Shakespeare*, ed. G. Blakemore Evans (Boston, Mass., 1974; rev. edn 1997); all references are to the second edition unless otherwise specified
Rowe	*Works*, ed. Nicholas Rowe, 7 vols (1709–10), vol. 1; Rowe's extra notes on *TGV* in vol. 7 are also referred to in the Introduction
Rowe²	*Works*, ed. Nicholas Rowe, 6 vols (1709)
Rowe³	*Works*, ed. Nicholas Rowe, 8 vols (1714)
Sanders	See Penguin
Schlueter	See Cam²
Signet	*The Two Gentlemen of Verona*, ed. Bertrand Evans (New York, 1964)
Singer	*Dramatic Works*, ed. Samuel W. Singer, 10 vols (1826)
Singer²	*Dramatic Works*, ed. Samuel W. Singer, 10 vols (1856)
Sisson	*Complete Works*, ed. C.J. Sisson (1954)
Staunton	*Plays*, ed. Howard Staunton, 3 vols (1858–62)

Steevens	*Plays*, ed. Samuel Johnson and George Steevens, 10 vols (1773)
Theobald	*Works*, ed. Lewis Theobald, 7 vols (1733)
Var. 1803	Johnson–Steevens Variorum, rev. Isaac Reed, 21 vols (1803)
Victor	Benjamin Victor, *The Two Gentlemen of Verona . . . With Alterations and Additions* (1763)
Warburton	*Works*, ed. William Warburton, 8 vols (1747)
White	*Works*, ed. Richard Grant White, 12 vols (Boston, Mass., 1857)

OTHER WORKS CITED

Abbott	E.A. Abbott, *A Shakespearian Grammar*, 3rd edn (1886)
ABT	A.B. Taylor, private communication
Adelman	Janet Adelman, 'Male Bonding in Shakespeare's Comedies', in Peter Erickson and Coppélia Kahn (eds), *Shakespeare's Rough Magic* (1985), 73–103
Allen	Mozelle S. Allen, 'Broke's *Romeus and Juliet* as a Source for the Valentine-Silvia Plot in *The Two Gentlemen of Verona*', *University of Texas Studies in English*, 18 (1938), 25–46
Amores	See *Heroides*
Aristotle	Aristotle, *Nichomachean Ethics*, trans. Horace Rackham (Cambridge, Mass., 1926)
Armstrong	Alan Armstrong, 'The 1997 Oregon Shakespeare Festival', *ShB*, 16.2 (1998), 33–7
Art	Ovid, *The Art of Love*, in *Ovid: The Art of Love, and Other Poems*, ed. J.H. Mozley (1929)
Astington	John Astington, ' "Fault" in Shakespeare', *SQ*, 36 (1985), 330–4
AT	Ann Thompson, private communication
Atheist's Tragedy	Cyril Tourneur, *The Atheist's Tragedy*, ed. Brian Morris and Roma Gill (1976)
Bacon	*Sir Francis Bacon: 'The Essayes or Counsels, Civill and Morall'*, ed. Michael Kiernan (Cambridge, Mass., 1985)
Bakhtin	Mikhail Bakhtin, *Rabelais and His World* (Cambridge, Mass., 1968)
Baldwin	T.W. Baldwin, *William Shakspere's Small Latine & Lesse Greeke*, 2 vols (Urbana, Ill., 1944)
Baldwin, *Company*	T.W. Baldwin, *The Organization and Personnel of the Shakespearean Company* (Princeton, N.J., 1927)
Barber	C.L. Barber, *Shakespeare's Festive Comedy* (Princeton, N.J., 1959)
Barber, L.	Lester E. Barber, 'Great Lakes Shakespeare', *SQ*, 30 (1979), 212–15

Barish   Jonas Barish, *The Antitheatrical Prejudice* (Berkeley, Calif., 1981)

Barkan   Leonard Barkan, *The Gods Made Flesh: Metamorphosis and the Pursuit of Paganism* (New Haven, Conn., 1986)

Bartholomew Fair Ben Jonson, *Bartholomew Fair* (1614), in Jonson, 4.1–122

Bate   Jonathan Bate, *Shakespeare and Ovid* (Oxford, 1993)

Bate, *Romantics* Jonathan Bate (ed.), *The Romantics on Shakespeare* (1992)

Beadle   Richard Beadle, 'Crab's Pedigree', in Michael Cordner, Peter Holland and John Kerrigan (eds), *English Comedy* (Cambridge, 1994), 12–35

Beaumont & *The Dramatic Works in the Beaumont and Fletcher Canon*,
 Fletcher   gen. ed. Fredson Bowers, vol. 1 (Cambridge, 1966)

Beckerman   Bernard Beckerman, 'Shakespeare's Dramaturgy and Binary Form', *Theatre Journal*, 33 (1981), 5–17

Belsey   Catherine Belsey, 'Disrupting sexual difference: meaning and gender in the comedies', in John Drakakis (ed.), *Alternative Shakespeares* (1985), 166–90

Boccaccio   Giovanni Boccaccio, *The Decameron*, trans. G.H. McWilliam (Harmondsworth, England, 1972), Day 10, Novel 8, 776–94

Bodenham   John Bodenham, *Bodenham's Belvedere or the Garden of the Muses* (1600)

Bradley   David Bradley, *From Text to Performance in the Elizabethan Theatre* (Cambridge, 1992)

Brathwait   Richard Brathwait, *The English Gentleman* (1630)

Braun   Georg Braun and Frans Hogenberg, *Civitates Orbis Terrarum* (Cologne, 1572–1618), reprinted 3 vols (Cleveland, Ohio, 1966)

Bray   Alan Bray, 'Homosexuality and the Signs of Male Friendship in Elizabethan England', in Jonathan Goldberg (ed.), *Queering the Renaissance* (Durham, N.C., 1994), 40–61

Brooks   Harold F. Brooks, 'Two Clowns in a Comedy (to say nothing of the Dog): Speed, Launce (and Crab) in *The Two Gentlemen of Verona*', *Essays and Studies*, n.s. 16 (1963), 91–100

Brown   John Russell Brown, 'Three Directors: A Review of Recent Productions', *SS 14* (1961), 129–37

Brown,   John Russell Brown, 'Free Shakespeare', *SS 24* (1971),
 'Free'   127–35

Bullough   Geoffrey Bullough (ed.), *Narrative and Dramatic Sources of Shakespeare*, 8 vols (1957–75)

Butler   Charles Butler, *The Feminine Monarchy or A Treatise Concerning Bees* (Oxford, 1609)

Byrne	Muriel St. Clare Byrne, 'The Shakespeare Season at the Old Vic, 1956–57 and Stratford-upon-Avon, 1957', *SQ*, 8 (1957), 461–92
Calvin	John Calvin, *Institutes of the Christian Religion*, ed. John T. McNeill, 2 vols (Philadelphia, Penn., 1960)
Campbell	O.J. Campbell, '*The Two Gentlemen of Verona* and Italian Comedy', in Eugene S. McCartney (ed.), *Studies in Shakespeare, Milton and Donne* (New York, 1925), 49–63
Campbell, 'Actors'	Kathleen Campbell, 'Shakespeare's Actors as Collaborators: Will Kempe and *The Two Gentlemen of Verona*', in Schlueter, *Essays*, 178–87
Carey, 'Oregon'	Robin B. Carey, 'Oregon Shakespearean Festival, 1974', *SQ*, 25 (1974), 419–21
Carlisle & Derrick	Carol J. Carlisle and Patty S. Derrick, '*The Two Gentlemen of Verona* on Stage: Protean Problems and Protean Solutions', in Michael J. Collins (ed.), *Shakespeare's Sweet Thunder: Essays on the Early Comedies* (1997), 126–54
Carroll, *Metamorphoses*	William C. Carroll, *The Metamorphoses of Shakespearean Comedy* (Princeton, N.J., 1985)
Carroll, '*Romeo*'	William C. Carroll, '"We were born to die": The Ending of *Romeo and Juliet*', *Comparative Drama*, 15 (1981), 54–71
Carroll, 'Virgin'	William C. Carroll, 'The Virgin Not: Language and Sexuality in Shakespeare', *SS 46* (1994), 107–19
Chambers, *Stage*	E.K. Chambers, *The Elizabethan Stage*, 4 vols (Oxford, 1951)
Chambers, *WS*	E.K. Chambers, *William Shakespeare: A Study of Facts and Problems*, 2 vols (Oxford, 1930)
Churchyard	Thomas Churchyard, *A Spark of Friendship and Warm Goodwill* (1588)
Cicero, *De Amicitia*	Cicero, *De Amicitia*, in Cicero, *De Senectute, De Amicitia, De Divinatione*, trans. W.A. Falconer (Cambridge, Mass., 1923)
Clayton	Thomas Clayton, 'The Climax of *The Two Gentlemen of Verona*: Text and Performance at the Swan Theatre, Stratford-upon-Avon, 1991', *ShB*, 9.4 (1991), 17–19
Clyomon	*The History of the Two Valiant Knights, Sir Clyomon . . . and Clamydes* (1599)
Cohn	Albert Cohn, *Shakespeare in Germany in the Sixteenth and Seventeenth Centuries* (Wiesbaden, 1865)
Coleridge, *Fragments*	Samuel Taylor Coleridge, *Shorter Works and Fragments*, ed. H.J. Jackson and J.R. deJ. Jackson, vol. 1 (Princeton, N.J., 1995)
Coleridge, *Lectures*	Samuel Taylor Coleridge, *Lectures 1808–1819 On Literature*, ed. R.A. Foakes, vol. 2 (Princeton, N.J., 1987)

Cook	Ann Jennalie Cook, *Making a Match: Courtship in Shakespeare and His Society* (Princeton, N.J., 1991)
Coryat	Thomas Coryat, *Coryat's Crudities* (1611), reprinted 2 vols (Glasgow, 1905)
Cotgrave	John Cotgrave, *The English Treasury of Wit and Language* (1655)
Cressy	David Cressy, *Bonfires and Bells: National Memory and the Protestant Calendar in Elizabethan and Stuart England* (Berkeley, Calif., 1989)
Daly	Augustin Daly, *Two Gentlemen of Verona. A Comedy in Four Acts by William Shakespeare. Re-arranged by Augustin Daly* (n.p., 1895)
D'Amico	Jack D'Amico, *Shakespeare and Italy: The City and the Stage* (Gainesville, Fla., 2001)
Damon and Pythias	Richard Edwards' *'Damon and Pithias'*, ed. D. Jerry White (1980)
Dekker	*The Dramatic Works of Thomas Dekker*, ed. Fredson Bowers, 4 vols (Cambridge, 1953–61)
Dent	R.W. Dent, *Shakespeare's Proverbial Language: An Index* (1981)
Derrick, 'Crucial'	Patty S. Derrick, '*Two Gents*: A Crucial Moment', *Shakespeare on Film Newsletter*, 16.1 (1991), 1, 4
Derrick, 'Depth'	Patty S. Derrick, 'Feminine "Depth" on the Nineteenth-Century Stage', in Schlueter, *Essays*, 178–87
Desens	Marliss Desens, *The Bed-Trick in English Renaissance Drama* (Newark, Del., 1994)
Diana	George of Montemayor, *Diana*, in Judith M. Kennedy (ed.), *A Critical Edition of Yong's Translation of George of Montemayor's 'Diana' and Gil Polo's 'Enamoured Diana'* (Oxford, 1968)
Disciplines	Peter Demetz, Thomas Greene and Lowry Nelson, Jr (eds), *The Disciplines of Criticism* (New Haven, Conn., 1968)
Doran	Madeleine Doran, *Endeavors of Art: A Study of Form in Elizabethan Drama* (Madison, Wis., 1954)
Dorke	Walter Dorke, *A Type or Figure of Friendship* (1589)
Draper	John W. Draper, 'Shakespeare and the Lombard Cities', *Rivista di Letterature Moderne e Comparate*, n.s. 4 (1953), 54–8
Duncan-Jones	Katherine Duncan-Jones (ed.), *Shakespeare's Sonnets* (Walton-on-Thames, 1997)
Eagles	Jonathan Eagles, *Watching Shakespeare: A Theatregoer's Review of the RSC, 1980–95* (1997)
Elam	Keir Elam, *Shakespeare's Universe of Discourse: Language-Games in the Comedies* (Cambridge, 1984)

ELH	*A Journal of English Literary History*
Eliot	*The George Eliot Letters*, ed. Gordon S. Haight, vol. 3 (New Haven, Conn., 1954), vol. 8 (New Haven, Conn., 1978)
ELR	*English Literary Renaissance*
Elyot	Sir Thomas Elyot, *The Boke Named the Governour*, ed. Henry H.S. Croft, vol. 2 (1883)
Enamoured Diana	See *Diana*
Erasmus	*The 'Adages' of Erasmus*, trans. Margaret Mann Phillips, in *Collected Works*, vol. 31 (Toronto, Ont., 1982)
Fleming	Abraham Fleming (trans.), *Of English Dogs . . . A Short Treatise written in Latin by Johannes Caius . . . newly drawn into English by Abraham Fleming* (1576)
Fletcher, 'Marriage'	Anthony Fletcher, 'The Protestant idea of marriage in early modern England', in Anthony Fletcher and Peter Roberts (eds), *Religion, Culture, and Society in Early Modern Britain* (Cambridge, 1994), 161–81
Foxe	*John Foxe: Titus et Gesippus*, ed. John Hazel Smith (New York, 1986)
FQ	*Spenser's Faerie Queene*, ed. J.C. Smith, 2 vols (Oxford, 1909)
Friedman	Michael D. Friedman, *'The World Must Be Peopled': Shakespeare's Comedies of Forgiveness* (Madison, N.J., 2002)
Frye	Northrop Frye, *A Natural Perspective: The Development of Shakespearean Comedy and Romance* (New York, 1965)
Garber	Marjorie Garber, *Coming of Age in Shakespeare* (1981)
Giamatti	A. Bartlett Giamatti, 'Proteus Unbound: Some Versions of the Sea God in the Renaissance', in *Disciplines*, 437–75
Girard	René Girard, 'Love Delights in Praises: A Reading of *The Two Gentlemen of Verona*', *Philosophy and Literature*, 13 (1989), 231–47
Goldberg	Jonathan Goldberg, *Voice Terminal Echo: Postmodernism and English Renaissance Texts* (New York, 1986), 68–100
Golding	*Ovid's 'Metamorphoses': The Arthur Golding Translation (1567)*, ed. John Frederick Nims (New York, 1965)
Greene	Thomas Greene, 'The Flexibility of the Self in Renaissance Literature', in *Disciplines*, 241–64
Grote	David Grote, *The Best Actors in the World: Shakespeare and His Acting Company* (2002)
Guare	*Two Gentlemen of Verona. Adapted from the Shakespeare Play by John Guare & Mel Shapiro* (New York, 1973)
Guinn	John A. Guinn, 'The Letter Device in the First Act of *The Two Gentlemen of Verona*', *University of Texas Studies in English*, 20 (1940), 72–81

Gurr, 'Localities'   Andrew Gurr, 'Shakespeare's Localities', in Agostino Lombardo (ed.), *Shakespeare a Verona e nel Veneto* (Verona, 1987), 55–66

Gurr, *Playgoing*   Andrew Gurr, *Playgoing in Shakespeare's London* (Cambridge, 1987)

Gurr, *Stage*   Andrew Gurr, *The Shakespearean Stage, 1574–1642*, 3rd edn (Cambridge, 1992)

Haight   Gordon S. Haight, *George Eliot: A Biography* (1968)

Hallett   Charles A. Hallett, '"Metamorphising" Proteus: Reversal Strategies in *The Two Gentlemen of Verona*', in Schlueter, *Essays*, 153–77

Harrison   T.P. Harrison, Jr, 'Shakespeare and Montemayor's *Diana*', *University of Texas Studies in English*, 6 (1926), 72–120

Haslem   Lori Schroeder Haslem, ' "O Me, The Word Choose!": Female Voice and Catechetical Ritual in *The Two Gentlemen of Verona* and *The Merchant of Venice*', *SSt*, 22 (1994), 122–40

Hayward   John Hayward, *Annals of the First Four Years of the Reign of Queen Elizabeth. Edited from a ms. in the Harleian collection, by John Bruce* (1840)

Hazlitt   William Hazlitt, *The Round Table and Characters of Shakespear's Plays*, ed. Catherine M. Maclean (1906)

Henslowe   *Henslowe's Diary*, ed. R.A. Foakes and R.T. Rickert (Cambridge, 1961)

Heroides   Ovid, *Heroides*, in *Heroides and Amores*, trans. Grant Showerman (1914)

Hinman   Charlton Hinman, *The Printing and Proof-Reading of the First Folio of Shakespeare*, 2 vols (Oxford, 1963)

Hoenselaars   A.J. Hoenselaars, 'Italy staged in English Renaissance drama', in Marrapodi, 30–48

Holland   Peter Holland, *English Shakespeares: Shakespeare on the English Stage in the 1990s* (Cambridge, 1997)

Honigmann, *Impact*   E.A.J. Honigmann, *Shakespeare's Impact on His Contemporaries* (Totowa, N.J., 1982)

Honigmann, *Texts*   E.A.J. Honigmann, *The Texts of 'Othello' and Shakespearian Revision* (1996)

Howard-Hill, 'Compositors'   T.H. Howard-Hill, 'The Compositors of Shakespeare's Folio Comedies', *SB*, 26 (1973), 61–106

Howard-Hill, *Crane*   T.H. Howard-Hill, *Ralph Crane and Some Shakespeare First Folio Comedies* (Charlottesville, Va., 1972)

Howard-Hill, 'Editor'   T.H. Howard-Hill, 'Shakespeare's Earliest Editor, Ralph Crane', *SS 44* (1992), 113–29

Hughey   Ruth Hughey, *John Harington of Stepney: Tudor Gentleman* (Columbus, Ohio, 1971)

Hunt	Maurice Hunt, '*The Two Gentlemen of Verona* and the Paradox of Salvation', *Rocky Mountain Review*, 36 (1982), 5–22
Hunter, *Comedy*	Robert G. Hunter, *Shakespeare and the Comedy of Forgiveness* (New York, 1965)
Hunter, *Lyly*	G.K. Hunter, *John Lyly: The Humanist as Courtier* (Cambridge, Mass., 1962)
Hutson	Lorna Hutson, *The Usurer's Daughter: Male Friendship and Fictions of Women in Sixteenth-Century England* (1994)
Jackson	Berners W. Jackson, 'Shakespeare at Stratford, Ontario, 1975', *SQ*, 27 (1976), 24–32
James	Mervyn James, *Society, Politics, and Culture: Studies in Early Modern England* (Cambridge, 1986)
James IV	Robert Greene, *James the Fourth*, ed. J.A. Lavin (1967)
Jardine	Lisa Jardine, *Still Harping on Daughters*, 2nd edn (New York, 1989)
Jardine, 'Companionate'	Lisa Jardine, 'Companionate marriage versus male friendship: anxiety for the lineal family in Jacobean drama', in Susan D. Amussen and Mark A. Kishlansky (eds), *Political Culture and Cultural Politics in Early Modern England* (Manchester, 1995), 234–54
Jeffrey	Violet Jeffrey, *John Lyly and the Italian Renaissance* (1928)
Jonson	*The Complete Plays of Ben Jonson*, ed. G.A. Wilkes, 4 vols (Oxford, 1982)
Jorgens	Jack Jorgens and Jan Levie, 'Champlain Shakespeare Festival', *SQ*, 29 (1978), 228–30
Kahn	Coppélia Kahn, *Man's Estate: Masculine Identity in Shakespeare* (Berkeley, Calif., 1981)
Kean	Charles Kean, *The Two Gentlemen of Verona. A Comedy* (New York, 1846)
Kean, Promptbook	Charles Kean, Promptbook of *The Two Gentlemen of Verona* (New York production, 1846) at the Folger Shakespeare Library, Washington, D.C. (Folger 2 Gent, 10)
Keats	*The Letters of John Keats*, ed. Maurice B. Forman, 2nd edn (1935)
Kemble	John Philip Kemble, *Shakespeare's Two Gentlemen of Verona, A Comedy* (1815); Kemble's adaptation used for his 1808 production
Kiefer	Frederick Kiefer, 'Love Letters in *The Two Gentlemen of Verona*', *SSt*, 18 (1986), 65–85
Kiernander	Adrian Kiernander, '*The Two* (?) *Gentlemen* (?) *of Verona* (?): Binarism, Patriarchy and Non-Consensual Sex Somewhere in the Vicinity of Milan', *Social Semiotics*, 4 (1994), 31–46

King	T.J. King, *Casting Shakespeare's Plays: London Actors and their Roles, 1590–1642* (Cambridge, 1992)
Knack	*A Knack to Know a Knave* (1594)
Kökeritz	Helge Kökeritz, *Shakespeare's Pronunciation* (New Haven, Conn., 1953)
Kyd	Thomas Kyd, *The Spanish Tragedy*, ed. J.R. Mulryne (1970)
Lamb	Charles and Mary Lamb, *Tales from Shakespeare* (1909)
Leishman	J.B. Leishman (ed.), *The Three Parnassus Plays (1598–1601)* (1949)
Levine	Laura Levine, *Men in Women's Clothing: Anti-theatricality and Effeminization, 1579–1642* (Cambridge, 1994)
Levith	Murray J. Levith, *Shakespeare's Italian Settings and Plays* (New York, 1989)
Lindenbaum	Peter Lindenbaum, 'Education in *The Two Gentlemen of Verona*', *Studies in English Literature*, 15 (1975), 229–44
Locatelli	Angela Locatelli, 'The fictional world of *Romeo and Juliet*: cultural connotations of an Italian setting', in Marrapodi, 69–84
Long	John H. Long, *Shakespeare's Use of Music* (Gainesville, Fla., 1955)
Lyly	*The Complete Works of John Lyly*, ed. R. Warwick Bond, 3 vols (Oxford, 1902)
MacCary	W. Thomas MacCary, *Friends and Lovers: The Phenomenology of Desire in Shakespearean Comedy* (New York, 1985)
McCauley	Janie Caves McCauley, 'The Two Gentlemen of Verona', *ShB*, 17.1 (1999), 11–12
Macfarlane	Alan Macfarlane, *Marriage and Love in England: Modes of Reproduction 1300–1840* (Oxford, 1986)
McPherson	David C. McPherson, *Shakespeare, Jonson, and the Myth of Venice* (Newark, Del., 1990)
Macready, Promptbook	William Charles Macready, Promptbook of *The Two Gentlemen of Verona* (Drury Lane production, London, 1841) at the Folger Shakespeare Library, Washington, D.C. (Folger 2 Gent, 11)
Magri	Noemi Magri, 'No Errors in Shakespere: Historical Truth and The Two Gentlemen of Verona', *The De Vere Society Newsletter*, 2.12 (1998), 9–22
Marlowe	*The Complete Works of Christopher Marlowe*, ed. Fredson Bowers, 2nd edn, 2 vols (Cambridge, 1981)
Marlowe, *Hero*	*Hero and Leander*, in Stephen Orgel (ed.), Christopher Marlowe, *The Complete Poems and Translations* (Harmondsworth, England, 1971)
Marrapodi	Michele Marrapodi (ed.), *Shakespeare's Italy* (Manchester, 1993)

Marston	John Marston, *The Insatiate Countess*, in Martin Wiggins (ed.), *Four Jacobean Sex Tragedies* (Oxford, 1998)
Masten	Jeffrey Masten, *Textual Intercourse: Collaboration, Authorship, and Sexualities in Renaissance Drama* (Cambridge, Mass., 1997)
Maurer	Margaret Maurer, 'Figure, Place, and the End of *The Two Gentlemen of Verona*', *Style*, 23 (1989), 405–29
Melchiori	Giorgio Melchiori, '"In fair Verona": *commedia erudita* into romantic Comedy', in Marrapodi, 100–11
Merry Devil	*The Merry Devil of Edmonton 1608*, ed. William A. Abrams (Durham, N.C., 1942)
Met.	Ovid, *Metamorphoses*, trans. Frank Justus Miller, 2 vols (1916). Vol. 1: Books 1–8; vol. 2: Books 9–15
Middleton	*The Works of Thomas Middleton*, ed. A.H. Bullen, 8 vols (1885)
Middleton, *Chaste Maid*	Thomas Middleton, *A Chaste Maid in Cheapside*, ed. Alan Brissenden (1968)
Middleton, *Women Beware*	Thomas Middleton, *Women Beware Women*, ed. William C. Carroll (1994)
Mills	Laurens J. Mills, *One Soul in Bodies Twain: Friendship in Tudor Literature and Stuart Drama* (Bloomington, Ind., 1937)
Montaigne	*Montaigne's Essays*, trans. John Florio (1603), reprinted 3 vols (1965)
Moryson	Fynes Moryson, *An Itinerary* (1617), reprinted 4 vols (New York, 1907)
Mucedorus	*A Most Pleasant Comedy of Mucedorus* (1598)
N&Q	*Notes and Queries*
Nashe	*The Works of Thomas Nashe*, ed. R.B. McKerrow, 5 vols (Oxford, 1958)
NB	Nicola Bennett, private communication
Nelsen	Paul Nelsen, '*The Two Gentlemen of Verona*', *ShB*, 9.4 (1991), 16
Nelsen, 'Prologue'	Paul Nelsen, 'Prologue Season at the New Globe: Polemics and Performance', *ShB*, 15.2 (1997), 5–8
Noble	Richmond Noble, *Shakespeare's Biblical Knowledge and Use of the Book of Common Prayer* (New York, 1935)
Nohrnberg	James Nohrnberg, *The Analogy of 'The Faerie Queene'* (Princeton, N.J., 1976)
Norland	Howard B. Norland, *Drama in Early Tudor Britain 1485–1558* (1995)
Norman & Stoppard	Marc Norman and Tom Stoppard, *Shakespeare in Love: A Screenplay* (New York, 1998)
Nosworthy	J.M. Nosworthy (ed.), *Cymbeline* (1955)
O'Connor	John S. O'Connor, 'Compositors D and F of the Shakespeare First Folio', *SB*, 28 (1975), 81–117

Odell	George C.D. Odell, *Shakespeare from Betterton to Irving*, 2 vols (New York, 1920)
OED	*Oxford English Dictionary*, ed. J.A. Simpson and E.S.C. Weiner, 2nd edn, 20 vols (Oxford, 1989)
Oliver	H.J. Oliver (ed.), *Timon of Athens* (1963)
Orgel	Stephen Orgel, *Impersonations: The Performance of Gender in Shakespeare's England* (Cambridge, 1996)
Osborne	Laurie E. Osborne, 'Rethinking the Performance Editions', in James C. Bulman (ed.), *Shakespeare, Theory, and Performance* (1996), 168–86
Østergaard	Claus B. Østergaard, 'Jealous Gentlemen: A Reappraisal of *The Two Gentlemen of Verona*', *SJW*, 131 (1995), 116–27
Parker	Patricia Parker, *Literary Fat Ladies: Rhetoric, Gender, Property* (1987)
Peele	*The Dramatic Works of George Peele*, ed. R. Mark Benbow, Elmer M. Blistein and Frank S. Hook, vol. 3 (New Haven, Conn., 1970)
Peterson[1]	Jean Peterson, 'The Two Gentlemen of Verona', *ShB*, 9.1 (1991), 33–4
Peterson[2]	Jean Peterson, 'The Taming of the Shrew-The Two Gentlemen of Verona', *ShB*, 11.1 (1993), 23–4
Peterson[3]	Jean Peterson, 'The Two Gentlemen of Verona', *ShB*, 13.2 (1995), 30–1
Pettigrew	John Pettigrew, 'Stratford 1975. I The Shakespeare Productions', *The Journal of Canadian Studies*, 11.1 (1976), 51–60
PMLA	*Publications of the Modern Language Association of America*
Potter	Lois Potter (ed.), *The Two Noble Kinsmen* (Walton-on-Thames, 1997)
Pressley	Nelson Pressley, 'Shakespeare in Jersey', *Washington Post*, 3 April 2001, Section C, 5
Rainoldes	John Rainoldes, *The Overthrow of Stage Plays* (Middelburg, 1599)
RenD	*Renaissance Drama*
Revenger's Tragedy	[Thomas Middleton?], *The Revenger's Tragedy*, ed. Brian Gibbons (1991)
Reynolds	Frederick Reynolds, *Songs, Duettos, Glees, and Choruses, Introduced in Shakspeare's Revived Play of the Two Gentlemen of Verona* (n.d. [1821])
Roaring Girl	Thomas Middleton and Thomas Dekker, *The Roaring Girl*, ed. Andor Gomme (1976)
Roberts, 'Crane'	Jeanne Addison Roberts, 'Ralph Crane and the Text of *The Tempest*', *SSt*, 13 (1980), 213–33
Roberts, 'D.C.'	Jeanne Addison Roberts, 'Shakespeare in Washington, D.C.', *SQ*, 29 (1978), 234–8

Roberts, *Wild*	Jeanne Addison Roberts, *The Shakespearean Wild* (Lincoln, Nebr., 1991)
Romeus	Arthur Brooke, *The Tragical History of Romeus and Juliet* (1562), in Bullough, 1.284–363
Roppolo	Joseph Patrick Roppolo, 'Shakespeare in New Orleans, 1817–1865', in Philip C. Kolin (ed.), *Shakespeare in the South: Essays on Performance* (Jackson, Miss., 1983), 112–27
Rossky	William Rossky, '*The Two Gentlemen of Verona* as Burlesque', *ELR*, 12 (1982), 210–19
Rowley, *Witch*	William Rowley *et al.*, *The Witch of Edmonton*, in Peter Corbin and Douglas Sedge (eds), *Three Jacobean Witchcraft Plays* (Manchester, 1986)
RP	Richard Proudfoot, private communication
RSC	Royal Shakespeare Company
Rubin	Gayle Rubin, 'The Traffic in Women: Notes on the "Political Economy" of Sex', in Rayna R. Reiter (ed.), *Toward an Anthropology of Women* (New York, 1975), 157–210
Rubinstein	Frankie Rubinstein, *A Dictionary of Shakespeare's Sexual Puns and their Significance*, 2nd edn (New York, 1995)
SAB	*The Shakspere Allusion-Book: A Collection of Allusions to Shakspere from 1591 to 1700*, ed. John Munro, 2 vols (1909)
Salgado	Gāmīni Salgado, *Eyewitnesses of Shakespeare: First Hand Accounts of Performances 1590–1890* (1975)
Salingar	Leo Salingar, *Shakespeare and the Traditions of Comedy* (Cambridge, 1974)
Sargent	Ralph M. Sargent, 'Sir Thomas Elyot and the Integrity of *The Two Gentlemen of Verona*', *PMLA*, 65 (1950), 1166–80
SB	*Studies in Bibliography*
Schafer	Elizabeth Schafer, *Ms-Directing Shakespeare: Women Direct Shakespeare* (1998)
Schlueter, *Essays*	June Schlueter (ed.), *Two Gentlemen of Verona: Critical Essays* (1996)
Scott	William O. Scott, 'Proteus in Spenser and Shakespeare: The Lover's Identity', *SSt*, 1 (1965), 283–93
Sedgwick	Eve Kosofsky Sedgwick, *Between Men: English Literature and Male Homosocial Desire* (New York, 1985)
Segal	Charles Segal, *Landscape in Ovid's Metamorphoses: A Study in the Transformation of a Literary Symbol* (Wiesbaden, 1969)
Shaaber	M.A. Shaaber (ed.), *A New Variorum Edition of Shakespeare: The Second Part of Henry the Fourth* (Philadelphia, Penn., 1940)

Shaltz	Justin Shaltz, 'The Two Gentlemen of Verona', *ShB*, 12.4 (1994), 34–5
Shannon	Laurie Shannon, *Sovereign Amity: Figures of Friendship in Shakespearean Contexts* (Chicago, Ill., 2002)
Shapiro, *Children*	Michael Shapiro, *Children of the Revels: The Boy Companies of Shakespeare's Time and their Plays* (New York, 1977)
Shapiro, *Gender*	Michael Shapiro, *Gender in Play on the Shakespearean Stage* (Ann Arbor, Mich., 1994)
ShB	*Shakespeare Bulletin*
Shershow	Scott Cutler Shershow, *Puppets and 'Popular' Culture* (Ithaca, N.Y., 1995)
Sidney	*The Poems of Sir Philip Sidney*, ed. W.A. Ringler, Jr (Oxford, 1962)
Simmons	J.L. Simmons, 'Coming Out in Shakespeare's *The Two Gentlemen of Verona*', *ELH*, 60 (1993), 857–77
Simpson	Claude M. Simpson, *The British Broadside Ballad and its Music* (New Brunswick, N.J., 1966)
SJW	*Shakespeare Jahrbuch (West)*
Skura	Meredith Anne Skura, *Shakespeare the Actor and the Purposes of Playing* (Chicago, Ill., 1993)
Slights	Camille Wells Slights, *Shakespeare's Comic Commonwealths* (Toronto, Ont., 1993), 57–73
Small	S. Asa Small, 'The Ending of *The Two Gentlemen of Verona*', *PMLA*, 48 (1933), 767–76
Smith, *Desire*	Bruce Smith, *Homosexual Desire in Shakespeare's England: A Cultural Poetics* (Chicago, Ill., 1991)
Smith, 'Festivals'	Peter D. Smith, 'The 1966 Festivals at Ashland, Oregon, and San Diego, California', *SQ*, 17 (1996), 407–17
Smith, 'Sign'	Peter J. Smith, 'Re(-)fusing the Sign: Linguistic Ambiguity and the Subversion of Patriarchy in *Romeo and Juliet* and *The Two Gentlemen of Verona*', in *Social Shakespeare: Aspects of Renaissance Dramaturgy and Contemporary Society* (1995), 120–45
Speaight	Robert Speaight, 'Shakespeare in Britain', *SQ*, 21 (1970), 439–49
Spivack	Bernard Spivack, *Shakespeare and the Allegory of Evil* (New York, 1958)
Spurgeon	Caroline F.E. Spurgeon, *Shakespeare's Imagery and What It Tells Us* (Cambridge, 1935)
SQ	*Shakespeare Quarterly*
SS	*Shakespeare Survey*
SSt	*Shakespeare Studies*

Stallybrass	Peter Stallybrass, 'Transvestism and the "body beneath": Speculating on the boy actor', in Susan Zimmerman (ed.), *Erotic Politics: Desire on the Renaissance Stage* (1992), 64–83
States	Bert O. States, 'The Dog on Stage: Theater as Phenomenon', *New Literary History*, 14 (1983), 373–88
Stow, *Annals*	John Stow, *The Annals, or General Chronicle of England* (1615)
Swinburne	Algernon Charles Swinburne, *A Study of Shakespeare* (1879)
Tannenbaum	S.A. Tannenbaum, *The New Cambridge Shakespeare and 'The Two Gentlemen of Verona'* (New York, 1939)
Taylor	Gary Taylor, ''Swounds Revisited: Theatrical, Editorial, and Literary Expurgation', in Gary Taylor and John Jowett (eds), *Shakespeare Reshaped, 1606–1623* (Oxford, 1993), 51–106
Taylor, *Ovid*	A.B. Taylor (ed.), *Shakespeare's Ovid: The 'Metamorphoses' in the Plays and Poems* (Cambridge, 2000)
Thacker, Promptbook	David Thacker, Promptbook of *The Two Gentlemen of Verona* (Swan Theatre production, Stratford-upon-Avon, 1991, transferred to the Barbican Theatre, London, 1992) at the Shakespeare Centre Library, Stratford-upon-Avon
Thaler	Alwin Thaler, 'Shakespeare and the Unhappy Happy Ending', *PMLA*, 42 (1927), 736–61
Thomas	Keith Thomas, *Man and the Natural World* (New York, 1983)
Thomas, *History*	William Thomas, *The History of Italy (1549)*, ed. George B. Parks (Ithaca, N.Y., 1963)
Thomas, *Stratford*	Viv Thomas, review of Edward Hall production, *Stratford Herald*, 26 February 1998
Thompson	Ann Thompson, 'Casting Sense between the Speech: Parentheses in the Oxford Shakespeare', *Analytical and Enumerative Bibliography*, n.s. 4 (1990), 72–90
Thomson, 'Necessary'	Peter Thomson, 'A Necessary Theatre: The Royal Shakespeare Season 1970', *SS 24* (1971), 117–26
Thynne	Francis Thynne, *Emblems and Epigrams* (1600)
Tilney	Edmund Tilney, *The Flower of Friendship: A Renaissance Dialogue Contesting Marriage*, ed. Valerie Wayne (Ithaca, N.Y., 1992)
Times	Review of Adrian Hall production, *The New York Times*, 19 August 1994, Section C, 2
Tobin, 'Nashe'	J.J.M. Tobin, 'Nashe and *The Two Gentlemen of Verona*', *N&Q* (1981), 122–3
Tottel	*Tottel's Miscellany (1557–1587)*, ed. Hyder E. Rollins, 2 vols (Cambridge, Mass., 1965)

Tristia	Ovid, *Tristia*, in *Tristia, Ex Ponto*, ed. Arthur L. Wheeler (1924); 2nd edn, rev. G.P. Goold (1988)
TxC	Stanley Wells, Gary Taylor *et al.*, *William Shakespeare: A Textual Companion* (Oxford, 1987)
Vaughan	Virginia Mason Vaughan and Alden T. Vaughan (eds), *The Tempest* (Walton-on-Thames, 1999)
Wall	Wendy Wall, 'Reading for the Blot: Textual Desire in Early Modern English Literature', in David M. Bergeron (ed.), *Reading and Writing in Shakespeare* (Newark, Del., 1996), 131–59
Warren[1]	Roger Warren, 'Interpretations of Shakespearian Comedy, 1981', *SS 35* (1982), 141–52
Warren[2]	Roger Warren, 'Shakespeare at Stratford, Ontario: The John Hirsch Years', *SS 39* (1987), 179–90
Webster, *Duchess*	John Webster, *The Duchess of Malfi*, ed. Elizabeth M. Brennan (1993)
Webster, *White Devil*	John Webster, *The White Devil*, ed. John Russell Brown (Cambridge, Mass., 1960)
Weimann	Robert Weimann, 'Laughing with the Audience: *The Two Gentlemen of Verona* and the Popular Tradition of Comedy', *SS 22* (1969), 35–42
Wells, 'Failure'	Stanley Wells, 'The Failure of *The Two Gentlemen of Verona*', *SJW*, 99 (1963), 161–73
Wells, *Re-Editing*	Stanley Wells, *Re-Editing Shakespeare for the Modern Reader* (Oxford, 1984)
Werstine[1]	Paul Werstine, 'Cases and Compositors in the Shakespeare First Folio', *SB*, 35 (1982), 206–34
Werstine[2]	Paul Werstine, 'Editing Shakespeare and Editing Without Shakespeare: Wilson, McKerrow, Greg, Bowers, Tanselle, and Copy-Text Editing', *TEXT*, 13 (2000), 27–53
Werstine[3]	Paul Werstine, 'McKerrow's "Suggestion" and Twentieth-Century Shakespeare Textual Criticism', *RenD*, 19 (1989), 149–73
Werstine[4]	Paul Werstine, Review of Stanley Wells, *Re-Editing Shakespeare for the Modern Reader*, *SSt*, 19 (1987), 329–32
Werstine[5]	Paul Werstine, 'Scribe or Compositor: Ralph Crane, Compositors D and F, and the First Four Plays in the Shakespeare First Folio', *Publications of the Bibliographical Society of America* (2001), 315–39
Whetstone	George Whetstone, *Promos and Cassandra* (1578), in Bullough, 2.442–513
Wiles	David Wiles, *Shakespeare's Clown: Actor and Text in the Elizabethan Playhouse* (Cambridge, 1987)
Williams	Gordon Williams, *A Glossary of Shakespeare's Sexual Language* (1997)

Wilson, 'Crane'	F.P. Wilson, 'Ralph Crane, Scrivener to the King's Players', *The Library*, 4th Series, 7 (1926–7), 194–215
Wilson, *Plague*	F.P. Wilson, *The Plague in Shakespeare's London* (Oxford, 1927)
Witches	*The Late Lancashire Witches, by Thomas Heywood and Richard Brome*, ed. Laird H. Barber (1979)
Woudhuysen	H.R. Woudhuysen (ed.), *Love's Labour's Lost* (Walton-on-Thames, 1998)
Wright	Herbert G. Wright (ed.), *Early English Versions of the Tales of 'Guiscardo and Ghismonda' and 'Titus and Gisippus'* (1937)
Yates	Francis A. Yates, *John Florio: The Life of an Italian in Shakespeare's England* (Cambridge, 1934)
Young	Alan R. Young, *The English Prodigal Son Plays: A Theatrical Fashion of the Sixteenth and Seventeenth Centuries* (Salzburg, 1979)

MODERN STAGE AND TELEVISION PRODUCTIONS CITED

Barton	RSC, Royal Shakespeare Theatre, Stratford-upon-Avon, directed by John Barton, 1981
BBC	BBC Television Shakespeare, directed by Don Taylor, 1983
Carey	Bristol Old Vic Theatre, directed by Denis Carey, 1952
Granville-Barker	Court Theatre, London, directed by Harley Granville-Barker, 1904
Hall, Adrian	New York Shakespeare Festival, Delacorte Theatre, New York, directed by Adrian Hall, 1994
Hall, Edward	RSC, Swan Theatre, Stratford-upon-Avon, directed by Edward Hall, 1998
Hall, Peter	RSC, Royal Shakespeare Theatre, Stratford-upon-Avon, directed by Peter Hall, 1960
Iden Payne	Shakespeare Memorial Theatre, Stratford-upon-Avon, directed by Ben Iden Payne, 1938
Langham	Old Vic Theatre Company, Old Vic, London, directed by Michael Langham, 1956
Phillips 1970	RSC, Royal Shakespeare Theatre, Stratford-upon-Avon, directed by Robin Phillips, 1970 (transferred to the Aldwych Theatre, London, 1970)
Phillips 1975	Shakespeare Festival Theatre, Stratford, Ontario, Canada, directed by Robin Phillips, 1975
Robinson	Royal National Theatre Company, Cottesloe Theatre, London, directed by Julie Anne Robinson, 1999
Rubin, Leon	Shakespeare Festival Theatre, Stratford, Ontario, Canada, directed by Leon Rubin, 1984

Shapiro	New York Shakespeare Festival, Delacorte Theatre, New York, directed by Mel Shapiro, 1971
Shepherd	Shakespeare's Globe Theatre, London, directed by Jack Shepherd, 1996
Thacker	RSC, Swan Theatre, Stratford-upon-Avon, directed by David Thacker, 1991 (transferred to the Barbican Theatre, London, 1992)
Wager	The Shakespeare Theatre, Washington, D.C., directed by Douglas C. Wager, 2001

INDEX

This index covers the Preface, Introduction, and Commentary. Characters in the play have separate entries.

313